Animals and Tourism

ASPECTS OF TOURISM

Series Editors: Chris Cooper, *Oxford Brookes University, UK*, C. Michael Hall, *University of Canterbury, New Zealand* and Dallen J. Timothy, *Arizona State University, USA*

Aspects of Tourism is an innovative, multifaceted series, which comprises authoritative reference handbooks on global tourism regions, research volumes, texts and monographs. It is designed to provide readers with the latest thinking on tourism worldwide and push back the frontiers of tourism knowledge. The volumes are authoritative, readable and user-friendly, providing accessible sources for further research. Books in the series are commissioned to probe the relationship between tourism and cognate subject areas such as strategy, development, retailing, sport and environmental studies.

Full details of all the books in this series and of all our other publications can be found on http://www.channelviewpublications.com, or by writing to Channel View Publications, St Nicholas House, 31–34 High Street, Bristol BS1 2AW, UK.

ASPECTS OF TOURISM: 67

Animals and Tourism

Understanding Diverse Relationships

Edited by
Kevin Markwell

CHANNEL VIEW PUBLICATIONS
Bristol • Buffalo • Toronto

Library of Congress Cataloging in Publication Data
Animals and Tourism: Understanding Diverse Relationships/Edited by Kevin Markwell.
Aspects of Tourism: 67
Includes bibliographical references and index.
1. Wildlife-related recreation. 2. Wildlife-related recreation—Moral and ethical aspects.
3. Wildlife-related recreation industry. 4. Wildlife-related recreation industry—Moral
and ethical aspects. 5. Tourism—Moral and ethical aspects. I. Markwell, Kevin.
SK655.A65 2015
338.4'759dc23 2014048023

British Library Cataloguing in Publication Data
A catalogue entry for this book is available from the British Library.

ISBN-13: 978-1-84541-504-4 (hbk)
ISBN-13: 978-1-84541-503-7 (pbk)

Channel View Publications
UK: St Nicholas House, 31–34 High Street, Bristol BS1 2AW, UK.
USA: UTP, 2250 Military Road, Tonawanda, NY 14150, USA.
Canada: UTP, 5201 Dufferin Street, North York, Ontario M3H 5T8, Canada.

Website: www.channelviewpublications.com
Twitter: Channel_View
Facebook: https://www.facebook.com/channelviewpublications
Blog: www.channelviewpublications.wordpress.com

The policy of Multilingual Matters/Channel View Publications is to use papers that are
natural, renewable and recyclable products, made from wood grown in sustainable forests. In the manufacturing process of our books, and to further support our policy, preference is given to printers that have FSC and PEFC Chain of Custody certification. The FSC
and/or PEFC logos will appear on those books where full certification has been granted
to the printer concerned.

Typeset by Techset Composition India (P) Ltd., Bangalore and Chennai, India.
Printed and bound in Great Britain by Short Run Press Ltd.

Contents

Part 2: Conflict, Contradiction and Contestation

Part 3: Shifting Relationships

Contributors

Editor

Kevin Markwell is a cultural geographer and associate professor in the School of Business and Tourism, Southern Cross University, Australia. He has published widely on topics relating to the social construction of tourists' experiences of nature and more recently he has focused specifically on human–animal interactions in the context of leisure and tourism. He co-authored *Snake Bitten, Eric Worrell and the Australian Reptile Park* (UNSW Press, 2010) with Nancy Cushing and was co-editor (along with Simone Fullagar and Erica Wilson) of *Slow Tourism: Experiences and Mobilities* (Channel View Publications, 2012).

Authors

Jane Bone is a senior lecturer at Monash University, Australia. Her main research area explores spirituality and ethics and she is internationally recognised for her work in this field. She is currently working with post-human theory as it provides a critical approach to connections between people, animals and the environment. Her research contributes to wider understandings about human–animal relationships, ethics and innovative methodologies.

Kate Bone is a research scholar at the Monash Injury Research Institute, Monash University, Australia. Kate has published in the field of tourism, specifically relating to research about wellness tourism. She is currently a PhD candidate. Kate's research interests centre on the wellbeing issues and experiences of individuals and groups in society through a critical sociological lens.

Georgette Leah Burns holds a joint position between Hólar University College, where she is an associate professor and head of the Department of Rural Tourism, and the Icelandic Seal Centre, where she is the head of tourism research. Her research focuses on the interactions between people and wildlife in nature-based tourism settings. In addition to numerous book chapters and journal articles on this topic, Leah is author of the book *Dingoes, Penguins and People: Engaging Anthropology to Reconstruct the Management of Wildlife Tourism Interactions* (Lambert Academic Publishing, 2010) and co-editor of *Engaging with Animals: Interpretations of a Shared Existence* (Sydney University Press, 2014).

Erik Cohen is the George S. Wise Professor of Sociology (emeritus) at the Hebrew University of Jerusalem, where he taught between 1959 and 2000. He has conducted research in Israel, Peru, the Pacific Islands and, since 1977, in Thailand. He is the author of around 200 publications. His recent books include *Contemporary Tourism: Diversity and Change* (Elsevier, 2004), and *Explorations in Thai Tourism* (Emerald, 2008). In 2012 he was awarded the UNWTO Ulysses Prize. Erik Cohen presently lives and does research in Thailand.

David Fennell teaches and researches in the Department of Tourism Management, Brock University, Canada. He has written widely on ecotourism, tourism ethics, and moral issues tied to the use of animals in tourism. His most recent book, *Tourism and Animal Ethics*, was published by Routledge in 2012. He is founding editor-in-chief of the *Journal of Ecotourism*.

Ulrike Gretzel is a professor in the UQ Business School, University of Queensland, Australia. Her research focuses on persuasion in human–technology interaction, information processing and decision making, the representation of sensory and emotional aspects of tourism experiences and issues relating to the development and use of intelligent systems and technology in tourism. She studies these concepts for different tourist groups including Chinese consumers and recreational vehicle travellers.

Anne Hardy is a senior lecturer at the Tasmanian School of Business and Economics, University of Tasmania. Anne's research activities cover a range of areas in tourism, including sustainable tourism issues, community involvement in tourism, interpretation and, more recently, drive tourism and the recreational vehicle market. She is also involved in research exploring the travel habits of international students in Australia.

James Higham holds the position of professor of tourism, University of Otago, Dunedin, New Zealand, and visiting professor of sustainable tourism, University of Stavanger, Norway. His research is situated in the broad field of tourism and global environmental change, which in recent years has focused on climate change, tourist behaviour and transitions to a low-carbon future.

John Jett has both a professional and educational background in the environmental sciences, with a focus on waterway management issues. As a killer whale trainer in the 1990s, John became aware of the serious health and behavioural consequences of killer whale confinement. Since that time he has engaged in evidence-based writing and speaking on the consequences of keeping whales in captivity for entertainment purposes.

Chantelle Jobberns is a PhD student at the University of Technology, Sydney (UTS) and works in the area of ethics in sustainable tourism. She received her honours degree at UTS for a thesis titled 'Animal rights in ecotourism: a case study of whale watching'.

Raynald Harvey Lemelin is an associate professor at Lakehead University, Canada. Harvey has showcased the various contributions of insects to tourism and leisure through publications, conferences and public outreach. His interest in insects has been recognised by the Social Sciences and Humanities Research Council of Canada, which has awarded him two national research grants. Harvey's most recent contribution to understanding human–insect encounters is *The Management of Insects in Recreation and Tourism* (Cambridge University Press, 2013).

Brent Lovelock is an associate professor in the Department of Tourism, University of Otago, Dunedin, New Zealand. His research addresses sustainable tourism and he is currently exploring the relationship between ethics and sustainability on a number of tourism fronts – including human rights, politics, global environmental change, the consumptive use of nature, and animal rights and welfare. Brent's edited book *Consumptive Wildlife Tourism* (Routledge, 2008) explores a range of issues around hunting, shooting and fishing, and his recently co-authored book *The Ethics of Tourism* (Routledge, 2013) further addresses the ethics of animal use in tourism. Brent is an avid (if not often successful) hunter and angler.

Muchazondida Mkono is a postdoctoral research fellow at the University of Queensland, Australia. Her research interests include the application of netnography in tourism studies, tourist experience and African tourism. She has also published works on authenticity and food experiences in tourism.

Katja Neves is currently associate professor in the sociology of the environment and social sustainability at Concordia University, Montreal, Canada. Her research addresses neoliberal conservation and socio-ecological sustainability. Katja's current SSHRC-funded research investigates the contemporary reinvention of botanical gardens as agents of social and ecological biodiversity conservation.

David Newsome is an associate professor in environmental science at Murdoch University, Australia. David's research and teaching focus on the sustainable recreational use of landscapes, maintaining the integrity of peri-urban reserves and the assessment and management of tourism activity in protected areas. He has co-authored and/or edited five books in the areas of natural area tourism, wildlife tourism and geotourism and is a member of the IUCN World Protected Areas Committee.

Taru Peltola is an environmental social scientist, currently on leave from the Finnish Environment Institute and working at the National Research Institute of Science and Technology for Environment and Agriculture (Irstea), France. Her main research interests include human–wildlife cohabitation and the role of scientific knowledge in governing natural resource use. She teaches environmental social science and science and technology studies courses at several universities and is a co-convener of the ALTER-Net summer school on biodiversity and ecosystem services.

Outi Ratamäki is a researcher in environmental policy and human–animal studies. Her main research focus has been on questions about large carnivores from the perspective of governance. She has also conducted research on ecosystem services while working for the Finnish Environment Institute. At the University of Eastern Finland she is known as an active promoter of the local and national human–animal studies research networks.

Jeffrey C. Skibins is an assistant professor in the Department of Horticulture, Forestry and Recreation Resources at Kansas State University, where he teaches graduate and undergraduate courses in the park management and conservation programme. His research focuses on the human dimensions of wildlife conservation. Jeffrey has conducted research in parks, protected areas and zoos and aquariums throughout the United States, Africa and Australia. These projects addressed the role of flagship species in ecotourism, visitor behaviours, interpretation and resource management.

Fernanda de Vasconcellos Pegas is a research fellow at the Griffith Institute for Tourism, Griffith University, Australia. Her research interests are ecotourism/sustainable tourism, endangered species conservation, cultural uses of wildlife and private protected areas.

Jeffrey Ventre is a medical doctor and a Diplomate of the American Board of Physical Medicine & Rehabilitation. He practices in Washington State, USA, treating patients with disabilities ranging from brain injury to low back pain. As a marine mammal trainer from 1987 until 1995 he witnessed significant health issues in every captive species he worked with, including killer whales, belugas, dolphins, false killer whales and pinnipeds.

Stephen Wearing is an associate professor at the University of Technology, Sydney (UTS). He has conducted numerous projects and lectures worldwide and is the author of 13 books and over 100 articles dealing with issues surrounding leisure and sustainable tourism. His practical experience as an environmental and park planner at local, state and international level has provided him with real-world experiences that he brings to his teaching and research. His research interests include ecotourism, community-based and volunteer tourism, environmentalism, the sociology of leisure and tourism and social sciences in protected area management.

Carlie S. Wiener is pursuing her PhD at York University, exploring human interactions with the Hawaiian spinner dolphin. She has worked for the past eight years in science communications, understanding human attitudes and perceptions towards ocean science and conservation topics. Carlie's research interests lie in the factors that contribute to the formation of attitudes towards non-human species and how these factors play a role in tourism and ocean conservation.

Figures

Tables

Acknowledgements

I would like first to thank the contributors to this volume who have provided a rich variety of scholarly perspectives on the relationships between tourism and animals. They have been a pleasure to work with – responding quickly and attentively to any queries that I posed to them and keeping to deadlines. I would also like to acknowledge and thank the researchers who submitted chapter proposals but who were not able to be included due to the inevitable size limitations on the publication.

Elinor Robertson, Sarah Williams and the team at Channel View Publications have always been very supportive and helpful and I thank them very much for their commitment to this book. I am also grateful to the anonymous reviewer of the book's manuscript for their insights, suggestions and advice which have hopefully improved the final book. Thanks also go to Brian and Michaela Gilligan, Mike Greenfelder and Betty Weiler who provided additional photographs.

My colleagues in the School of Business and Tourism at Southern Cross University provide me with a stimulating and friendly environment in which to work. I thank Diana Sims for preparing Figure 1 and for always providing formatting advice so cheerfully. I thank my colleagues and friends, Professors John Jenkins and Betty Weiler (Southern Cross University) and David Rowe and Deborah Stephenson (University of Western Sydney) for their mentorship over almost two decades which has contributed in many ways to my intellectual growth and development.

Finally, I thank my partner, Steve Harrison, for his love and support, and for being so willing to accommodate my animal-oriented interests when we holiday, and my parents, Bert and Elaine Markwell, for encouraging my early interests in animals by taking me to places in order to see them, giving me books to read about them and letting me keep some as pets.

1 Birds, Beasts and Tourists: Human–Animal Relationships in Tourism

Kevin Markwell

Introduction

Animals (and the products derived from their bodies) are so much a part of our day-to-day lives that we often fail to register their presence, or, when we do, they are frequently relegated to the background. Regardless of whether we live in highly urbanised cities or rural villages, non-human animals co-habit these spaces with us. Some we regard as companions to be loved and cared for, inhabiting the intimate spaces of home, while others we construct as pests and try our best to exclude or even exterminate them from our domestic lives. Still others co-exist with us, sharing spaces and other resources, but not impacting on our own lives in any direct way.

Given the ubiquitous involvement of animals in our everyday lives, it should not be surprising that they inhabit tourism spaces and experiences in equally diverse arrangements. Animals contribute to tourism in multiple ways: as attractions in their own right – alive or dead, wild or captive; as forms of transportation; symbolically as destination icons; as travel companions; and as components of regional cuisine. Some, like leeches and flies, irritate us while we walk through forests admiring flamboyant butterflies and birds, while others, such as crocodiles and tigers, regard us as prey. Breaching humpback whales migrating along coastlines evoke feelings of awe and wonderment and sustain a rapidly expanding industry with substantial returns to regional economies, while the presence, real or imagined, of great white sharks can close beaches and damage the reputations of destinations. As will become evident, animals, whether invertebrate or vertebrate, cold-blooded or warm-blooded, friendly or otherwise, intersect with tourists and tourism in a multitude of diverse ways.

The ambition of this book, therefore, is to make a meaningful contribution to the growing body of knowledge concerning the relationships between animals, tourists and the tourism industry and to contribute to current debates about their involvement. By doing so I hope that the theoretically informed and empirically rich chapters that comprise the book will help to highlight key research questions and stimulate other researchers and students to reflect critically on the place of animals within tourism spaces, experiences, practices and structures. Given the numerous intersections between animals and tourism and the growing awareness more generally of issues relating to the use of animals, it is timely to consider critically our relations with animals within the domain of tourism.

The critical interrogation of human–animal relations more generally is the object of the emerging field of study known as human–animal studies or anthrozoology. This intellectually exciting field of inquiry examines the complex interrelationships between humans and animals constituted within the social and cultural worlds that they share with each other (DeMello, 2010; Shapiro, 2008). It seeks to reveal the diversity of relationships between humans and animals, the ways in which those relationships are changing and the meanings that are attached to those relationships. Human–animal studies questions our use of animals: as workers, performers and companions; as experimental subjects and as components of food; as living targets; and as subjects of art, literature and popular culture. It illuminates the contradictions, inconsistencies and ambiguities that characterise our relations with animals and highlights the implications these have for animal welfare, wildlife conservation, food security and public health (Bulliet, 2005; DeMello, 2010; Fennell, 2012; Franklin, 1999; Herzog, 2010). This scholarship challenges us to create more ethical and sustainable ways of living with, and among, animals.

Contemporary human–animal studies scholarship provides new insights into the ambiguous and multifaceted relationships that exist between humans and non-human animals – relationships that, as I mentioned previously, have tended to be taken for granted, backgrounded and not often subject to critical analysis. This is not to deny the rich scholarship that has already occurred and the field is indebted to the conceptual understandings revealed by scholars working in a range of disciplines such as anthropology, history, sociology, cultural studies, geography and psychology.

DeMello (2010) provides a detailed account of the emergence of human–animal studies and identifies key authors whose work has helped shape the field of study and the questions that it poses. These authors include John Berger (*Why Look at Animals?* 1980) Yi-Fu Tuan (*Dominance and Affection, The Making of Pets,* 1984), James Serpell (*In the Company of Animals,* 1996), Harriet Ritvo (*The Animal Estate,* 1987) and Donna Haraway (*Primate Visions: Gender, Race and Nature in the World of Modern Science,* 1989). The 1980s appears to have been a particularly important decade for the publication of important books that helped build the foundations of human–animal relations. Other works of significance that followed included, among others, Steve Baker's *Picturing the Beast: Animals, Identity and Representation* (1993), Arnold Arluke and Clinton Sanders' *Regarding Animals* (1996), Jennifer Wolch and Jody Emel's edited collection, *Animal Geographies: Place, Politics and Identity in the Nature–Culture Borderlands* (1998), Adrian Franklin's *Animals and Modern Cultures: A Sociology of Human–Animal Relations in Modernity* (1999), Chris Philo and Chris Wilbert's edited collection, *Animal Spaces, Beastly Places* (2000) and Richard W. Bulliet's *Hunters, Herders and Hamburgers: The Past and Future of Human–Animal Relationships* (2005).

Over the past decade many more titles (and journal articles) have been published which continue to address questions arising from human–animal relations. Some of these have been targeted at more general readerships reflecting the rapidly growing interest in the topic outside academia. These include *Why We Love Dogs, Eat Pigs and Wear Cows* by Melanie Joy (2010), *Some We Love, Some We Hate and Some We Eat* by Hal Herzog (2010) and, more specifically related to tourism, *Wild Ones* by Jon Mooallem (2013). Michael Pollan's *The Omnivore's Dilemma: A Natural History of Four Meals* (2006) and Jonathan Safran Foer's *Eating Animals* (2009) have done much to encourage people to think more critically about the food choices they make and the implications of these to the ways we treat animals. It is clear then from these lists of publications that the field of human–animal studies is attracting greater levels of attention from scholars working in a diverse range of disciplinary areas and fields of study. One of these is the field of tourism studies and the following section will provide a brief overview of work that has been conducted on the intersections of tourism and animals.

Human–Animal Relationships in Tourism

Cohen (2009) argues that tourism is an ideal context for the exploration of human–animal relationships because of the opportunities it affords for various forms of interaction, such as viewing, hunting, fishing, playing and, indeed, eating. However, Cohen's attention is directed primarily at wildlife tourism where, admittedly, much of the human–animal interaction in tourism occurs. But tourism, as a system of representations and organised and embodied social and economic practices, intersects with animals in a diversity of ways beyond their role as attractions. As Fennell (2012) makes clear, the involvement of animals in tourism includes their role in transportation and gastronomy and as hazards to be avoided or managed. Animals feature in the travel narratives that excite our imaginations and help create the desire to visit places where we might see them at first hand; some become icons that contribute to the creation of place identity and help to market destinations and, for others, their bodies are manufactured into tourist souvenirs.

Surely, one of the most successful and most popular animal icons in tourism marketing must be Mickey Mouse, who continues to play a major role in the global popularity of Disneyland Park and Walt Disney World (Figure 1.1).

While the focus of this book is on the intersections of animals in contemporary tourism forms and practices, animals have been involved in recreational travel in one way or another since its earliest beginnings in ancient civilisations. Travel across long distances was complicated not only by the presence of thieves and thugs but also, in some places, by dangerous animals. Beasts of burden such as donkeys, oxen, horses and camels transported goods and wealthier travellers. Ancient Romans took pet birds such as exotic parrots with them when they travelled (Johnson, pers. comm, 2014) and no doubt dogs were included in some travel parties for companionship and as protection against dangerous animals and thieves. However, it is the incorporation of animals into the spectacles of death that took place in the ancient Roman arenas that has attracted most attention from scholars. While there does not appear to be any evidence that the Romans enjoyed viewing animals in their own habitats and for their own sake, their collective gaze was, instead, directed towards the bloody performances in the arenas. As Kalof (2007: 27) observed, 'for more than 450 years ... the public slaughter of animals (and humans) was a celebrated form of Roman entertainment'. Public displays of exotic animals in menageries and 'zoos' occurred in ancient Egypt and Greece (Kalof, 2007) and in Rome (Kalof, 2007; Kyle, 1998).

Figure 1.1 Two of the most iconic tourism 'animal ambassadors', Mickey and Minnie Mouse, welcome visitors to Walt Disney World
Photo: Author.

Research into contemporary forms of human–animal interactions in tourism has tended to focus on (live) animals as attractions and much of the initial research attention was aimed at understanding the impacts of tourism on certain species. The literature concerning the ecological impacts of tourism on animals and their habitats (principally through wildlife tourism) emerged in the late 1970s, corresponding broadly with Jafari's (2001) 'cautionary platform'. The bulk of this early research, which embraced recreational and tourism impacts, was not undertaken by social scientists, understandably, but by ecologists, who began to observe that the consequences of persistent encounters with wildlife through tourism and recreation activities could have adverse effects on the ecology and behaviour of certain species. Over the course of the past 40 years or so a considerable body of literature has been built up on a diverse range of taxa including cetaceans (whales and dolphins) (see, for example, Christiansen et al., 2010; Lusseau & Higham, 2004; Orams, 2000) nesting seabirds (Burger & Gochfield, 1993; Fowler, 1999; McClung et al., 2004) and marine turtles (Jacobson & Lopez, 1994; Johnson et al., 1996), great white sharks (Laroche et al., 2007), gorilla (Muyambi, 2005) and Komodo dragons (Walpole, 2001).

The research effort across taxa is far from even, however, and there are substantial difficulties in undertaking field-based studies on the effects of tourism on many species, particularly if they are relatively small and occur in fewer numbers. As can be seen from the small sample of research given above, studies have tended to be made on species that are relatively large, readily observable and/or occur in reasonably large numbers. Elucidating the factors affecting individuals and populations of animals that derive from tourism and not from other ecosystem influences is challenging and it is usually difficult if not impossible to control for these other variables in field-based projects. Funding opportunities for this kind of research are usually limited and the meagre funds that are available tend to be targeted at those species that demonstrate high economic value. The findings of ecological, behavioural and physiological research are crucial, however, if the negative effects of tourism are to be understood and managed.

Appropriate management of tourist–animal interactions depends not just on understanding the effects of tourism on the animal species but also, just as critically, understanding the human dimension of those interactions. Over the past couple of decades a considerable body of social science research has accumulated that examines the experiences of tourists encountering animals. Given that much of the most obvious interaction takes place within wildlife tourism, it is not surprising that a very strong theme has focused on wildlife-based tourism, with several books and hundreds of journal articles published (see, for example, Higginbottom, 2004; Newsome et al., 2005; Shackley, 1996). An important sub-theme of this scholarship has focused specifically on the display of captive animals as visitor attractions. This research on wildlife tourism including captive displays, feeding wildlife and educational outcomes constitutes the bulk of literature dealing with tourism–animal relationships. Indeed, in a special issue on animals in the tourism and leisure experience of the journal, *Current Issues in Tourism* (edited by Neil Carr, 2009), two-thirds of the articles were about some form of wildlife tourism. The remaining articles concerned hunting and angling, which comprise another theme within the tourism–animal literature that is slowly growing in terms of the number of publications (see, for instance, Brent Lovelock's *Tourism and the Consumption of Wildlife*, 2008). The final coherent, although not yet well developed, theme that I can discern in the literature concerns the ethics of using animals in tourism. David Fennell's seminal *Tourism and Animal Ethics* (2012) gives a comprehensive overview of the research that has been undertaken both outside and within tourism studies.

A Model of Tourism–Animal Relationships

Figure 1.2 depicts a model of tourism–animal relationships. It is organised, following Leiper (2004), spatiotemporally into the tourist-generating region (TGR), tourist transit region (TTR) and the tourist destination region (TDR). These regions broadly correspond with the constituent phases of the tourist experience: pre-travel decision making; travel to destination; at-destination experiences; and post-travel remembering, and feeds into the decision-making process for forthcoming trips.

Tourist generating region: Pre-departure

During the pre-travel phase in the TGR, prospective tourists engage in decision-making behaviours concerning their forthcoming holiday. Animals become involved in this phase mostly, but not only, through their representations in literature and the media. Popular culture such as fiction and non-fiction books and magazines, travelogues, television programmes and Web 2.0 forms such as blogs, postings on social media and photo- and video-sharing platforms are important ways by which animals enter into the tourist's imagination and influence decisions about where to travel and what to see and experience. Indeed, the title of this chapter is derived from the title of one of the books by British naturalist, Gerald Durrell, *Birds, Beasts and Relatives*, which humorously recounts his idyllic childhood on the Greek island of Corfu. Durrell's immensely popular books – about his childhood in Corfu, his adventures capturing animals for zoos in Africa and South America and his later books on his own zoo on Jersey – motivated many to travel to seek their own adventures with wildlife. His books on Corfu were so popular that they are regarded as being a factor in increasing tourism to the island – something that the author apparently 'deeply regretted' (Horrocks, 2012, np).

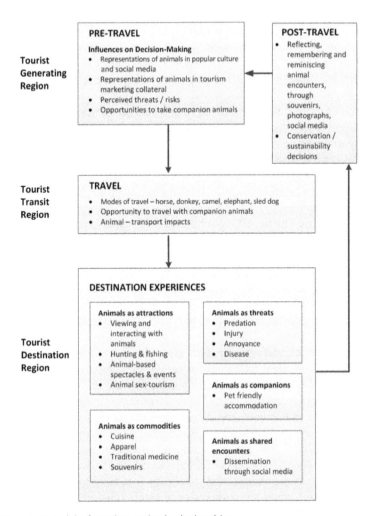

Figure 1.2 A model of tourism–animal relationships

These representations of animals, whether textual or visual, not only fuel our desire to see these animals 'for real', but they also powerfully shape our constructions and understandings of them. As Baker (1993) has argued, our understandings of animals are moulded largely by cultural representations of them and many of us unselfconsciously pack these understandings with us when we travel in search of them. For those of my generation, our childhood understandings of dolphins were constructed through watching *Flipper*, chimpanzees through *The Hathaways* and, as an Australian, my early understandings of kangaroos came from the television series *Skippy, the Bush Kangaroo*. Shot though lenses smeared with an anthropomorphic gel, these television programmes accentuated the human-ness of these animals which appeared to live happy and contented lives intertwined with the lives of humans. The programmes represented close, friendly relationships between the animals and their human best friends. It is no surprise then that many of us yearn for these innocent, friendly, close-up encounters with wild animals when we travel.

We also encounter representations of animals in the marketing collateral produced and disseminated by destination management organisations and tour companies. Animals are utilised in the place-branding strategies used by destination marketing authorities. Animals symbolise qualities such as power, strength, exoticism, friendliness, ferocity and joy and their representations can be harnessed or co-opted into marketing strategies. The estuarine crocodile has been used to market tourism, at least domestically, in Australia's Northern Territory (Ryan, 1998), while other destinations employ salmon (Forrestal & Lehto, 2009), cicada (Forrestal *et al.*, 2014) and kangaroo (Simons, 2013). While some tourists see these images of animals at face value, for others the images signify more abstract values or aspirations such as freedom, adventure, Otherness and the exotic. Images of animals, then, represent the species depicted, the destinations at which they can be found, and the hopes and dreams that are, in part at least, motivating the tourist to travel in the first place.

The desire to see and interact with animals, shaped as it is by popular culture, can be a motivating factor for travel, but negative perceptions of certain animals can perform an entirely opposite role in dissuading people from visiting some destinations. The deleterious effects of animals on tourism experiences has been the subject of analysis in a small number of studies (see, for example, Durrheim & Leggat, 1999; Gautret *et al.*, 2007; Moscardo *et al.*, 2006), but deaths or injuries caused by animals to tourists are tiny in comparison to other causes such as drowning and vehicular accidents (Figure 1.3). Nevertheless, the possibility that they might encounter a dangerous animal such as shark or snake or catch a disease such as malaria is sufficient to deter at least some tourists from visiting destinations where such threats exist. Sometimes this fear is turned into a marketing opportunity. For example, there are a variety of t-shirt and tea towel designs which celebrate the dangerous animals that can be encountered in Australia. This is a whimsical reconfiguration of the perceived threat that these animals pose to some tourists contemplating travel to this country.

Finally, for those who have a companion animal, decisions have to be made during this stage concerning whether to leave them behind or to take them along on the trip. There is a rapidly growing market for pet-friendly accommodation in particular; many establishments ranging from caravan parks through more luxurious resorts and hotels actively and enthusiastically welcome pet dogs and cats as well as service or guide dogs. Robbins (2014) asserts that approximately 60% of all American hotels now allow dogs to stay in hotel rooms with their owners. *National Geographic* published their own guidebook,

Figure 1.3 Some animals present a danger to tourists; signs are used to alert tourists to the potential danger of crocodiles and guide their behaviour in Kakadu National Park, Australia
Photo: Author.

Dog Lover's Guide to Travel (Carter, 2014) for people who want to travel with their pets, and various travel insurance plans are available which cover pets. For those pets that don't get to travel with the family, a range of pet hotels and 'resorts' accommodate these not-so-lucky companion animals.

Transit route

Within tourist transit routes, animals are most commonly involved in the provision of transportation, which may also be part of the attraction for tourists. Pack animals such as donkeys, horses and camels as well as sled dogs transport tourists and their luggage, particularly in mountainous, remote or rugged areas where there are often few alternatives (Cousquer & Allison, 2012). On some Greek islands, such as Santorini and Hydra, donkeys transport tourists and/or their luggage up the steep roads to the town perched high above the coastline. Using pack animals no doubt adds to the rustic charm and perceived authenticity of the holiday for some tourists. Aware of the value of novelty in the tourism experience, some tour operators incorporate a pack animal experience to give themselves a competitive advantage over other operators. Tourists, for example, can choose to access the Grand Canyon in Arizona, USA, through a number of means: on foot, by helicopter, by boat or by mule.

It is as beasts of burden that animals are most directly and clearly 'at work', labouring for the benefit of tourists. Cousquer and Allison (2012) argue that in many instances these animals are placed under considerable stress and are not looked after at all well, sometimes being made to work very long hours under very difficult circumstances. A number of websites highlight the poor conditions under which some of these animals are maintained and warn against hiring them (see, for example, mygreecetravelblog. com and right-tourism.com).

While many pet dogs and cats accompany their owners in private vehicles, some will need to be transported by aeroplane or train. Many airlines now offer 'pet-friendly' options that include small dogs or cats as part of free luggage allowances, while others issue a special 'pet ticket' at an additional cost. For other tourists, the presence or absence of pet-friendly camping grounds, motels and resorts, as well as transportation modes, will shape their choice of transit route and itinerary.

Lastly, animals are impacted by, and can themselves seriously impact modes of transport that are used to convey tourists from their origins to destinations. Animals are obviously the victims of road, rail and boating incidents and the impacts of these can be exacerbated in certain touristic spaces and at particular times or seasons. For instance, a very popular visitor activity in Australia's Kakadu National Park is to view the sunset from Ubirr Rock, a rocky outcrop on the edge of a vast floodplain. At late afternoon during the dry season the car park is filled to capacity or beyond with visitors' vehicles. Once the sun has set, visitors drive off down the one road that then connects with the rest of the park's road system. Unfortunately, it is at this time that snakes and lizards emerge to warm themselves on the bitumen road and many are subsequently run over by this large convoy of vehicles (Figure 1.4). Conversely, bird strikes are a significant hazard for aircraft and,

Figure 1.4 Many small animals, especially reptiles that seek out sealed roads at dusk to warm themselves, are killed by tourist traffic on its way to or from a tourist attraction
Photo: Author.

while it is difficult to accurately estimate their cost, one author has calculated that globally these incidents cost between US$1bn–1.5bn (Allan, 2002) and occasionally result in human fatalities.

Tourist destination region

It is at the TDR that the intersections between animals and tourists are most obvious and frequent. It is here that animals are manufactured into 'tourism products' for the consumption, either metaphorically or materially, by tourists. The special interest tourism experience called 'wildlife tourism' is the most popular form of animal-based tourism, although there are others that will be discussed shortly. Wildlife tourism can be defined as tourism in which tourists deliberately seek out relatively close encounters with wildlife in settings that range from completely wild and free through semi-wild to completely contrived or manufactured or constructed settings (Cohen, 2009; Hall *et al.*, 2003; Higginbottom, 2004; Newsome *et al.*, 2005; Shackley, 1996). The dominant mode of engagement is visual and tourists gain satisfaction and enjoyment from seeing these animals at close range and collecting their own images through photography, which they can share instantaneously with friends and family through social media (Figure 1.5). However, hunting and fishing are activities that are sometimes included under the umbrella of wildlife tourism, in which case the engagement goes beyond the visual to the tactile and gustatory.

Figure 1.5 Tourism provides many opportunities for observing and photographing animals in the wild. A tourist photographs a giant anteater in the Pantanal Wetland, Brazil. The handkerchief is protection against cold winds
Photo: Mike Greenfelder.

Several authors (see, for example, Beardsworth & Bryman, 2001; Cohen, 2009; Hall *et al.*, 2003; Orams, 1996; Reynolds & Braithwaite, 2001) have put forward various schema that describe the modes or forms of interactions in relation to the settings in which the interactions occur. These range from wilderness areas and the open ocean where obvious human interventions in the landscape are virtually non-existent and where animal–tourist interactions are largely shaped by the actions of the animals themselves, through to national parks and nature reserves in which modifications such as walking tracks and viewing platforms create opportunities to more easily see animals, to urban parks where animals are semi-wild and provisioned with food to encourage them to stay. Finally, settings in which animals are held in captivity and exhibited for the benefit of tourists include zoos and aquaria, and circuses.

Other forms of animal-based tourism beyond wildlife tourism include: farm stays where visitors interact with domestic animals such as cattle, sheep, alpacas, horses and chickens; viewing bullfights in Spain and Portugal and Indonesian cock-fights; attending horse, camel and dog races; visiting museums to gaze at skeletons of prehistoric animals and taxidermied versions of extant ones (Figure 1.6); and the tourism associated with animal-based special events and festivals such as birding meetings, pet shows and

Figure 1.6 It's not only living animals that attract tourists. These two taxidermied lions are the famous 'Tsavo Lions', the subjects of a non-fiction book, *The Man-Eaters of Tsavo*, and the Hollywood movie, *The Ghost and the Darkness*. Their notoriety produced through popular cultural forms such as books and film encourages tourists to travel to the Field Museum of Natural History, Chicago, IL, to view their mounted hides
Photo: Author.

the various 'rattlesnake roundups'. At some destinations, so-called 'doctor fish' (usually *Garra rufa*, a fish native to Turkey), are the basis of fish spas where people dangle their legs in large tanks for the fish to nibble at the skin of their legs and feet (Figure 1.7). While some people attend the spas because they believe there are health benefits, for others, particularly tourists, the attraction is in the novelty offered by the experience. The tourist–animal relationship in this instance, however, is not one based on visual consumption of the animal but instead the animal, the fish, is 'at work', feeding off the skin of the humans and the tourists derive pleasure through the novelty of the experience and the physical sensations created as the fish scrape away at their skin with their teeth.

Finally, reports have appeared in the media about 'animal-sex tourism' in which people travel to destinations such as Denmark and Norway, where so-called 'animal brothels' are not illegal (Digens, 2014; Olafsson, 2008; also Fennell, 2012). Given the capacity of the internet to connect people with shared interests, and the proliferation of pornographic sites, some of which include animal–human sex, it is not impossible that such tourism could continue to grow, if at very low levels. While the greater majority would find this form of tourism activity abhorrent, social scientists should not shy away from examining it as another form of human–animal interaction. Indeed, a

Figure 1.7 'Doctor fish' enthusiastically scraping dead skin off the author's feet and legs at a fish spa in Singapore
Photo: Author.

publication of the International Society for Anthrozoology specifically focused on the topics of bestiality and zoophilia in 2005 (Podberscek & Beetz, 2005).

Animals also turn up on the dinner plates of tourists. The act of eating food within tourism is both an everyday necessity and an attraction in itself (Quan & Wang, 2004; Figure 1.8). Exotic cuisines attract gourmet travellers and food tourists seeking new culinary experiences. The basis for some of these exotic meals is local animals that may not always be harvested in a sustainable or ethical way. Additionally, in order to support high levels of tourism activity at destinations, reliable sources of meat have to be available in order to satisfy demand. Questions arise relating to the welfare of the animals raised for food and the ways in which the meat is stored and processed. Eating ethically can be a challenge for tourists who wish to do so.

Components of some animal species are also used in traditional medicines and, while some tourists travel to destinations specifically to take such medications, many others may be tempted to try a medicine incidentally to the purposes of their holiday. Concerns relate to animal welfare as well as the sustainability of harvesting some of these animals from the wild. Conservation and animal welfare organisations strongly oppose the use of animals in traditional medicines and it is clear that there are significant ecological and animal welfare problems associated with the use of many of these animal species.

Figure 1.8 Restaurants sometimes display living fish, crabs and other seafood in aquariums to entice diners. These animals are then killed on demand and prepared for diners to enjoy
Photo: Author.

There are also significant concerns about the use of animals as souvenirs. Souvenirs are, for many tourists, an important aspect of the tourist experience and animals or their representations are easily commoditised into saleable items that tourists can purchase as a keepsake of their holiday. For example, at the rattlesnake roundups mentioned above, tourists may purchase all kinds of rattlesnake-derived souvenirs including cans of rattlesnake meat, open-mouthed dried rattlesnake heads, and rattlesnake heads and tails embedded in resin, as well as snakeskin wallets and boots. At international terminals of Australian airports, money bags made from the scrotal skin of red kangaroos are available for purchase.

But it is at destinations in the developing world, many of which are not subject to animal protection legislation or those which are subject are not properly policed, where the greatest range of animal-based souvenirs can be purchased by tourists. Taxidermied animals, resin-embedded scorpions, dried butterflies and spiders, tortoiseshell, shrunken monkey heads, 'snake-wine', among many other examples, are available. The most extreme (and surely the cruellest) form of animal-based souvenir is the plastic packets of live fish, salamanders and baby turtles that are apparently sold in some destinations in China, including Beijing. The animals are sealed in the packet containing a liquid supposedly infused with special nutrients that will keep them alive for several months and sold as key rings and living 'animal adornments'. Unless rescued from their plastic prison, however, the animals soon die through lack of oxygen (CNN, 2011).

At some destinations tourists have the opportunity to be photographed holding or touching charismatic animals such as gibbons, pythons, baby elephants and parrots. Many tourists, perhaps through a combination of naivety or lack of awareness, are ignorant of the 'back story' of how these animals came to be in captivity, or how they are treated in captivity, and are simply happy to have the opportunity to encounter these animals and be photographed with them. For others, who are aware of the controversy surrounding these 'photo-prop' animals (see bornfree.org.uk), the encounter is perhaps so surreal or liminal – outside the boundaries of everyday life – that they surrender to it, even if their enjoyment may sometimes be tinged with guilt.

Animals can also negatively affect the destination experience, either directly or indirectly. Flies, mosquitoes, sand flies, leeches, ticks and midges irritate swimmers, walkers and those wishing to eat outdoors. Mosquitoes and ticks can have a much more serious effect by transmitting debilitating or even lethal viruses into humans. Flocks of pigeons and sparrows annoy tourists at many famous monuments and public places throughout the world and their faeces can be both a hazard to human health and a hazard to the integrity of the monuments. Dangerous animals sometimes attack and kill (and very occasionally eat) tourists. The threat of death or injury by wild animals perceived by some tourists is sufficient to dissuade them from visiting certain destinations or from engaging in activities such as swimming in an ocean or walking through forests.

Finally, for those tourists travelling with their pets, pet-friendly accommodation has to be found at destinations. This search is made much easier today with guidebooks such as the *Dog Lover's Guide to Travel* (Carter, 2014) and an array of blogs and other internet sites that provide up-to-date information and advice to pet-accompanied tourists. The inclusion of pets on holiday can also act as a constraint on the activities of tourists, although some hotels now offer pet-minding services and private individuals can be hired to take dogs for walks.

Tourist-generating region: Post-trip recollections

In the final stage of the tourism experience, recollection and reflection, which mostly occurs back home at the tourist-generating region, tourists share their memories, souvenirs and their photos and videos with friends and family. Through social media and photograph- and video-sharing platforms they can share their experiences with a global audience. Increasing numbers of tourists use sites such as TripAdvisor to post reviews of attractions, restaurants and the performances of tour guides which influence the travel decision-making of others. The memories and mementos of the holiday lay the foundation for future travel and serve to stimulate friends and family to travel as well and completes the 'circle of representation' (Jenkins, 2003) which commences with viewing images of animals in the pre-departure phase. It is also during this phase that some people will join or donate money to conservation organisations and modify aspects of their everyday life in order to reduce their impacts on the environment.

Structure of the Book

Before I give an account of the structure of this book it is important to note that many contemporary scholars in human–animal studies, recognising the power relations inherent in the use of language, employ terms such as 'non-human animal', 'animals other than human' and 'more than human' to emphasise that humans are indeed a form of animal and that many taxa share the capacity for pain, pleasure, anxiety and contentment, with humans. The use of these terms acknowledges the shared characteristics between 'human' and 'animal' rather than emphasising difference and Otherness. Indeed, it is not only in animal rights discourses and in humanities and social science scholarship that these terms are being used, for there are an increasing number of journal articles in science and medicine that employ the term 'non-human animal' (see, for example, O'Brien & Gardner, 2005). Some authors in the book have chosen to use one or other of these terms whereas others have not and I made the editorial decision for each author to retain the right to express the concept 'animal' or 'non-human animal' in the way they preferred.

The book is organised into three major parts, based on the themes of 'Ethics and Welfare', 'Conflict, Contradiction and Contestation' and 'Shifting Relationships'. Contributors to 'Ethics and Welfare' examine critically the treatment of animals within tourism and consider questions around our use of animals to create pleasure and enjoyment as well as the effects on animals' welfare of being incorporated into tourism. This part commences with a comprehensive overview of the dominant ethical approaches towards human–animal relations by David Fennell. Each of these approaches is described and a detailed discussion of the criticisms that have been made against each is provided. By mapping out the key differences between these ethical approaches and through an examination of how each of these approaches has been used to examine tourism–animal interactions, Fennell's chapter offers a theoretically informed foundation for further studies that critically analyse the moral and ethical implications of tourism–animal interactions.

In Chapter 3, Georgette Leah Burns picks up some of the threads of the preceding chapter by interrogating the ways by which tourism has tradition-ally conceived of animals as objects that can be exploited for the hedonistic pleasures of tourists. Burns argues that tourism has largely comprehended animals in an anthropocentric and instrumental way and this has led to the marginalisation of animals' interests. She applies seven principles of what she calls 'an ecocentric approach to wildlife tourism' to two specific cases of tourist–animal interactions. These two chapters provide the conceptual scaf-folding for a series of empirical studies that follow which explore the ethical and moral issues that arise from the use of animals in tourism.

In Chapter 4, Kate Bone and Jane Bone examine the exploitation of women and elephants within the Thai tourism economy. These authors argue that there are similarities in the ways by which the tourism industry exploits women as sex workers and animals as performers for the tourist gaze. They support their argument through an empirical analysis of the 'dart trick', an act performed by both elephants and female sex workers for the amusement of (at least some) tourists. Underpinned by post-human theory, their analysis reveals that these human and non-human animals are oppressed through a process of Othering, which renders them objects of an exploitative tourist gaze.

Stephen Wearing and Chantelle Jobberns examine, in Chapter 5, the extent to which ecotourism based on viewing whales has led to an improve-ment in the rights of whales. Situating ecotourism within a neoliberal model of capitalist production, they argue that whales are transformed into prod-ucts for tourist consumption and that such a process can lead to unethical treatment of individual whales and unsustainable futures for species as a whole. They propose a 'decommodified approach' that moves away from the utilitarian and instrumental approaches that underpin the orthodox theory and practice of ecotourism. The final chapter in this section deals with the contentious topic of hunting, and specifically the ethics of 'heli-hunting', in which trophy animals are hunted from helicopters. Brent Lovelock's analysis in Chapter 6 uncovers a number of ethical and moral disturbances that underpin core debates about recreational hunting and its highly commercialised and commodified form in tourism. The considerable tensions that have emerged between the various stakeholders are revealed through the analysis of three narratives that demonstrate the range of ethical positions on this form of hunting.

The second part of the book, 'Conflict, Contradiction and Contestation' focuses attention on the instabilities, inconsistencies and ambiguities that so often characterise human–animal relations in tourism. This section leads off with a provocative chapter by James Higham and Katja Neves that examines critically some of the paradoxes and contestations of whale watching as a form of ecotourism that is considered a part of the larger capitalist project. In particular, they interrogate the contradictions that exist in the dependence of whale watching on the oil industry. Their analysis offers original and often uncomfortable insights into the difficulties that the industry has in achieving the conservation and sustainable economic and social development goals it aspires to attain.

The involvement of whales in tourism, specifically the captive exhibition of killer whales, is also addressed by Jeffrey Ventre and John Jett in Chapter 8. The 'stars' of oceanaria around the world, the whales find themselves in the centre of a multi-million dollar entertainment industry which continues to draw many millions of visitors annually. The authors' central argument, informed in part by their previous employment as killer whale trainers, is that the keeping of killer whales in captivity cannot be justified. They argue that the harm that captivity causes to the whales' physical and mental well-being cannot be compensated for by any social good arising out of their exhibition in terms of public education and a strengthened concern for whale conservation. Continuing the focus on cetaceans, in Chapter 9 Carlie Wiener explores the tensions inherent in human–dolphin relations within tourism contexts. She discusses the great appeal that dolphins have for Westerners in particular, for whom dolphins represent a range of material and abstract values. The desire to be close to these animals has led to a diversity of tourist experiences that create opportunities for proximity and intimacy but at the same time can lead to harmful impacts on the dolphins themselves.

Erik Cohen focuses his attention, in Chapter 10, on the involvement of young elephants in Thai tourism. He details the harsh treatment given to these animals in order to fashion an amiable, compliant animal performer whose own interests become secondary to those of their handlers and to the tourists who pay to see them perform. He shows how anthropomorphic discourses assist in the maintenance of such practices by encouraging tourists to think of the elephants as human children eager to learn new 'tricks' and show them off. Outi Ratamäki and Taru Peltola present an interesting case study in Chapter 11 of the performances of animals (carnivores such as wolverines and bears) and humans in a tourism space known as Erä-Eero in northern Finland. Their study reveals the complex web of interrelationships and resulting tensions that emerge between the various actors (human and animal) that create this particular tourist space. The authors demonstrate how the agency of the various animals involved in the tourist performances creates the tourist attraction space – the animals are active participants in the making of this tourist spectacle.

In Chapter 12, the conflicts that are often present between the cultural and individual expectations of Indigenous peoples and the requirements of ecotourism are brought into focus by David Newsome in his examination of birdwatching tourism in Papua New Guinea. Newsome details the challenges in the creation and maintenance of a sustainable birdwatching industry in that country that include disputes over land, the important role that hunting has traditionally played in the cultures of PNG and its effect on certain bird species and the tremendous pressures being placed on biodiversity through extractive industry development such as mining and forestry.

This part of the book closes with a chapter by Muchazondida Mkono that examines the practice of eating animals within the tourism experience. It is the consumption of animals as food that brings into sharp relief the inconsistencies, contradictions and ambiguities that are emblematic of human–animal relations. Mkono situates her analysis at wildlife tourism destinations where tourists have opportunities to eat 'game meats', meat from non-domesticated animals. She employs the concept of cognitive dissonance as a theoretical tool to reveal how tourists negotiate the internal conflict between appreciating both the living animal which is the focus of the tourist gaze and the dead animal consumed as part of a meal.

The final part of the book, 'Shifting Relationships', explores the transformations that characterise humans and non-human animal relationships. Our relationships with animals, whether at the level of society, culture or the individual, are always fluid, dynamic and shifting. The collection of chapters reveals some of these changes. Harvey Lemelin, in Chapter 14, seeks to redress the overwhelming attention on vertebrates by the tourism industry and by most human–animal research by focusing on tourism based on experiences with invertebrates. He shows that there is a diversity of attractions that are based on encounters with these fascinating and often spectacular animals. Through well-managed close encounters with invertebrates such as butterflies, dragonflies and spiders, Lemelin argues that appreciation of these animals can be enhanced, leading to significant conservation outcomes.

In Chapter 15, Fernanda de Vasconcellos Pegas also focuses on a group of animals that are not often considered as particularly endearing to many tourists – sea turtles. She presents a case study of how the social construction of these endangered reptiles has shifted significantly at a major ecotourism destination in Brazil, Praia do Forte. Formerly extensively harvested for meat and eggs, the turtles are now valued for their role in the ecotourism industry which attracts increasing numbers of tourists to the village. The turtles are now valued as living animals upon whose continued existence the livelihood of the residents depends to a great extent. de Vasconcellos Pegas argues that reptiles such as sea turtles can act as flagship species that help promote biodiversity conservation more generally.

The notion of flagship species is also taken up in the next chapter by Jeffrey Skibins. He argues that charismatic fauna such as the great apes, big cats, large African land animals such as elephant and giraffe, and marsupials such as kangaroo and koala have traditionally been seen as attractions that serve to draw tourists to destinations and tourist spaces within destinations such as zoos, aquaria and national parks. More recent configurations of these and other animals with mass appeal within tourism, Skibins argues, embrace explicit conservation roles for these species, transforming them from mere attractions to 'ambassadors' for nature. Tourists can be exposed to broader conservation messages that are designed around the appeal of these flagship species.

The concluding contribution to this set of chapters addresses pet keeping and its changing relationship with tourism. The empirical focus of Chapter 17 by Ulrike Gretzel and Anne Hardy is the recreational vehicle community and the desire by many to travel with their pets. For many of the RVers interviewed, the opportunity to travel with their pets was central to their enjoyment while travelling. Their pets enhanced their travel experience as well as contributing to their sense of 'home' on the road. The inclusion of pets within the travel party came at a cost, however, and routes had to be planned that included pet-friendly camping sites.

Finally, in Chapter 18, I draw out the main themes that have arisen from the chapters and explore some of the implications for tourism as well as identifying further areas for research.

References

Allan, J.R. (2002) The costs of bird strikes and bird strike prevention. In L. Clark, J. Hone, J.A. Shivik, R.A. Watkins, K.C. Vercauteren and J.K. Yoder (eds) *Human Conflicts with Wildlife: Economic Considerations*, Proceedings of the Third NWRC Special Symposium (pp. 147–153). Fort Collins, CO: National Wildlife Research Centre.

Arluke, A. and Sanders, C.R. (1996) *Regarding Animals*. Philadelphia, PA: Temple University Press.

Baker, S. (1993) *Picturing the Beast: Animals, Identity and Representation*. Manchester: Manchester University Press.

Beardsworth, A. and Bryman, A. (2001) The wild animal in late modernity: The case of the Disneyzation of zoos. *Tourist Studies* 1 (1), 83–104.

Berger, J. (1980) *About Looking*. New York: Pantheon Books.

Bulliet, R.W. (2005) *Hunters, Herders and Hamburgers: The Past and Future of Human – Animal Relationships*. New York: Columbia.

Burger, J. and Gochfield, M. (1993) Tourism and short-term behavioural responses of nesting masked, red-footed and blue-footed boobies in the Galapagos. *Environmental Conservation* 20 (3), 255–259.

Carr, N. (ed.) (2009) Special issue: Animals in the tourism and leisure experience. *Current Issues in Tourism* 12 (5–6), 409–587.

Carter, K.E. (2014) *The Dog Lover's Guide to Travel.* Washington, DC: National Geographic.

Christiansen, F., Lusseau, D., Stensland, E. and Berggren, P. (2010) Effects of tourist boats on the behaviour of Indo-Pacific bottlenose dolphins off the south coast of Zanzibar. *Endangered Species Research* 11, 91–99.

CNN (2011) Live animals sold as key rings in China. *CNN International*, 15 April. See http://edition.cnn.com/2011/WORLD/asiapcf/04/14/china.animal.keyring/ (accessed 2 July 2014).

Cohen, E. (2009) The wild and the humanized: Animals in Thai tourism. *Anatolia* 20 (1), 100–118.

Cousquer, G. and Allison, P. (2012) Ethical responsibilities towards expedition pack animals. The mountain guide's and expedition leader's responsibilities towards pack animals on expedition. *Annals of Tourism Research* 39 (4), 1839–1858.

DeMello, M. (ed.) (2010) *Teaching the Animal: Human–animal Studies Across the Disciplines.* New York: Lantern Books.

Digens, A. (2014) 'Is Denmark actually the animal sex tourism capital of the world?'. *Vice*, 2 April. See www.vice.com/en_uk/read/its-legal-to-have-sex-with-dogs-in-denmark (accessed 2 July 2014).

Durrheim, D.N. and Leggat, P.A (1999) Risk to tourists posed by wild mammals in South Africa. *Journal of Travel Medicine* 6 (3), 172–179.

Fennell, D.A. (2012) *Tourism and Animal Ethics.* London and New York: Routledge.

Foer, J.S. (2009) *Eating Animals.* London: Hamish Hamilton.

Forrestal, L.J. and Lehto, X.Y. (2009) Place branding with native species: Personality as a criterion. *Place Branding and Public Diplomacy* 5, 213–225.

Forrestal, L.J., Lehto, X.Y. and Lee, G. (2014) The contribution of native species to sense of place. *Current Issues in Tourism* 17 (5), 414–433.

Fowler, G.S. (1999) Behavioural and hormonal responses of Magellanic Penguins (*Spheniscus magellanicus*) to tourism and nest-site visitation. *Biological Conservation* 90 (2), 143–149.

Franklin, A. (1999) *Animals and Modern Cultures: A Sociology of Human–animal Relations in Modernity.* London: Sage.

Frost, W. (ed.) (2011) *Zoos and Tourism: Conservation, Education, Entertainment?* Clevedon: Channel View Publications.

Gautret, P., Schwartz, E., Shaw, M., *et al.* (2007) Animal-associated injuries and related diseases among returned travellers: A review of the GeoSentinel Surveillance Network. *Vaccine* 25 (14), 2656–2663.

Hall, D., Roberts, L., Wemelsfelder, F. and Farish, M. (2003) Animal attractions, welfare and the rural economy. In D. Hall, L. Roberts and M. Mitchell (eds) *New Directions in Rural Tourism* (pp. 90–101). London: Ashgate.

Haraway, D.J. (1989) *Primate Visions. Gender, Race, and Nature in the World of Modern Science.* London and New York: Routledge.

Herzog, H. (2010) *Some We Love, Some We Hate, Some We Eat.* New York: Harper Collins.

Higginbottom, K. (ed.) (2004) *Wildlife Tourism: Impacts, Management and Planning.* Altona, Melbourne: Common Ground and Sustainable Tourism CRC.

Horrocks, J. (2012) My family and Durrell's Corfu: Jane Horrocks explores the naturalist's Mediterranean island. *The Independent*, 13 July. See www.independent.co.uk/travel/europe/my-family-and-durrells-corfu-jane-horrocks-explores-the-naturalists-mediterranean-island-7939781.html (accessed 2 July 2014).

Jacobson, S.K. and Lopez, A.F. (1994) Biological impacts of ecotourism: Tourists and nesting turtles in Tortuguero National Park, Costa Rica. *Wildlife Society Bulletin* 22, 414–419.

Jafari, J. (2001) The scientification of tourism. In V.L Smith and M. Brent (eds) *Hosts and Guests Revisited: Tourism Issues in the 21st Century* (pp. 28–41). New York: Cognizant.

Jenkins, O. (2003) Photography and travel brochures: The circle of representation. *Tourism Geographies* 5 (3), 305–328.

Johnson, M. (2014) Personal communication with the author, 25 June. University of Newcastle, NSW, Australia.

Johnson, S.A., Bjorndal, K.A. and Bolten, K.B (1996) Effects of organised turtle watches on loggerhead (*Caretta caretta*) nesting behaviour and hatchling behaviour in Florida. *Conservation Biology* 10 (2), 570–577.

Joy, M. (2010) *Why We Love Dogs, Eat Pigs and Wear Cows*. San Francisco, CA: Canari Press.

Kalof, L. (2007) *Looking at Animals in Human History*. London: Reaktion Books.

Kyle, D.G. (1998) *Spectacles of Death in Ancient Rome*. New York: Routledge.

Laroche, R.K., Kock, A.A., Dill, L.M. and Oosthuizen, W.H. (2007) Effects of the provisioning of ecotourism activity on the behaviour of white sharks, *Carcharidon carcharias. Marine Ecology Progress Series* 338, 199–209.

Leiper, N. (2004) *Tourism Management* (3rd edn). Frenchis Forest, Sydney: Pearson Education.

Lovelock, B. (ed.) (2008) *Tourism and the Consumption of Wildlife: Hunting, Shooting and Sport Fishing*. London and New York: Routledge.

Lusseau, D. and Higham, J.E.S. (2004) Managing the impacts of dolphin-based tourism through the definition of critical habitats: The case of bottlenose dolphins (*Tursiops* spp.) in Doubtful Sound, New Zealand. *Tourism Management* 25 (6), 657–667.

McClung, M.R., Seddon, P.J., Massaro, M. and Setiawan, A.N. (2004) Nature based tourism impacts on yellow eyed penguins, *Megadyptes antipodes*: Does unregulated visitor access affect fledging weight and juvenile survival? *Biological Conservation* 119 (2), 279–285.

Mooallem, J. (2013) *Wild Ones*. New York: Penguin Books.

Moscardo, G., Travener, M. and Woods, B. (2006) When wildlife encounters go wrong: Tourist safety issues associated with threatening wildlife. In Y. Mansfield and A. Pizam (eds) *Tourism, Security and Safety: From Theory to Practice* (pp. 209–227). Burlington, VT: Elsevier.

Muyambi, F. (2005) The impact of tourism on the behaviour of mountain gorillas. *Gorilla Journal* 30, 14–15.

Newsome, D., Dowling, R. and Moore, S. (2005) *Wildlife Tourism*. Clevedon: Channel View Publications.

O'Brien, C.P and Gardner, E.L. (2005) Critical assessment of how to study addiction and its treatment: Humans and non-human animal models. *Pharmacology & Therapeutics* 108 (1), 15–58.

Olafsson, O. (2008) Animal brothels legal in Denmark. *Ice News*, 20 May. See www.icenews.is/2008/05/20/animal-brothels-legal-in-denmark/ (accessed 2 July 2014).

Orams, M.B. (1996) A conceptual model of tourist–wildlife interaction: The case for education as a management strategy. *Australian Geographer* 27, 39–51.

Orams, M.B. (2000) Tourists getting close to whales, is it what whale watching is all about? *Tourism Management* 21 (6), 561–569.

Philo, C. and Wilbert, C. (eds) (2000) *Animal Places, Beastly Spaces, New Geographies of Human–animal Geographies*. London: Routledge.

Podberscek, A.L. and Beetz, A.M. (eds) (2005) *Beastiality and Zoophilia: Sexual Relations with Animals*. West Lafayette, IN: Purdue University Press.

Pollan, M. (2006) *The Omnivore's Dilemma: A Natural History of Four Meals*. New York: Penguin Books.

Quan, S. and Yang, N. (2004) Towards a structural model of the tourist experience: An illustration from food experiences in tourism. *Tourism Management* 25 (3), 297–305.

Reynolds, P.C and Braithwaite, D. (2001) Towards a conceptual framework for wildlife tourism. *Tourism Management* 22 (1), 31–42.

Ritvo, H. (1987) *The Animal Estate: The English and Other Creatures in the Victorian Age.* Cambridge, MA: Harvard University Press.

Robbins, J. (2014) Hotels roll out red carpet for jet-setting pooches. *Calgary Herald,* 28 April. See http://cached.newslookup.com/cached.php?ref_id=125&siteid=2117&id=5842509&t=1398690812#_federated=1 (accessed 28 June 2014).

Ryan, C. (1998) Saltwater crocodiles as tourist attractions. *Journal of Sustainable Tourism* 6 (4), 314–327.

Serpell, J. (1996) *In the Company of Animals: A Study of Human–animal Relationships.* Cambridge, MA: Cambridge University Press.

Shackley, M. (1996) *Wildlife Tourism.* London: International Thomson Business Press.

Shapiro, K.J. (2008) An introduction to human–animal studies. In C.P. Flynn (ed.) *Social Creatures: A Human and Animal Studies Reader* (pp. 3–6). Brooklyn, NY: Lantern Books.

Simons, J. (2013) *Kangaroo.* London: Reaktion Books.

Tuan, Y.-F. (1984) *Dominance and Affection: The Making of Pets.* New Haven, CT: Yale University Press.

Walpole, M.J. (2001) Feeding Komodo dragons in Komodo National Park: A tourism tool with conservation complications. *Animal Conservation* 4 (1), 67–73.

Wolch, J. and Emel, J. (eds) (1998) *Animal Geographies: Place, Politics and Identity in the Nature-Culture Borderlands.* New York: Verso.

Part 1

Ethics and Animal Welfare

2 The Status of Animal Ethics Research in Tourism: A Review of Theory *Introduction*

David A. Fennell

Introduction

The purpose of this chapter is to explore the current status of animal ethics research in tourism. It is a topic of interest in view of the fact that animals are used in so many different capacities to facilitate the needs of tourists and the tourism industry. One would be hard pressed to find a destination where animals were not used in some capacity for tourism purposes – animals held in captivity, circuses, rodeos, racing, fighting, pursued in sports, and as workers. It is a matter of concern because up until recently there has been very little interest on the part of tourism theorists in these types of uses. In this chapter I *briefly* examine five main animal ethics theories that have emerged in the literature. In doing so I draw liberally on recent work by Fennell (2012a, 2012b, 2013a, 2013b) and Yudina and Fennell (2013), who have applied all of these theories in a tourism context (see also Çalik & Çiftci, 2013; Fennell, 2012c, for a more comprehensive look at the moral issues tied to the use of animals in tourism). I summarise these theories in Table 2.1, according to the main proponent(s) of the theory, basis of the theory, examples of the theory used in tourism research, examples in tourism practice and the range of the theory's use in tourism.

Animal Welfare

Animal welfare is a family of perspectives that deal with scientific and moral questions regarding the use of animals (see Fennell, 2013b). Minimally, it has been defined as 'the state of an animal as regards its attempts to cope

Table 2.1 Summary of animal ethics theories

Theory and main proponent(s)	Basis of theory	Examples in tourism research	Examples in tourism practice	Range of use in tourism
Animal welfare Many theorists	Morally acceptable to use animals as long as mental and physical needs are taken care of. A focus on maintaining or improving the quality of their lives while in use. The use of animal-specific standards now being developed to maintain or enhance welfare.	Many examples: general, Orams (2002); Fennell (2013b); hunting, Lovelock (2003); zoos, Turley (1999), Mason (2000), Catibog-Sinha (2008), Ryan and Saward (2004); cetaceans, Hughes (2001), Orams (2004), Garrod (2007), Higham and Lusseau (2007); tigers, Cohen (2013); elephants, Duffy and Moore (2010, 2011).	Many examples: *Animals Asia*, wrong to use animals for entertainment; *World Society for the Protection of Animals*, acceptable to use animals for entertainment, with welfare recommendations; *The Brooke*, acceptable to use equines, with welfare recommendations.	Applies to all types of tourism that use animals.
Animal rights Tom Regan	Theory based on inherent value – individuals (human and non-human) exist as ends-in-themselves, i.e. they have value in their own right. Based on respect and justice: we deserve the same respect equally, and one individual is no more deserving of higher moral regard than another.	Few examples: Hughes (2001) on the captive dolphin industry; Orams (2002) on human provisioning of food for animals; Lovelock (2008) on rights and hunting and fishing; Wearing and Jobberns (2011) on ecotourism; Shani and Pizam (2008) in comparison to welfare and environmental ethics; Fennell (2012a).	More examples than in theory. Most rights issues identified in the popular media. Examples include tiger tourism in India (Nolan, 2012); bear baiting in Pakistan (Drake, 2011); the Tiger Temple in Thailand (Garland, 2012); watching crocodiles eat other animals alive (Watts, 2011).	Would reject most types of tourism that use animals. Possible acceptance of some forms of ecotourism.

Utilitarianism Peter Singer	Equal consideration of interests. The suffering of a being is counted equally with the like suffering of any other being to avoid being speciesist. Sentience including suffering and pain given primary consideration.	Very few examples: Dobson (2011) on balancing costs and benefits in marine wildlife tourism; Fennell and Sheppard (2011) on sled dog tourism; Fennell (2012b) on utilitarian theory and zoos; Fennell (2012b).	Theory not used specifically. Related cases include Catalonia's vote and ban on bullfighting (BBC News, 2010); the politics of fox hunting in the UK (Benn, 2010); the killing of released zoo animals in Ohio (Associated Press, 2011).	Would reject all forms of tourism that cause suffering in animals.
Ecocentrism Aldo Leopold	Value is placed on whole systems. Boundaries of the moral community are extended to include all living and non-living things. If activities like hunting are deemed to be good for the whole system, they are morally acceptable – as long as they don't compromise the integrity of the system.	Few examples: Fennell and Nowaczek (2010) on fish and ecotourism; Kontogeorgopoulos (2009) on elephant camp tourism in northern Thailand; Burns et al. (2011) on tourism and dingoes at Fraser Island; Holland et al. (1998, 2000); Fennell (2000) on the legitimacy of billfish angling as a form of ecotourism; Fennell (2013a).	Few examples on ecocentrism specifically. Typical examples include hunting and fishing, but also orang-utans boxing in front of tourists in Bangkok (Aljazeera, 2006); captive black market tigers at Thai temples (Dell'Amore, 2008); endangered shark species (McKie, 2009); hare coursing as a blood sport (Bowcott, 2010).	Would support wide use of animals, with no emphasis on individual interests.
Animal rights Tom Regan	Value is placed on an ethic of responsibility/care, with emphasis on compassion, equity and need. Ecofeminists are critical of moral theories that emphasise a masculine connection to the rest of nature. This often includes recognition of the oppression of animals.	Very few examples. A direct connection to the ethics of care in Swain (2004), Fennell (2006), Holden (2007), Smith and Duffy (2003). Direct connection to animals in Bulbeck (2005), Yudina and Fennell (2013).	Virtually non-existent. Links to the entertainment industry including circuses and zoos by mainly non-tourism focused individuals. Food tourism shows an absence of work on moral issues tied to meat eating.	Would reject animal consumption (food) in tourism and other forms that oppress animals.

with its environment' (Hill & Broom, 2009: 532), and it is typically measured on a scale of very poor to very good.

Animal welfarists maintain that it is morally acceptable to sacrifice the interests of animals for the benefit of humans (Garner, 1993). As such, there is concern over the quality of animals' lives, not over whether animals should be used by humans (Bekoff & Nystrom, 2004). There are two important points raised by Bekoff and Nystrom. First is the aspect of quality of life. If animals are doing well, i.e. well fed, free of pain and hunger, humans are fulfilling their obligations to animals. Secondly, the question of whether humans ought to use animals is a moot point. The pleasures, pain, suffering and sometimes death that animals experience is justified because of the benefits that humans derive from this use. The principal concern is that we should not use these animals badly (Kistler, 2004): in the lab, on the farm, in zoos or in any other way.

Hewson (2003) argues that contemporary definitions of animal welfare fall into three categories: natural living, physiology and feelings/mental/behaviour. Natural living focuses on allowing animals to perform the full range of their natural behaviours. According to this view, physical suffering such as thermal stress, food deprivation and emotional suffering is acceptable (see for example Lund, 2006). The physiological approach (health of skin and fur) and physical environment measures (e.g. food and shelter) are centred on the health and productivity of an animal. If an animal is measured as being healthy and producing well it is said to have good welfare. The third aspect of welfare is feelings. Using this metric, if an animal feels well, it is faring well, and this can be measured by behavioural outcomes. (See Dawkins, 2004, who argues that welfare ought to be defined according to whether animals have what they want and they are happy.) The 'Five Freedoms' is an accepted method by which to gauge animal welfare. Animals are said to be faring well (mentally and physically) if they have: freedom from hunger and thirst; freedom from discomfort; freedom from pain, injury and disease; freedom to express normal behaviours; and freedom from fear and distress.

Criticisms

Kistler (2004) argues that animal welfare may be criticised because of the use of blanket assessments and applications, i.e. what is good for one animal or in one situation is good for all. Added to this is the fact that animals are used in so many different ways, allowing for a wide spectrum of interpretation (Garner, 1993). This diversity has been highlighted by Bloom (2008) in reference to the Australian Animal Welfare Strategy, which provides a 'national framework to identify priorities, coordinate stakeholder action and improve consistency across all animal use sectors' (Department of Agriculture, 2014, np), where animal welfare is subject to shifting interests, including economics, environment, governmental planning, human health and tourism and entertainment.

Singer (2009) highlights the aforementioned issues in the context of animal welfare societies, and how these organisations have yet to prevent cruelty towards animals. He argues that, even though these organisations developed historically to prevent the abuse of animals, they have slowly changed their practices in line with political and economic pressures. As they grew in membership, wealth and respectability, Singer adds, they slowly lost their radical nature and became more a function of the establishment – including close ties with people of prominence in government, research and industry. The more these groups protected their own interests (e.g. scientists working for the food industry, and government protecting food industry interests), the more they compromised their more stringent principles on the treatment of animals. Instead of instigating broad campaigns against any type of cruelty to animals, their mandate has switched to an emphasis on safer activities, 'like collecting stray dogs and prosecuting individual acts of wanton cruelty' (Singer, 2009: 218). Table 2.1 provides an overview of some examples of not-for-profit tourism organisations involved in animal welfare work.

Animal Rights

The most articulate argument in support of the animal rights view in contemporary times is Regan's (2004) *The Case for Animal Rights* (see Fennell, 2012a). Regan's theory is based on inherent value, which means that individuals exist as ends-in-themselves, i.e. they have value in their own right. Regan argues that inherent value is categorical in the sense that individuals either have it or they do not. The criteria used by Regan to ascribe rights includes consciousness, intentionally and sentience (being 'capable of experiencing positive and negative affective states', as defined by Duncan, 2006: 11). For those in possession of these characteristics, Regan argues that all are subjects-of-a-life.

If they have beliefs and desires; perception, memory, and a sense of the future, including their own future; an emotional life together with feelings of pleasure and pain; preference- and welfare-interests; the ability to initiate action in pursuit of their desires and goals; a psychophysical identity over time; and an individual welfare in the sense that their experiential life fares well or ill for them, logically independently of their utility for others and logically independently of their being the object of anyone else's interest. Those who satisfy the subject-of-a-life criterion themselves have a distinctive kind of value – inherent value – and are not to be viewed or treated as mere receptacles. (Regan, 2004: 243)

Respect is a cornerstone of Regan's theory, which is derived from formal justice in a way that is deemed egalitarian (i.e. we deserve the same respect equally) and non-perfectionist (i.e. one individual is no better and therefore more deserving of a higher level of moral regard than anyone else). We should never use others as resources or as a means to an end. The justice principle demands that we not only treat individuals with respect in the manner described above, but we also have a *prima facie* duty to help those who are victims of injustice from the deeds of others, and to never harm individuals.

Regan continues by illustrating that if we have a moral right we are in a position to claim something that is owed to us – we are entitled to treatment of a certain kind (McCloskey, 1965). This means that if one has a moral right, such as the right not to be physically harassed, then others have a direct duty in reference to this right. That is, if one has a moral right to just treatment, then others have a direct duty to uphold this right. Regan argues that it is not simply humans who are deserving of this right, but all beings categorised as having inherent value, as detailed above.

In subsequent work, Regan (1997) enlists Ronald Dworkin's (1977) claim that in democratic societies individual rights 'trump' collective interests. There are actions that, morally speaking, cannot be done to individuals if the collective stands to gain from these actions. By parallel, Regan suggests that if animals have rights, these rights override the benefits that would be derived by the collective (humans) for gain. This means that the use of animals for experimentation, or for entertainment in zoos and circuses, is morally unjustifiable. As such, if the rights of the individual trump all else, and if animals have rights, then all uses of animals that infringe upon their basic rights for human gain must be abolished.

Criticisms

Much of the criticism waged against the animal rights view stems from ideas presented by McCloskey (1965), who argues that there are two conditions that must be in place for the granting of rights. The first is that only a being that can possess things can possess rights. Secondly, only a being that can possess interests can possess rights. In reference to the animal rights debate, McCloskey (1979) contends that rights assume equality, reciprocity and responsibility. If animals cannot assume these capacities, they are not deserving of rights.

Perhaps the most outspoken critic of the animal rights perspective is Carl Cohen (1997), who argues that the granting of rights should be done on a species-specific basis, not on the basis of individuals. Humans are granted rights because they are capable of distinguishing between their own interests on the basis of some external notion of right or wrong. Humans have the ability to comprehend the rules of society as different, perhaps, from what is in their best interests. Animals can't do this. As such, Cohen feels that animals are completely amoral – they simply have nothing close to any concept of morality.

Utilitarianism

Utilitarianism is a teleological or ends-based theory that focuses on the optimum outcomes, ends or consequences of an action. An act is deemed good if it produces or intends to produce at least as great a balance of good over bad as other alternative acts (Frankena, 1963). An act is wrong if it tends to do otherwise. The original configuration of this theory emphasised group happiness (hedonic utilitarianism), i.e. an act is good if it produces more group happiness than other alternatives.

The leading proponent of the utilitarian perspective as it applies to animal ethics is Peter Singer, whose landmark book, *Animal Liberation*, provided the groundwork for an emerging sensitivity towards the interests of animals (Singer, 2009; see also Fennell, 2012b). The bulk of Singer's book examines animals as experimental subjects, and the evil of factory farms – animals viewed as instruments of the trade, no different perhaps from tables or desks – without any regard whatsoever for the fact that they are 'living, suffering creatures' (Singer, 2009: 69). But he also observes that activities like hunting, the capture and presentation of animals for human entertainment, the circus and rodeos, are all practices that fail to take into consideration animal interests.

Singer (2009) argues that there are other things in life besides the calculation of pain and pleasure that are intrinsically valuable (hedonic utilitarianism). Some people are willing to forego times of happiness or pleasure if in doing so this contributes to the satisfaction of other preferences. For Singer, 'The right act is the one that will, in the long run, satisfy more preferences than it will thwart, when we weigh the preferences according to their importance for the person holding them' (Singer, 2003: 527).

Singer's main theoretical premise is equality, which follows from the early pioneers of utilitarianism. Bentham, for example, argued for a system of morality based on 'Each to count for one and none for more than one' (Singer, 2009: 5). This idea suggests that any assessment of the goodness or badness of an act should only take place in consideration of the interests of all of those affected by the action, and weighing these interests equally. Singer argues that this perspective should apply to animals as much as it applies to humans, because both share the capacity to experience pain and suffering. The argument Singer defends is that the interests that non-human animals have in not suffering outweigh the many marginal interests (of their use) for human benefit. This means that those beings, animal or human, made to suffer more, should be accorded a higher level of treatment over those suffering less.

> If a being suffers there can be no moral justification for refusing to take that suffering into consideration. No matter what the nature of the being, the principle of equality requires that its suffering be counted equally with the like suffering – insofar as rough comparisons can be

made – of any other being. If a being is not capable of suffering, or of experiencing enjoyment or happiness, there is nothing to be taken into account. So the limit of sentience ... is the only defensible boundary of concern for the interests of others. To mark this boundary by some other characteristic like intelligence or rationality would be to mark it in an arbitrary manner. (Singer, 2009: 9)

There is evil when we choose to use animals instrumentally in the most inhumane ways even though there is ample evidence that animals do in fact experience pain and can suffer (see also Rollin, 2011). Sentience is thus a core characteristic of Singer's position, and applies to those beings 'capable of subjectively perceiving or feeling by means of the senses. This includes not only being capable of the feeling of being happy and/or unhappy, but also includes beings just capable of perceiving things without having any affective feelings' (Clarke & Ng, 2006: 408). There are important welfare considerations built into the difference between beings that are affective sentients and those determined to be non-affective sentients. Kangaroos, as Clarke and Ng (2006) illustrate, would be an example of affective sentient beings. Bugs may not be.

Singer's (2009) theory has yielded many issues of practical importance. For example, pains that are equal in intensity and duration are equally bad, no matter the species under consideration. If we slap a horse to get it to move, this may not have the effect that a slap with the same force would have on a baby. One is wrong and not necessarily the other. It would be wrong to slap the horse with so much force that it would generate the same level of pain that would cause the baby severe discomfort. In addition, it is important to recognise that Singer's views on equality are not anti-exploitation. If the consequences of an act justify the exploitation of animals, the act would be sanctioned. For example, if a single experiment on an animal or group of animals were to lead to the cure of a horrible human disease, Singer would support such a use. The consequences justify the means. But he also argues that we should be prepared to use humans for these experiments to avoid the charge of speciesism.

Criticisms

A criticism that applies to all theories of animal ethics that use sentience as a key feature, and this includes rights theory as well as utilitarianism, is that sentience is not a sufficient condition for moral consideration (Methany, 2006). For some, there are other more important criteria including language, rationality, intelligence and the ability to reciprocate on a moral level, which we ought to use in extending moral concern to a being or species. The response to this criticism is hard to ignore. Methany asks us how we can be justified in ignoring the pain of another being – which is likely very similar to the type and intensity of pain that we would feel under similar circumstances – especially when we are patently unsure about the inner workings of these animal others (see Nagel, 1974).

More to utilitarianism specifically, Frey (1983) identifies a number of other practical considerations in an attempt to refute Singer's preference utilitarianism, especially Singer's views on agriculture and vegetarianism. One of Frey's key arguments concerns the pain caused to animals as being unfounded, based on his belief that the eater of meat bears no responsibility for how or why animals are killed.

> Suppose my neighbour shoots and kills a turkey: even if it was wrong of him to kill it, is it wrong for me to eat it? It is not obvious how the argument from killing ... can show that it is, when the person who does the eating is different from the person who does the killing, which is the case, of course, with meat we buy in the supermarket. After all, where killing or violating rights or inflicting suffering is concerned, it is normally the person who does these things who is morally suspect. And even if we allow that most abattoirs would not exist if most people did not eat meat, it does not follow that the wrongness of the slaughterer's act of killing, if it is wrong, somehow mystically transfers to the consumer's act of eating. It is true that animals are killed in order to be eaten; but it is killing, not eating, which carries the moral force in the argument from killing and which is being condemned. (Frey, 1983: 28–29)

Frey appears to be more concerned about the many workers who would lose their jobs if the practice of large-scale slaughter were somehow suddenly ended, rather than about the rights or welfare of animals. Here then, is a focus on the interests of workers over the interests of animals.

Ecocentrism

The field of environmental ethics has advanced through the development and refinement of a diverse range of theories that have been organised according to the degree in which they place emphasis on human- and ecologically centred values (see Fennell, 2013a). Curry (2011) has organised these theories into three categories: light green, mid-green and deep green. The first two of these are summarised in brief, with the final category most relevant to the following discussion.

Light green or shallow environmental ethics places direct value on humans (Curry, 2011), and can take one of two general forms: weak and strong. An example of the weak perspective includes enlightened self-interest, which reflects society's need to maintain a healthy environment simply for the purpose of maximising human health and comfort (e.g. ecosystem services such as soil generation, water purification and oxygen production, according to Hull *et al.*, 2003) today and for the future. Although there are good reasons to protect various elements of nature, it is always the interests of humans that take precedence over the interests of these other entities (living or non-living).

Mid-green environmental ethics is characterised as non-anthropocentric but not entirely ecocentric (Curry, 2011). Value is not just placed on humans, but the extension of value also does not extend so far as to include ecosystems. The focus of the mid-green perspective is said by Curry (2011) to be more on animals and, more specifically, individual animals (see animal rights and utilitarianism, above). This type of ethics 'extends moral considerability to (primarily) animals, which are therefore perceived as possessing independent moral status, and therefore as deserving protection for their own sakes, regardless of whether they matter to human beings' (Curry, 2011: 72).

While the mid-green perspective places more emphasis on the value of individual animals, deep green or ecocentric environmental ethics instead places value on whole systems. Examples of this perspective include the self-development and self-realisation components of deep ecology (Naess, 1984), the Gaia hypothesis (Lovelock, 1979), and the land ethic (Leopold, 1970).

Aldo Leopold (1970) has had a significant impact on the way we think about ecocentrism. His sketches and observations on the land ethic took shape in the early 1930s (Leopold, 1933a, 1933b) and culminated in his landmark work, *A Sand County Almanac*, in 1949 (Leopold, 2004). His main maxim, i.e. 'A thing is right when it tends to preserve the integrity, stability, and beauty of the biotic community. It is wrong when it tends otherwise' (Leopold, 1970: 262), has been a mainstay for environmentalists since its publication. Leopold extends the boundaries of the moral community to include animals and plants, rocks, water, soil, and everything else that collectively comprises the land (Nelson, 2004). As long as the consequences of our actions do not compromise the integrity of the biotic community, i.e. if we act in a way that promotes the good, and not harm, of the biotic community on the whole, these actions are morally praiseworthy.

From a practical standpoint, there is no limit to the types of activities that might take place in nature. If hunting, trapping, fishing and other consumptive activities do not adversely disrupt ecological systems, these activities would be deemed morally acceptable. In this capacity, Rowe (1997) argues that we ought to feel more pain at the devastation of wild ecosystems than over the death of individual organisms. This perspective has been adopted by Loftin (1985), who writes that it makes little sense to doctor sick animals because value should be placed not on individual animals but rather on the entire ecosystem. He argues that time, money and other resources would be better channelled into habitat protection or other measures that would protect the integrity of ecosystems.

Criticisms

The main criticism of ecocentrism is that there is deliberate subordination of the wellbeing of all creatures according to the needs of the broader community (Regan, 2004). Individuals may be sacrificed for the greater good of the biotic community, according to Regan (and Brown, 1995, above), in maintaining the stability and integrity of the natural world. Collections of systems like forests might have inherent value, but Regan (2004) finds it difficult to understand how moral rights are attributed to collections of trees or ecosystems. These are not individuals and, as such, are not deserving of moral status (see Steverson, 1994). O'Neil (2000) writes that non-sentient environmental entities like rocks and trees may have intrinsic value, but they don't have moral standing. Moral standing is extended to those beings that can be benefited or harmed – if something works for or against their interests. A sentient being, like a dog, can have moral standing and intrinsic value. By contrast, a beautiful picture may have intrinsic value if it has a good outside of the pleasure it may bring, but not moral standing.

Ecofeminism

While there is no single philosophy of ecofeminism (Kheel, 2009), it is possible to identify core 'presuppositions, principles, precepts, or beliefs that shape ecofeminist thought' (Howell, 1997: 233; see also Yudina & Fennell, 2013). Ecofeminists insist on an interconnection between the domination of women and the domination of nature in patriarchal society. Underlying these oppressions is a series of dualisms: culture/nature, male/female, mind/body, reason/emotion, universal/particular, self/other (Plumwood, 1993). The first of each pair is deemed superior, while the second is not only inferior but in service to the first (Adams, 1993). As Adams (1993) explains, ecofeminist scholars have attributed the dualisms that underpin Eurocentric patriarchal culture to: (i) classical thought and Jewish and Christian religious traditions; (ii) the resulting emphasis of the scientific revolution on autonomy and objective knowledge; and (iii) the abandonment and devaluation of earth-based spiritualities in favour of a sky-god. Men exist separately from and outside of nature, while women and nature are the 'Other'; they do not conform to the masculine norm, and they are objects and property that exist as means to an end (Kheel, 2009).

Many have studied the division of males from the feminine, but most influential is the work of Gilligan (1993), who found that men and women tend to have a different core sense of self. Women tend to identify themselves relationally, as part of an interconnected web. Men, by contrast, tend to identify themselves through separation and individuation, 'since separation from the mother is essential for the development of masculinity' (Gilligan, 1993: 8).

Gilligan (1993) explains that these differences also affect how men and women conceive morality. Women tend towards an ethic of responsibility, which 'relies on the concept of equity, the recognition of differences in need' (Gilligan, 1993: 164) and 'rests on an understanding that gives rise to compassion and care' (Gilligan, 1993: 165). Men tend toward an ethic of rights, 'a manifestation of equal respect, balancing the claims of other and self,' and 'predicated on equality and centered on the understanding of fairness' (Gilligan, 1993: 164–165).

Ecofeminists are thus critical of ethics theories that emphasise a more masculine human connection to the rest of nature (Kheel, 2008: 2). Holist philosophies such as ecocentrism 'typically care about "species", "the ecosystem" or "the biotic community" over and above individual beings' (Kheel, 2008: 2); two of the most influential philosophers of animal advocacy, Singer (1981) and Regan (2001), both 'devalue personal and affective ties' (Kheel, 2008: 17). In these theories there is no room for 'kindness, affection, delight, wonder, respect, generosity, or love' (Vance, 1995: 172).

Some ecofeminists explicitly recognise the oppression of other-than-human animals as a significant aspect of the domination of nature (Gaard, 2002). These theorists – referred to as vegetarian ecofeminists – examine the various contexts of dietary choices given that animals are most commonly oppressed and violated through the practice of meat eating. Vegetarian ecofeminism suggests that we express our feelings for others through concrete action, such as refusing to eat meat through the practices of vegetarianism and veganism. As such, vegetarianism (consumption of dairy and eggs, but not animal flesh) and veganism (avoidance of all animal products for food, clothing, personal care and the like) are not just diets; they constitute 'an embodied response that expresses our feelings for others through concrete actions' (Kheel, 2009: 48).

Contextual moral vegetarianism considers a number of contextual variables – race, gender, class, geography, climate, and so on – in the making of dietary decisions. It is not a 'static, universal, or absolute moral state, but rather a dynamic moral direction' (Gaard, 2002: 134). Gaard and Gruen (1995: 238) note that 'To suggest, for example, that indigenous Aleutians must now grow broccoli because some academic ecofeminist has decided such behavior is the moral high ground is patently absurd'. Instead, contextual ecofeminists encourage us to make our food choices 'more consciously, coherently, and contextually' (Gaard, 2002: 135).

Criticisms

Several theorists have voiced concern about the ethic of care as proposed by ecofeminism. Regan (2001: 60) questions the ecofeminist understanding of the reason/emotion dichotomy. Maintaining that 'emotions without reason can be blind', he asserts that '[t]he task of checking the factual and inferential basis of the emotions we feel exceeds both the reach and the grasp of our power to feel them'. In Regan's view, emphasising reason over emotion does not denigrate emotion, and it is less than obvious why such a dualism or hierarchy between the two is 'a bad thing' (Regan, 2001: 60). Johnson and Johnson (1994) question whether this failure to care in any particular situation frees us from moral responsibility. Even though we may care more for those closest to us, it does not mean that we do not care for those outside our own circle of morality (Singer, 1981).

King (1991: 80) approaches this issue differently, saying that the problem is not so much that we fail to care but that 'there is a plurality of "natures" and a plurality of forms of caring'. This creates a challenge given that many ecofeminists advocate the relevance of personal narrative and storytelling as a way of raising philosophical issues and expressing and fostering a caring relationship with the rest of nature (see Payne, 1994; Vance, 1995; Warren, 2000). In expressing his concern over how we are to navigate and incorporate these lived experiences into a coherent ethical position, King (1991: 84) asks: 'whose voice should we be listening to: the resort developer's, the agribusiness entrepreneur's, the hunter's, the tourist's, the weekend athlete's? These voices are not all compatible with one another, nor are they all interested in the well-being of the natural world.'

Conclusions

The magnitude of animals used in the service of global tourism is incalculable. Up until quite recently animals entered into tourism research discussion in the context of ecotourism or wildlife tourism. And even in these types, little concern has been demonstrated on the part of both researchers and practitioners with regard to the interests of non-human animals. This suggests that animals are generally accorded instrumental value instead of intrinsic value – they are objects or means to an end, rather than subjects – and this is represented in how animals are commodified for the benefit of tourists and operators (Wearing & Jobberns, 2011; the issue of commodification is also addressed by a number of authors in this volume including Burns, Chapter 3; Bone and Bone, Chapter 4; Wearing and Jobberns, Chapter 5; Higham and Neves, Chapter 7; and Cohen, Chapter 10).

In conclusion, much more research is required in the areas of animal welfare, animal rights, utilitarianism, ecocentrism and ecofeminism, for the purpose of deciding how or even if we should use animals in the service of tourism. This research needs to focus on various scales of use (from the local to the cosmopolitan) and how political, economic, social, cultural, historic and environmental forces influence these uses. It is also prudent to suggest that tourism organisations that have not traditionally held animals in any regard (e.g. UNWTO) ought to do so in their efforts to promote truly responsible and sustainable forms of tourism.

References

Adams, C.J. (1993) Introduction. In C.J. Adams (ed.) *Ecofeminism and the Sacred* (pp. 1–6). New York: Continuum Publishing.

Aljazeera (2006) Blow to Thailand monkey business. *Aljazeera*, 23 April. See www.aljazeera.com/archive/2006/04/200841092626122565.html (accessed 8 November 2012).

Associated Press (2011) Ohio police faced charging animals after preserve owner set them free. *The Guardian*, 4 November. See www.guardian.co.uk/world/2011/nov/04/ohio-police-faced-charging-animals (accessed 27 June 2012).

BBC News (2010) Catalonia bans bullfighting in landmark Spain vote. *BBC News*, 28 July. See www.bbc.co.uk/news/world-europe-10784611 (accessed 28 June 2012).

Bekoff, M. and Nystrom, J. (2004) The other side of silence: Rachel Carson's views of animals. *Zygon* 39 (4), 861–883.

Benn, H. (2010) The Hunting Ban is Here to Stay. See http://www.guardian.co.uk/commentisfree/2010/feb/18/hunting-ban-tory-return (accessed 28 June 2012).

Bloom, G. (2008) *Regulating Animal Welfare to Promote and Protect Improved Animal Welfare Outcomes Under the Australian Animal Welfare Strategy*. AAWS International Animal Welfare Conference, Gold Coast, 1 September. See http://www.australiananimalwelfare.com.au/app/webroot/files/upload/files/The%20role%20of%20law%20in%20promting%20and%20protecting%20improved%20animal%20welfare.pdf

Bowcott, O. (2010) Northern Ireland bans hare coursing. *The Guardian*, 23 June. See www.guardian.co.uk/uk/2010/jun/23/northern-ireland-bans-hare-coursing (accessed 9 November 2012).

Brown, C.S. (1995) Anthropocentrism and ecocentrism: The quest for a new worldview. *Midwest Quarterly* 36 (2), 191–202.

Bulbeck, C. (2005) *Facing the Wild: Ecotourism, Conservation and Animal Encounters*. London: Earthscan.

Burns, G.L., MacBeth, J. and Moore, S. (2011) Should dingoes die? Principles for engaging ecocentric ethics in wildlife tourism management. *Journal of Ecotourism* 10 (3), 179–196.

Çalik, A.O. and Çiftci, G. (2013) Animal ethics in tourism. *International Journal of Business and Management Studies* 5 (1). See www.academia.edu/4106557/CALIK_A.O_CIFTCI_G_2013_._ANIMAL_ETHICS_IN_TOURISM._The_International_Journal_of_Business_and_Management_Studies_Vol.5_No.1_ISSN_1309_8047_Online_.

Catibog-Sinha, C. (2008) Zoo tourism: Biodiversity conservation through tourism. *Journal of Ecotourism* 7 (2 and 3), 160–177.

Clarke, M. and Ng, Y.-K. (2006) Population dynamics and animal welfare: Issues raised by the culling of kangaroos in Puckapunyal. *Social Choice and Welfare* 27, 407–422.

Cohen, C. (1997) Do animals have rights? *Ethics and Behavior* 7 (2), 91–102.

Cohen, E. (2013) Buddhist compassion and animal abuse in Thailand's Tiger Temple. *Society & Animals* 21, 266–283.

Curry, P. (2011) *Ecological Ethics: An Introduction* (2nd edn). Cambridge: Polity Press.

Dawkins, M.S. (2004) Using behaviour to assess animal welfare. *Animal Welfare* 13, S3–S7.

Dell'Amore, C. (2008) Black market tigers linked to Thai temple, report says. *National Geographic News*, 20 June. See http://news.nationalgeographic.com/news/2008/06/080620-tiger-temple.html (accessed 8 November 2012).

Department of Agriculture (2014) *Australian Animal Welfare Strategy*. Department of Agriculture, Australian Government. See www.daff.gov.au/animal-plant-health/welfare/aaws (accessed 31 January 2014).

Dobson, J. (2011) Towards a utilitarian ethic for marine wildlife tourism. *Tourism in Marine Environments* 7 (3–4), 213–222.

Drake, M. (2011) Help stop bear baiting in Pakistan. *Care2*, 4 June. See www.care2.com/causes/help-stop-bear-baiting-in-pakistan.html (accessed 23 March 2012).

Duffy, R. and Moore, L. (2010) Neoliberalising nature? Elephant-back tourism in Thailand and Botswana. *Antipode* 42 (3), 742–766.

Duffy, R. and Moore, L. (2011) Global regulations and local practices: The politics and governance of animal welfare in elephant tourism. *Journal of Sustainable Tourism* 19 (4–5), 589–604.

Duncan, I.J.H. (2006) The changing concept of animal sentience. *Applied Animal Behaviour Science* 100, 11–19.

Dworkin, R. (1977) *Taking Rights Seriously*. Cambridge, MA: Harvard University Press.

Fennell, D.A. (2000) Ecotourism on trial – the case of billfish angling as ecotourism. *Journal of Sustainable Tourism* 8 (4), 341–345.

Fennell, D.A. (2006) *Tourism Ethics*. Clevedon: Channel View Publications.

Fennell, D.A. (2012a) Tourism and animal rights. *Tourism Recreation Research* 37 (2), 157–166.

Fennell, D.A. (2012b) Tourism, animals and ethics: Utilitarianism. *Tourism Recreation Research* 37 (3), 239–249.

Fennell, D.A. (2012c) *Tourism and Animal Ethics*. London: Routledge.

Fennell, D.A. (2013a) Tourism, animals and ecocentrism: A re-examination of the billfish debate. *Tourism Recreation Research* 38 (2), 189–202.

Fennell, D.A. (2013b) Tourism and animal welfare. *Tourism Recreation Research* 38 (3), 325–340.

Fennell, D.A. and Nowaczek, A. (2010) Moral and empirical dimensions of human–animal interactions in ecotourism: Deepening an otherwise shallow pool of debate. *Journal of Ecotourism* 9 (3), 178–189.

Fennell, D.A. and Sheppard, V.A. (2011) Another legacy for Canada's 2010 Olympic and Paralympic winter games: Applying an ethical lens to the post-games' sled dog cull. *Journal of Ecotourism* 10 (3), 197–113.

Frankena, W.K. (1963) *Ethics*. Englewood Cliffs, NJ: Prentice-Hall.

Frey, R.G. (1983) *Rights, Killing and Suffering*. Oxford: Basil Blackwell.

Gaard, G. (2002) Vegetarian ecofeminism: A review essay. *Frontiers* 23 (3), 117–146.

Gaard, G. and Gruen, L. (1995) Comment on George's 'Should Feminists be Vegetarians?' *Signs: Journal of Women in Culture and Society* 21 (1), 230–239.

Garland, I. (2012) Shocking footage of tourists 'teasing' drugged tigers slammed by animal rights groups. *The Sun*, 11 September. See www.thesun.co.uk/sol/homepage/news/4532530/footage-of-tourists-teasing-drugged-tigers-animal-rights-groups.html (accessed 24 January 2013).

Garner, R. (1993) Political animals: A survey of the animal protection movement in Britain. *Parliamentary Affairs* 46 (3), 333–352.

Garrod, B. (2007) Marine wildlife tourism and ethics. In J. Higham and M. Lück (eds) *Marine Wildlife and Tourism Management* (pp. 257–271). Wallingford: CABI.

Gilligan, C. (1993) *In a Different Voice: Psychological Theory and Women's Development*. Cambridge, MA: Harvard University Press.

Hewson, C.J. (2003) What is animal welfare? Common definitions and their practical consequences. *Canadian Veterinary Journal* 44 (6), 496–499.

Higham, J. and Lusseau, D. (2007) Urgent need for empirical research into whaling and whale watching. *Conservation Biology* 21 (2), 554–558.

Hill, S.P. and Broom, D.M. (2009) Measuring zoo animal welfare: Theory and practice. *Zoo Biology* 28, 531–544.

Holden, A. (2008) *Environment and Tourism*. London: Routledge.

Holland, S.M., Ditton, R.B. and Graefe, A.R. (1998) An ecotourism perspective in billfish fisheries. *Journal of Sustainable Tourism* 6 (2), 97–116.

Holland, S.M., Ditton, R.B. and Graefe, A.R. (2000) A response to 'Ecotourism on Trial: The Case of Billfish Angling as Ecotourism'. *Journal of Sustainable Tourism* 8 (4), 346–351.

Howell, N.R. (1997) Ecofeminism: What one needs to know. *Zygon* 32 (2), 231–241.

Hughes, P. (2001) Animals, values and tourism – structural shifts in UK dolphin tourism provision. *Tourism Management* 22, 321–329.

Hull, R.B., Richert, D., Seekamp, E., Robertson, D. and Buhyoff, G.J. (2003) Understandings of environmental quality: Ambiguities and values held by environmental professionals. *Environmental Management* 31 (1), 1–13.

Johnson, D.K. and Johnson, K.R. (1994) The limits of partiality: Ecofeminism, animal rights, and environmental concern. In K.J. Warren (ed.) *Ecological Feminism* (pp. 106–119). London: Routledge.

Kheel, M. (2008) *Nature Ethics: An Ecofeminist Perspective.* Lanham, MD: Rowman & Littlefield.

Kheel, M. (2009) Communicating care: An ecofeminist view. *Media Development* 56 (2), 45–50.

King, R.J.H. (1991) Caring about nature: Feminist ethics and the environment. *Hypatia* 6 (1), 75–89.

Kistler, J.M. (2004) Introduction. In J.M. Kistler (ed.) *Animals Are the Issues: Library Resources on Animal Issues* (pp. 1–6). New York: Haworth Press.

Kontogeorgopoulos, N. (2009) Wildlife tourism in semi-captive settings: A case study of elephant camps in northern Thailand. *Current Issues in Tourism* 12 (5–6), 429–449.

Leopold, A. (1933a) *Game Management.* New York: MacMillan.

Leopold, A. (1933b) The conservation ethic. *Journal of Forestry* 31, 634–641.

Leopold, A. (1970) *A Sand County Almanac with Essays on Conservation from Round River.* New York: Ballantine Books.

Leopold, A. (2004) Living with the land ethic. *BioScience* 54 (2), 149–154.

Loftin, R.W. (1985) The medical treatment of wild animals. *Environmental Ethics* 7, 231–239.

Lovelock, B. (2003) International and domestic visitors' attitudes as constraints to hunting tourism in New Zealand. *Journal of Sport Tourism* 8 (3), 197–203.

Lovelock, B. (2008) An introduction to consumptive wildlife tourism. In B. Lovelock (ed.) *Tourism and the Consumption of Wildlife: Hunting, Shooting and Sport Fishing* (pp. 3–30). London: Routledge.

Lovelock, J.E. (1979) *Gaia: A New Look at Life on Earth.* Oxford: Oxford University Press.

Lund, V. (2006) Natural living – a precondition for animal welfare in organic farming. *Livestock Science* 100, 71–83.

Mason, P. (2000) Zoo tourism: The need for more research. *Journal of Sustainable Tourism* 8 (4), 333–339.

McCloskey, H.J. (1965) Rights. *Philosophical Quarterly* 15 (59), 115–127.

McCloskey, H.J. (1979) Moral rights and animals. *Inquiry* 22, 23–54.

McKie, R. (2009) Shark fin ban ends cruel slaughter. *The Guardian,* 11 October. See www.guardian.co.uk/environment/2009/oct/11/uk-shark-finning-ban-extinct (accessed 8 November 2012).

Methany, G. (2006) Utilitarianism and animals. In P. Singer (ed.) *In Defense of Animals: The Second Wave* (pp. 13–25). Oxford: Blackwell.

Naess, A. (1984) A defence of the Deep Ecology movement. *Environmental Ethics* 6 (3), 265–270.

Nagel, T. (1974) What is it like to be a bat? *Philosophical Review* 83 (4), 435–450.

Nelson, M.P. (2004) Teaching the land ethic. *Worldviews* 8 (2–3), 353–365.

Nolan, S. (2012) India bans tiger tourism amid animal-rights push, outraging some. *Globe and Mail,* 2 September. See www.theglobeandmail.com/news/world/india-bans-tiger-tourism-amid-animal-rights-push-outraging-some/article4515569/ (accessed 24 January 2013).

O'Neil, R. (2000) Animal liberation versus environmentalism: The care solution. *Environmental Ethics* 22, 183–190.

Orams, M. (2002) Feeding wildlife as a tourism attraction: A review of issues and impacts. *Tourism Management* 23 (3), 281–293.

Orams, M. (2004) Why dolphins may get ulcers: Considering the impacts of cetacean-based tourism in New Zealand. *Tourism in Marine Environments* 1 (1), 17–28.

Payne, P. (1994) Restructuring the discursive moral subject in ecological feminism. In K.J. Warren (ed.) *Ecological Feminism* (pp. 139–157). London: Routledge.

Plumwood, V. (1993) *Feminism and the Mastery of Nature*. New York: Routledge.

Regan, T. (1997) The rights of humans and other animals. *Ethics and Behavior* 7 (2), 103–111.

Regan, T. (2001) *Defending Animal Rights*. Urbana and Chicago, IL: University of Illinois.

Regan, T. (2004) *The Case for Animal Rights*. Berkeley, CA: University of California Press.

Rollin, B.E. (2011) Animal pain: What it is and why it matters. *Journal of Ethics* 15, 425–437.

Rowe, J.S. (1997) From reductionism to holism in ecology and Deep Ecology. *The Ecologist* 27 (4), 147–151.

Ryan, C. and Saward, J. (2004) The zoo as ecotourism attraction – visitor reactions, perceptions and management implications: The case of Hamilton Zoo, New Zealand. *Journal of Sustainable Tourism* 12 (3), 245–266.

Shani, A. and Pizam, A. (2008) Towards an ethical framework for animal-based attractions. *International Journal of Contemporary Hospitality Management* 20 (6), 679–693.

Singer, P. (1981) *The Expanding Circle: Ethics and Sociobiology*. New York: Farrar, Straus and Giroux.

Singer, P. (2003) Voluntary euthanasia: A utilitarian perspective. *Bioethics* 17 (5 and 6), 526–541.

Singer, P. (2009) *Animal Liberation: The Definitive Classic of the Animal Movement*. Toronto: Harper Perennial.

Smith, M. and Duffy, R. (2003) *The Ethics of Tourism Development*. London: Routledge.

Steverson, B.K. (1994) Ecocentrism and ecological modelling. *Environmental Ethics* 16, 71–88.

Swain, M. (2004) (Dis)embodied experience and power dynamics in tourism research. In J. Phillimore and L. Goodson (eds) *Qualitative Research in Tourism: Ontologies, Epistemologies, and Methodologies* (pp. 102–118). London: Routledge.

Turley, S.K. (1999) Conservation and tourism in the traditional UK zoo. *Journal of Tourism Studies* 10 (2), 2–13.

Vance, L. (1995) Beyond just-so stories: Narrative, animals, and ethics. In C.J. Adams and J. Donovan (eds) *Animals and Women: Feminist Theoretical Explorations* (pp. 163–191). Durham, NC: Duke University Press.

Warren, K.J. (2000) *Ecofeminist Philosophy: A Western Perspective on What it is and Why it Matters*. Lanham, MD: Rowman & Littlefield.

Watts, A. (2011) Croc of gold: Latest tourist show is watching animals eaten alive. *Sydney Morning Herald*, 20 August. See http://newsstore.smh.com.au/apps/viewDocument.ac;jsessionid=C0BC770A107910E68EA3A6CCEE0BB426?sy=afr&pb=all_ffx&dt=selectRange&dr=1month&so=relevance&sf=text&sf=headline&rc=10&rm=200&sp=brs&cls=221&clsPage=1&docID=SMH110820HC3GD6GTRPB (accessed 23 March 2012).

Wearing, S. and Jobberns, C. (2011) Ecotourism and the commodification of wildlife: Animal welfare and the ethics of zoos. In W. Frost (ed.) *Zoos and Tourism: Conservation, Education, Entertainment?* (pp. 47–58). Bristol: Channel View Publications.

Yudina, O. and Fennell, D.A. (2013) Ecofeminism in the tourism context: A discussion of the use of other-than-human animals as food in tourism. *Tourism Recreation Research* 38 (1), 55–69.

3 Animals as Tourism Objects: Ethically Refocusing Relationships Between Tourists and Wildlife

Georgette Leah Burns

Introduction

Tourism is based on the human pursuit of personal satisfaction. It exists within an ethical framework that is instrumental in approach: that is, the industry is based on valuing its product by its use to the tourist (refer to Chapter 2 for a comprehensive overview of ethical positions in relation to animals and tourism). The product is an object constructed for human consumption. When that product is an animal, appreciating it only for its extrinsic value downgrades, or even denies, its capacity for independent agency.[1] In this situation, tourism can exemplify an anthropocentrically focused relationship that objectifies animals and leaves them as the underprivileged counterparts.

This chapter examines the role of animals as tourism objects and the changes offered to human and animal relations as a result of the movement toward more ethically responsible forms of tourism. It explores what the emergence of 'responsible' tourism means for objectifying and commoditising animals, especially in wildlife tourism contexts. Although research on the commoditisation and objectification of wildlife in captive tourism settings is widespread (e.g. Spotte, 2008; Wearing, 2011), it is still largely absent within the context of wildlife in nature-based tourism settings. This chapter discusses literature on objectification, and on responsible tourism, before turning to how engagement with these terms might provide a useful explanatory tool for the current relationships between tourists and wildlife.

As tourism scholars and practitioners look toward more responsible ways to engage with tourism objects, be they people, landscapes or animals, they increasingly turn to the field of environmental ethics. Focusing on examples of human and animal interactions in nature-based wildlife tourism settings, this chapter reviews literature at the intersection of tourism, ethics and animal studies. It then examines a set of ecocentric principles designed to guide the interactions between tourists and wildlife. The principles aim to refocus relations to recognise the intrinsic value of animals, and the need for informed moral reasoning and obligation by people. The guiding principles also stress the interconnectedness between humans and animals, and the need for ethical self-reflection by managers and tourists alike.

Empirically, the chapter draws on case studies from Fraser Island in Australia and the Vatnsnes peninsula in Iceland. Both regions contain significant nature-based wildlife tourism attractions. Dingoes are one of many tourist attractions on Fraser Island, whereas seals are the principal attraction on the Vatnsnes peninsula. Both regions are rural and have small resident human populations: approximately 200 on Fraser Island and 600 on the Vatnsnes peninsula. They are also remote locations, situated several hours' travel from the nearest capital city. These cases illustrate both the need, and the tools, to re-evaluate the way humans interact with animals in wildlife tourism settings.

Objects in Tourism

Discussion of humans as objects was a common theme in early anthropological discourse. In their goal of obtaining a holistic and comparative understanding of humanity, famous anthropologists such as Margaret Mead (1928) traditionally studied the 'exotic Other': those who were different from the usually Western culture from which the anthropologist originated. This approach was subject to a radical epistemological critique sparked by the work of Edward Said (1978) on cultural misinterpretations in post-colonial studies. Johannes Fabian (1983) claimed that anthropological rhetoric served to distance ethnographers from the people they researched, blocking anthropology's awareness of its own politicised context (Marcus, 1984) as well as facilitating a process of subjugation. As part of its response to these critiques, the discipline became closely aligned with sociology in its adoption of a more self-reflexive gaze. Anthropology is not the only field to objectify its subjects. The practice is also commonly seen in tourism, and in fact could be argued is a necessary component of it.

In the context of tourism, people, as individuals and as members of a culture, may be treated as objects for consumption. This is common, for example, in tourist destinations such as cultural centres where both individuals and their culture are displayed for tourists. Much has been written about this phenomenon, about its advantages and disadvantages for the 'Othered' culture, the tourists and the tourism industry more generally (e.g. Desmond,

1999; Greenwood, 1989; Ritsma & Ongaro, 2000). Missing from the litera-ture is the exploration of this notion of 'Otherness' to animals in tourism and, most particularly, to wildlife. Perhaps this is because animals are fre-quently constructed as 'Other' in relation to humans, as part of a cognitive distancing between 'us' and 'them' (Burns, 2014). Reduction to a status as an economic commodity treats animals as 'nothing more than lifeless or non-sentient resources' for our use (Linzey, 2009: 136). Tourism is just one of many ways we use animals and the ethics of our engagement with them in other contexts influences how we perceive animals in tourism. Thus, the 'Othering' of animals in tourism contexts is deserving of investigation.

Objectification has been defined historically as a process of subjugation whereby people, like objects, are treated as a means to an end (Gruenfeld *et al.*, 2008). Objectification theory is commonly discussed in relation to women's studies and gender relations (e.g. Fredrickson & Roberts, 1997); however, the underlying concepts are also pertinent to human–animal stud-ies. As Lopez (1986: 200) notes, 'Because we have objectified animals, we are able to treat them impersonally'.

Objectifying animals nicely serves the purposes of tourism. Tourism is fundamentally a hedonistic activity (Calver & Page, 2013; Fennell, 2008). Tourists are on holiday, with the desire to escape from their normal daily lives and to experience different places and activities that enhance their sense of personal wellbeing and happiness. This basis has meant that for a very long time (and arguably, still) the majority of tourism has been underpinned by an instrumental approach: that is, the industry has been based on valuing its products by their use to tourists. Of course these products constitute many things but, when the product is an animal, the instrumental approach ensures that we appreciate the animal in the context of tourism only for its extrinsic value. As Wearing (2011) notes, economic rationalist approaches often place economic incentive before the intrinsic and intangible values of nature which in turn results in the inappropriate development or use of natu-ral resources. Ignoring the intrinsic value of animals downgrades, or even denies, their capacity for independent agency and can result in the inappro-priate use of them. Objectifying them as a product available for consumption firmly places animals as the underprivileged counterparts in tourism power relations.

Consumption of Wildlife

A huge and diverse industry supports human desires for engaging with non-human animals in different forms of tourism and many scholars have suggested typologies or frameworks to categorise these different forms (e.g. Beardsworth & Bryman, 2001; Cohen, 2009). The focus here is on that part of the industry which includes wildlife (undomesticated animals) in nature-based tourism settings, but does not include hunting or fishing. Wildlife tourism is often segregated into two types based on its purpose of either being consumptive or non-consumptive (Fennell, 2012; Higginbottom, 2004; Lovelock, 2008; Tremblay, 2001), where consumptive is taken to mean the deliberate killing of animals by tourist activities such as hunting and fishing. However, literature on the tourist gaze (Urry, 1990, 2002) and objectification in tourism leads to use of 'consumption' to denote the processes of commoditisation and commercialisation in contexts where natural and cultural features are perceived as the multitude of products experienced by tourists. In this definition of consumptive action, nothing is deliberately killed. It is my contention that wildlife watching, where animals are the tourism product, can also be meaningfully discussed as a form of consumption. Therefore, for the purposes of this work, consumption is used in its more general and broad sense. Deliberately killing animals for tourism purposes comes with a set of ethical stances and assumptions towards wildlife that is worthy of investigation, but is beyond the scope of this chapter (see Chapter 6, this volume, for a discussion of the ethics of trophy hunting).

In the 1990s John Urry brought Foucault's (1976) work on the medical gaze to tourism studies and introduced the notion of a constructed tourist gaze (Urry, 1990, 2002). Urry sees the tourist gaze as responsible for demarcating the 'Other', although he confines his discussion largely to features of townscape and landscape (Urry, 2002). His work forms part of a substantial body of literature that focuses on people as tourism objects, as discussed above, especially in the context of cultural tourism (e.g. Biddlecomb, 1981; Williams, 2011). Tourism can 'Other' or objectify almost anything, and this 'Othering' is strongly related to the concept of commodification. Tourism turns its objects, the focus of the tourist gaze, into marketable items that can be bought and sold. Souvenirs are an obvious example of this, but the objectification and commoditisation also extends to experiences, cultures and animals. They become commodities and have a market price. So they too become objectified, valued as an object for tourist consumption, and such valuation may change their former values.

In wildlife tourism, some arguments claim that promoting wildlife for tourism consumption can bring substantial benefits for the wildlife, most commonly in the form of contributions to conservation (Higginbottom & Tribe, 2004). For example, gorillas in Rwanda have long been objects of a tourist gaze and gorilla tourism is credited with successfully providing many benefits for both the species and the local communities (Figure 3.1) (Nielsen & Spenceley, 2010). There is also considerable evidence that watching wildlife is psychologically good for people (Curtin, 2009) and that such recognition, in turn, has positive implications for environmental conservation (Figure 3.2). This argument for wildlife tourism development, however, firmly positions the welfare and interests of the people above that of the animals. It is an anthropocentric viewpoint that focuses on the

Figure 3.1 The income derived from gorilla tourism helps to sustain a local economy that values the gorillas as living animals that need protecting
Photo: Betty Weiler.

Figure 3.2 Viewing wild animals is an activity enjoyed by many tourists and can lead to greater involvement in nature conservation through donations of money or changes to lifestyles to reduce environmental impacts
Photo: Brian Gilligan.

instrumental value of the wildlife. We conserve them because they can do positive things for us.

Despite positive arguments, objectifying within tourism can also be negative. It is part of an instrumental approach concerned only with extrinsic value. Without intrinsic value the wildlife lack agency and are considered worthwhile only in terms of what they can do for humans. By extension, if the wildlife no longer serves a purpose for humans or in any way threatens our safety or hedonistic pursuit of happiness, then we are less likely to feel morally obligated to consider them as valued stakeholders in tourism processes.

More Ethically Responsible Tourism

Tourism scholarship, like anthropology, is dynamic. Lovelock and Lovelock (2013) ask what changes in tourism have generated the recent interest in ethics. The search for answers requires moving beyond a focus solely on tourism to the movement towards consideration of ethics across a range of disciplines. Social science, for example, has been influenced in the 21st century by a 'critical turn' that directed research to subjects like values and ethics (Tribe, 2010). The changes may have arisen out of growing claims that the three pillars approach to sustainability constitutes little more than another branding opportunity for tourism growth and has been largely a 'policy failure' (Hall, 2011). A broader approach to ethics has the potential to go beyond the three pillars concept (Wedden, 2002). In the last decade, scholarship around the topic of ethics in tourism has increased significantly and branched increasingly into more areas of tourism. Jafari's four platforms of tourism, devised in 1990 and revised in 2001, for example, were the object of scrutiny by Macbeth (2006), who suggested adding a fifth platform on sustainable development and a sixth on ethics. Regardless of the reason for the shift in interest, many labels have arisen that attempt to describe it. One of these labels is responsible tourism.

The 2002 Cape Town Declaration on Responsible Tourism (Responsible Tourism Partnership, 2002) is commonly cited as comprising the defining tenets of responsible tourism, despite discussions around the notion of responsible tourism existing previously (e.g. D'Amore, 1993; Lea, 1993). The declaration contains seven key characteristics of responsible tourism that attempt to address some of the power differentials between different tourism stakeholders (Table 3.1).

Absent from this list, which covers people as well as natural and cultural objects of tourism, are animals. In trying to find a place for animals in responsible tourism, the fourth of these characteristics, 'make positive contributions to the conservation of natural and cultural heritage, to the maintenance of the world's diversity', seems the most relevant, particularly for

Table 3.1 The seven key characteristics of responsible tourism from the Cape Town Declaration on Responsible Tourism

Characteristic	Description
(1)	Minimise negative economic, environmental and social impacts
(2)	Generate greater economic benefits for local people and enhance the wellbeing of host communities; improve working conditions and access to the industry
(3)	Involve local people in decisions that affect their lives and life chances
(4)	Make positive contributions to the conservation of natural and cultural heritage, to the maintenance of the world's diversity
(5)	Provide more enjoyable experiences for tourists through more meaningful connections with local people, and a greater understanding of local cultural social and environmental issues
(6)	Provide access for physically challenged people
(7)	Is culturally sensitive, engenders respect between tourists and hosts and builds local pride and confidence

Source: Responsible Tourism Partnership (2002).

wildlife. One could assume that the intent is to include them as natural heritage, even though this is not explicitly stated. However, inclusion in this way, as an assumed part of something else, is not sufficient. Despite playing significant roles as tourism attractions on all continents, animals are rarely considered in broad managerial-type guidelines. Perhaps most significantly (a point made by Fennell, Chapter 2, in this volume as well), animals are also missing from the UN World Tourism Organisation's Global Code of Ethics for Tourism (WTO, 2014; see http://ethics.unwto.org/en/content/global-code-ethics-tourism) (Table 3.2).

Adopted in 1999, the 10 articles in the WTO code are designed to guide tourism development and, as such, stand as a valuable referential framework, although they are not legally binding. A notable absence in the code's recognition of rights accorded to various stakeholders such as workers, tourists and hosts, is consideration of animals. In this way its approach is anthropocentric, mirroring the dominant ideological justifications for most current and longstanding ethical approaches to tourism study and practice.

Animals are not only ignored, or at best assumed to be included under labels of nature (in juxtaposition to humans as part of culture), in these characteristics of responsible and ethical tourism. They are also not considered as tourism stakeholders, even in models that attempt a wide inclusion of interested parties (e.g. Burns & Howard, 2003; Reynolds & Braithwaite, 2001). These exclusions compound the lack of recognised rights and agency afforded to animals as vital components of tourism.

Table 3.2 The WTO's Global Code of Ethics for Tourism

Article	Description
(1)	Tourism's contribution to mutual understanding and respect between peoples and societies
(2)	Tourism as a vehicle for individual and collective fulfilment
(3)	Tourism, a factor of sustainable development
(4)	Tourism, a user of the cultural heritage of mankind and contributor to its enhancement
(5)	Tourism, a beneficial activity for host countries and communities
(6)	Obligations of stakeholders in tourism development
(7)	Right to tourism
(8)	Liberty of tourist movements
(9)	Rights of the workers and entrepreneurs in the tourism industry
(10)	Implementation of the principles of the Global Code of Ethics for Tourism

Source: WTO (2014).

Dingoes and Ethical Tourism

Although lacking focus on animals, an opportunity derived from the push toward responsibility in tourism practice is that it gives us scope to consider what this means ethically. How can we engage ethically with animals as objects of the tourist gaze? As tourism scholars and practitioners look toward more responsible ways to engage with tourism objects, they increasingly turn to the field of environmental ethics.

Ethical engagement with wildlife has been explored in the case of dingoes in Australia (Burns *et al.*, 2011). Fraser Island, the largest sand island in the world, is part national park and part World Heritage Area. It is home to approximately 150 dingoes who have lived on the island for at least 1000, but possibly as much as 4000 years. The island is visited each year by approximately 400,000 tourists who come to fish, camp, relax on the beach and view the natural features that earned the island its world heritage listing. Increasing numbers of tourists have led to increased interactions with dingoes, and not all of these interactions are positive (Figure 3.3). Dingoes steal food from campgrounds and have bitten people. A child died in 2001 after being chased and attacked by two juvenile dingoes (Burns & Howard, 2003).

The island is managed by the Queensland Parks and Wildlife Service. The response of this government agency has been to shoot dingoes that frequent human areas and are identified as being a problem, increase fines for people who directly or indirectly feed dingoes, and to build fences to keep dingoes out of designated human spaces (Hytten & Burns, 2007). This met with strong public opposition. The policies on which the Fraser Island management

Figure 3.3 Interactions between people and dingoes on Fraser Island can present considerable management problems
Photo: Jennifer Parkhurst.

action is based are human focused, with the intention of maximising the tourism benefits of the destination for humans. The goal of Burns *et al.* (2011) was to explore how the tourist experience on Fraser Island could be structured in a more responsible manner that was less human focused in its ethical stance. They developed a set of seven principles that would enable management policies to shift focus toward a more ecocentric approach (Table 3.3).

Applied to tourism on Fraser Island, Principle 1, the intrinsic value principle, advocates shifting the perception of the value of dingoes from instrumental to intrinsic. This enables an ideological shift away from a preoccupation with what dingoes can offer tourists and allows dingoes to be viewed as valuable simply because they exist on Fraser Island. This move towards intrinsic value recognition is crucial for enacting the other six principles (Burns *et al.*, 2011).

Adopting the principle of moral obligation, a change to human expectations of the destination can be facilitated by encouraging consideration of their obligation to wildlife. This principle advocates informing visitors to the destination of the consequences of their actions. On Fraser Island, visitors need to be aware of the potentially fatal consequences for the dingoes as objects of the tourist gaze. This is connected with the third principle of moral reasoning that suggests that educational material for visitors to Fraser Island should include information about environmental ethics and about the dingoes and their habitat. This is likely to assist the development of moral reasoning in the management and experience of Fraser Island as a wildlife tourism destination (Burns *et al.*, 2011).

Table 3.3 Seven principles for an ecocentric approach to wildlife tourism

Principle	Description
(1) Intrinsic value	Wildlife has inherent value, independent of its usefulness to human activities
(2) Moral obligations	Awareness of the environmental consequences of their actions can compel tourists to change their behaviour through a sense of moral obligation
(3) Moral reasoning	Information on environmental ethics can assist tourists in engaging in ecocentric moral reasoning
(4) Precautionary	If a wildlife tourism action has a suspected risk of causing harm to animals or their habitat, in the absence of scientific consensus that the action is harmful, then the burden of proof that it is not harmful falls on those proposing the action
(5) Avatar	The interconnectedness of humans and nature requires management of both in a more holistic framework as part of shared ecosystems
(6) Belong in nature	Humans must acknowledge that wildlife belongs in and with nature and that humans are visitors to the habitat
(7) Reflective manager	Managers need to self-reflect on how their ethical position is constructed and could potentially change over time

Source: Adapted from Burns et al. (2011).

Implementing the fourth, the precautionary principle, is especially crucial on Fraser Island. There are serious knowledge gaps about the location's dingoes, including crucial data on exact population numbers. If dingo numbers are low, managing behaviour by killing individuals could have detrimental outcomes for the population as a whole. In the face of these unknowns, the precautionary principle places the onus on managers to prove that the action of continued killing is justifiable (Burns et al., 2011).

Management on Fraser Island focuses on the negative effect that interactions between dingoes and visitors could have for people and therefore attempts to separate dingoes and visitors, despite considerable evidence that visitors value the positive experiences of seeing dingoes in the wild (Burns, 2009). Here the Avatar principle[2], that all life is interconnected, encourages an acknowledgement that not all interactions are negative and facilitates the management of positive interactions in a more interconnected and holistic framework (Burns et al., 2011).

In accordance with the sixth principle of belonging in nature, Fraser Island would not be marketed solely as a safe, human-dominated destination. Instead, the intrinsic value and place of dingoes within the ecosystem would be emphasised. Informed that dingoes belong in the ecosystem that the people are visiting, and that dingoes may be aggressive, situates dingoes as more than just objects for tourism consumption and leaves visitors with the choice of whether to venture to this tourist destination (Burns, 2009; Burns *et al.*, 2011).

The strategies that guide the management of human–dingo interactions on Fraser Island have been revised and revisited many times in the last 15 years but remain essentially anthropocentric. Future management decisions on the island could benefit from acknowledging this, and from encouraging managers to be reflexive about their ethical positions (Principle 7). Increased understanding about how ethical positions are constructed, and how they alter over time, can assist with facilitating change (Burns *et al.*, 2011).

Seals and Ethical Tourism

Dingoes and tourists have interacted on Fraser Island for many decades, yet organised seal watching in Iceland is much more recent. It is also growing rapidly in popularity, perhaps indicative of the huge growth in marine tourism activities worldwide (Cater, 2010). Despite strong geographic and demographic similarities between these two wildlife tourism destinations, as outlined in the introduction, there are significant differences in species, behaviour and management. These differences provide a fertile testing ground to examine the ecocentric principles in different contexts.

Iceland has a history of killing seals for human use, following a very instrumental ethical approach to interacting with the species. Seal hunting most likely started at settlement when abundant seal colonies would have provided an important resource of meat and skins for early settlers (Hauksson & Einarsson, 2010: 341). More recently, seal products have been used to supplement other economic resources for rural communities. The new use of seals for tourism provides a further economic supplement, following the continued pattern of an instrumental or extrinsic view of the species as objects for consumption.

Seal hunting was traditionally a legal right for farmers whose land was adjacent to water frequented by seals. A license to shoot them was not required and no quota system on them existed (Hauksson & Einarsson, 2010). As seal watching gained popularity, studies demonstrated that seal behaviour was affected by the presence of tourists (Granquist & Sigurjonsdottir, 2014) and some farmers chose to close their land to tourists to protect seal rookeries. On the Vatnsnes peninsula, three seal watching sites are promoted to tourists and another site is closed to protect the seals. Each of the four sites is owned by a different farmer.

Despite a significant reduction in seal hunting in recent years, declining harbour seal numbers led to a call by marine biologists for Iceland to consider promoting some seal rookeries to tourists interested in watching wildlife as a method for maintaining the population (Hauksson & Einarsson, 2010).

Seal watching must be properly regulated, however, to avoid harassment to the animals (Hauksson & Einarsson, 2010) and provide an attractive and sustainable experience for the tourists.

Considered in the light of the seven ecocentric principles, the change in resource use of seals gives us a chance to rethink the way we interact with this species. The intrinsic value principle advocates recognition of an inherent value of seals that does not exclude their role in tourism but establishes their value beyond this single purpose. As seal watching tourism is a relatively new product in Iceland (the Icelandic Seal Center, established in 2005, is the country's first formal seal tourism organisation), the opportunity exists to inform tourists of their moral obligations when wildlife watching in Iceland and to provide educational material and messages to facilitate moral reasoning towards seals and their habitat.

Seal census data suggest that harbour seal populations in Iceland are in decline so, because of the recent introduction of seal watching, the precautionary principle is of particular importance. The impacts of increased tourism on seal populations are currently unknown. They are likely to be more positive than hunting; nevertheless, precautions should be undertaken and it is especially important to plan ahead to ensure that tourism now and into the future provides conservation benefits.

Employing the Avatar principle enables us to act now in tourism settings to redress the power imbalance between humans and seals that has existed in Iceland since settlement. Recognition of the interconnection between seals and humans grounds the tourism in a more holistic footing. Combined with the belonging in nature principle, these principles remind stakeholders that messages provided to tourists about their wildlife encounter should inform them that they are entering habitat that is natural for, and home to, the seals.

Finally, the reflective manager principle in this case applies mainly to landowners, usually farmers, rather than the government agency discussed previously in the case of Fraser Island. The landowners should be provided with tools to assist them to think about their ongoing ethical relationship with seals as tourism products. This could also be extended to organisations such as the Icelandic Agricultural Advisory Centre who offer advice for farmers on how to utilise resources, including seals.

The situation with harbour seals on the Vatnsnes peninsula is very different from that of dingoes on Fraser Island but offers no less compelling a case in which to apply the ecocentric principles outlined in Table 3.3. In both locations, people seek experiences in nature and are keen to watch wildlife. Despite these similarities in the type of tourism, the management structures employed are very different. This is partly due to Icelandic cultural practices of landowners being the ultimate caretakers of their land. Seal watching destinations on the Vatnsnes peninsula, and elsewhere in Iceland, are most often on private land. Government bodies, such as local municipalities, have little influence on what occurs at these sites. This arrangement has worked well in the past when tourism has been minimal or non-existent, but may not be as effective as tourist numbers increase. In Iceland wildlife tourism has developed without overarching planning, policy and guidelines and thus the opportunity currently exists to begin planning stages with a consideration of underlying ethical principles.

Conclusions

Tourism is traditionally a hedonistic activity, with animals viewed as one of its many 'objects'. As a tourist product, animals have extrinsic value but this does not mean we should deny them intrinsic value. With a focus on making positive contributions to the conservation of natural heritage and diversity, responsible tourism allows us to consider alternative ethical stances for how we engage with wildlife.

Humans need to be responsible towards animals in tourism contexts and move beyond treating them as mere objects for our consumption. However, characteristics in the Cape Town Responsible Tourism Declaration (Table 3.1) do not readily facilitate this. Despite the global importance of this Declaration, and the much cited articles in the WTO Global Code of Ethics for Tourism, they are inadequate for explaining and managing interactions between people and animals in tourism contexts. The existence of animals as tourism objects requires specific inclusion in these strategic documents. Animals are important stakeholders in tourism and recognising them as such would provision them with agency. A much needed ethical component can be added to the three pillars of sustainability and the six platforms discussed by Macbeth (2006), through employing the ecocentric principles examined in this chapter.

As demonstrated through the two case studies of dingoes and seals, adopting ecocentric principles allows us to refocus relations in order to recognise the intrinsic value of animals, and the need for informed moral reasoning and obligation by people. The case studies also demonstrate the advantages of engagement with a precautionary principle, and recognition that nature-based tourism takes place in habitat where wildlife belong; it is their home. The guiding principles also stress interconnectedness (rather than separation) between humans and animals, and the need for ethical self-reflection by managers and tourists alike.

The global move towards more responsible, and more ethical, forms of tourism as well as the absence of concern about animals in these discourses highlights the need to consider animals while also providing the opportunity to be informed about the importance of ethical stances as we move forward to plan new wildlife tourism attractions and revisit strategies for existing ones. By ethically refocusing the relationships between tourists and wildlife, through integrating more ecocentric principles into management policies, practices and planning, we can move away from a preoccupation with seeing wildlife solely as objects for consumption as tourism products.

Notes

(1) See Plumwood (2002) for further discussion on animal agency and its relationship with instrumentalism.
(2) The Avatar principle stresses the interconnectedness of humans, other species and nature as part of shared ecosystems (Burns *et al.*, 2011: 187). The principle was named after a 2009 science fiction film with the same name that featured this type of interconnectedness.

References

Beardsworth, A. and Bryman, A. (2001) The wild animal in late modernity: The case of the Disneyzation of zoos. *Tourist Studies* 1 (1), 83–104.

Biddlecomb, C.Z. (1981) *Pacific Tourism: Contrasts in Values and Expectations*. London: CAB Direct.

Burns, G.L. (2009) Managing wildlife for people or people for wildlife? A case study of dingoes and tourism on Fraser Island, Queensland, Australia. In J. Hill and T. Gale (eds) *Ecotourism and Environmental Sustainability: Principles and Practice* (pp. 139–155). Farnham: Ashgate.

Burns, G.L. (2014) Animals and anthropomorphism in the anthropocene. In G.L. Burns and M. Paterson (eds) *Engaging with Animals: Interdisciplinary Essays on Shared Existence* (pp. 3–20). Sydney: Sydney University Press.

Burns, G.L. and Howard, P. (2003) When wildlife tourism goes wrong: A case study of stakeholder and management issues regarding dingoes on Fraser Island, Australia. *Tourism Management* 24 (6), 699–712.

Burns, G.L., Macbeth, J. and Moore, S. (2011) Should dingoes die? Principles for engaging ecocentric ethics in wildlife tourism management. *Journal of Ecotourism* 10 (3), 179–196.

Calver, S.J. and Page, S.J. (2013) Enlightened hedonism: Exploring the relationship of service value, visitor knowledge and interest, to visitor enjoyment at heritage attractions. *Tourism Management* 39, 23–36.

Cater, C. (2010) Any closer and you'd be lunch! Interspecies interactions as nature tourism at marine aquaria. *Journal of Ecotourism* 9 (2), 133–148.

Cohen, E. (2009) The wild and the humanized: Animals in Thai tourism. *Anatolia: An International Journal of Tourism and Hospitality Research* 20 (1), 100–118.

Curtin, S. (2009) Wildlife tourism: The intangible, psychological benefits of human–wildlife encounters. *Current Issues in Tourism* 12 (5–6), 451–474.

D'Amore, L.J. (1993) A code of ethics and guidelines for socially and environmentally responsible tourism. *Journal of Travel Research* 32 (3), 64–66.

Desmond, J. (1999) *Staging Tourism: Bodies on Display from Waikiki to Sea World*. Chicago, IL: University of Chicago Press.

Fabian, J. (1983) *Time and the Other: How Anthropology Makes Its Object*. New York: Columbia University Press.

Fennell, D.A. (2008) Responsible tourism: A Kierkegaardian interpretation. *Tourism Recreation Research* 33 (1), 3–12.

Fennell, D.A. (2012) *Tourism and Animal Ethics*. London: Routledge.

Foucault, M. (1976) *The Birth of the Clinic*. London: Tavistock.

Fredrickson, B.L. and Roberts, T.-A. (1997) Objectification theory: Toward understanding women's lived experiences and mental health risks. *Psychology of Women Quarterly* 21 (2), 173–206.

Granquist, S.M. and Sigurjonsdottir, H. (2014) The effect of land based seal watching tourism on the haul-out behaviour of harbour seals (*Phoca vitulina*) in Iceland. *Applied Animal Behaviour Science* 156, 85–93.

Greenwood, D.J. (1989) Culture by the pound: An anthropological perspective on tourism as cultural commoditization. In V. Smith (ed.) *Hosts and Guests: The Anthropology of Tourism* (2nd edn) (pp. 171–185). Philadelphia, PA: University of Pennsylvania Press.

Gruenfeld, D.H., Inesi, M.E., Magee, J.C. and Galinsky, A.D. (2008) Power and the objectification of social targets. *Journal of Personality and Social Psychology* 95 (1), 111–127.

Hall, C.M. (2011) Policy learning and policy failure in sustainable tourism governance: From first and second to third order change? *Journal of Sustainable Tourism* 19 (4–5), 649–671.

Hauksson, E. and Einarsson, S.T. (2010) Review on utilization and research on harbor seal (*Phoca vitulina*) in Iceland. *NAMMCO Scientific Publications* 8, 314–353.

Higginbottom, K. (2004) Wildlife tourism: An introduction. In K. Higginbottom (ed.) *Wildlife Tourism: Impacts, Management and Planning* (pp. 1–14). Altona, Australia: Common Ground Publishing.

Higginbottom, K. and Tribe, A. (2004) Contributions of wildlife tourism to conservation. In K. Higginbottom (ed.) *Wildlife Tourism: Impacts, Management and Planning* (pp. 99–124). Altona, Australia: Common Ground Publishing.

Hytten, K. and Burns, G.L. (2007) Deconstructing dingo management on Fraser Island, Queensland: The significance of social constructionism for effective wildlife management. *Australasian Journal of Environmental Management* 14, 40–49.

Lea, J. (1993) Tourism development ethics in the Third World. *Annals of Tourism Research* 20, 701–715.

Linzey. A. (2009) *Why Animal Suffering Matters: Philosophy, Theology, and Practical Ethics.* New York: Oxford University Press.

Lopez, B. (1986) *Arctic Dreams: Imagination and Desire in a Northern Landscape.* New York: Charles Scribner.

Lovelock, B. (2008) An introduction to consumptive wildlife tourism. In B. Lovelock (ed.) *Tourism and the Consumption of Wildlife: Hunting, Shooting and Sport Fishing* (pp. 3–30). New York: Routledge.

Lovelock, B. and Lovelock, K. (2013) *The Ethics of Tourism: Critical and Applied Perspectives.* New York: Routledge.

Macbeth, J. (2006) Towards an ethics platform for tourism. *Annals of Tourism Research* 32 (4), 962–984.

Marcus, G.E. (1984) Review of 'Time and the Other: How Anthropology Makes Its Object' by Johannes Fabian. *American Anthropologist* 86 (4), 1023–1025.

Mead, M. (1928) *Coming of Age in Samoa: A Psychological Study of Primitive Youth for Western Civilization.* New York: William Morrow.

Nielsen, H. and Spenceley, A. (2010) The success of tourism in Rwanda – gorillas and more. World Development Report 2011 Background Paper. Washington, DC and The Hague: World Bank and SNV.

Plumwood, V. (2002) *Environmental Culture: The Ecological Crisis of Reason.* London: Routledge.

Responsible Tourism Partnership (2002) *The Cape Town Declaration*, International Conference on Responsible Tourism in Destinations, Cape Town. See www.responsibletourismpartnership.org/CapeTown.html (accessed 23 June 2014).

Reynolds, P.C. and Braithwaite, D. (2001) Towards a conceptual framework for wildlife tourism. *Tourism Management* 22 (1), 31–42.

Ritsma, N. and Ongaro, S. (2000) The commoditisation and commercialisation of the Maasai culture: Will cultural Manyattas withstand the 21st century? Proceedings of the ATLAS Africa International Conference, December, Mombasa, Kenya (pp. 127–135).

Said, E. (1978) *Orientalism*. New York: Vintage Books.

Spotte, S. (2008) *Zoos in Postmodernism: Signs and Simulation*. Madison, NJ: Fairleigh Dickinson University Press.

Tremblay, P. (2001) Wildlife tourism consumption: Consumptive or non-consumptive? *International Journal of Tourism Research* 3 (1), 81–86.

Tribe, J. (2010) Tribes, territories and networks in the tourism academy. *Annals of Tourism Research* 37 (1), 7–33.

Urry, J. (1990) *The Tourist Gaze: Leisure and Travel in Contemporary Societies*. London: Sage.

Urry, J. (2002) *The Tourist Gaze* (2nd edn). London: Sage.

Wearing, S. (2011) Ecotourism and the commodification of wildlife: Animal welfare and the ethics of zoos. In W. Frost (ed.) *Zoos and Tourism: Conservation, Education, Entertainment?* (pp. 47–58). Bristol: Channel View Publications.

Weddon, C. (2002) Ethical tourism: An opportunity for competitive advantage? *Journal of Vacation Marketing* 8 (2), 141–153.

Williams, I. (2011) Impact of eco-tourism on African societies – case study of the Maasai. Social Science Research Network. See http://ssrn.com/abstract=1972668 (accessed 23 June 2014).

WTO (World Tourism Organisation) (2014) *Global Code of Ethics for Tourism*. Madrid: UNWTO. See http://ethics.unwto.org/en/content/global-code-ethics-tourism (accessed 23 June 2014).

4 The Same Dart Trick: The Exploitation of Animals and Women in Thailand Tourism

Kate Bone and Jane Bone

Introduction

The exploitation of animals and women in Thailand's tourism industry is both disturbing and disturbingly similar. Thailand is a major tourist site well known for its pristine white sand beaches, ancient temples and fresh food. However, these surface attractions are shadowed by tourist experiences centred on the sex industry and animal abuse. In this chapter we examine the relationships between the sex industry and animal abuse through 'the same dart trick', that we argue oppresses women and animals, in this case, elephants. The dart trick (woman) is a sexualised performance for tourists whereby a dart is fired into a balloon from the woman's vagina. The dart trick (elephant) is performed by an elephant using its trunk to throw the dart to burst the balloon. We play on the word 'trick' as both a term referring to 'a clever or dexterous feat intended to entertain, amuse', often related to what animals can be taught to do, and 'trick' in slang relating to the act of prostitution (Dictionary.com, 2010).

Our argument is that the construction, through the tourist gaze, of animal and female in Thailand is about Othering (Pritchard & Morgan, 2000; Said, 1995). The post-human and feminist perspectives we are adopting enable us to consider both woman and elephant. It is important to note that Thailand's sex tourism industry does not exclusively involve women as it is common for children (Child Wise, 2014) and transgender or *kathoey* people to be involved in sex tourism (Ocha & Earth, 2012). However, the 'dart trick' that oppresses women and animals is the central focus of this chapter.

We argue in this chapter that there are parallels between the treatment of these woman and animal Others as objects of *consumption* (Urry, 1990). Edensor (2007) claims that tourists are also performers in tourism; they bring their privileges and cultural expectations to different contexts. This may mean that tourists indulge in extreme behaviours on the *stage* (Edensor, 2001) of the popular tourist destination of Thailand. The complexity of the tourist role is explored here using 'the same dart trick' as a focus.

Internationally Thailand is well known as a tourist destination and according to the official Tourism Authority of Thailand website:

> Thailand is a wondrous kingdom, featuring Buddhist temples, exotic wildlife, and spectacular islands. Along with a fascinating history and a unique culture that includes delectable Thai food and massage, Thailand features a modern capital city, and friendly people who epitomize Thailand's 'land of smiles' reputation. (Tourism Authority of Thailand, 2013)

This excerpt highlights the desire of the tourism authority to represent the Thai people as eager to please, happy and carefree, serving the 'deserving' tourists. In actuality, Thailand is a country whose people face profound inequality (World Bank, 2013), widespread corruption (Transparency International, 2013), and growing political instability. Writing for the Institute of Human Rights and Business (IHRB), Barnett (2011) notes the ambiguous relationship between tourist and destination in places like Thailand where the environment and the local population become exploited by people who view the experience as an unproblematic holiday. Our work supports a growing concern for the treatment and representation of animals in tourism (Bertella, 2013; Fennell, 2013) and particularly the role of the elephant in Thailand's tourism industry (Cohen, 2010; Duffy & Moore, 2010; Kontogeorgopoulos, 2009; see also Cohen, Chapter 10, this volume). Taking a post-human (Haraway, 2008) and feminist perspective (Adams, 1995, 2003, 2010) we problematise 'the same dart trick' in terms of its implications for animals and women in Thailand tourism.

Theoretical Perspective

This chapter uses post-human and feminist perspectives to analyse the oppressive features of exploitative spectacles that feature women and animals in Thailand's tourism industry. Tourism proves to be an agent through which patriarchal ideals are mobilised and enforced upon performers (including the tourists themselves) acting within the tourist's realm (Edensor, 2000). This chapter calls for a sense of 'response-ablity' (Haraway, 2008: 88) in terms of tourism, and recognises that tourists might find certain experiences aversive (Howard, 2009). In Haraway's (2008) use of the term 'response-ability' she emphasises that, in comparison to the taken-for-granted word, responsibility, response-*ability* highlights the *ability* to act, to go beyond one's duty and realise that one must be in a respectful relationship with the Other (in this case women and animals in Thailand). In the context of this chapter, 'response-ability' acknowledges the power of the tourist to react and respond in a way that is respectful instead of going along with exploitative practices and accepting them as a new 'norm'. A feminist perspective calls for recognition that 'feminist defences of animals insist that we must acknowledge and accept accountability for what we do to others' bodies' (Adams, 1995: 13). Adams (2003) drew the parallel between the female body and the animal in terms of meat. She used images and phrases and noted that:

> Women are called by the names of other beings who are not free to determine their own identity, 'pets', (sex) kitten, (Playboy) bunny, dog, beast, bird, bitch, heifer, sow, lamb, cow. Abusive epithets for young women have included hen, bird, flapper, quail, columbine, and, of course, chick – tasty or otherwise. (Adams, 2003: 31)

Adams' (2003) work highlights the similarities between the way women and animal bodies are represented. Haraway's (2008) work is used in terms of post-human theorising. Post-human theory disrupts the boundary between human and animal or machine and disturbs the idea that the human is at the top of the hierarchical chain. The animal as 'more than human' or 'other than human' marks these distinctions. The phrase 'more than human' makes the point that the human is part of the category 'animal' and that this is not without its limitations. Haraway's (2008) work calls for both to be respected as human and animal. Taking a post-human perspective enables us to disturb tourist complacency and question the acceptance of practices which exist within the tourist 'bubble', constituting a short period of touristic fantasy that we argue has longer term implications.

Post-human theory breaks down the category of human and everything else; it is not about simple comparisons but is a means to claim the possibility of different relationships for both the human and non-human animal. Post-human theory, according to Haraway (2008: 18), explores beyond the humanist, and is relevant here because:

> The discursive tie between the colonised, the enslaved, the noncitizen, and the animal – all reduced to type, all Others to rational man, and all essential to his bright constitution – is at the heart of racism and flourishes, lethally, in the entrails of humanism. (Haraway, 2008: 18)

The exploration undertaken here is an aspect of 'response and respect' (Haraway, 2008: 19), made possible when boundaries are blurred between species and when we learn to do what Haraway stresses is so important, namely, to 'pay attention' (Haraway, 2008: 19). She insists that we pay attention to the fact that, whether human or non-human, 'ways of living and dying matter' (Haraway, 2008: 88). Respect is *respecere* – looking back, holding in regard, understanding that meeting the look of the other is a condition of having faced oneself. All of this is what I am calling "sharing suffering". It is not a game ...' (Haraway, 2008: 88).

Methodology

Critical content analysis was the methodology used to analyse the data to generate findings that support the critique presented here. Information was found on official governmental websites, blog sites, web pages and Google web and image searches. Urry (1994: 235) supports this methodology as he argues that 'images replace ideologies' in the *'visualisation of culture'* (Urry's italics). In research about specific tourist sites, Urry (1994: 238) recommends interpreting texts through qualitative techniques: 'to identify the discursive structures which give rise to and sustain, albeit temporarily, a given tourist site'. Destination branding is managed by organisations involved in promotion, unlike destination imaging, which is 'owned by tourists' as they interpret a context (Munar, 2011: 293).

Websites play an important role in destination branding and a content analysis methodology is appropriate to explore the influential nature of these representations (Horng & Tsai, 2010). User-generated content websites (blogs, TripAdvisor forums and YouTube) aid in the creation of destination imaging (Munar, 2011). Content analysis is a subjective research methodology as the signs from these website sources have been filtered through our own researcher perspective (see Urry, 1994: 238). The process of cultural interpretation was influenced by our position as Western female academics with a disposition toward animal and human rights activism. Urry (1994: 233) advocates for the methodological approach used in this chapter as he claims that tourist practices are *'cultural,* that is, they comprise signs, images, texts and discourse' (authors' italics). In using this methodological approach we take advantage of information flows which, according to Szerszynski and Urry (2006: 117), comprise 'knowledge, money, commodities, people and images'.

Othering as a Process of Oppression

The interchangeability of discourse and ideologies surrounding the representations of female and animal bodies has been explored in the literature (see Jones, 2004; Kalof *et al.*, 2004; Power & Watts, 1997). Uncomfortable and confronting parallels between the female and animal body as sites of exploitation were proposed by Adams (2003) in *The Pornography of Meat.* Adams demonstrates that the same images and languages are used to designate both. She notes 'a young prostitute is known as *fresh meat;* an older prostitute, *dead meat'*

(Adams, 2003: 11; author italics). The divorce of the body of the animal from meat is a commonplace observation in Western society where the abattoir is separate from the supermarket, the field from the plate, and caricatures of feminised chickens advertise their own flesh – roasted, grilled or fried.

To exemplify these feminised animals, a local hot-chicken shop in Australia is called 'Best Legs in Town' (Best Legs in Town, 2013). The shop-front on the internet site is like a sex shop with a backlit sign of a chicken with long red hair, its feathers formed into a minidress, legs crossed, with red high heels being donned instead of chicken feet. The words 'tasty fresh and tender roast chickens' describe what is for sale along with offers for party catering services and party orders, much like strippers are ordered for celebrations. A small Australian flag is stabbed into the body of the roast chicken so that this product is connected to the national identity. It is worth noting that 'chicken' is also slang for an attractive woman, an older woman may be described as 'no spring chicken', and it is a term also used for a prostitute whose speciality is oral sex (Urban Dictionary, 2014).

Our content analysis of the Thailand tourism industry reinforced these links between the interchangeability of women and animals in tourism spectacles. Discourses regarding tourist attitudes towards women and animals in Thailand, as found on blog sites and other public web pages, were equally as violently and sexually charged and a website (now banned by Google) revolved around real tourist shooting ranges where people can pay to fire guns or rocket launches at targets or, for a higher cost, chickens or cows. This clearly demonstrates the attitudes and actions of some tourists towards animals and people in developing countries and problematises tourist performance.

Both women and animals in Thailand suffer from similar oppressive techniques such as being contained within cages and controlled through abuse to assist in their docility in order to enable tourist amusement. A *Care for the Wild International* (CWI, 2008) report found a popular tourism 'Tiger Temple' kept tigers in horrific conditions; 'Tigers are dragged into position by their tail and even punched or beaten to adopt particular postures... Temple staff stay close to the animals at all times to maintain control by use of tiger urine squirted from a bottle into the animal's face...' (CWI, 2008: 3). Such confinement and control echoes the treatment of Thai bar girls as they are confined within the bar, disciplined through fines and ultimately controlled through patriarchy. The women in Thai sex bars wear number badges as identification so that men can 'order' the woman they would like to 'buy' and if the women fail to wear their number badges they are fined by the bar owner (Manderson, 1992: 459). The identity badges and nudity implicit to the women's role as prostitutes in Thailand strip the women of any identity outside of that attributed to them through the male gaze (Manderson, 1992; Pritchard & Morgan, 2000). In bar settings control is embodied by the male patrons as their ejaculation drives the degradation of the women just as the urine spray controls the tigers.

The similarity between sexual discourse and that of violence is clearly displayed here and has been found in other research that supports Adams' (2003) arguments. Kalof *et al.* (2004) found that violence and sexuality were clearly linked in the discourse of sport hunting magazines. For instance, the magazines describe the death of the animal as a 'climax' or 'score' and hunting as 'hot and heavy action'. The discourse described here is problematic for all parties involved in Thailand's tourism industry including organisations like Animals Asia (2012) that actively resist violence against animals.

Performance

In this chapter, while the spectacle of tourism in Thailand is discussed, the critique is also focused on the performance of tourists both during their visits and after their return home. Due to the inequalities marked by the privileged tourist, tourism becomes an agent for oppression. Edensor (2000) claims that performances are located in the tourists' originating culture rather than the host culture, and therefore the primary critique of tourist performances refers back to the culture of the tourists' homeland. Certain practices designated unacceptable or illegal in the homeland are tolerated and even celebrated in places where these social controls cease to operate, when 'opportunities are available to transgress ordinary morality, to consume excessively and perform in a carnivalesque spirit' (Edensor, 2007: 199).

Tourist typologies

While there are clearly defined sex tourist typologies (ECPAT, 2010), tourists who engage in animal tourism may be equally diverse. Some may become inadvertent supporters of an abusive tourism industry (Tourism Concern, 2013) and find themselves caught up in unexpected street performances with endangered and exploited species in Thailand, such as, for example, gibbons. In some instances, animal tourism may be the sole purpose of their trip, for example, wildlife or jungle safari tours (Thailand Uncovered, 2014). Not all forms of animal tourism are necessarily abusive, but Tourism Concern (2013) describes the challenge for 'adventurous' and 'animal lover' tourists not to fall into the 'traps' of exploiting animals when travelling overseas:

> As a nation of animal lovers, temptation to get up close to such exotic animals as gibbons, slow lorises, snakes, bears and even lions and tigers is often too much. But, by doing so tourists can inadvertently be supporting a lifetime of abuse for these animals and encouraging an industry that causes suffering, killing and cruelty for the exact creatures that we love so much. (Tourism Concern, 2013)

From this perspective, tourists are not passive entities; rather, they are performing agents and, far from leaving everyday life behind them, they 'carry out particular habits and practices as tourists' (Edensor, 2007: 201). From a post-human feminist perspective we suggest that this should involve taking response-ability (Haraway, 2008) for what they see, buy and do, despite being elsewhere. Edensor (2007: 202–203) claims that 'when tourists enter particular stages, they are usually informed by pre-existing discursive, practical, embodied norms which help to guide their performative orienta-tions and achieve a working consensus about what to do'. This argument proposes that tourists are accountable for their actions. However, it seems that as soon as the tourist enters Thailand's tourism stage, morality and social norms are cast aside for erotic and exotic experiences (Fennell, 2013; Pritchard & Morgan, 2000).

This observation is supported through the 'anonymity' that being a tour-ist brings about (The United States Department of Justice, 2015). Travelling and being a tourist breaks down the boundaries of what is classed as accept-able behaviour. Thailand, as an away-from-home context, offers tourists new expectations and, at the same time, it offers no expectations at all (Edensor, 2000, 2001). In this sense tourism spaces can become 'liminal playgrounds' (Larsen et al., 2007: 246), offering new zones for unregulated experimentation. This type of experience is analysed using the example of 'the same dart trick'.

Stage: The Same Dart Trick

An example of the oppression of animals and women in Thailand is the tourist performance known as the dart trick. In this performance the female sex worker at a bar shoots darts out of her vagina which fly through the air and pop balloons (Mai, 2005). Elephants also perform a dart trick: 'the elephants demonstrate a variety of skills, most of them simulations of human leisure activities: sitting on chairs, throwing darts on balloons, or driving a tricycle' (Cohen, 2009: 28; see also Chapter 10, this volume). Elephants are trained to do these tricks as this is not a natural animal behaviour. There is a long rela-tionship between people and elephants in Thailand. One of the mediators of this behaviour and a traditional means of training the elephant is 'the crush'.

The crush

The subduing of the elephant body is carried out in a torturous process known as 'the crush'. The only way that an elephant would be able to per-form tricks such as throwing darts onto balloons is by being traumatised from a young age and this works by a process of pain and fear. According to a commentator, 'once they have their souls stomped out, they are simply vessels entertaining people. They are chained' (Pipa, 2013, np). As Fennell

(2013: 326) points out, 'the pleasures, pain, suffering and sometimes death that animals experience is justified because of the benefits that humans derive from this use' but, as he says, this does not absolve us from moral obligations or the requirement to think ethically about what Haraway (2008: 74) calls our 'relations of use'. 'The crush' torture is described on the *National Geographic* website as follows:

> It's a sound not easily forgotten. Just before dawn in the remote high-lands of northern Thailand, west of the village Mae Jaem, a four-year-old elephant bellows as seven village men stab nails into her ears and feet. She is tied up and immobilized in a small, wooden cage. Her cries are the only sounds to interrupt the otherwise quiet countryside.
>
> The cage is called a 'training crush'. It's the centerpiece of a centuries-old ritual in northern Thailand designed to domesticate young elephants. In addition to beatings, handlers use sleep-deprivation, hunger, and thirst to 'break' the elephants' spirit and make them submissive to their owners. (Hile, 2002, np)

These elephants are taken from their mothers at a young age in order to entertain tourists for the rest of their lives. According to Pipa (2013, np) tourists 'send a clear message to the elephant tourism industry that shows they support the torture these animals go through early in their life, as well as the horrific conditions they live in as cogs in the tourism wheel'. The evidence of this torture is shown in photographs and videos portraying the beatings and torments inflicted on the baby elephants (Pipa, 2013). Natural elephant behaviour does not include throwing darts at balloons as a tourist spectacle; they are forced to enact such degrading tricks through fear and dominance.

The elephant show

There are cautions on TripAdvisor about elephant shows in Thailand. For example, *Nong Nooch Tropical Botanical Garden* is one tourist attraction that is warned to be a site where animal abuse is reported and tourists have been allegedly injured and killed by the animals there (TripAdvisor, 2014). Tourist reactions about this attraction are mixed. The TripAdvisor website has reviews from 1298 tourists of which the rating table shows 782 reports of 'Excellent' in comparison to 18 who judged the attraction 'Terrible'. Tourists commented from the 'Excellent' perspective that their visit was 'awesome', 'unforgettable', 'stunning', 'a great day out for the kids' and a 'must visit' location. In comparison, most of the 'Terrible' reviews were based on concerns for animal welfare. They described tigers and elephants being chained up, in small cages, drugged; animals in a sorry state, thin, the owners being only interested in making money and the appalling treatment of the animals. Some tourists reported emotional reactions such as: 'one of my friends wept on the way home'. Disturbingly, while the animal abuses are clearly observed, a disproportionate number of reviews were positive regardless of the maltreatment of the animals.

The contested nature of reactions to such tourist shows is evident on a YouTube (2007) clip, *Elephant Darts*, which shows elephants performing the dart trick. In one dialogue, the extreme difference in perspective is evident:

'who cares about the elephants welfare, I want to see some fucking elephants throwing darts!'

'fuck.'

'I don't find throwing darts that tortuous, the elephant should be glad it's even allowed to play darts.'

'I would take pleasure in putting you through the same torture that elephant went through.' (YouTube, 2007)

Many tourists see elephant shows and animal encounters as an acceptable part of their Thailand experience, while others (seemingly a smaller number) are morally outraged and emotionally upset by witnessing animals they see as suffering, confined and drugged. With Fennell (2013: 326), we support asking 'new questions about the moral acceptability of using so many animals for purposes of personal comfort and entertainment'. There must be some critique of the moral position claimed by one contributor on TripAdvisor (2014), who said about a Bangkok Elephant Theme show: 'this is a great show – you have to put your morals down by a little and think: "when in Rome . . ."' and so forth. If you like elephants this is the place to be.' This 'setting aside' of moral considerations seems to permeate the tourist experience in Thailand and helps to support what happens to the body of the Other.

Patriarchal dominance

Even the instruments used in such tricks, i.e. darts, embody gendered connotations. The elephant performing the dart trick entertains tourists because of the anthropomorphic qualities of an elephant throwing darts. However, we argue that the dart denotes male penetration as the elephants have been tortured by men who stab them and force them to throw the darts when in a submissive state. Through an anthropocentric lens (where humans are placed at the top of the hierarchy), the elephant dart trick might be seen as acceptable or 'cute' because it mimics a human activity. In contrast, post-human theory stipulates that 'we are in a knot of species co-shaping one another in layers of reciprocating complexity all the way down' (Haraway, 2008: 42). This theory challenges hierarchies of domination. Instead, post-human theory suggests recognition that we are 'beings-in-encounter' and 'knotted beings' (Haraway, 2008: 5). In the case of the same dart trick the hierarchies are maintained to ensure that the body of the woman and the elephant demonstrate submission. Post-human theorising suggests another way rather than humanism because humanism constructs everything that 'lies outside the bright territory of man' (Haraway, 2008: 18) as Other.

The dart

The same dart trick is performed by both animals and women, thus suggesting that these 'entertainers' are positioned to fulfil the desires of the all-pervasive tourist gaze (Urry & Larsen, 2011). The tourist is exempt from performing such humiliating tricks. Tricks performed by animals and women in the spectacle reinforce animal and female roles of submission and ridicule that are inherent to patriarchal society. Tourism proves to be an agent through which patriarchal ideals are mobilised and enacted. The dart trick for the women may appear to be more demeaning but because of the training involved for the elephant the suffering is not less. From the perspective of post-human theory, taking response-ability involves a sharing of suffering regardless of species (Haraway, 2008).

Kalof et al. (2004) found in their analysis of hunting discourse that bows and arrows are often attributed feminised or masculinised characteristics. Kalof et al. (2004: 245) describe how 'the active, projectile arrow was imbued with stereotypically male characteristics and depicted as an extension or embodiment of the (male) hunter, the bow was feminized and sexualized, often described as beautiful, smooth, and dependable'. The arrow/dart projects through the air and bursts the balloons with ejaculation-like symbolism. The woman is instrumental to the dart as the medium through which the dart/phallus obtains its status and climax. The tourist may embody different behaviours when, in a particular tourist context, however, it is argued by many that such behaviours emerge 'out of dispositions that evolve around class, gender, ethnicity and sexuality' (Edensor, 2001: 60). A hierarchy exists within tourist stages deeming some actors worthy of having their privileged desires met, albeit at the cost of the rights and dignity of Others; these Others, in this case, women and elephants, are made to fulfil their role, pleasing the tourist, as a submissive and degrading spectacle.

Visual stagings and the spectacle

Western society is a 'society of the spectacle' (Edensor, 2001: 68). The spectacle object can be a human body or an animal body – nothing is exempt from the spectator's gaze: 'even while the body is celebrated as the location of pleasure, fertility and generative new life, it too, is the object of ridicule and debasing' (Morris, 1994: 21). Cohen (2009) notes that animals are an important constituent of many tourist attractions – sometimes even the mascot for tourist destinations. The same can be said of women and children in Thailand as they are portrayed like mascots in tourism advertisements (Stout, 2014). Pritchard and Morgan (2000: 886) suggest that 'the ways in which landscapes and destinations are imaged have significant implications for how those places and their peoples are perceived'. Advertising supports the patriarchal nature of tourism in Thailand and in turn generates the tourist's expectations of the spectacle in Thailand.

Urry (1999: 35) argues that the 'embodied nature of our relationship to the world has come to be narrowly "focused" upon the visual sense which incorporates the "specularisation of life"'. The privileged patriarchal, heterosexual male gaze encompasses the making of 'gendered space' in tourism – Thailand embodies the Western desire of a feminised, exotic, erotic space (Pritchard & Morgan, 2000: 885). Manderson (1992: 452) speaks of the dilution of the ability of acts (and arguably all facets of life) to tantalise; over time acts become more explicit, 'wandering to the margins of lewdness and violence'. Cohen (2009) writes about the spectacle performances of animals which are driven by tourism. Tourists' interests in animals are centred on two contrasting themes: the wild animals' Otherness and the performing animals' humanisation (Cohen, 2009). Cohen differentiates the attractive qualities tourists place upon their experience of either the 'wild' or the 'humanised' animal in tourism:

> The wild animal, encountered in a natural setting, seems to offer an authentic experience of fascinating Otherness, while the humanized animal seems to offer a ludic, entertaining and funny experience, provoked by the incongruity between its animality and apparent performance of human activities. (Cohen, 2009: 3)

Cohen (2009) argues that tourists prefer (by far) interacting with animals in 'contrived settings' where the tourist is entertained by the animal rather than as an observer of the animal in a natural setting (Cohen, 2009: 24–25). This preference results in the creation of establishments which offer shows to satisfy the tourists' desire to be entertained by animals – such establishments are built to attract tourists and they are particularly popular with international Asian tourists (Cohen, 2009: 25). The shows act to mediate the interaction between the tourists and animals in much the same way as women are mediated through bar managers (Cohen, 2009; Manderson, 1992).

Internet sites show that tourists enjoy having their photo taken with the animals just as men enjoy having their photo taken with young Thai women. Images often show the image of the male tourist with Thai women who are not only participating in tourist performances but who have to show that they are enjoying it. In some of these examples the male has his identity protected by a pixilated image or a black-out strip over the eyes; the women are not granted this privileged privacy. From such images it is evident that the women are young, beautiful, and often appear intoxicated. Contrastingly, the tourist is white, elderly, smiling and posing for the photograph with the intent of 'bragging' about his experiences upon returning home. In another example, drunken young men are shown with a baby elephant. The elephant will have been trained through 'the crush', ensuring submission (Hile, 2002; Cohen, this volume). The elephant is being hugged and the trunk grasped, surrounded by a group of drunken tourists it is not familiar with. This is its role from now on, as is the role of many other animals in Thailand (Tourism Concern, 2013). Edensor (2001: 70) claims that photographs are cultural stagings; such imagery 'inevitably raises controversies about the reproduction of stereotypes associated with primitivism, exoticism and eroticism'. The women and animals are unprotected in these stagings; neither is respected and their role in this spectacle is as a consumable object and souvenir.

Implications and Disturbances

Thailand's ethical tourism trades, such as spiritual, eco and cuisine tourism, are damaged and undermined by the tourist-driven exploitation of animals and women. Elephants are at risk of extinction in Thailand due to their use in the tourism trade (Doksone, 2012). Tourists actively support illegal animal trades and increased extinction rates by becoming an audience for activities like the same dart trick. By being implicated in shows with wild and often endangered animals, tourists provide their poachers with the finances to continue such trades:

> These animals are taken from the wild and exploited as tourist attractions. In the case of wild gibbons, the parents are killed in order to obtain the baby gibbon. The baby gibbon does not always survive the fall from the canopy once the mother is killed, so in most cases, many gibbons are killed to obtain just one baby. If these actions continue to be financially supported by tourists, gibbons will one day be extinct. (WARF, 2007: np)

Tasci (2011: 118) describes how 'countries, along with their names, flags and related symbols, historic and current political relationships, policies, and unique and common features represent global destination brands'. Destinations can also become blemished when the country or its residents are portrayed negatively (Tasci, 2011). Thailand is a unique destination that offers many high-quality experiences for visiting tourists. However, we have argued that portrayals of the country relating to the exploitation of women and animals, especially with regard to 'the same dart trick', adversely affect Thailand's tourism reputation despite global efforts to make tourism ethical (Ethical Traveler, 2014). Ethical Traveler (2014) compiles a report of ethical sites and included animal welfare in its list of criteria for the first time. These criteria also include human rights and the environmental record of each country. Thailand is not included in the list (Greenwald et al., 2013).

Conclusions

We have been intentionally focused on 'the same dart trick' while knowing that exploitation in Thailand is not confined to women and animals and that such tricks may also take place beyond Thailand. In this chapter we do not want to reinscribe women or animals as victims but rather pay tribute to them as (sometime) survivors in desperate circumstances. Through discussion of the concepts of *consumption, performance* and the *stage* we have drawn attention to the shared experience of these two touristic performers, the female sex worker and the elephant, whose bodies are inscribed with the manifestations of exploitation and Othering. We advocate for places like Thailand to become ethical tourist destinations and urge tourists to take note of the warnings that are clearly available to them on websites and to take response-ability (Haraway, 2008) for what they see and do.

When tourists support 'the same dart trick', whether performed by the female or elephant body, they show a blatant disregard for others. The ethical response-ability of tourists is to be critical of what is offered at tourism destinations and not engage in practices that support abuse and exploitation. Tourist relationships in the destination have the potential to create change. Our argument is supported by a post-human and feminist perspective whereby we do not engage dualisms of 'saint' or 'sinner' (Smith, 2013). Instead, and through the notion of response-ability, we argue for the possibility 'to hold in regard, to respond, to look back reciprocally, to notice, to pay attention, to have courteous regard for, to esteem: all of that is tied to polite greeting, to constituting the polis, where and when species meet' (Haraway, 2008: 19).

References

Adams, C. (1995) *Neither Man nor Beast: Feminism and the Defence of Animals.* New York: Continuum.

Adams, C. (2003) *The Pornography of Meat.* New York: Continuum.

Adams, C. (2010) Why feminist-vegan now? *Feminism & Psychology* 20 (3), 302–317.

Animals Asia (2012) Our work. *Animals Asia.* See www.animalsasia.org/au/ (accessed 18 February 2014).

Barnett, P. (2011) Time for tourism industry to put human rights on its agenda. *Institute for Human Rights and Business.* See www.ihrb.org/commentary/time-for-tourism-industry-to-put-human-rights-on-agenda.html (accessed 9 January 2014).

Bertella, G. (2013) Ethical content of pictures of animals in tourism promotion. *Tourism Recreation Research* 38 (3), 281–295.

Best Legs in Town (2013) What we're famous for. *Best Legs in Town.* See www.bestlegs.com.au/ (accessed 9 January 2014).

Care for the Wild (CWI) (2008) *Exploiting the Tiger: Illegal Trade, Animal Cruelty and Tourists at Risk at the Tiger Temple.* See http://www.careforthewild.com/wp-content/uploads/2012/05/tigertemplereport08_final_v11.pdf (accessed 7 January 2015).

Child Wise (2014) Child Wise tourism program. *Child Wise.* See www.childwise.net/page/13/child-wise-tourism-program (accessed 10 January 2014).

Cohen, E. (2009) The wild and the humanized: Animals in Thai tourism. *Anatolia* 20 (1), 100–118.

Cohen, E. (2010) Panda and elephant – contesting animal icons in Thai tourism. *Journal of Tourism and Cultural Change* 8 (3), 154–171.

Dictionary.com (2010) Trick. *Dictionary.com*. See http://dictionary.reference.com/browse/trick (accessed 15 April 2010).

Doksone, T. (2012) Elephant meat in Thailand poses extinction threat to animal. *HuffPost*, 26 January. See www.huffingtonpost.com/2012/01/26/elephant-meat-thailand_n_1233487.html (accessed 13 January 2014).

Duffy, R. and Moore, L. (2010) Neoliberalising nature? Elephant-back tourism in Thailand and Botswana. *Antipode* 42 (3), 742–766.

ECPAT (2010) *Child Sex Tourism in Thailand*. London: ECPAT UK. See www.ecpat.org.uk/sites/default/files/thailand05.pdf (accessed 20 April 2010).

Edensor, T. (2000) Staging tourism: Tourists as performers. *Annals of Tourism Research* 27 (2), 322–344.

Edensor, T. (2001) Performing tourism, staging tourism. *Tourist Studies* 1 (1), 59–81.

Edensor, T. (2007) Mundane mobilities, performances and spaces of tourism. *Social & Cultural Geography* 8 (2), 199–215.

Ethical Traveler (2014) Empowering travelers to change the world. *Ethical Traveler*. See www.ethicaltraveler.org (accessed 15 January 2014).

Fennell, D. (2013) Tourism and animal welfare. *Tourism Recreation Research* 38 (3), 325–341.

Greenwald, J., Hoover, C. and Lefevre, N. (2013) The world's ten best ethical destinations – 2014. *Ethical Traveler*. See www.ethicaltraveler.org/explore/reports/the-worlds-best-ethical-destinations-2014/ (accessed 15 January 2014).

Haraway, D.J. (2008) *When Species Meet*. Minneapolis, MN: University of Minnesota Press.

Hile, J. (2002) Activists denounce Thailand's elephant 'crushing' ritual. *National Geographic*, 16 October. See http://news.nationalgeographic.com.au/news/2002/10/1016_021016_phajaan.html (accessed 10 January 2014).

Horng, J. and Tsai, C. (2010) Government websites for promoting East Asian culinary tourism: A cross-national analysis. *Tourism Management* 31 (1), 74–85.

Howard, R. (2009) Risky business? Asking tourists what hazards they actually encountered in Thailand. *Tourism Management* 30 (3), 359–365.

Jones, R. (2004) Becoming-hysterical – becoming-animal – becoming-woman in *The Horse Impressionists*. *Journal of Visual Art Practice* 3 (2), 123–138.

Kalof, L., Fitzgerald, A. and Baralt, L. (2004) Animals, women, and weapons: Blurred sexual boundaries in the discourse of sport hunting. *Society and Animals* 12 (3), 237–251.

Kontogeorgopoulos, N. (2009) Wildlife tourism in semi-captive settings: A case study of elephant camps in northern Thailand. *Current Issues in Tourism* 12 (5–6), 429–449.

Larsen, J., Urry, J. and Axhausen, K. (2007) Networks and tourism: Mobile social life. *Annals of Tourism Research* 34 (1), 244–262.

Mai, C. (2005) Bangkok ping pong! Yikes! *TravelPod*, 26 June. See www.travelpod.com/travel-blog-entries/maia/world_tour_2004/1119804360/tpod.html (accessed 23 April 2014).

Manderson, L. (1992) Public sex performances in Patpong and explorations of the edges of imagination. *Journal of Sex Research* 29 (4), 451–475.

Morris, P. (1994) *The Bakhtin Reader*. London: Edward Arnold.

Munar, A. (2011) Tourist-created content: Rethinking destination branding. *International Journal of Culture, Tourism and Hospitality Research* 5 (3), 291–305.

Ocha, W. and Earth, B. (2012) Identity diversification among transgender sex workers in Thailand's sex tourism industry. *Sexualities* 16 (1/2), 195–216.

Pipa, C. (2013) Elephant cruelty in Thailand. *Alternative Way*, 6 April. See www.alternative way.net/blogs/activism-stories-from-the-web-worth-reading/7644599-elephant-cru elty-in-thailand (accessed 14 February 2014).

Power, C. and Watts, I. (1997) The woman with the zebra's penis: Gender, mutability and performance. *Journal of the Royal Anthropological Institute* 3 (3), 537–560.

Pritchard, A. and Morgan, N. (2000) Privileging the male gaze: Gendered tourism landscapes. *Annals of Tourism Research* 27 (4), 884–905.

Said, E.W. (1995) *Orientalism*. London: Penguin.

Smith, P. (2013) In defence of tourism: A reassessment. *Tourism Recreation Research* 38 (3), 362–369.

Stout, D. (2014) *Thailand Was Never the Land of Smiles, Whatever the Guidebooks May Have Told You*. See http://time.com/6597/thailand-was-never-the-land-of-smiles/ (accessed 7 January 2015).

Szerszynski, B. and Urry, J. (2006) Visuality, mobility and the cosmopolitan: Inhabiting the world from afar. *British Journal of Sociology* 57 (1), 113–131.

Tasci, A. (2011) Destination branding and positioning. In Y. Youcheng and A. Pizam (eds) *Destination Marketing and Management: Theories and Applications* (pp. 113–127). Wallingford: CABI.

Thailand Uncovered (2014) Highlighted tours. *Thailand Uncovered*. See www.thailand-uncovered.com/ (accessed 9 January 2014).

The United States Department of Justice (2015) *Child Exploitation and Obscenity Section*. See http://www.justice.gov/criminal/ceos/subjectareas/child-sex-tourism.html (accessed 7 January 2015).

Tourism Authority of Thailand (2013) About Thailand. *Tourismthailand.org*. See www.tourismthailand.org/Thailand (accessed 3 January 2014).

Tourism Concern (2013) *For Traveling Animal Lovers, the Temptations to get up Close to Exotic Animals as Gibbons, Bears, Reptiles and Even Lions and Tigers is Often too Much*. See https://www.facebook.com/tourismconcern/posts/680570285292815 (accessed 7 January 2015).

Transparency International (2013) Corruption perceptions index 2013. *Transparency International*. See http://cpi.transparency.org/cpi2013/results/ (accessed 9 January 2014).

TripAdvisor (2014) Nong Nooch Tropical Botanical Garden. *TripAdvisor.com*. See www.tripadvisor.com.au/Attraction_Review-g293919-d669526-Reviews-Nong_Nooch_Tropical_Botanical_Garden-Pattaya_Chonburi_Province.html#REVIEWS (accessed 17 February 2014).

Urban Dictionary (2014) Chicken. *Urban Dictionary*. See www.urbandictionary.com/define.php?term=chicken (accessed 9 January 2014).

Urry, J. (1990) The 'consumption' of tourism. *Sociology* 24 (1), 23–35.

Urry, J. (1994) Cultural change and contemporary tourism. *Leisure Studies* 13 (4), 233–238.

Urry, J. (1999) Sensing leisure spaces. In D. Crouch (ed.) *Leisure/tourism Geographies: Practices and Geographical Knowledge* (pp. 34–45). London: Routledge.

Urry, J. and Larsen, J. (2011) *The Tourist Gaze 3.0*. London: Sage.

WARF (2007) *Gibbon Rehabilitation Project*. Phuket: Wild Animal Rescue Foundation of Thailand. See www.gibbonproject.org/ (accessed 13 January 2014).

World Bank (2013) *Thailand Overview*. Washington, DC: World Bank. See www.worldbank.org/en/country/thailand/overview (accessed 9 January 2014).

YouTube (2007) Elephant darts. *YouTube.com*, 25 September. See www.youtube.com/watch?v=H5YO56LD_dY (accessed 17 February 2014).

5 From *Free Willy* to SeaWorld: Has Ecotourism Improved the Rights of Whales?

Stephen Wearing and Chantelle Jobberns

Introduction

This chapter will argue that neoliberalist models of tourism based on commodified agendas continue to hold dominance in both the theory and practice of ecotourism. Tourism in the free market economy represents the commercialisation of the human need to travel and can exploit natural and cultural resources as a means of profit accumulation. The World Tourism Organisation has proposed a 'Global Code of Ethics for Tourism' as the organisation feels it is necessary to ensure the provision of social justice and equity for local communities over commodified, neoliberalist approaches to tourism and such a code could be a mechanism to change industry practice. But what voice within this code of ethics will be given to the animals that ecotourism bases much of its commercial enterprise on? This chapter discusses the ways in which the commodification of whales through ecotourism has increasingly seen the unethical treatment and valuing of these animals through the production, consumption and industrialisation process that tourism subjects them to. We maintain that, without ethical valuing through a de-commodified approach, the treatment of whales and other animals in ecotourism can reach a level of mistreatment that denies the contribution of ecotourism to sustainability.

We examine the commodification of whales and compare captive whale viewing programmes with whale watching. The chapter explores both of these in an effort to determine the issues surrounding their economic and social viability as forms of sustainable marine tourism activities. We acknowledge that commodification of nature will occur through ecotourism (Wearing & Neil, 2009) but explore how we might seek improved outcomes if closer regard is given to the treatment of animals. Therefore we ask, what do captive whale viewing programmes and whale watching contribute to the rights of whales? Does whale watching hold the potential for sustainable practice, one that is both ecological and profitable? Or is whale watching creating a 'tragedy of the commons' and only further commodifying whales in the process? Responsible whale watching is seen by many as a clean, green industry that simultaneously promotes whale education, and conservation, while supporting local economies. Captive whale viewing programmes are viewed as educational and accessible, enabling a large percentage of the population to experience whales with little impact on the environment and the use of fewer whales.

Better Than It Was?

Viewed by the International Whaling Commission (IWC) in 1983 as an alternative 'use' for whales, whale watching has been recognised as a legitimate form of ecotourism (Orams, 2000), and is the fastest growing sector of the ecotourism industry (Corkeron, 2004; Curtin, 2003). In 2001 the international whale watching industry was valued at over US$1bn (Hoyt, 2001), and attracted over nine million people annually. By 2008, this number had grown to US$2.1bn and over 13 million people participating in over 119 countries (IFAW, 2010). Whale watching focuses on the aesthetic consumption of whales through a largely visual experience that is supposed to be educative in nature. Some types of whale watching are more tactile, notably the programmes that offer the chance to swim with dolphins. Whether viewing whales from a promontory point on land or from the bow of a boat, this activity is considered to foster both an appreciation of these animals and a use that is sustainable in nature.

Traditionally considered a mass tourism activity, marine parks and aquariums are now sometimes classified as a form of ecotourism but, given that they generally cater to large numbers of tourists, this raises a range of issues (see also Ventre & Jett, this volume). For example, marine parks/aquaria have the benefit of not disturbing wild populations, thus minimising potential negative impacts to surrounding environments (Ryan & Saward, 2004; Tremblay, 2008). However, marine parks/aquaria are consumptive in nature, where live capture still accounts for many of the animals featured (Casamitjana, 2004; Engelbrecht & Smith, 2004). The visitor is given an 'up close and personal' experience with the animals, through various swim with dolphin programmes, petting pools and 'trainer for a day' experiences. Marine parks/aquaria focus heavily on entertainment, with daily shows, rides and merchandise sales. Stakeholders and supporters of the public display industry maintain that captive viewing contributes to education and conservation and insist that they create a strong supporter basis for a wider population of animals (Carwardine, 2001; Hoyt, 1992; Smith, 2003; Williams, 2001).

The Environmental Movement and Ecotourism

The environmental movement has a complex and discursive history based on many factors. Environmental NGOs have evolved into more autonomous, vocal and politically active organisations. Many environmental groups are working within a new political space, created by the shared language of 'sustainability' and a more mainstream environmental agenda. Many environmental issues have come into prominence because they represent the broader critique of modern society at large, especially the relationships between human societies and environmental risks, many of which are undetectable (Macnaghten & Urry, 1998).

During the 1960s, nature figured prominently in development projects, including such things as the creation of parks, nature resorts and entertainment. By the 1970s environmentalism and animal rights became more firmly established in the West. This led to the questioning of anthropocentricism and the search for more sustainable practices. The 1970s saw an increased sensitivity to environmental issues, popularised by leading environmentalists, such as the fear of nuclear fallout, the oil shock of 1973 and the growing perception that the future of humanity was tied to the future of the environment. This growing realisation contributed to the growth of conservation groups such as the Sierra Club, as well as environmental activist groups such as Friends of the Earth, Earth First, Greenpeace and Sea Shepherd.

Ecotourism experienced a growth in popularity during the 1980s, leading up to the International Year of Ecotourism in 2002. It was believed that tourists had begun to question tourism products and were willing to pay more for tourism products that were perceived to be ethical (Boo, 1990; Cole, 2007; King & Stewart, 1996; Wight, 1993). Wight (1994: 41) found that ecotourists were willing to spend '8.5% more for services and products provided by environmentally responsible suppliers'. Yet such findings remain contested. Cunningham (2007) found that only one out of four lodgers were willing to pay an additional 10–20% to stay at an ecolodge, even though nearly 60% of the same respondents indicated the desire to stay at one. Similarly, Kirk (1996) found that 71% of the respondents he surveyed claimed that they would prefer to stay in hotels that showed concern for the environment, but were not willing to pay extra for it. Hobson and Essex (2001: 145) report that few guests showed any regard for environmental practices carried out by hotels and usually only required a 'clean, comfortable bed' with a 'good breakfast'.

Sustainable Growth for a Common Future

Although whale watching is part of the global tourism trade, it is really a community-level industry. Whale watching tourists support local economies through their purchases: from whale watching tickets to associated expenses for travel, food, hotels and souvenirs. Beyond economics, the whale watching industry offers communities a sense of identity and cultural pride and helps foster an appreciation for the marine environment. This supports local businesses, creating jobs and providing income (IFAW, 2010). Ramage adds, 'While governments continue to debate the future of whaling, the bottom line is increasingly clear: responsible whale watching is the most sustainable, environmentally-friendly and economically beneficial "use" of whales in the 21st century' (IFAW, 2010: 9).

There are many advantages of this kind of ecotourism; if conducted within certain parameters this activity is relatively benign (Blewitt, 2008; Jensen *et al.*, 2009; Lusseau *et al.*, 2009; Noren *et al.*, 2009). Through proper management, whale watching has proved to be profitable and sustainable. This approach provides a resource for ongoing cetacean research as well as a context in which to promote an appreciation of the marine environment and to explore conservation issues in the public discourse (Greenpeace, 2010).

There is growing concern, however, about the inadvertent damage caused by whale watching. The questions that scientists, policy makers and the tourism industry are facing are how to determine the conditions under which whale watching becomes detrimental to the animals it targets and how best to protect them (Simmonds & Isaac, 2007). Higham and Lusseau (2007, 2008) have highlighted the urgent need for empirical research into whale watching and Zeppel and Muloin (2008) echo the call for further research examining the educational component of marine wildlife tourism in order to be able to assess whether or not there is an increase in tourist knowledge and whether there are any associated attitudinal shifts or lifestyle changes that help to conserve marine wildlife. In a meta-analysis of guided tourist encounters with whales, dolphins and marine turtles from 1996 to 2007, Zeppel and Muloin (2008) conclude that mediated encounters with marine wildlife contribute to pro-environmental attitudes and improved on-site behaviour, with some longer term intentions to engage in conservation actions that benefit marine species.

In order to ensure the viability of whale watching in the future within an ecotourism context, we need to examine the educative elements of this activity and the social impact it has upon the participants. While whale watching is widely assumed to enhance people's awareness and appreciation of whales – and perhaps lead to a greater commitment to conservation and the protection of the environment – if it is to be considered under the ecotourism banner it is necessary to evaluate the educational impact of this activity. In their examination of whale watching experiences in New South Wales, Australia, Stamation *et al.* (2007: 41) found that 'the current education provided lacks structure, there are no clear conservation objectives, and there is limited addition to knowledge and conservation behaviours of whale watchers in the long term'.

In order to justify this ecotourism activity and to validate its claims of inspiring conservation and environmental awareness, the whale watching industry needs to address these issues. For example, in his investigation of dolphin-swim tours in New Zealand, Lück (2003) found a demand for structured interpretation programmes on marine mammal tours, with respondents clearly indicating that they would have liked to have received more information, in particular about the wider marine environment.

It has been suggested at a broader level that to effectively manage wildlife tourism, the biological impacts, as well as the needs of tourists, industry and other stakeholders need to be taken into consideration. Stamation (2008) suggests that an adaptive management system that is both integrative and holistic be adopted in the management of whale watching. This would allow for the study of both the human and animal dimensions of this activity by incorporating biological and social sciences. Such an approach would provide a framework for maximising the benefits of whale watching, while at the same time minimising the adverse effects on whales. Incorporating a holistic and global approach to attractions such as whale watching fosters environmental enhancement, deep understanding and the transformation of behaviour (Weaver, 2005: 439). We argue that this model can best promote global sustainability by accommodating selective 'hard' and 'soft' characteristics, thereby taking advantage of the economies of scale offered by the latter, leading to a de-commodified framework.

In comparison, captive animal viewing is most popular with domestic tourists; an estimated 130 million Americans visit zoos, marine parks and aquariums in that country each year. The majority of visitors are children on school excursions and families with young children, who are drawn to marine parks and aquariums to view the more popular dolphins, killer whales and beluga whales (Winiarskyj, 2004). While often criticised by animal welfare groups and researchers for exhibiting such large and socially complex animals (Engelbrecht & Smith, 2004; Hoyt, 1992; Rose et al., 2009; Williams, 2001), Kirby (2012: 18) notes that 'the public display industry should be credited for changing our attitudes toward killer whales from contempt to admiration and even affection'. In 1973, for instance, US Navy diving manuals described killer whales as 'extremely ferocious', who 'will attack human beings at every opportunity' (Kirby, 2012: 15), and were used as practice targets by the Royal Canadian Air Force (Kirby, 2012). Of the killer whales captured during the 1960s and 1970s, nearly one-quarter had bullet wounds (Kirby, 2012). So we find that over time the interactions with this species through tourism have changed our attitudes toward them.

SeaWorld Parks exhibit captive killer whales at three sites in the US: San Diego, Orlando and San Antonio. They claim to be 'striving to provide an enthusiastic, imaginative and intellectually stimulating atmosphere to help students and guests develop a lifelong appreciation, understanding and stewardship [of] our environment' (Engelbrecht & Smith, 2004: 5). Wary of the sensitive topic of captivity, Orlando staff are instructed to stay away from words such as 'captured', 'cage', 'tank' and 'captivity' and instead to use 'acquired', 'enclosure', 'aquarium' and 'controlled environment'. Employees are also instructed to feign ignorance in the event that they are asked about the welfare of any particular animal (Engelbrecht & Smith, 2004). There are no international guidelines to govern the keeping of captive whales and dolphins, and living conditions vary among marine parks and aquariums (Carwardine, 2001; Hoyt, 1992; Smith, 2003; Williams, 2001). Captive marine mammals in the United States are protected under the *Animal Welfare Act and Animal Welfare Regulations* (2013), issued by the US Department of Agriculture (USDA). The Act sets out guidelines for facilities and operating standards, animal health and husbandry standards and transportation standards (USDA, 2013).

A study examining the effects of captivity on wide-ranging carnivores found that species such as polar bears and tigers display significant stress-related behaviours, and concludes that, while some species thrive in captivity, others are 'prone to health problems that include poor health, repetitive stereotypic behaviour and breeding difficulties' (Clubb & Mason, 2003: 473); the authors argue that the keeping of such animals should be greatly improved or phased out. These results can also be applied to dolphins and killer whales, who travel upward of 40–100 km per day, and display stress-induced behaviours including aggression toward other animals and humans, apathy and repetitive movements (Engelbrecht & Smith, 2004).

Captive animal viewing raises questions of ethics and rights, particularly if contextualised within an ecotourism framework. Do the potential benefits to wildlife and their natural habitats justify their becoming commodified and being kept in captivity? Or does the loss of freedom and other welfare considerations of individual animals deem captivity unjustifiable? Here we will leave the questions around commodification as they have been dealt with before (see Wearing & Jobberns, 2011; Wearing & Wearing, 1999; Wearing *et al.*, 2012) but will examine the programmes that exist using captive populations. Critics of captivity disagree with the common sentiment that the social and conservation benefits of holding animals in aquariums and marine parks outweigh the cost to the individual welfare and rights of the animal, in order to educate, protect and conserve wild populations and habitats (DeGrazia, 2002; Kuehn, 2002).

Conservation and education place great emphasis on species preservation in both wild and captive populations, and in the process disregard individual animal welfare and the rights of individual animals (Millar & Houston, 2008). Bekoff's (2013) writings on compassionate conservation give consideration to those animals in captivity where their welfare has been overlooked for the future wellbeing of the species. Compassionate conservation 'is concerned with the humane treatment and welfare of individual animals within the framework of traditional conservation biology in which the focus is on species, populations, or ecosystems' (Tobias, 2013, np). The conservation of animals through captive breeding programmes, and the establishment of captive populations, is a human desire. Upon the extinction of a species, the animal itself is not harmed, and they are unaware of their species' impending extinction (Mullin, 1999). By classifying captive animal viewing as ecotourism, we risk diminishing the standard of ecotourism, and its positive contribution to genuine sustainable tourism (Fennell, 2012).

Reviewing the Literature: Ecotourism and Whale Watching

In their research into ecotourist activities in Kaikoura, New Zealand, Cloke and Perkins (2005) examined the non-human agency of nature and the role it plays in the performance and meaning of place. The recent boom in ecotourism at this location has been 'co-constituted by the networked agency of whales and dolphins, whose charismatic animal appeal is a magnet for tourists' (Cloke & Perkins, 2005: 903) and plays a role in the mediation of the meaning of place. This research poses significant questions about the ability of actor networks and relational networks to fully capture the power of non-humans to evoke 'sublime emotional and aesthetic relations with humans' (Cloke & Perkins, 2005: 903).

Wearing and Neil (2009) suggest that the ecotourist is concerned with development and fulfilment, including self-education. This desire has led to an increase in the number of nature-based activities and interpretive programmes in marine-based ecotourism (Zeppel & Muloin, 2008). Tisdell and Wilson (2005) have identified the importance of learning and the interaction of tourists with wildlife as contributors to their pro-conservation sentiments and actions. The growing presence of ecotourism, and the activity of whale watching, provides an opportunity for sustainable growth. Furthermore, pursuing the visual consumption of whales may help to advance the culturally sensitive issues associated with the practice of whaling by aligning use, sustainability and profit.

Whales and dolphins are increasingly the focus of tourism activities in many coastal locations; however, the impacts of these activities remain largely unknown. Human interaction with cetaceans can cause short-term changes in the behaviour of these creatures such as alterations to foraging strategies or reduced maternal care, which in the long term can lead to their displacement from preferred habitats or reduced reproductive success (Blewitt, 2008). For this reason, a variety of strategies have been implemented in an effort to manage and control whale watching activities throughout Australia – and other whale watching locations. These strategies include regulations, permit and licensing systems, industry guidelines, education and interpretation. An important component supporting these management systems is research.

A growing number of studies have investigated the impact of vessel noise on cetacean communication. Jensen *et al.* (2009) suggest that the increasing number and speed of vessels may have reduced the habitat quality of cetaceans by increasing underwater noise levels. Lusseau *et al.* (2009) report that vessel traffic has disrupted the foraging behaviour of southern killer whales resident around San Juan Island, Washington, USA. Noren *et al.* (2009) focused on the same group of whales, reporting that the surface-active behaviours (SABs) of these whales were affected by the proximity of vessels in the area. The authors conclude that the minimum approach distance of 100 m in whale watching guidelines may be insufficient in preventing behavioural responses from whales.

Weinrich and Corbelli (2009) studied the potential impacts of vessel exposure on the calving rate of humpback whales off the coast of southern New England (USA) but found no direct evidence for negative effects. They posit that any 'short-term disturbance may not necessarily be indicative of more meaningful effects on either individuals or populations' (Weinrich & Corbelli, 2009: 2931). Sousa-Lima and Clark (2008) found an important negative effect of boat traffic on singing activity. Adaptive management should aim at reducing the number of noise events per boat, which can improve the whale watching experience and reduce the impact on male singing behaviour. Stamation *et al.* (2010) found that calf pods were more sensitive to the presence of vessels than non-calf pods, and that dive times and the overall percentage of time whales spent submerged were higher in the presence of vessels. The authors caution that, since the long-term impacts of the effects of vessels are unknown, management of the humpback whale watching industry should adopt a conservative approach.

In his investigation of bottlenose dolphins living in similar fjords but exposed to different levels of tourism activities, Lusseau (2004) compared the impacts of boat interactions upon these cetaceans. In particular, the author examined short-term avoidance strategies and the threshold at which those strategies were no longer effective. According to Lusseau, the resting state was the most sensitive to interactions whereas socialising was less sensitive. Short-term displacement or in extreme cases area avoidance were typical responses to boat exposure, yet the author contends that the overall behaviour of the dolphins remained largely unchanged.

The call for the monitoring and management of whale watching extends to the frigid waters of the Antarctic. Shipboard visitors are routinely rewarded with whale sightings. However, careful management and dedicated research are needed to ensure that the growing Antarctic marine tourism industry does not inadvertently harm these populations. Responsible tourism has a substantial contribution to make to Antarctic whale conservation and research through collaboration (Williams & Crosbie, 2007: 195).

A review of the whale watching research (Corkeron, 1996; Scarpaci *et al.*, 2008) revealed that so far most studies have concentrated on the biological and behavioural aspects of whales, with little recognition being given to the social aspects. This is hardly surprising, as most research concerning human–wildlife interactions has come from the biological sciences (Muloin, 1998).

Duffus and Dearden (1993) were among the first researchers to investigate the 'human' dimensions of whale watching in the context of managing human interaction with these creatures. They stress that both the human and ecological dimensions of whale watching must be understood and balanced at all stages of management. Recent research has explored the activity of whale watching in terms of human–animal interaction and the impact on whales (Noren et al., 2009; Tosi & Ferreira, 2009; Vieira & Brito, 2009; Weinrich & Corbelli, 2009; Williams et al., 2009), on the income of fishing communities (Einarsson, 2009), and on how to manage whale watching (Stamation, 2008).

Learning more about wildlife users (e.g. whale watchers) in terms of their motivations, expectations and satisfaction would allow for more effective management strategies (Stamation, 2008). In particular, a better understanding of the 'human dimension' of whale watching would guide educational and interpretive programmes aimed at whale watching participants (Amante-Helweg, 1996; Orams, 1999; Stamation et al., 2007). A few studies have specifically examined factors relating to visitor satisfaction with cetacean watching (mainly involving whales). In an Australian study, Foxlee (2001) found that the factors contributing to visitor satisfaction, in order of importance were: (i) numbers of whales seen; (ii) distance from whales; (iii) whale activity; (iv) information about whales; (v) information available about other marine life; and (vi) the style in which the information was presented.

Exploring touristic interaction with dwarf minke whales in the Great Barrier Reef, Valentine et al. (2004) found that most of the participants had low expectations about whale encounters, with only one out of four coming specifically to swim with the whales and nearly half of the participants being content to learn about the whales on board the vessel. The authors cited a number of factors that contributed to visitor satisfaction, including the diving experience and particular dive sites, the most significant factor being the closeness of approaches by the whales, total number of whales seen, and total time spent with whales.

Packer and Ballantyne (2012) compared four marine-based wildlife tourism sites in Australia – two captive and two non-captive sites. While tourists at both the captive and non-captive sites had similar pre-existing knowledge of the environment and shared interests and behaviours, their motivations were remarkably different. Learning and educational aspects were most important to the non-captive viewers, whereas visitors to captive sites were more interested in the entertainment and social element. Packer and Ballantyne (2012: 1243) concluded that 'visitors perceive zoos and aquariums more as a site for a social, relaxing or enjoyable outing with family or friends, while they perceive non-captive viewing more as an opportunity to experience and learn about the natural world'.

Until research addresses the ecological and human dimensions of whale watching more thoroughly, it is likely that the resource and the recreational experience will be degraded (Clark *et al.*, 2007; Higham & Lusseau, 2007). Long-term strategic planning would help to mitigate the impact of tourism on targeted animals and ensure a responsible and sustainable approach in appreciating cetaceans and their environment (Higham *et al.*, 2008).

Has Ecotourism Improved the Plight of Whales?

Ecotourism creates a market value for the observation of animals through the commodification of wildlife and its habitats. However, the commodification and consumption of animals through whale watching and captive whale viewing has been criticised on ethical grounds (Scarpaci *et al.*, 2008), especially the commercial live capture of whales for the display industry. Movies such as *Free Willy*, in which a lone captive killer whale is released into the wild and reunited with his family (Wincer, 1993), increased public awareness about welfare issues and the ethics of exhibiting captive whales. Public outrage resulted in Keiko the movie's star being released into the wild; however, the film failed to initiate public discussion concerning all captive marine mammals, particularly other captive whales, and such exhibits continue to draw crowds (Scarpaci *et al.*, 2008; Wearing *et al.*, 2011).

Displaying killer whales is a profitable business, and critics claim that the health and wellbeing of the whales are compromised. SeaWorld parks attract approximately 10 million people annually, and receive US$400m–500m per year from visitor revenue (Williams, 2001). SeaWorld estimates that as much as 70% of their income derives directly from visitor interest in killer whales. Hoyt (1992) implies that the state-of-the-art medical treatment administered to their whales is geared more toward economic benefits for the business, rather than the welfare of the whales; they are protecting their multimillion-dollar investments. The mortality rate in captivity is high, and these whales die far younger than their wild relatives (Carwardine, 2001; Hoyt, 1992; Smith, 2003; Williams, 2001). SeaWorld maintain that their whales live stress-free lives in controlled environments and free from 'dangers such as shortages of food, parasites and threats from humans' (Smith, 2003: 2).

Wild killer whales live in tight-knit communities called pods, constructed of blood relatives, whom they stay with for life. There are no complete pods in captivity, and whales are forced to interact with whales from different pods and oceans who communicate in different dialects (Carwardine, 2001; Hoyt, 1992; Kirby, 2012; Williams, 2001). With regulations now governing the capture of killer whales in most waters, and increasing public disapproval, marine parks and aquariums are focusing on captive breeding programmes to maintain their captive numbers (Carwardine, 2001; Hoyt, 1992; Kirby, 2012; Smith, 2003; Williams, 2001). SeaWorld's breeding programme is the most successful, but has been criticised for high mortality rates and the regular removal of calves from their mothers before the age of five, whereas in the wild calves stay with their mothers for life (Hoyt, 1992; Williams, 2001). Minimum pool sizes are stipulated in the Animal Welfare Act and Animal Welfare Regulations (USDA, 2013), although some argue that current standards were set to coincide with the size of existing pools in marine parks (Carwardine, 2001; Hoyt, 1992; Smith, 2003; Williams, 2001). Wild orcas swim up to 160 km every day; an adequate pool size is the equivalent of 9000 times the size of all the interconnecting pools at San Diego SeaWorld (Hoyt, 1992). Killer whales are highly acoustic and life in a tank has been likened to 'a human living in a small room with mirrors on all walls and on the floor' (Williams, 2001: 35).

Viewed within the current debate between Australia and Japan over whaling, and the constraints of captivity discussed above, perhaps the non-consumptive commercialisation of whales through the activity of whale watching might provide a common ground for the sustainable use of whales. Sustainability needs practices that can move beyond conflict. It needs to be able to demonstrate a future that is enabling and co-existent. Competing values should be brought together in processes that acknowledge cultural differences and resolve political conflicts. Whale watching provides the opportunity to demonstrate the potential of sustainable development while at the same time honouring the principles of conservation, but we must see this in practice.

Given the political nature of nature (see Latour, 1993), we must be wary of substituting whale watching for whaling, and then industrialising whale watching, so that we once again see the whales jeopardised. One avenue would be to look at how a discourse, such as the promotion of whale watching, addresses the variety of conditions and beliefs at the local level. Lawrence and Phillips (2004) examined this question using a case study of the development of commercial whale watching on the western coast of Canada. The authors argued that the emergence of this activity was made possible through the influence of macro-cultural discourse upon local actors in the creation of new institutional structures. They argued that the changing conceptualisation of the whale in North America, along with the 'geographically distinct institutional fields that emerged depended on local action and the process of structuration that those actions supported' (Lawrence & Phillips, 2004: 689).

The conceptual shift from hunting whales to whale watching is due, in part, to the dialogue on nature management and conservation. Rapid growth in the demand for tourist interactions with cetaceans in the wild constitutes a challenge to management, as short-term animal behaviour changes can have long-term biological consequences for individual animals and populations. Whale watching management therefore encompasses macro, meso and micro dialogues that contribute to the way we view whales at the global and local levels.

Developing a global code of ethics might go a long way in regulating the consumption of nature, but this is complicated by different cultural values.

Adopting the developmental model of ecotourism, with its built-in code of ethics, would provide a vehicle to pursue whale watching for sustainable economic gain – while at the same time adhering to the general principles of conservation. Ecotourism provides a business model that would provide an avenue for economic growth and the development of political capital. It would allow whale watching to be repositioned as an economic activity, rather than as a contested cultural activity.

Promoting whale watching through the ecological and economic developmental model of ecotourism would act upon the local and global discourses on conservation. The intersection of these discourses marks the cutting edge of this narrative and points to the future. In spite of the contested nature of the Japanese scientific whaling programme – and the contested nature of 'use' versus 'conservation' – this discourse seems to be moving in favour of the latter, particularly given the current concern about global warming and other related issues. Rather than giving in to political pressure to stop commercial whaling, the promotion of whale watching provides the opportunity for Japan and other whaling countries to pursue the fastest growing segment of ecotourism (and tourism in general), and at the same time reaffirm their commitment to the preservation and conservation of natural resources.

Conclusions

There is little doubt that ecotourism has seen the commodification of wildlife internationally and has created a market value for the viewing of nature. At the same time, it has led to a contested view of nature through the economic evaluation of the outputs from ecotourism. It now sits between the absolutes of conservation and commercial sale, where the direct human 'gaze' of wildlife is central to the experience with all of the possibilities for disruption that such viewing brings (Ryan & Saward, 2004: 246). Given its alignment with alternative tourism (Wearing & Neil, 2009), ecotourism should also provide a mechanism to improve animal welfare and to conserve nature in general. Since whale watching is a category of ecotourism, whale watching, with strong environmental protection objectives, may lead to a positive image in terms of animal welfare and attract more whale watching tourists (Kuo et al., 2009: 6).

We have also explored the allied role of marine parks and aquariums and raise issues about the inclusion of these as a form of ecotourism. The captive animal debate will continue to be a prominent one as to its value in the spectrum of nature opportunities available to tourism and this will continue to be debated with regard to captive whale programmes being included in ecotourism practice. We would suggest that the consumptive process of ecotourism and the global commodification of animals make the argument for developing whale watching that is in line with neoliberal principles

(Macnaghten & Urry, 1998; see also Higham & Neves, Chapter 7, this volume). While the use of nature is highly contested, whale watching might provide a sustainable economic incentive to pursue this activity – while at the same time building political capital upon the world stage, if we can find guidelines which ensure that the rights of the whale are respected.

Finding common ground between the interests of Australia and other non-whaling countries and Japan and other whaling countries must eventually come to the gradual displacement of whaling. If we accept that commercial whale watching only really started in 1955 and now involves 119 countries worldwide (IFAW, 2010) it offers an opportunity to seek common ground in the future between all the countries interested in the future of the whale. In the intervening years continued debate must be had on what is feasible in terms of existing practice. With sound negotiation this could not only provide Japan with ample time to further develop and promote whale watching, which has already proven to be a profitable activity – and one that more people can enjoy – but to also phase out whaling with some acknowledgement of the cultural issues under which they operate. It would also aid Australia and Japan in moving on from the conflict surrounding them concerning the current situation about scientific whaling on the world stage.

References

Amante-Helweg, V. (1996) Ecotourists' beliefs and knowledge about dolphins and the development of cetacean ecotourism. *Aquatic Mammals* 22 (2), 131–140.

Bekoff, M. (ed.) (2013) *Ignoring Nature No More: The Case for Compassionate Conservation*. London: University of Chicago Press.

Blewitt, M. (2008) Dolphin–human interactions in Australian waters. *Australian Zoologist* 34, 197–210.

Boo, E. (1990) *Ecotourism: The Potentials and Pitfalls* (Vols 1 & 2). Washington, DC: WorldWide Fund for Nature.

Bulbeck, C. (2005) *Facing the Wild: Ecotourism, Conservation and Animal Encounters*. London: Earthsean.

Carwardine, M. (2001) *Killer Whales*. London: BBC Worldwide.

Casamitjana, J. (2004) *Aquatic Zoos: A Critical Study of UK Public Aquaria in the Year 2004*. Salford: Captive Animals Protection Society.

Clark, J., Simmonds, M. and Williams-Grey, V. (2007) Close encounters: Whale watching in the UK. *Biologist* 54 (3), 134–141.

Cloke, P. and Perkins, H.C. (2005) Cetacean performance and tourism in Kaikoura, New Zealand. *Environment and Planning D: Society and Space* 23 (6), 903–924.

Clubb, R. and Mason, G. (2003) Captivity effects on wide-ranging carnivores. *Nature* 425 (6957), 473–474.

Cole, S. (2007) Implementing and evaluating a code of conduct for visitors. *Tourism Management* 28 (2), 443–451.

Corkeron, P.J. (1996) Research priorities for whale watching in Australia: A scientist's viewpoint. In K. Cogan, S. Presser and A. Jeffery (eds) *Encounters with Whales – 1995 Proceedings* (pp. 123–135). Canberra: Australian Nature Conservation Agency.

Corkeron, P.J. (2004) Whale watching, iconography, and marine conservation. *Conservation Biology* 18 (3), 847–849.

Cunningham, P.A. (2007) Baselining sustainable practices in Ogasawara. *Rikkyo Daigaku Kankogakubu Kiyo* 9, 44–49.

Curtin, S. (2003) Whale-watching in Kaikoura: Sustainable destination development? *Journal of Ecotourism* 2 (3), 173–195.

DeGrazia, D. (2002) *Animal Rights: A Very Short Introduction*. Oxford: Oxford University Press.

Duffus, D.A. and Dearden, P. (1993) Recreational use, valuation and management of killer whales (*Orcinus orca*) on Canada's Pacific coast. *Environmental Conservation* 20 (2), 149–156.

Einarsson, N. (2009) From good to eat to good to watch: Whale watching, adaptation and change in Icelandic fishing communities. *Polar Research* 28 (1), 129–138.

Engelbrecht, T. and Smith, J. (2004) Dying to entertain us. *The Ecologist*, 1 October, 6.

Fennell , D.A. (2012) *Tourism and Animal Ethics*. London, New York: Routledge.

Foxlee, J. (2001) Whale watching at Hervey Bay. *Parks and Leisure Australia* 4 (3), 17–18.

Greenpeace (2010) Iceland whaling. *Greenpeace.org*. See http://www.greenpeace.org/australia/en/news/whales/iwcwrap-280610/ (accessed 26 April 2010).

Higham, J.E.S. and Lusseau, D. (2007) Urgent need for empirical research into whaling and whale watching. *Conservation Biology* 21 (2), 554–558.

Higham, J.E.S. and Lusseau, D. (2008) Slaughtering the goose that lays the golden egg: Are whaling and whale-watching mutually exclusive? *Current Issues in Tourism* 11 (1), 63–74.

Higham, J.E.S., Bejder, L. and Lusseau, D. (2008) An integrated and adaptive management model to address the long-term sustainability of tourist interactions with cetaceans. *Environmental Conservation* 35 (4), 294–302.

Hobson, K. and Essex, S. (2001) Sustainable tourism: A view from accommodation businesses. *Service Industries Journal* 21 (4), 133–146.

Hoyt, E. (1992) *The Performing Orca – Why the Show Must Stop. An In-depth Review of the Captive Orca Industry*. Bath: Whale and Dolphin Conservation Society.

Hoyt, E. (2001) *Whale Watching 2001: Worldwide Tourism Numbers, Expenditures and Expanding Benefits*. Yarmouth Port, MA, USA: International Fund for Animal Welfare. See http:/www/cetaceanhabitat.org/pdf_bin/hoyt_ww_2001_report.pdf (accessed 12 February 2015).

IFAW (2010) *The Booming Whale Watching Industry*. London: International Foundation for Animal Welfare. See www.mywhaleweb.com/?page_id=289 (accessed 6 April 2010).

Jensen, F.H., Bejder, L., Wahlberg, M., Soto, N.A., Johnson, M. and Madsen, P.T. (2009) Vessel noise effects on delphinid communication. *Marine Ecology Progress Series* 395, 161–175.

King, D.A. and Stewart, W.P. (1996) Ecotourism and commodification: Protecting people and places. *Biodiversity and Conservation* 5, 293–305.

Kirby, D. (2012) *Death at Seaworld*. New York: St Martin's Press.

Kirk, D. (1996) *Environmental Management for Hotels*. Oxford: Butterworth.

Kuehn, B.M. (2002) Is it ethical to keep animals in zoos? *Journal of the American Veterinary Medical Association* 221 (11), 1528–1529.

Kuo, H., Chen, C.C. and McAleer, M. (2009) Estimating the impact of whaling on global whale watching. *Social Science Research Network*, 1 August. See http://ssrn.com/abstract=1442444.

Latour, B. (1993) *We Have Never Been Modern*. Cambridge, MA: Harvard University Press.

Lawrence, T.B. and Phillips, N. (2004) From Moby Dick to Free Willy: Macro-cultural discourse and institutional entrepreneurship in emerging institutional fields. *Organization* 11 (5), 689–711.

Lück, M. (2003) Education on marine mammal tours as agent for conservation – but do tourists want to be educated? *Ocean and Coastal Management* 46 (9–10), 943–956.

Lusseau, D. (2004) The hidden cost of tourism: Detecting long-term effects of tourism using behavioral information. *Ecology and Society* 9 (1). See www.ecologyandsociety.org/vol9/iss1/art2.

Lusseau, D., Bain, D.E., Williams, R. and Smith, J.C. (2009) Vessel traffic disrupts the foraging behavior of southern resident killer whales *Orcinus orca*. *Endangered Species Research* 6 (3), 211–221.

Macnaghten, P. and Urry, J. (1998) *Contested Natures*. London: Sage.

Millar, R. and Houston, C. (2008) Zoo rocked by abuse allegations. *The Age*, 19 January. See http://www.theage.com.au/news/national/zoo-rocked-by-abuse-allegations/2008/01/18/1200620212113.html?page=fullpage (accessed 24 October 2009).

Mullin, M.H. (1999) Mirrors and windows: Sociocultural studies of human–animal relationships. *Annual Review of Anthropology* 28, 201–224.

Muloin, S. (1998) Wildlife tourism: The psychological benefits of whale watching. *Pacific Tourism Review* 2, 199–213.

Noren, D.P., Johnson, A.H., Rehder, D. and Larson, A. (2009) Close approaches by vessels elicit surface active behaviors by southern resident killer whales. *Endangered Species Research* 8 (3), 179–192.

Orams, M.B. (1999) *Marine Tourism: Development, Impacts and Management*. London: Routledge.

Orams, M.B. (2000) Tourists getting close to whales, is it what whale-watching is all about? *Tourism Management* 21 (6), 561–569.

Packer, J. and Ballantyne, R. (2012) Comparing captive and non-captive wildlife tourism. *Annals of Tourism Research* 39 (2), 1242–1245.

Rose, N.A., Parsons, E.C.M.P. and Farinato, R. (2009) *The Case against Marine Mammals in Captivity*. Boston, MA: Humane Society of the United States.

Ryan, C. and Saward, J. (2004) The zoo as ecotourism attraction – visitor reactions, perceptions and management implications: The case of Hamilton Zoo, New Zealand. *Journal of Sustainable Tourism* 12 (3), 245–266.

Scarpaci, C., Parsons, E.C.M. and Lück, M. (2008) Recent advances in whale-watching research: 2006–2007. *Tourism in Marine Environments* 5 (1), 55–66.

Simmonds, M.P. and Isaac, S.J. (2007) The impacts of climate change on marine mammals: Early signs of significant problems. *Oryx* 41 (1), 19–26.

Smith, J. (2003) Captive killer whales. *The Ecologist*, 33, 24.

Sousa-Lima, R.S. and Clark, C.W. (2008) Modeling the effect of boat traffic on the fluctuation of humpback whale singing activity in the Abrolhos National Marine Park, Brazil. *Canadian Acoustics – Acoustique Canadienne* 36 (1), 174–181.

Stamation, K. (2008) Understanding human–whale interactions: A multidisciplinary approach. *Australian Zoologist* 34, 211–224.

Stamation, K.A., Croft, D.B., Shaughnessy, P.D., Waples, K.A. and Briggs, S.V. (2007) Educational and conservation value of whale watching. *Tourism in Marine Environments* 4 (1), 41–55.

Stamation, K.A., Croft, D.B., Shaughnessy, P.D., Waples, K.A. and Briggs, S.V. (2010) Behavioral responses of humpback whales (*Megaptera novaeangliae*) to whale-watching vessels on the southeastern coast of Australia. *Marine Mammal Science* 26 (1), 98–122.

Tisdell, C. and Wilson, C. (2005) Perceived impacts of ecotourism on environmental learning and conservation: Turtle watching as a case study. *Environment, Development and Sustainability* 7 (3), 291–302.

Tobias, M.C. (2013) Compassionate conservation: A discussion from the frontlines with Dr Marc Bekoff. *Forbes*, 9 May. See www.forbes.com/sites/michaeltobias/2013/05/09/compassionate-conservation-a-discussion-from-the-frontlines-with-dr-marc-bekoff/ (accessed 12 March 2014).

Tosi, C.H. and Ferreira, R.G. (2009) Behavior of estuarine dolphin, *Sotalia guianensis* (Cetacea, Delphinidae), in controlled boat traffic situation at southern coast of Rio Grande do Norte, Brazil. *Biodiversity and Conservation* 18 (1), 67–78.

Tremblay, P. (2008) Wildlife in the landscape: A Top End perspective on destination-level wildlife and tourism management. *Journal of Ecotourism* 7 (1–2), 179–196.

USDA (US Department of Agriculture) (2013) *Animal Welfare Act and Animal Welfare Regulations.* Washington, DC: United States Congress.

Valentine, P.S., Birtles, A., Curnock, M., Arnold, P. and Dunstan, A. (2004) Getting closer to whales – passenger expectations and experiences, and the management of swim with dwarf minke whale interactions in the Great Barrier Reef. *Tourism Management* 25 (6), 647–655.

Vieira, N. and Brito, C. (2009) Past and recent sperm whales sightings in the Azores based on catches and whale watching information. *Journal of the Marine Biological Association of the United Kingdom* 89 (5), 1067–1070.

Wearing, S.L. and Jobberns, C. (2011) Ecotourism and the commodification of wildlife: Animal welfare and the ethics of zoos. In W. Frost (ed.) *Zoos and Tourism: Conservation, Education, Entertainment?* (pp. 47–58). Bristol: Channel View Publications.

Wearing, S.L. and Neil, J. (2009) *Ecotourism: Impacts, Potential and Possibilities* (2nd edn). Oxford: Butterworth-Heinemann.

Wearing, S.L and Wearing, M. (1999) Decommodifying ecotourism: Rethinking global–local interactions with host communities. *Loisir & Societe* 22 (1), 39–70.

Wearing, S.L., Buchmann, A. and Jobberns, C. (2011) Free Willy: The whale-watching legacy. *Worldwide Hospitality and Tourism Themes* 3 (2), 127–140.

Wearing, S.L., Wearing, M. and McDonald, M. (2012) Beyond commodification – slow'n down the town to let nature grow: Ecotourism, social justice and sustainability. In S. Fullagar, K. Markwell and E. Wilson (eds) *Slow Mobilities: Experiencing Slow Travel and Tourism* (pp. 36–52). Bristol: Channel View Publications.

Weaver, D.B. (2005) Comprehensive and minimalist dimensions of ecotourism. *Annals of Tourism Research* 32 (2), 439–455.

Weinrich, M.T. and Corbelli, C. (2009) Does whale watching in Southern New England impact humpback whale (*Megaptera novaeangliae*) calf production or calf survival? *Biological Conservation* 142, 2931–2940.

Wight, P. (1993) Ecotourism: Ethics or eco-sell. *Journal of Travel Research* 31 (3), 3–9.

Wight, P. (1994) Environmentally responsible marketing of tourism. In E. Cater and G. Lowman (eds) *Ecotourism: A Sustainable Option?* (pp. 39–55). New York: Wiley.

Wincer, S. (1993) *Free Willy.* Motion picture, Warner Bros., Burbank, CA.

Winiarskyj, L. (ed.) (2004) *Animals in Entertainment.* Washington, DC: National Association for Humane and Environmental Education.

Williams, R. and Crosbie, K. (2007) Antarctic whales and Antarctic tourism. *Tourism in Marine Environments* 4 (2–3), 195–202.

Williams, R., Bain, D.E., Smith, J.C. and Lusseau, D. (2009) Effects of vessel on behaviour patterns of individual southern resident killer whales *Orcinus orca. Endangered Species Research* 6 (3), 199–209.

Williams, V. (2001) Captive Orcas 'Dying to Entertain You': The Full Story. Chippenham: Whale and Dolphin Conservation Society.

Zeppel, H. and Muloin, S. (2008) Conservation benefits of interpretation on marine wildlife tours. *Human Dimensions of Wildlife: An International Journal* 13 (4), 280–294.

6 Troubled-Shooting: The Ethics of Helicopter-assisted Guided Trophy Hunting by Tourists for Tahr

Brent Lovelock

Introduction

Within many jurisdictions, hunting is a strongly contested activity and, likewise, within many destinations it can be a contentious form of tourism. Indeed, hunting is seen by some as a 'disgusting sport that recalls and rehearses the worst in human behavior' (Vitali, 1990: 69), and trophy hunting in particular is 'widely condemned in the environmental ethics literature' (Gunn, 2001: 75). Animal rights and animal welfare advocates oppose hunting on ethical grounds, employing the argument that animals have sentience and thus moral consideration. Hunters defend their activity through arguments based upon various combinations of personal benefits, cultural rights or ecosystem benefits (e.g. through maintaining 'balance'). Overarching these concerns, however, is the fact that hunting is a multimillion-dollar, global tourism activity. In the UK, for example, hunting is said to generate 33,000 jobs (BFSS, nd, in Gunn, 2001) and in New Zealand, the site of this study, recreational hunting and other associated forms of consumptive wildlife tourism generate several thousand jobs (Gunn, 2001). In a range of other jurisdictions, from Africa to the Canadian arctic, the value of trophy hunting to local communities through trophy fees, employment of locals as guides and in various other aspects of hunting, along with the provision of game meat to communities, has been well documented (e.g. Dowsley, 2009; Foote & Wenzel, 2008; Gunn, 2001; Lovelock, 2008; Mbaiwa, 2008). However, the ethical aspects of hunting tourism are such that morally they cannot be avoided, and pragmatically they are likely to have increasingly profound impacts upon the ability of destinations and tourism operators to continue promoting and practising hunting tourism.

Heli-hunting

'Heli-hunting' or, more formally, helicopter-assisted guided trophy hunting, is a niche tourism activity practised within some public conservation lands (e.g. national parks) and private hunting estates of New Zealand. Tourist-hunters (predominantly wealthy middle-aged male Americans) are transported by helicopter into the habitat of the target species (mainly Himalayan tahr, *Hemitragus jemlahicus*) high in the mountains. The helicopter may then be used to herd and haze (hazing is where a helicopter is used to chase a game animal potentially to the point of exhaustion) the animals into a position from which the animals can be shot. Because of this, the activity has been criticised on animal welfare grounds, and labelled 'unethical' by NGOs and domestic hunters. Yet the activity is supported by the tourism industry as an example of a profitable niche tourism product. It is also supported by protected area managers as a means of 'pest' control (tahr is an introduced species, and legislation calls for their extermination). Thus heli-hunting is seen by conservation managers and the tourism industry as an innovative way to generate a high-yield income from tourists while also contributing to ecological integrity.

More recently, heli-hunting has been introduced in Texas, USA, as a means by which hunter-tourists can hunt wild hogs (pigs). Hogs are considered by farmers to be pests and, in a similar way to New Zealand, tourism operators have taken advantage of this status to offer hunting as a tourist experience. High celebrity hunter-tourists such as rock star Ted Nugent have participated in highly inflammatory heli-hunting expeditions where they claim to use machine guns to kill hundreds of pigs. Not surprisingly, this has gained the attention of the animal rights movement, with the activity becoming ethically and politically contested. Meanwhile, the tourist-hunters defend their activity on the basis of providing help to Texan ranchers, and by contributing some wild pork to charity.

This chapter explores touristic heli-hunting – as a case of a tourism activity that is ethically ambiguous, and one which raises questions about animal rights and welfare. We observe how the use of helicopters and the involvement of international hunter-tourists have exacerbated opposition to what some consider 'just another hunt'. Interestingly, the use of technology (helicopters) has made it more difficult for the tourist operators and hunters to ethically justify an activity (hunting per se) which they have historically defended on the grounds of an inherent traditional and cultural right to fulfil an atavistic need and (for some) to provide sustenance for themselves, their family and/or to the needy. The chapter discusses the ethical tensions that arise from the employment of animals in what appears to be on one level a highly unethical tourism activity, but when considered from a more holistic perspective, one which may indeed be justifiable on a number of ecological, economic, social and cultural grounds.

The chapter begins with a brief overview of the ethical arguments for and against hunting in general and then more specifically trophy hunting (see also Fennell, Chapter 2, in this volume). Then the case of heli-hunting in New Zealand is discussed in greater detail and the surrounding narratives addressed. The chapter suggests ways forward to address ethical and related problems around hunting tourism, and to advance the sustainability of this niche tourism activity.

The Ethics of Hunting

Space does not permit a detailed coverage of the ethics of hunting here, but rather a brief background is provided (for a fuller coverage see, for example, Curnutt, 1996; Dickson, 2009; Dobson, 2012; Fennell, 2012; Lovelock & Lovelock, 2013; Regan, 2004; Reis, 2009; Singer, 2001).

Overall, there seem to be more arguments against hunting than for it. And this applies more so to sport, recreational or touristic hunting than to primal or subsistence forms of hunting. Arguments against hunting are largely centred on animal rights (Regan, 2004) and animal welfare (Singer, 2001), while acknowledging that there is some overlap between the two. As noted by Gunn (2001), a successful or 'authentic' hunt usually involves the death of the target animal, and it is the form and nature of this death, and indeed that we could even contemplate this death occurring, that form the central criticisms of hunting and of trophy hunting in particular (Dobson, 2012). Arguments are made on the basis of causing harm to sentient beings and around recognising the intrinsic (rather than utilitarian) value of animals.

Compared to the non-consumptive tourism activity of wildlife viewing, consumptive activities such as hunting and fishing are highly controversial on ethical grounds, with the moral integrity of the consumptive act itself being questioned (Oian, 2013). Basically, the question around hunting relates to the more profound issue of 'what exactly can be done to other animals in the name of human interests?' (Aaltola, 2005: 20). Gunn (2001: 68) notes that at one end of the spectrum 'is the view that hunting is justified only for self-protection and for food, where no other reasonable alternative is available'.

Thus touristic trophy hunting seems to attract a more intense critique than other forms of hunting, and as Gunn (2001: 68) notes, 'Nowhere in the literature ... is hunting for fun, for the enjoyment of killing, or for the acquisition of trophies defended'. Causey (1989: 340) describes in obviously distasteful tones the trophy hunter who 'runs down his panicked prey with a Land Rover, shoots it with a semi-automatic weapon, then removes the head to decorate his office wall, while letting the carcass rot'. Such a lack of respect for the animal is central to many of the concerns around trophy hunting, exemplified by Taylor's (1996: 263) musing that 'There are circumstances in which the killing of a human being may be justified, but to mount this person's head on a wall is usually not acceptable'.

However, many writers agree that hunting can be justified in scenarios where hunting is a part of a cultural tradition, for the psychological wellbeing of the hunter, or when introduced destructive species are threatening the ecosystem values of endangered species (Gunn, 2001; Loftin, 1984). Gunn (2001: 69) advocates that we are entitled to kill animals, but 'only in order to promote or protect some non-trivial human interest and where no reasonable alternative strategy is available'. Hunting has also been morally justified on the basis of the virtues that are espoused or acquired through the practice. These may include 'tenacity, courage, moderation and discipline, and the achievement of a heightened respect for the biotic community in which the hunt takes place' (List, 2004). However, some (see, for example, Lovering, 2006) criticise such a virtue ethics approach, believing that it fails to provide sufficient justification for hunting. While not yet addressed within the literature, the contemporary practice of tourist hunters, who undertake their hunt within a highly time-constrained, commercialised, guided, managed (and often mechanised) context, challenges the idea that virtues may be acquired in such scenarios. This aspect is further addressed below in the context of heli-hunting for tahr in New Zealand.

Nor do the primitivist or neo-primitivist arguments for hunting really hold up in such a touristic context. Ortega y Gasset's (1972: 139) description of hunting as an atavistic 'vacation from the human condition', an escape from 'the miserable convenience of modern life' does not really hold water within the modern touristic context. It is arguable how much 'carving away [of] modernity' (Morris, 2013: 298) the cosseted, guided (and in the case of heli-hunting – *airborne*) tourist hunter actually experiences, as they are comforted away up into the alpine habitat of the tahr on a waft of jet-aviation fuel.

A suitable ethical framework for hunting tourism?

The contextual variety of hunting is immense, ranging from subsistence hunting (perhaps located at one end of an 'ethical hunting continuum') to high-tech, 'canned' trophy hunting at the other, but with the added intricacies of local versus touristic, endangered species versus pest, use versus non-use (meat, skins, etc.) and local economic contribution versus foreign managed, owned and controlled (and leaked). In response to this complexity, Aaltola (2005) (who considers human–non-human relations in general), proposes a model that we could apply to help resolve the ethical conflicts around hunting tourism. The model recognises that there are multiple bases of value (e.g. life, sentience, ecology, moral agency, humanity, community) and that these would need to be accounted for when making decisions about the appropriateness of any hunting tourism activity. Similarly, in an attempt to address some of the ethical problems around wildlife tourism, Burns *et al.* (2011) in their provocatively titled paper, *Should dingoes die?*, proposed a set of principles for an ecocentric approach to wildlife tourism. While their principles are focused on non-consumptive wildlife tourism, they may also be applicable to hunting tourism – in particular, those that refer to the intrinsic value of wildlife, the moral obligations of visitors, and managers and tourism operators self-reflecting on their ethical position (Burns *et al.*, 2011).

Himalayan Tahr in New Zealand

Tahr as a precious tourism commodity

Tahr were introduced to New Zealand in 1904, an outcome of the national tourism organisation's goal of encouraging visits from wealthy European and North American hunter-tourists. Several species of deer were also introduced around this time, along with moose, and today these contribute to a strong hunting tourism industry. Tahr encountered no natural enemies in New Zealand. They steadily colonised the high alpine areas of the Southern Alps, reaching a population of around 40,000 by the 1970s, and have had a substantial impact upon alpine ecosystems by overgrazing. Since 1993 tahr have been managed under a statutory plan that limits their numbers to 10,000 over about 5000 km^2 of the Alps (Moore, 2014; Parkes, 2006). Today tahr are described (by some) as a national and international hunting and conservation resource. New Zealand has the only substantial wild herd of tahr outside of their native Himalayan range, and is the only destination where tahr can be hunted in a free-range natural environment (Moore, 2014).

Tahr as a pest

New Zealand is typical of many Western or Western-influenced jurisdictions in that its conservation ideology is dominated by preservationist ideals of restoring and/or maintaining a pre-human natural state. Indeed, the country's tourism product is sold to international visitors over the strapline '100% Pure', which appears on all promotional material from Tourism New Zealand, the national tourism organisation. Our conservation ideology also drives our human–animal relations in that we attempt to reduce the impact of introduced species, such as tahr, on natural ecosystems because we acknowledge a sense of ethical responsibility for this ecological disturbance (Sadlier, 1990).

Thus tahr in New Zealand are also perceived as a pest species, classified as such under legislation, and their control is sought by the Department of Conservation (DoC) on the grounds of their impact upon natural biota

(Parkes, 2006). However, their popularity for recreational and touristic hunting creates conflicting management goals.

Exotic versus natural species

In general, the ethical theories addressing concern for animals do not 'allow any morally significant distinctions between native and exotic species, or to attribute any overriding moral significance to the protection of unique indigenous species and ecosystems' (Eggleston *et al.*, 2003: 362). But an ecocentric understanding of ethical responsibility places greatest moral significance on the protection of entire ecosystems, thus overriding the welfare or rights of individual organisms (Eggleston *et al.*, 2003: 362). Such an approach would recognise animal welfare as being only of secondary concern, and hunting could thus be employed as a valid approach to wildlife management. But the issue is complex and Eggleston *et al.* draw upon bioethics to help inform decisions around hunting tourism. They propose a set of principles for the management of wild animals. Of particular relevance to touristic tahr hunting is the 'harm principle' (from 19th-century English philosopher, J.S. Mill).

The freedom granted to hunter-tourists results in harm to others – prima facie gratuitous harm to sentient creatures – and therefore harms interests of ethical significance (Eggleston *et al.*, 2003: 371). But counter to this, hunters can claim that hunting performs a necessary 'ecologically therapeutic function that may even benefit aggregate animal welfare' (Eggleston *et al.*, 2003: 371). It is argued that so-called 'therapeutic hunting' can even be *morally required* under certain circumstances (Callicott, 1980; Gunn, 2001). This may especially apply to those species (e.g. tahr) that regularly exceed the capacity of their range, causing harm to other species (Varner, 1994). In such cases we can identify an overlap between the goals of sport/touristic hunting and therapeutic hunting – the situation for hunting tahr in New Zealand – whereby sporting/touristic hunters can acquire trophy animals while also contributing to ecosystem management goals. While touristic trophy hunting may be considered a legitimate way to kill these animals, to be considered an ethical means of control would entail that it comes 'at no cost to society' (Gunn, 2001: 80).

Heli-hunting of Tahr

Helicopter-assisted guided hunting operations targeting tahr, with tourist clients, have been underway for several years. In 2011, on public conservation land, this involved 212 flights with 255 guided clients (mainly international visitors), recovering 376 trophies (DoC, 2011a). Additional non-trophy animals were also culled as a condition of the operators' permits. Helicopter-assisted guided hunting generates income for the DoC, generating NZ$199,000 in 2011. Additional savings to the DoC were made through the cull requirement of operators' permits, resulting in 'free' tahr control for the DoC to the value of around NZ$27,000 (DoC, 2011a).

In 2012 a study of the economic impact of heli-hunting (Lovelock *et al.*, 2012) showed that, for a modest number of clients, helicopter-assisted guided hunting produces a relatively high total output (revenue/sales) of NZ$5.6m. Visitor spend is high on the activity, with client expenditure while based with the hunting operator averaging NZ$16,780 – far greater than that of the average international visitor (currently NZ$2421 average expenditure per trip for international visitors to New Zealand – see MED, 2011). The client spend associated with the entire activity – based upon respondents' estimates of client expenditure on all hunting-related services (e.g. transport, taxidermy, and hospitality, some of which is provided by other businesses), is estimated to be in the order of NZ$9.7m (Lovelock *et al.*, 2012). Importantly, a significant proportion of clients indicated to operators that their primary motivation for visiting New Zealand was to engage in helicopter-assisted guided hunting. The potential loss of direct spending to New Zealand helicopter-assisted guided hunting operators from those clients who may seek alternative international hunting destinations if the activity were not available is approximately NZ$2.2m (Lovelock *et al.*, 2012).

Given the study's findings, heli-hunting would appear to meet the criteria for 'high yield' tourism, as advocated in the *New Zealand Tourism Strategy 2015*, which contains the objective: 'To develop existing products and services so that they increase the value of the visitor experience and encourage higher levels of spending' (TIANZ, 2007). Additionally, heli-hunting is a highly seasonal activity, providing income to operators during the 'low season' (March–September) for international and domestic tourist activity in New Zealand (Lovelock *et al.*, 2012). However, the DoC acknowledges that a number of 'social effects' arise from heli-hunting: 'In particular, [local] ground hunters have been vocal in 2011 in their opposition to tourist heli-hunting' (DoC, 2011b: 9). Apart from possible impacts upon ground hunting, concern has been expressed over the ethics of helicopter-assisted guided hunting, along with opposition to operations in Wilderness Areas.

Herding, hazing and fair chase

In heli-hunting, helicopters are potentially used to herd and haze (chase) animals – so that this maximises the opportunity for the hunter client, who has been transported to an advantageous shooting position – to kill their chosen trophy animal. On this point, recreational hunters (mainly domestic foot hunters) and animal welfare advocates are united in their opposition to this practice, arguing that tahr are stressed and harassed and that there is no element of 'fair chase' in such hunts. Fair chase refers to hunts being undertaken in such conditions that animals have an unrestricted capacity to evade the hunter, thus granting no hunter an advantage over another in terms of potential to bag a trophy (Lovelock, 2008). While introduced by hunting clubs over 100 years ago to 'level the playing field' for trophy hunters, the fair chase code has also (probably unintentionally) granted some degree of animal rights and welfare protection to game animals. Fair chase includes proscriptions against shooting animals from aircraft, boats, land vehicles, against herding animals towards shooters, the use of 'cheater technology', and the shooting of fenced-in animals. Heli-hunting would appear to breach fair chase criteria.

While herding is permitted (but in a manner that does not place the animal under adverse duress), heli-hunting operators maintain that hazing, where a helicopter chases a game animal potentially to the point of exhaustion, is not practised. Hazing is banned both under the industry code of practice and their DoC concessions, as is aerial shooting (unless a wounded animal needs to be dispatched humanely). Whether performed or not, narratives have emerged that incorporate and perpetuate the existence of such unethical practices.

Heli-hunting Narratives

A number of conflicting narratives persist within the heli-hunting domain. Variously, these narratives demonstrate a range of ethical positions with regard to the relationship between the hunter, the hunted and the hunting ground, and establish the context within which the future of touristic heli-hunting for tahr will be debated and decided.

The tourism industry narrative

The tourism industry peak body, the Tourism Industry Association New Zealand (TIANZ), supports the hunting industry in general. Many heli-hunting operators are TIANZ members. TIANZ representatives attend the annual Safari Club International (SCI) convention in Las Vegas, promoting New Zealand as a hunting destination. The TIANZ notes that New Zealand is regarded as being in the world's top five international hunting destinations and that hunting guides '... are well placed to help leverage this awareness into visitors staying longer and spending more when they plan their next visit to New Zealand' (TIANZ, 2014).

The heli-hunting operators' narrative centres around prestige, comfort, convenience and universality of access for their tourist clients, who may demonstrate a range of physical mobilities.

Tahr are arguably one of the most impressive game animals in the world and are the highlight of a hunter's trip to New Zealand. Our hunting methods vary depending on the level of fitness of individual hunters, personal preference and time frames. We can use helicopters to get up into the high alpine hunting country or do on foot walk up hunts. (www.mtcooktrophyhunting.co.nz/project_category/game/)

Access to these alpine trophies can be by walking, four-wheel drive vehicle or helicopter, thereby allowing hunters of all physical abilities the chance to take these exceptional mountain trophies. (www.johnberry hunting.com/newzealand.htm)

... if the going gets a little tough for the alpine species we can supply helicopter transport. Excellent numbers of game sighted and top sized trophies taken, all with private comfortable accommodations included. (www.nzwildhunt.com/trophy-gallery/private-land-hunting)

Our hunting methods match the level of fitness of individual hunters. We can take a helicopter daily from comfortable lodgings, or do wilderness spike camps. (http://newzealandtrophyhunting.com/index.php/eng/page/hunting/tahr)

Heli-hunting client testimonies offer a range of justifications for their use of helicopters for tahr hunting, including having minimal time, poor ground access, or having family members along on the hunt, e.g. 'We used a helicopter to get back in and out, made sense since my wife was along and helps you to get away as road access is minimal' (http://onyourownadventures.com/hunttalk/showthread.php?t=248547).

Heli-hunting operators' promotional materials also stress the 'free-range' (and thus ethical) nature of the hunting: 'Our private land hunts are undertaken across 10,000's of acres to hunt these species' (www.nzwildhunt.com/trophy-gallery/private-land-hunting).

However, not all hunting tourism operators use helicopters. This may be from choice, lack of capacity to invest in a helicopter, inability to partner with a helicopter operator or simply because there are a limited number of heli-hunting permits issued by DoC. Some companies stress their use of more traditional – and thus ethical – modes of hunting, even using this as a 'point of difference':

At Kiwi Safaris we pride ourselves on hunting 95% of all our tahr on foot – without the need for helicopter access. Don't be fooled by the 'Helicopter assisted' hype that some may promote. It is completely unnecessary to have to use a helicopter to hunt Tahr. A tahr hunt, while being quite physical, is achievable by most people. www.kiwisafaris.co.nz

The anti-hunting heli-hunting narrative

This narrative sees an unlikely selection of interest groups, including recreational hunters, conservationists, environmental NGOs and even conservation QANGOs all loosely united in their opposition to heli-hunting. Recreational hunters are the most vocal of these, having organised petitions and gained the support of politicians to help ban the practice. One such petition calls for a ban on heli-hunting on the grounds that it is 'unethical', impinges on the rights of other users, and is detrimental to New Zealand's destination image and tourism industry (Carle, 2010). Recreational hunters have been successful in gaining political support for their cause to the extent that the New Zealand Government recently enacted legislation (Game Animal Council Act, 2013) that will purportedly ensure that 'herd-and-chase style heli-hunting becomes a thing of the past' (Collins, 2013, np).

Opposition has also been expressed by a range of conservation interests including the DoC's own advisory boards, who are concerned about animal welfare and New Zealand's international reputation. Even the Parliamentary Commissioner for the Environment has expressed opposition to the practice, on animal welfare grounds, likening heli-hunting to fox-hunting (which is now banned in England and Scotland) (PCE, 2012). It is notable that conservation interests are not supportive of heli-hunting despite the acknowledged negative impacts of tahr on natural ecosystems. The Royal New Zealand Forest and Bird Protection Society (the country's largest environmental NGO) belittles the conservation benefits of heli-hunting, describing it as a commercial activity for private benefit, rather than a conservation management activity for the public good. They say that it has limited conservation benefits, with only small numbers of trophy animals taken, and that it impacts negatively upon back-country tourism and recreation.

However, in reality, the 'anti' narrative has really been driven not by animal welfare or rights concerns, nor by destination image concerns, but by recreational hunters wishing (oxymoronically) to protect the tahr population from touristic hunting so more are available for their own use. This has been veiled within an ethical argument that heli-hunting is not 'fair chase' which, while a legitimate concern for many hunters, may be secondary to their desire to defend their 'rights' of fair access to the tahr resource.

The public narrative

The issue of heli-hunting has appeared in the media regularly over recent years, and has generally been portrayed in a negative light. A recent editorial in a regional daily newspaper is fairly typical, referring to heli-hunting as a:

> ... practice carried out for the gratification of indolent, affluent tourists effortlessly and lazily killing animals ... as an approximation of actual hunting it still ranks somewhere behind the activities of obese couch-bound gamers playing some of the more realistic computer games out there.... Critics are right to portray it, essentially, as just vainglorious

killing, in conditions that allow the targeted animal ... virtually no chance of escape. (Southland Times, 2013, np)

In another national weekly, it is noted that 'A hunter hunts: a rich tourist in a helicopter is engaged in another pursuit entirely' (Blundell, 2008: 19–21).

Discussion and Conclusions

Vitali (1990) argues that sport (or touristic) hunting does not violate any animal's moral rights and is a natural and moral good. The exercise of human skill is 'sufficient good to compensate for the evil that results from it, namely the death of the animal' (Vitali, 1990: 69). For touristic hunting activities, however, the extent to which human skill is exercised, at least on the part of the actual hunter, is debatable. A raft of support is put in place for the tourist hunter, from drivers and pilots to guides, cooks and cleaners, and physical discomforts are removed to the extent that the hunter is cosseted and effectively insulated from any real hunting experience. In terms of the relationship between the hunter, the hunted and the hunting ground, there comes a disconnection that leads us to question the extent to which commercialised touristic hunting can be considered to be virtuous – and therefore ethical.

That is not to say that all hunter-tourists seek or experience such cosseting and distancing from the hunted and the hunting ground, but it is quite apparent that the type of hunting considered here – heli-hunting – is an extreme example of this, to the extent that many question whether heli-hunting is hunting at all.

Commercialised touristic hunting is a highly competitive niche activity where operators compete in the provision of convenience and comfort to their clients. The time compression in commercialised touristic hunting, where there are often highly time-constrained itineraries, provides further rationale for the reduction or elimination of certain elements of the hunt that in other circumstances (perhaps back 'home') would collectively contribute to the ethical integrity of the hunt (e.g. prior research on the game species, habits and habitat; slow and careful familiarisation with the hunting ground; physical discomfort and exertion with travelling to and through the hunting ground; survival and bush craft skills; patience during the stalk; skill with the shooting and kill; skill with the dressing and taking of meat and trophies; fortitude with recovering meat and trophy from the hunting ground).

Also, the therapeutic (to the ecosystem) aspect of this type of hunting is largely a distraction, and the economic value generated, while substantial, comes at the price of devaluing the hunting experiences of many thousands of domestic non-tourist hunters, while also impacting upon the back-country experiences of non-hunting tourists and recreationists. For heli-hunting the blatant absence of the above elements, together with direct competition with the local use of the resource (the tahr and their natural environment) by recreational hunters and other nature-based tourists/recreationists, make this activity dedicated to what could be described as the 'trivial human interest' (Gunn, 2001) of a handful of wealthy tourists, extremely vulnerable to criticism and attack.

But this problem goes beyond heli-hunting and ultimately challenges the legitimacy (and therefore political sustainability) of a range of commercial tourist hunting activities, depending upon the extent to which the hunter-tourist is cosseted, or self-reliant, and exercising their authentic hunting skills and sensitivities – and by doing so, becoming virtuous. In the mainly touristic contexts in which hunting does not have an obvious role in terms of subsistence, its legitimacy 'depends on cultural, moral and political views and definitions, and is therefore potentially fragile and ready to be challenged' (Oian, 2013: 183).

That hunting can be successfully challenged and in some cases eliminated has already been clearly demonstrated. Lovelock (2008) predicts that it will be the animal rights advocates who determine the future of commercial touristic hunting, as evidenced already in some destinations (e.g. England, Scotland and arguably in some African destinations, where such interests have worked alongside international environmental interests who have based their conservation campaigns on the protection of charismatic megafauna from hunting; see Martin, 2012). However, there are others who believe that the future of hunting (and by extension the future of hunting tourism) will be determined by the non-hunting, non-animal-rights advocate majority (Peterson, 2004). According to Peterson, it is the social legitimacy of hunting rather than its moral legitimacy that is important, and this will determine its ability to persist. Leader-Williams (2009) concurs, noting that tourism industry practitioners need to address those aspects of their activity that are most likely to cause public concern, and to explain the benefits of hunting. One mechanism to do so is through hunting operator certification, which may promote good practice, discourage those that are unethical or unsustainable, and foster moral reflection on the part of visitors, managers and tourism operators. Concepts such as humane killing and fair chase may be 'legitimate and helpful ethical variables to be included in certification criteria' (Child & Wall, 2009: 351).

It was noted earlier that heli-hunting has also arisen in Texas. While the activity there is not without its detractors, in Texas, however, it is clearly acknowledged by operators (who bring in out-of-state hunter-tourists) that:

> This service is not sport hunting but a depredation hunt to help the landowner control his population of feral hogs. This means that as a private hunter, you are now allowed by the State of Texas to pay for the right to perform as the gunner and shoot feral hogs from a helicopter as part of a feral hog depredation program. (www.texasvarminthunting.com/TexasHelicopterPigHunting.html)

Such a transparent approach, where there are clear economic and ecological imperatives to control the target species, and where these are clearly conveyed to the public and to the hunter-tourist participants, is preferable to situations such as heli-hunting where 'shooting' is disguised as hunting, and as being an ethical and virtuous activity, where arguably it is not. To try to extend the legitimacy of local subsistence and/or recreational hunting to commercialised touristic hunting may be a weak argument that will ultimately undermine efforts to achieve sustainable hunting tourism activities.

References

Aaltola, E. (2005) Animal ethics and interest conflicts. *Ethics & the Environment* 10 (1), 9–48.

Blundell, S. (2008) The war on tahr. *The Listener*, 19 January.

Burns, G.L., MacBeth, J. and Moore, S. (2011) Should dingoes die? Principles for engaging ecocentric ethics in wildlife tourism management. *Journal of Ecotourism* 10 (3), 179–196.

Callicott, J.B. (1980) Animal liberation: A triangular affair. *Environmental Ethics* 2 (4), 311–338.

Carle, J. (2010) Say NO to heli hunting in New Zealand. *Mountain Man*, 11 January. See www.mountainman.co.nz/articles/article/36 (accessed 2 February 2014).

Causey, A.S. (1989) On the morality of hunting. *Environmental Ethics* 11 (4), 327–343.

Child, B. and Wall, B. (2009) The application of certification to hunting: A case for simplicity. In B. Dickson, J. Hutton and W.M. Adams (eds) *Recreational Hunting, Conservation and Rural Livelihoods: Science and Practice* (pp. 341–360). Oxford: Wiley-Blackwell.

Collins, J. (2013) Game Animal Council Bill — second reading, in committee, third reading. *Hansard and Journals*, 19 November. Wellington: New Zealand Parliament. See www.parliament.nz/en-nz/pb/debates/debates/50HansD_20131120_00000016/game-animal-council-bill-%E2%80%94-second-reading-in-committee (accessed 21 February 2014).

Curnutt, J. (1996) How to argue for and against sport hunting. *Journal of Social Philosophy* 27 (2), 65–89.

DoC (2011a) *Final Report on 2011 Heli-hunting Operations*. Wellington: Department of Conservation, New Zealand Parliament. See www.doc.govt.nz/upload/documents/parks-and-recreation/hunting/2011-heli-hunting-report.pdf (accessed 21 November, 2012).

DoC (2011b) *Report to the Deputy Director General Research and Development*. Wellington: Department of Conservation, New Zealand Parliament. See www.doc.govt.nz/upload/documents/aboutdoc/news/issues/heli-hunting/decision-makers-reportheli hunting-april11.pdf (accessed 21 November, 2012).

Dickson, B. (2009) The ethics of recreational hunting. In B. Dickson, J. Hutton and W.M. Adams (eds) *Recreational Hunting, Conservation and Rural Livelihoods: Science and Practice* (pp. 59–72). Oxford: Wiley-Blackwell.

Dobson, J. (2012) Ethical issues in trophy hunting. In O. Moufakkir and P.M. Burns (eds) *Controversies in Tourism* (pp. 86–98). Wallingford: CABI.

Dowsley, M. (2009) Inuit organized polar bear sport hunting in Nunavut Territory, Canada. *Journal of Ecotourism* 8 (2), 161–175.

Eggleston, J.E., Rixecker, S.S. and Hickling, G.J. (2003) The role of ethics in the management of New Zealand's wild mammals. *New Zealand Journal of Zoology* 30 (4), 361–376.

Fennell, D.A. (2012) *Tourism and Animal Ethics*. London, New York: Routledge.

Foote, L. and Wenzel, G. (2008) Conservation hunting concepts, Canada's Inuit, and polar bear hunting. In B.A. Lovelock (ed.) *Tourism and the Consumption of Wildlife: Hunting, Shooting and Sport Fishing* (pp. 115–128). London: Routledge.

Gunn, A.S. (2001) Environmental ethics and trophy hunting. *Ethics and the Environment* 6 (1), 68–95.

Leader-Williams, N. (2009) Conservation and hunting: Friends or foes? In B. Dickson, J. Hutton and W.M. Adams (eds) *Recreational Hunting, Conservation and Rural Livelihoods: Science and Practice* (pp. 9–24). Oxford: Wiley-Blackwell.

List, C.J. (2004) On the moral distinctiveness of sport hunting. *Environmental Ethics* 26 (2), 155–169.

Loftin, R.F. (1984) The morality of hunting. *Environmental Ethics* 6, 241–250.

Lovelock, B.A. (ed.) (2008) *Tourism and the Consumption of Wildlife: Hunting, Shooting and Sportfishing*. London: Routledge.

Lovelock, B. and Lovelock, K.M. (2013) *The Ethics of Tourism: Critical and Applied Perspectives*. London: Routledge.

Lovelock, B., Kahui, V. and O'Sullivan, O. (2012) Estimating the value of helicopter-assisted guided hunting. Unpublished report. Centre for Recreation Research, School of Business, University of Otago, Dunedin.

Lovering, R. (2006) The virtues of hunting: A reply to Jensen. *Philosophy in the Contemporary World* 13 (1), 68–76.

Martin, G. (2012) *Game Changer: Animal Rights and the Fate of Africa's Wildlife*. Oakland, CA: University of California Press.

Mbaiwa, J. (2008) The success and sustainability of consumptive wildlife tourism in Africa. In B.A. Lovelock (ed.) *Tourism and the Consumption of Wildlife: Hunting, Shooting and Sportfishing* (pp. 141–154). London: Routledge.

MED (Ministry of Economic Development) (2011) *Tourism Research and Data*. Wellington: Ministry of Business, Innovation & Employment, New Zealand Government. See www.med.govt.nz/sectors-industries/tourism/tourism-research-data (accessed 20 December 2011).

Moore, K. (2014) Tahr 100 years in New Zealand. *Twizel Update* 470 (6 February), 1.

Morris, S.P. (2013) Challenging the values of hunting: Fair chase, game playing, and intrinsic value. *Environmental Ethics* 35, 295–331.

Oian, H. (2013) Wilderness tourism and the moralities of commitment: Hunting and landscapes in Norway. *Journal of Rural Studies* 32, 177–185.

Ortega y Gasset, J. (1972) *Meditations on Hunting*. New York: Charles Scribner.

Parkes, J.P. (2006) Does commercial harvesting of introduced wild mammals contribute to their management as conservation pests? *Ecological Studies* 186, 407–420.

PCE (Parliamentary Commissioner for the Environment) (2012) *Speech to Otago University Symposium Public Conservation Lands 2040: Prosperity or Posterity? The Future of Conservation Land*. Wellington: Parliamentary Commissioner for the Environment. See www.pce. parliament.nz/media/speeches/speech-to-otago-university-symposium-public-con servation-lands-2040 (accessed 2 November 2013).

Peterson, M.N. (2004) An approach for demonstrating the social legitimacy of hunting. *Wildlife Society Bulletin* 32 (2), 310–321.

Regan, T. (2004) *The Case for Animal Rights*. Berkeley, CA: University of California Press.

Reis, A.C. (2009) More than the kill: Hunters' relationships with landscape and prey. *Current Issues in Tourism* 12 (5/6), 573–578.

Sadlier, R.M.S.F. (1990) Proposals and principles (perhaps?). In B. McFadgen and P. Simpson (eds) *Research Directions for Conservation Science*. Science & Research Series No. 37. Wellington: Department of Conservation, New Zealand Parliament.

Singer, P. (2001) *Animal Liberation*. New York: Harper Collins.

Southland Times (2013) Editorial: Indolent thrills and effortless kills. *Southland Times*, 20 November. See www.stuff.co.nz/southland-times/opinion/9419498/Editorial-Indolent-thrills-and-effortless-kills (accessed 20 February 2014).

Taylor, A. (1996) Animal rights and human needs. *Environmental Ethics* 18, 249–264.

TIANZ (Tourism Industry Association New Zealand) (2007) *New Zealand Tourism Strategy 2015*. Wellington: New Zealand Tourism Industry Association. See www.tianz.org.nz/content/library/final_nzts2015_hr.pdf.

TIANZ (Tourism Industry Association New Zealand) (2014) Hunting business in Las Vegas. *TIA News Updates*, 21 February.

Varner, G.E. (1994) Can animal rights activists be environmentalists? In C. Pierce and D. Van De Veer (eds) *People, Penguins and Plastic Trees* (pp. 254–273). Belmont, CA: Wadsworth.

Vitali, T.R. (1990) Sport hunting: Moral or immoral? *Environmental Ethics* 12 (1), 69–82.

Part 2

Conflict, Contradiction and Contestation

7 Whales, Tourism and Manifold Capitalist Fixes: New Relationships with the Driving Force of Capitalism

James Higham and Katja Neves

Introduction

Ecotourism is a powerful, but highly contentious, form of contemporary economic development (Cater, 2006; Wheeller, 1994). It expresses a strong desire among the alienated middle classes in post-industrial societies to get back in touch with nature (Fletcher, 2014). It also reflects an attempt to overcome individual anxiety relating to irreversible environmental degradation and biodiversity loss caused by capitalism (Žižek, 2011) through the conflation of eco-consumption with biodiversity conservation (Duffy, 2008; Neves, 2010a). Within this context, wildlife tourism, it may be argued, represents one of a range of new strategies of capital accumulation and expansion (Fletcher & Neves, 2012; Neves & Igoe, 2012).

This chapter addresses the capacity of ecotourism to employ capitalist mechanisms to address some of the more acute problems of capitalism itself. It addresses ecotourism in terms of a range of capitalist 'fixes' including: economic stagnation due to over-accumulation (time/space fix); limitations on capital accumulation resulting from ecological degradation (environmental fix); growing inequality and social unrest (social fix); and a widespread sense of alienation between humans and non-human natures (psychological fix). We consider the widespread advocacy of ecotourism as a panacea for the diverse social and environmental problems of capitalism in terms of endorsement of its potential as a manifold capitalist fix. In doing so, we find that, rather than coming to fruition as solutions to the shortcomings of capitalist processes, these promised fixes tend to reproduce and exacerbate existing socio-ecological problems (e.g. Neves & Igoe, 2012; see also Silva, 2013).

Within the context of ecotourism development, we contemplate wildlife tourism – specifically whale watching – as a manifold capitalist fix through a series of local and global considerations. We then extend our discussion by paying particular attention to old and new relationships between whales and the most sacred capitalist commodity – petroleum. In doing so, we suggest that the construction of contemporary relations between wildlife and capitalism in tourism as the non-material dual opposite of the deadly intersection of capitalism and wildlife during industrial capitalism amounts to an ideological construct that legitimises and promotes contemporary forms of capitalist accumulation (Neves, 2010a). Notwithstanding fundamental and important differences between whale hunting and whale watching, these two 'whale-related' industries can be described as recursively linked through the (re)production of specific historically situated modes of capitalist production. These links raise concerns regarding the welfare of whales, human social justice, alienation and equity (Neves & Igoe, 2012). Moreover, we bring to light important parallels between the history of the contrasting whale industries, as well as the intersection of ecotourism and the expansion of petroleum-based industries – namely aviation and whale watching itself. In doing so we highlight the paradoxes entailed in the contemporary expansion of ecotourism as a panacea for the contradictions of capitalism that is simultaneously dependent on dwindling petroleum reserves.

(Eco)tourism and Capitalism

In recent decades the limitations and contradictions of capitalism have become increasingly difficult to ignore. At the core of this recognition, both critics and proponents of capitalism have come to recognise the paradoxical nature of capitalist logic and practices (Harvey, 2010a). Two fundamental contradictions sustain the paradoxical nature of capitalism: a contradiction between capital's dictum to grow and expand exponentially through a variety of value extraction processes, and secondly its tendency to destroy the very resources that capitalist modes of production extract and transform. The growing levels of resource scarcity that these contradictions entail have led to increased costs of production, inflationary economic effects and, most importantly, to social and ecological degradation. While opponents of capitalism have argued for centuries that capitalism is neither socially, economically nor ecologically sustainable, defenders of capitalist ideology and practices have found temporary solutions to the limitations of capitalism (Harvey, 2010a). This has been achieved by means of displacing the aforementioned contradictions temporally into the future, spatially through geographic global expansion, and ontologically by extending capitalist accumulation into new realms. Such realms include the previously untapped domains of the human psyche and/or the human body (Fletcher & Neves,

2012), the financialisation of ecological services such as CO_2 capturing, deep-ocean or outer-space mining, or even through the conceptualisation and material production of entirely new realms for capitalist extraction and accumulation (e.g. genetically modified organisms).

Britton (1991: 451) has explained that the global tourism industry is 'a major internationalised component of Western capitalist economies' and it is within this context that ecotourism and wildlife tourism have emerged as mass capitalist 'industries'. The emergence of these industries must be understood as part of the rise of economic neoliberalism since the 1980s (Harvey, 2010a). In this sense, ecotourism constitutes a prime example of a system of economic thinking and acting that deregulated the global circulation of people, goods and financial investment in an attempt to overcome capitalism's spatio-geographic limitations (Harvey, 2005, 2010a, 2010b). As the dynamics of neoliberal ideology have unfolded, ecotourism has been increasingly presented as an ideal solution to manifold capitalist contradictions (Fletcher, 2011; Fletcher & Neves, 2012).

Ecotourism lies at the cutting edge of the commodification of natural resources around the globe (Bandy, 1996; West & Carrier, 2004). It is implicated in capitalism's 'ecological phase' (O'Connor, 1994), embodying such paradigmatic free market principles as decentralisation and deregulation of natural resource governance (or, more precisely, re-regulation from states to non-state actors) as well as resources' marketisation, privatisation, and commodification as tourism 'products' (see Bianchi, 2005, 2009; Carrier & Macleod, 2005; Cater, 2006; Davis, 1997; Duffy, 2002, 2008, 2010, 2012; Duffy & Moore, 2010; Fletcher, 2009, 2011; Mowforth & Munt 2008; Neves, 2004, 2010b; Vivanco, 2001, 2006). Ecotourism is characterised by 'the institutional expression of particular sets of late capitalist values in a particular political-economic climate' (West & Carrier, 2004: 484). Cater (2006) describes ecotourism as a 'Western construct' expanding the hegemony of global capitalism. Duffy (2012: 17) explains that ecotourism 'is not just reflective of global neoliberalism, but constitutes one of its key drivers, extending neoliberal principles to an expanding range of biophysical phenomena'.

These authors describe an increasing trend toward neoliberalisation within natural resource management with a specific focus on environmental conservation (e.g. Brockington & Duffy, 2010; Brockington et al., 2008; Büscher, 2010; Büscher et al., 2012; Dressler & Roth, 2010; Fletcher, 2010; Igoe & Brockington, 2007; Neves, 2010a, 2010b; Sullivan, 2006, 2009). While extractive industry creates value by transforming natural resources into commodities that can be exported to global consumer markets, environmental conservation commodifies resources *in situ* (Neves, 2010a). Considerable extraction value is generated by virtue of the necessity of transporting consumers to the site of production (Büscher et al., 2012), through which ecotourism has become a powerful driving force of neoliberal conservation. In doing so, ecotourism offers to placate or overcome the considerable anxieties arising from the irreversible environmental costs of capitalism (Žižek, 2011). The conflation of eco-consumption with biodiversity conservation through ecotourism had proved a powerful mechanism underpinning this avenue of economic development (Duffy, 2008; Neves, 2010a, 2010b).

Ecotourism and Manifold Capitalist Fixes

As an expression of neoliberal capitalism, ecotourism has been seen to offer a number of potential 'fixes' (Harvey, 1989, 2006) to address contradictions inherent to the accumulation process (Cater, 2006; Fletcher, 2011). It provides a range of ecological, psychological and social fixes to capitalist shortcomings in addition to the spatial and temporal fixes just described. With the claim that ecotourism contributes to conservation *par excellence*, ecotourism promises to contribute to the preservation of non-human species while contributing to the social welfare of the peoples living within or near these resources (Fletcher & Neves, 2012). It thus promises to deliver crucially important social and ecological fixes to the negative outcomes of earlier forms of capitalism.

A crisis of capitalism arises from the ecological limits of a finite natural resource base (O'Connor, 1988, 1994). Generating profit through ever-increasing production results in rapid degradation of the resource base. This crisis can be addressed through a series of 'environmental fixes' (Castree, 2008), primarily through the commodification and trading of new forms of natural capital. These environmental fixes have entailed replacing state control of resources with capitalist markets; intensifying exploitation of a given natural resource to yield increased short-term profits; and/or transferring resource governance responsibility (and thus revenues) from state to non-state actors (Fletcher & Neves, 2012).

Ecotourism provides particularly fertile ground for the pursuit of environmental fixes (Fletcher, 2011; Robbins & Fraser, 2003). It creates new markets for natural capital through spatial expansion into relatively uncommodified new destinations. Privatisation offers much scope to transfer resource control from states to capitalist markets (Langholz & Lassoie, 2001). Increasing visitation augments revenue generation at the destination and its natural resource base. NGOs and private consultancy firms act as intermediaries in the ecotourism development process, cementing the shift in revenue generation from state to non-state actors (Butcher, 2006). Ecotourism offers scope for additional environmental fixes by harnessing resource degradation itself (Fletcher, 2011; Neves, 2010a; Neves-Graca, 2002), whereby additional value is derived from increasing scarcity. Reflecting the notion of 'disaster capitalism' (Klein, 2007), an environmental fix is available through the increasing scarcity value of dwindling resources. Wildlife species, like ecotourism destinations themselves (Mowforth & Munt, 2008), may be marketed in ways that highlight the probability that they will cease to exist at some point in the not too distant future. This capitalist environmental fix is illustrated by growth in demand for 'extinction tourism' and 'last chance tourism' (Lemelin *et al.*, 2011) whereby capitalist value is explicitly derived from the prospect of imminent disappearance (Leahy, 2008).

Pushing this line of analysis further, ecotourism development can be seen to provide a variety of other fixes to problems intrinsic to capitalist development. Ecotourism may deliver a 'social fix' (Doane, 2010) by providing the opportunity for an income to producers and, therefore, redress the inequalities and social unrest created by capitalist markets. Inequality and poverty (e.g. pro-poor tourism) can be harnessed as a source of increased value to assuage the inequality that exists in communities that are bypassed by conventional development. It also offers a 'psychological fix' by way of connecting humans with non-human natures (Braun, 2003; Fletcher, 2009; Neves, 2004; Neves-Graca, 2002; West & Carrier, 2004). Marx (1973) recognises that capitalist production creates a 'metabolic rift' whereby producers and consumers are alienated from the non-human natures that serve as the resource base of production (Bellamy Foster, 2000). Ecotourism promises the possibility of addressing this form of human/non-human alienation (Braun, 2003), and therefore a 'psychological' fix for the existential crisis created by capitalist development (Fletcher & Neves, 2012). A further psychological fix can be found in ecotourism's promise to deliver the extraordinary experiences of mystery and enchantment that are lacking in everyday life (Arnould & Price, 1993; Arnould *et al.*, 1999; Neves, 2004; Neves-Graca, 2005). Ecotourism development offers a package of manifold spatial, temporal, environmental, social and psychological capitalist fixes (Fletcher & Neves, 2012).

Wildlife Tourism, Cetaceans and the Manifold Capitalist 'Fixes'

The theoretical context of ecotourism as a manifold capitalist fix provides a useful framework for critically considering cetaceans and wildlife tourism development. Cetaceans – the various species of marine mammals that include whales, dolphins and porpoises – trigger sentiments of awe, inspiration and excitement (Garrod & Fennell, 2004; see also Ventre & Jett, Chapter 8, in this volume). The fact that 'few creatures carry more emotion . . . than whales; and few issues arouse as much passion as whaling' (Hammond, 2006: 54) signals at least two reasons why, through wildlife tourism development, cetaceans have been subject to a periodic transformation in the global capitalist economy (Neves, 2010a; see also Wearing & Jobberns, Chapter 5, this volume). The aura of intrigue associated with whales delivers the 'extraordinary experiences of mystery and enchantment' that the alienated middle classes of post-industrial societies are routinely denied (Neves, 2004; Neves-Graca, 2005). Furthermore, the emotions aroused by whale hunting (in terms of both historical and contemporary hunting practices; see Neves-Graca, 2005), further inspire the desire to consume the experiences that these animals offer (Corkeron, 2014). In these ways, whale watching provides a psychological fix to redress deep-set human alienation from non-human natures. This is a case of old capitalism (hunting) inspiring new capitalism in the form of industrial-scale whale watching.

Whale-watching – commercial experiences of cetaceans in the wild – may be seen as the commodification of nature and the trading of new forms of natural capital. This avenue of development has provided capitalism with a phenomenal environmental fix. Twelve percent per annum growth in global whale watch numbers occurred throughout the 1990s, growing from two to nine million tourists (Hoyt, 2001). Tourist expenditure grew at the rate of 18.6% per annum across the same timeframe (Garrod & Fennell, 2004). Whale watching is now a US$2.1bn per year industry, with 13 million whale watchers supporting 13,000 full-time equivalent jobs (O'Connor et al., 2010). This growth trajectory has been fuelled by the removal of laws constraining the circulation of goods, people and financial investment to facilitate the expansion of capitalist accumulation at global level (Harvey, 2010a). Meanwhile, parallel processes of re-regulation have taken place to ensure the fruition of the specific economic and political interests of a growing corporate elite (Igoe et al., 2010). In whale watching, for example, laws have been developed to foster the interests of specific capitalist business models to the detriment of others that are more socially and ecologically oriented (Neves, 2010b; Neves-Graca, 2002, 2004, 2006; Neves & Igoe, 2012).

Whale watching has also provided a remarkable spatial fix (Fletcher & Neves, 2012). The growth of whale watching has initially been in regional coastal communities in the developed world (Hoyt, 2001). The continuing growth of whale watching now centres on the developing world (Higham et al., 2014), in countries such as Cambodia/Laos (Beasley et al., 2014) and Indonesia (Mustika et al., 2012). The analysis of Cisneros-Montemayor et al. (2010) suggests that an additional US$413m and 5700 jobs could potentially exist in the global whale watching system, with much of the remaining untapped capacity in developing world nations (Mustika et al., 2012). This existing and latent capacity equates to a whale watch industry of over US$2.5bn, supporting 19,000 jobs globally (Cisneros-Montemayor et al., 2010), particularly in regional, peripheral and developing world contexts, thereby providing a social fix to those who are bypassed by conventional development.

Whales and Petroleum: The Driving Force of Capitalism

More broadly, capitalism's manifold fixes can be critically explored in terms of the relationship between whales and petroleum – the driving force of capitalism. Whales have a longstanding association with capitalism. Commercial whale hunting dates to the 16th century in the North Atlantic and to the late 18th century in the Pacific (Hammond, 2006). Commercial whale hunting was the original 'oil rush' (WDCS, 2010). It dramatically reduced the population stocks of, initially, species of right (*Eubalaena* spp.) and bowhead (*Balaena* spp.) whales, the grey whale (*Eschrichtius robustus*) and sperm whale (*Physeter macrocephalus*). Hammond (2006) dates modern whaling to 1863 when Norwegian whalers brought together the industrial technologies of the explosive-tipped harpoon and steam-powered whaling vessel to devastating effect. The faster swimming species including blue (*Balaenoptera musculus*), fin (*B. physalus*), sei (*B. borealis*) and humpback (*Megaptera novaeangliae*) whales, and more spatially dispersed pelagic populations became the focus of industrial-scale whaling. In the 40 years from 1928 to 1968 over a million whales were slaughtered in the Southern Ocean for their blubber and other fatty tissues, which were rendered down into oil (WDCS, 2010). The oil of 200,000 whales was extracted in the boilers of the Deception Island (Antarctica) whale-processing factory before its abandonment in 1931 (Hammond, 2006).

Whale hunting practices, which brought many populations of great whales dangerously close to extinction (Williams, 2014), were pursued in response to the demand for oil products such as candles and fuel for lamps. The richness and chemical complexity of whale oil provided 'a veritable pharmacopeia of raw materials for a fast industrializing world' (WDCS, 2010: np). From the 1920s, whale oil served an increasing range of purposes that included animal feed, machine lubricants, glycerine-based explosives, soap, detergents and margarine. Later, whale oil was used as a lubricant for high-precision guns during WWII (Neves-Graca, 2002) and for the aerospace programme (WDCS, 2010). Whale oil was a driving force of industrial capitalist production. The closure of whale-processing factories was due to 'economic extinction' – the depletion of stocks to the point of commercial non-viability (Hammond, 2006). It is claimed that continuing 'scientific' and commercial whale hunting by Norwegian, Japanese and Icelandic fleets is associated with the development of new industrial uses for whales including pharmaceuticals, health supplements and cosmetic products (WDCS, 2010).

The Contradictions of Whale Watching and Capitalism

The near obliteration that industrial whale hunting brought about has raised the scarcity value of whales in relation to Klein's (2007) notion of 'disaster capitalism'. Whales became the '... standard bearers of marine environmental issues' (Corkeron, 2006: 161), inspiring an original form of 'extinction tourism'. Whale watching began in a commercial sense in California in 1952 (Hoyt, 2001). Since then, and particularly following the International Whaling

Commission (IWC) moratorium on commercial whaling in 1982, the public appetite for viewing cetaceans in the wild has been insatiable. In 1993 the IWC '... formally recognised whale-watching as a legitimate tourism industry which provided for the *sustainable* [emphasis added] use of these animals' (Orams, 2000: 561). Reflecting the earlier hunting technologies of the explosive-tipped harpoon and steam-powered whaling vessel, the industrial technologies of whale watching include GPS, electronic communications and fast surface transportation. These tools ensure that target animals can be swiftly located, endlessly tracked and constantly engaged (Constantine, 2014).

It is important to critically address capitalism's environmental fix in the context of whale watching through a series of local and global considerations. At the local level, the growth of whale watching has been accompanied by extensive field-based behavioural studies that examine the impacts of human interactions with cetaceans in the wild (e.g. Bejder *et al.*, 2006; Blane & Jaakson, 1995; Nowacek *et al.*, 2001). In addressing this issue Bejder *et al.* (2009) have applied aspects of evolutionary theory for decision-making under the risk of predation to make predictions about how individual animals respond to non-lethal forms of human disturbance. This approach assumes that animals use analogous decision processes to evaluate responses to the risks presented by natural predators and those presented by anthropogenic agents of disturbance, such as hunting and tourism (Bejder *et al.*, 2009). These authors conclude that individual animals take the same ecological considerations into account when they experience human disturbance as they do when they perceive any risk of predation.

Extensive field-based behavioural studies have conclusively shown that cetaceans behave evasively when approached by whale watching boats. This reflects the behaviour of other species when seeking to avoid predators (Williams *et al.*, 2002). Groups of animals commonly tighten when boats are present (Bejder *et al.*, 2006) or engage in active avoidance by way of changes in movement patterns (Nowacek *et al.*, 2001), increases in dive intervals (Baker *et al.*, 1988; Bejder *et al.*, 2006) and increases in swimming speed (Blane & Jaakson, 1995; Williams *et al.*, 2002). The net effect of repeated disturbance is a reduction of time engaged in critical behaviours such as resting and feeding (Lusseau & Higham, 2004). These studies draw the legitimacy of whale watching as a *sustainable* use of wild animals into question (Higham *et al.*, 2014). Despite the findings of over 25 years of observational and experimental science, and in an effort to curtail continuing whale hunting practices, the focus of environmental NGOs has been to portray whale watching as a 'quintessentially and uniformly benign activity' (Neves-Graca, 2002). Without the acknowledgement and acceptance that whale watching may cause altered behaviours that have broader biological and ecological consequences (Corkeron, 2006; Neves, 2004, 2010a) whale watching has continued to grow in the almost complete absence of regulatory and management frameworks (Higham *et al.*, 2009).

Whale Watching: New Oil Dependencies

Notwithstanding the problematic relationship between whale hunting and capitalism that resulted in the quasi obliteration of entire species of whales from our planet's oceans, histories of whaling have been objectified and fetishised into commodity form as former whaling towns and villages re-invent themselves in museumified form (Neves, 2004; Neves-Graca, 2002, 2006). Most interestingly, many of the whale watching destinations that have emerged from the 1970s onwards have appropriated and constructed whaling legacies as a component of their whale-related product offerings – even in places where whale hunting had been incipient or barely existent (Neves-Graca, 2006). While in many of these locales the co-existence of whale hunting legacies with whale watching is contentious, fraught with tension and subject to complex political negotiation (Neves, 2004; Neves-Graca, 2002, 2005, 2006), it can be argued that the 'newly' invented whale watching industry has played a key role in rendering the whale oil industry a desirable tourism product. Thus, whale watching has helped facilitate the conditions for capital profit to be made anew from the whale oil industry, this time as a commoditised history-rendered component of ecotourism packages. In effect, tourists have come to increasingly expect the inclusion of multifarious amalgamations of history, epicurean delights, nature adventure and 'ethnographic' entertainment in ecotourism offers.

In turn, while it has been noted that whale watching has developed as an appealing economic alternative to the practice of industrial whale hunting (IFAW, 1995), here we argue that whale watching is also implicated in bringing about new relationships with petroleum – the driving force of capitalism. Much science has attended to locally contextualised, site-specific impacts of whale watching (Bejder et al., 2006; Lusseau & Higham, 2004). In terms of oil, the local effects of vessel exhaust fumes on killer whales has been addressed by Lachmuth et al. (2011). Christiansen and Lusseau (2014) also consider the impacts of whale watch vessel engine noise on cetaceans' song vocalisations and echolocation. Injury from collisions with whale watch vessels is a growing concern as the volume and speed of surface transportation increases in areas where whales are present (Lammers et al., 2013). The findings of a 36-year study of collisions data in Hawaii confirmed that the majority of collisions occurred at boat speeds of 10–19 knots because vessels travelling to viewing locations travel too fast to avoid collisions with the very whales that tourists come to view (Lammers et al., 2013; Morell, 2013).

More broadly, whale watching encapsulates a paradoxical relationship with oil. Whale watching is presented as an environmentally sustainable economic alternative to whale hunting (Neves, 2004, 2010a; Neves-Graca, 2002, 2006). However, Becken and Schellhorn (2007) observe that the focus on local biophysical and socio-economic impacts has meant that macro-environmental global effects have hitherto been largely ignored. They call for an 'open-system' approach which 'deeply challenges the widely accepted link between ecotourism and nature conservation' (Becken & Schellhorn, 2007: 99). Herein lies a deeply paradoxical relationship between whale watching and petroleum. Tourism is an oil-intensive industry (Becken, 2010) that is co-dependent on aviation. Flying, which is a necessary requirement for most tourists to reach their destinations, is explicitly material (i.e. it has a high carbon cost) (Peeters & Williams, 2009). This raises serious questions about the dispersed and global environmental risks associated with travel consumption (Higham *et al.*, 2013).

The spatial fix offered by global ecotourism has created a particularly deeply entrenched form of co-dependence between the tourism and aviation industries. In this sense it may be argued that whale watching, and other forms of ecotourism development, have created new tourism oil dependencies (Hall, 2007). These arise from the demands of the environmentally conscious bourgeoisie of the global north to consume the experiences of the tourism-dependent economies of the global south (Becken & Schellhorn, 2007). International tourist flows largely originate from developed countries, in particular Europe, which accounts for 57.8% of all international travel. While 'north–south' flows are comparatively minor (about 11% of all international travel; Scott *et al.*, 2011), they nevertheless are of critical economic importance to ecotourism destinations (Becken, 2010; Becken & Schellhorn, 2007; Hall, 2007).

Little scholarly attention has been paid to the relationship between whale watching and global climate change (Lambert *et al.*, 2012) although Neves (2010a) does contemplate the ecological footprint of 10 million ecotourists. In fact it has been estimated that the global aviation industry consumes 243 million tonnes of fuel per year, which is the equivalent of 6.3% of world refinery production (Becken, 2010; Nygren *et al.*, 2009). Of the 4.4% of global carbon emissions for which tourism is directly accountable (Peeters & Dubois, 2010), 40% can be conservatively attributed to tourist air travel (Gössling *et al.*, 2009). The whale watching spatial fix is directly implicated in the concomitant release of massive amounts of CO_2.

The fossil-fuel burn associated with people travelling to engage in nature-based tourism activities contributes to the globally dispersed consequences of anthropogenic climate change (Hall, 2007; Peeters & Dubois, 2010). Within this context, whale watching clearly exacerbates the challenge of avoiding dangerous climate change (Becken & Schellhorn, 2007; Hall, 2007; Scott *et al.*, 2011), which necessitates that temperature rise is stabilised below an increase of 2°C from the pre-industrial baseline (IPCC, 2013; Higham *et al.*, 2014). The current evidence suggests that the tourism and aviation industries will fall short of this challenge. The jet engine has reached a stage of 'evolutionary sophistication' that does not allow for further efficiencies (Holloway *et al.*, 2009) and CO_2-e (carbon dioxide equivalent) projections from tourism are expected to increase by more than 130% over 2005 levels by 2035 (UNWTO-UNEP-WMO, 2008).

The sustainability of high-volume, high-velocity, long-distance transportation is now under intense scrutiny (Peeters & Dubois, 2010). The consequences for nature-based tourism destinations have been addressed in reference to the northern high latitudes (Johnston, 2006), Antarctica (Eijgelarr et al., 2010), ski resorts (Hopkins, 2014), snow-covered vistas (Lemelin et al., 2011), coral reefs (Scott et al., 2011) and polar bears (Dawson et al., 2010). The current evidence relating to whale watching signals changes in the distribution and abundance of cetaceans in response to modified sea surface temperatures, with implications for the presence and frequency of cetacean species and migration patterns (Lambert et al., 2012). Acidification of the world's oceans due to the absorption of atmospheric carbon presents the possibility of wholesale food chain alteration (Lambert et al., 2012). These aspects of the relationship between whale watching and climate change deeply compromise the self-identity of the environmentally responsible consumer due to the material environmental impacts of air travel (Barr et al., 2010; Higham & Cohen, 2011). Perversely, it also creates an environmental fix in terms of 'extinction tourism'.

Tourism, whale watching and oil exploration

Western governments have to date been unwilling to respond meaningfully to the tourism transport emissions challenge. The best efforts of the EU have failed to bring international aviation into the Europe's ETS while IATA (2013) remains committed to continued growth in aviation based on a vision of sustainability achieved through technical, operational and biofuel solutions (IATA, 2013; see Duval, 2013). The aviation industry remains single minded in its focus on massive growth targets for aircraft production (Holloway et al., 2009). Broader issues relate to the scarcity of fossil fuels (Becken & Schellhorn, 2007), whereby tourism activities such as whale watching are implicated in perpetuating and securing the demand side of this crucial capitalist commodity. It is ironic that whale watching is implicated in driving demand for both disappearing nature experiences (Lemelin et al., 2011) and, simultaneously, dwindling fossil fuel resources. The latter now extends to new oil extraction techniques such as fracking and deep-sea drilling, expanding the spatial range of petroleum exploration into increasingly marginal coastal and pelagic environments, posing a significant threat to water quality and heightening the risk of ecological disasters in the marine environment (Becken, 2010).

The consequences of oil exploration and recovery for cetaceans are significant. In terms of the first phase (exploration and seismic survey), Jepson et al. (2003) were the first to raise the possibility of a link between occurrences of mass cetacean strandings (predominantly with species of beaked whales) and the deployment of sonar. The linking of acute and chronic tissue damage in stranded cetaceans and the deployment of military sonar challenged the prevailing view at that time that marine mammals do not suffer decompression sickness. It also implicated acoustic factors in the aetiology of bubble-related disease in marine mammals (Jepson *et al.*, 2003). During the Austral summer of 2013/2014, and amid significant public protests, the Anadarko test drill ship, the *Nobel Bob Douglas*, conducted seismic surveys of coastal Taranaki (New Zealand) waters, home of the critically endangered Maui's dolphin (*Cephalorhynchus hectori maui*). It subsequently conducted deep-sea seismic surveying on the eastern South Island coast. During this time a 4.5-m long-fin pilot whale (*Globicephala melas*) died after beaching at Kaka Point (South Otago). The cost of conducting a necropsy (animal autopsy) on the dead animal was met by the Shell Oil Company, due to an existing agreement with the Department of Conservation (part of the conditions laid to undertake seismic surveying off the Otago coastline) (de Reus, 2014). This agreement arises from a marine mammal impact assessment that highlighted the uncertainty of the impacts of oil exploration on the morbidity and mortality of cetaceans.

The second phase of oil exploration (drilling and recovery) is associated with the risk of ecological disaster in terms of both oil spill and, typically, the widespread use of dispersants at or below the surface of the ocean. The 2010 Deepwater Horizon/BP oil spill in the Gulf of Mexico vividly highlights the catastrophic risks associated with deep-sea oil drilling and recovery (Williams *et al.*, 2011). Relatively modest environmental impacts were implied by the reporting of 101 marine mammal mortalities; however, Williams *et al.* (2011: 228) claim that marine mammal carcasses are '... recovered, on an average, from only 2% (range: 0–6.2%) of cetacean deaths. Thus, the true death toll could be 50 times the number of carcasses recovered, given no additional information.' They also call for more rigorous analytical methods to account for the low probability of carcass recovery from other fatal events including acoustic trauma. Schwacke *et al.* (2014) report equally shocking findings of cetacean morbidity associated with petroleum hydrocarbon exposure and toxicity in the Gulf of Mexico. These activities contribute to the transformation of the marine environment through the development of transportation (e.g. vessel strike, noise and emissions), compromise of the acoustic environment (e.g. through seismic surveying), and the heightened risk of environmental disaster associated with oil drilling and recovery. These elements of transformation are clearly implicated in ecotourism's manifold capitalist fixes.

Conclusions

In this chapter we attempt to show that mainstream ecotourism is quintessentially a capitalist mode of production and, as such, it tends to recreate and reproduce the very problems and contradictions it purports to fix. First of all, although whale watching manifests and materialises a plethora of philosophies and practices, capitalist modes of production have come to dominate this form of ecotourism (Neves, 2010b; Neves-Graca, 2006), as in fact has been the case in ecotourism more generally (Fletcher, 2014). As such, profit-oriented goals tend to override ecological conservation objectives as well as concerns with social equity and human wellbeing. Hence, while the ecotourism industry often conflates its activities with biodiversity conservation and social development, it is frequently associated with the spread of 'uneven development' (Neves & Igoe, 2012) and negative ecological impacts (e.g. Higham, 2007; Neves-Graca, 2006). Secondly, ecotourism facilitates the extension of capitalist accumulation into previously untapped realms, particularly non-human natures (Fletcher & Neves, 2012) as well as into the human body and psyche, while re-attributing economic value to former capitalist industries now re-cast as a commoditised historical legacy. Finally, ecotourism constitutes a renewal and expansion of capitalism's dependency on a petroleum-based economy by facilitating capitalist expansion and accumulation through an exponential growth in international travel (Becken, 2010).

While ecotourism may have the potential to raise environmental awareness and commitment to a socio-ecological ethic, we argue that extant dominant capitalist modes of ecotourism production/consumption tend to undermine this potential. In cases where ecotourism does indeed facilitate the fruition of socio-ecological goals – such as increased social equity and ecological learning – profit maximisation and accelerated growth have come to dominate (Neves, 2004, 2010a). Arguing precisely against dogmatic discourses about the inevitability of specific capitalist arrangements – especially those that neoliberal ideology promotes – we call for a closer investigation of existing and emerging alternatives to the hegemonic forms of ecotourism described in this chapter. The formulation of new models of ecotourism, wildlife tourism and whale watching – which must include an uncoupling from the petroleum industry – is urgently required.

References

Arnould, E.J. and Price, L.L. (1993) River magic: Extraordinary experiences and the extended service encounter. *Journal of Consumer Research* 20, 24–45.

Arnould, E.J., Price, L.L. and Otnes, C. (1999) Making consumption magic: A study of white-water river rafting. *Journal of Contemporary Ethnography* 28, 33–68.

Baker, C.S., Perry, A. and Vequist, G. (1988) Humpback whales of Glacier Bay, Alaska. *Whalewatcher*, Fall, 13–17.

Bandy, J. (1996) Managing the other of nature: Sustainability, spectacle, and global regimes of capital in ecotourism. *Public Culture* 8, 539–566.

Barr, S., Shaw, G., Coles, T. and Prillwitz, J. (2010) 'A holiday is a holiday': Practicing sustainability, home and away. *Journal of Transport Geography* 18 (3), 474–481.

Beasley, I., Bejder, L. and Marsh, H. (2014) Cetacean-watching in developing countries: A case study from the Mekong River. In J.E.S. Higham, L. Bejder and R. Williams (eds)

Whale-watching: Sustainable Tourism and Ecological Management (pp. 307–322). Cambridge: Cambridge University Press.

Becken, S. (2010) A critical review of tourism and oil. *Annals of Tourism Research* 38, 359–379; doi:10.1016/j.annals.2010.10.005.

Becken, S. and Schellhorn, M. (2007) Ecotourism, energy use and the global climate: Widening the local perspective. In J.E.S. Higham (ed.) *Critical Issues in Ecotourism: Understanding a Complex Tourism Phenomenon* (pp. 85–101). Oxford: Elsevier.

Bejder, L., Samuels, A., Whitehead, H. *et al.* (2006) Relative abundance of bottlenose dolphins (*Tursiops* sp.) exposed to long-term anthropogenic disturbance. *Conservation Biology* 20 (6), 1791–1798.

Bejder, L., Samuels, A., Whitehead, H., Finn, H. and Allen, S. (2009) Impact assessment research: Use and misuse of habituation, sensitisation and tolerance in describing wildlife responses to anthropogenic stimuli. *Marine Ecology Progress Series* 395, 177–185.

Bellamy Foster, J. (2000) *Marx's Ecology: Materialism and Nature*. New York: Monthly Review Press.

Bianchi, R.V. (2005) Tourism restructuring and the politics of sustainability: A critical view from the European periphery (The Canary Islands). *Journal of Sustainable Tourism* 12 (6), 495–529.

Bianchi, R.V. (2009) The 'critical turn' in tourism studies: A radical critique. *Tourism Geographies* 11 (4), 484–504.

Blane, J.M. and Jaakson, R. (1995) The impact of ecotourism boats on the Saint Lawrence beluga whales. *Environmental Conservation* 21 (3), 267–269.

Braun, B. (2003) 'On the raggedy edge of risk': Articulations of race and nature after biology. In D.S. Moore, J. Kosek and A. Pandian (eds) *Race, Nature, and the Politics of Difference* (pp. 175–203). Durham, NC: Duke University Press.

Britton, S.G. (1991) Tourism, capital, and place: Towards a critical geography of tourism. *Environment and Planning D* 9, 451–478.

Brockington, D. and Duffy, R. (eds) (2010) Special issue on 'Capitalism and Conservation'. *Antipode* 42 (3).

Brockington, D., Duffy, R. and Igoe, J. (2008) *Nature Unbound: Conservation, Capitalism and the Future of Protected Areas*. London: Earthscan.

Büscher, B. (2010) Seeking 'telos' in the 'transfrontier'? Neoliberalism and the transcending of community conservation in Southern Africa. *Environment and Planning A* 42, 644–660.

Büscher, B., Brockington, D., Igoe, J., Neves, K. and Sullivan, S. (2012) Towards a synthesized critique of neoliberal biodiversity conservation. *Capitalism Nature Socialism* 23 (2), 4.

Butcher, J. (2006) Natural capital and the advocacy of ecotourism as sustainable development. *Journal of Sustainable Tourism* 14 (6), 529–544.

Carrier, J.G. and Macleod, D.V.L. (2005) Bursting the bubble: The socio-cultural context of ecotourism. *Journal of the Royal Anthropological Institute* 11, 315–334.

Castree, N. (2008) Neoliberalising nature: The logics of deregulation and reregulation. *Environment and Planning A* 40, 131–152.

Cater, E. (2006) Ecotourism as a Western construct. *Journal of Ecotourism* 5 (1–2), 23–39.

Christiansen, F. and Lusseau, D. (2014) Understanding the ecological effects of whale-watching on cetaceans. In J.E.S. Higham, L. Bejder and R. Williams (eds) *Whale-watching: Sustainable Tourism and Ecological Management* (pp. 177–192). Cambridge: Cambridge University Press.

Cisneros-Montemayor, A.M., Sumaila, U.R., Kaschner, K. and Pauly, D. (2010) The global potential for whale-watching. *Marine Policy* 34, 1273–1278.

Constantine, R. (2014) Whale-watching and behavioural ecology. In J.E.S Higham, L. Bejder and R. Williams (eds) *Whale-watching: Sustainable Tourism and Ecological Management* (pp. 193–205). Cambridge: Cambridge University Press.

Corkeron, P.J. (2006) How shall we watch whales? In D.M. Lavigne (ed.) *Gaining Ground: In Pursuit of Ecological Sustainability* (pp. 161–170). Guelph, ON: International Fund for Animal Welfare.

Corkeron, P.J. (2014) Human attitude and values: Tradition and transformation and zombies. In J.E.S Higham, L. Bejder and R. Williams (eds) *Whale-watching: Sustainable Tourism and Ecological Management* (pp. 48–56). Cambridge: Cambridge University Press.

Davis, S.G. (1997) *Spectacular Nature: Corporate Culture and the Sea World Experience.* Berkeley, CA: University of California Press.

Dawson, J., Stewart, E.J., Lemelin, H. and Scott, D. (2010) The carbon cost of polar bear viewing in Churchill, Manitoba, Canada. *Journal of Sustainable Tourism* 18 (3), 319–336.

de Reus, H. (2014) Shell to pay cost of whale necropsy. *Otago Daily Times*, 22 February. See www.odt.co.nz/regions/south-otago/292612/shell-pay cost-whale-necropsy (accessed 24 February 2014).

Doane, M. (2010) Maya coffee: Fair Trade markets and the 'social fix'. Paper presented at The American Anthropological Association Annual Conference, New Orleans, LA, 17–21 November.

Dressler, W. and Roth, R. (2010) The good, the bad, and the contradictory: Neoliberal conservation governance in rural Southeast Asia. *World Development* 39 (5), 851–862.

Duffy, R. (2002) *Trip Too Far: Ecotourism, Politics, and Exploitation.* London: Earthscan.

Duffy, R. (2008) Neoliberalising nature: Global networks and ecotourism development in Madagascar. *Journal of Sustainable Tourism* 16 (3), 327–344.

Duffy, R. (2010) *Nature Crime.* New Haven, CT: Yale University Press.

Duffy, R. (2012) The international political economy of tourism and the neoliberalisation of nature: Challenges posed by selling close interactions with animals. *Review of International Political Economy* 20 (3), 605–626; doi:10.1080/09692290.2012.654443.

Duffy, R. and Moore, L. (2010) Neoliberalising nature? Elephant-back tourism in Thailand and Botswana. *Antipode* 42 (3), 742–766.

Duval, D.T (2013) Critical issues in air transport and tourism. *Tourism Geographies* 15 (3), 494–510.

Eijgelaar, E., Thaper, C. and Peeters, P. (2010) Antarctic cruise tourism: The paradoxes of ambassadorship 'last chance tourism' and GHG emissions. *Journal of Sustainable Tourism* 18 (3), 337–354.

Fletcher, R. (2009) Ecotourism discourse: Challenging the stakeholders theory. *Journal of Ecotourism* 8 (3), 269–285.

Fletcher, R. (2010) Neoliberal environmentality: Towards a poststructuralist political ecology of the conservation debate. *Conservation and Society* 8 (3), 171–181.

Fletcher, R. (2011) Sustaining tourism, sustaining capitalism? The tourism industry's role in global capitalist expansion. *Tourism Geographies* 13 (3), 443–461.

Fletcher, R. (2014) *Romancing the Wild: Cultural Dimensions of Ecotourism.* Durham, NC: Duke University Press.

Fletcher, R. and Neves, K. (2012) Contradictions in tourism: The promises and pitfalls of ecotourism as a manifold capitalist fix. *Environment and Society: Advances in Research* 3, 60–77.

Garrod, B. and Fennell, D.A. (2004) An analysis of whale-watching codes of conduct. *Annals of Tourism Research* 31 (2), 334–352.

Gössling, S., Haglund, L., Kallgren, H., Revahl, M. and Hultman, J. (2009) Swedish air travellers and voluntary carbon offsets: Towards the co-creation of environmental value. *Current Issues in Tourism* 12 (1), 1–19.

Hall, C.M. (2007) Scaling ecotourism: The role of scale in understanding the impacts of ecotourism. In J.E.S. Higham (ed.) *Critical Issues in Ecotourism: Understanding a Complex Tourism Phenomenon* (pp. 243–255). Oxford: Elsevier.

Hammond, P. (2006) Whale science – and how (not) to use it. *Significance*, June, 54–58.

Harvey, D. (1989) *The Condition of Postmodernity: An Inquiry into the Origins of Cultural Change*. Oxford: Basil Blackwell.

Harvey, D. (2005) *A Brief History of Neoliberalism*. Chicago, IL: University of Chicago Center for International Studies.

Harvey, D. (2006) *Spaces of Global Capitalism: A Theory of Uneven Geographical Development*. London: Verso.

Harvey, D. (2010a) *The Enigma of Capital*. London: Profile Books.

Harvey, D. (2010b) *A Companion to Marx's Capital*. London: Verso.

Higham, J.E.S. (ed.) (2007) *Critical Issues in Ecotourism: Understanding a Complex Tourism Phenomenon*. Oxford: Elsevier.

Higham, J.E.S. and Cohen, S.A. (2011) Canary in the coalmine: Norwegian attitudes towards climate change and extreme long-haul air travel to *Aotearoa*/New Zealand. *Tourism Management* 32 (1), 98–105.

Higham, J.E.S., Bejder, L. and Lusseau, D. (2009) An integrated and adaptive management model to address the long-term sustainability of tourist interactions with cetaceans. *Environmental Conservation* 35 (4), 294–302.

Higham, J.E.S., Cohen, S.A., Peeters, P. and Gössling, S. (2013) Psychological and behavioural approaches to understanding and governing sustainable mobility. *Journal of Sustainable Tourism* 21 (7), 949–967.

Higham, J.E.S., Bejder, L. and Williams, R. (eds) (2014) *Whale-Watching, Sustainable Tourism and Ecological Management*. Cambridge: Cambridge University Press.

Holloway J.C., Humphreys, C. and Davidson, R. (2009) *The Business of Tourism* (8th edn). Harlow: Pearson Education.

Hopkins, D. (2014) The sustainability of climate change adaptation strategies in New Zealand's ski industry: A range of stakeholder perceptions. *Journal of Sustainable Tourism* 22 (1), 107–126.

Hoyt, E. (2001) *Whale-Watching 2000: Worldwide Tourism Numbers, Expenditures, and Expanding Socioeconomic Benefits*. Crowborough: International Fund for Animal Welfare.

IATA (2013) II. Resolution on the implementation of the aviation 'CNG2020' strategy. See http://ec.europa.eu/clima/consultations/0020/organisation/iata_en.pdf.

Igoe, J. and Brockington, D. (2007) Neoliberal conservation: A brief introduction. *Conservation and Society* 5 (4), 432–449.

Igoe, J., Neves, K. and Brockington, D. (2010) Engaging the hegemonic convergence of capitalist expansion and biodiversity conservation: A theoretical framework for social scientific investigation. Special issue on Capitalism and Conservation. *Antipode* 42 (3), 486–512.

International Fund for Animal Welfare (IFAW) (1995) *Report of the Workshop on the Scientific Aspects of Managing Whale-watching*. Italy: International Fund for Animal Welfare, Montecastello di Vibio.

IPCC (2013) *Climate Change 2013: The Physical Science Basis*. Geneva: Intergovernmental Panel on Climate Change. See www.ipcc.ch/report/ar5/wg1/#.Uu70df0p8ds (accessed 28 November).

Jepson, P.D., Arbelo, M., Deaville, R., *et al.* (2003) Gas-bubble lesions in stranded cetaceans: Was sonar responsible for a spate of whale deaths after an Atlantic military exercise? *Nature* (425), 574-575.

Johnston, M.E. (2006) Impacts of global environmental change on tourism in the polar regions. In S. Gössling and C.M. Hall (eds) *Tourism and Global Environmental Change: Ecological, Social, Economic and Political Interrelationships* (pp. 37–53). London: Routledge.

Klein, N. (2007) *The Shock Doctrine: The Rise of Disaster Capitalism*. New York: Metropolitan Books.

Lachmuth, C.L., Barrett-Lennard, L.G., Steyn, D.Q. and Milsom, W.K. (2011) Estimation of southern resident killer whale exposure to exhaust emissions from whale-watching vessels and potential adverse health effects and toxicity thresholds. *Marine Pollution Bulletin* 62 (4), 792–805.

Lambert, E., Hunter, C., Pierce, G.J. and MacLeod, C.D. (2012) Sustainable whale-watching tourism and climate change: Towards a framework of resilience. *Journal of Sustainable Tourism* 18 (3), 409–427.

Lammers, M.O., Pack, A.A., Lyman, E.G. and Espiritu, L. (2013) Trends in collisions between vessels and North Pacific humpback whales (*Megaptera novaeangliae*) in Hawaiian waters (1975–2011). *Journal of Cetacean Resource Management* 13 (1), 73–80.

Langholz, J.A. and Lassoie, J.P. (2001) Perils and promise of privately protected areas. *BioScience* 51 (12), 1079–1085.

Leahy, S. (2008) Extinction tourism: See it now before it's gone. *Stephen Leahy website.* See http://stephenleahy.net/2008/01/18/extinction-tourism-see-it-now-before-its-gone (accessed 8 January 2012).

Lemelin, H., Dawson, J., Stewart, E.J., Maher, P. and Lueck, M. (2011) Last chance tourism: The boom, doom and gloom of visiting vanishing destinations. *Current Issues in Tourism* 13 (5), 477–493.

Lusseau, D. and Higham, J.E.S. (2004) Managing the impacts of dolphin-based tourism through the definition of critical habitats: The case of bottlenose dolphins (*Tursiops* spp.) in Doubtful Sound, New Zealand. *Tourism Management* 25 (5), 657–667.

Marx, K. (1973) *Grundrisse: Foundations of the Critique of Political Economy.* Harmondsworth: Penguin.

Morell, V. (2013) ScienceShot: When whale watching turns deadly. *Science Magazine,* 24 December. See http://news.sciencemag.org/plants-animals/2013/12/scienceshot-when-whale-watching-turns-deadly (accessed 27 December 2013).

Mowforth, M. and Munt, I. (2008) *Tourism and Sustainability: New Tourism in the Third World* (3rd edn). London: Routledge.

Mustika, P.L.K., Birtles, A., Everingham, Y. and Marsh, H. (2012) The human dimensions of wildlife tourism in a developing country: Watching spinner dolphins at Lovina, Bali, Indonesia. *Journal of Sustainable Tourism* 21 (2), 1–23.

Neves, K. (2004) Revisiting the Tragedy of the Commons: Whale watching in the Azores and its ecological dilemmas. *Human Organization* 63 (3), 289–300. [Also published under the author surname Neves-Graca.]

Neves, K. (2010a) Cashing in on cetourism: A critical ecological engagement with dominant E-NGO discourses on whaling, cetacean conservation, and whale watching. *Antipode* 42, 719–741.

Neves, K. (2010b) Critical business and uncritical conservation: The invisibility of dissent in the world of marine ecotourism. *Current Conservation* 3 (3), 18–21.

Neves, K. and Igoe, J. (2012) Accumulation by dispossession and uneven development: Comparing recent trends in the Azores and Tanzania. *Journal of Economic and Social Geography* 103 (2), 164–179.

Neves-Graca, K. (2002) A whale of a thing: Transformations from whale hunting to whale watching in Lajes do Pico, Azores. Dissertation published online, York University, Ontario.

Neves-Graca, K. (2004) Revisiting the Tragedy of the Commons: Whale watching in the Azores and its ecological dilemmas. *Human Organisation* 63 (3), 289–300. [Also published under the author surname Neves.]

Neves-Graca, K. (2005) Chasing whales with Bateson and Daniel. *Ecological Humanities Corner of the Australian Humanities Review Journal* 35, June.

Neves-Graca, K. (2006) Politics of environmentalism and ecological knowledge at the intersection of local and global processes. *Journal of Ecological Anthropology* 10, 19–32.

Nowacek, S.M., Wells, R.S. and Solow, A.R. (2001) Short-term effects of boat traffic on Bottlenose Dolphins, *Tursiops truncatus*, in Sarasota Bay, Florida. *Marine Mammal Science* 17 (4), 673–688.

Nygren, E., Aleklett, K. and Höök, M. (2009) Aviation fuel and future oil production scenarios. *Energy Policy* 37, 4003–4010.

O'Connor, J. (1988) Capitalism, nature, socialism: A theoretical introduction. *Capitalism Nature Socialism* 1 (1), 11–38.

O'Connor, J. (1994) Is sustainable capitalism possible? In P. Allen (ed.) *Food for the Future: Conditions and Contradictions of Sustainability* (pp. 125–137). New York: Wiley-Interscience.

O'Connor, S., Campbell, R., Cortez, H. and Knowles, T. (2010) *Whale-Watching Worldwide: Tourism Numbers, Expenditures and Expanding Economic Benefits*. Special report for the International Fund for Animal Welfare prepared by Economists at Large. Yarmouth, MA: International Fund for Animal Welfare.

Orams, M.B. (2000) Tourists getting close to whales, is it what whale-watching is all about? *Tourism Management* 21, 561–569.

Peeters, P. and Dubois, G. (2010) Tourism travel under climate change mitigation constraints. *Journal of Transport Geography* 18 (3), 447–457.

Peeters, P. and Williams, V. (2009) Calculating emissions and radiative forcing: Global, national, local, individual. In S. Gössling and P. Upham (eds) *Climate Change and Aviation* (pp. 69–87). London: Earthscan.

Robbins, P. and Fraser, A. (2003) A forest of contradictions: Producing the landscapes of the Scottish Highlands. *Antipode* 35 (1), 95–118.

Schwacke, L.H., Smith, C.R., Townsend, F.I. *et al.* (2014) Health of common bottlenose dolphins (*Tursiops truncatus*) in Barataria Bay, Louisiana following the *Deepwater Horizon* oil spill. *Environmental Science and Technology* 48 (1), 93–103.

Scott, D., Hall, C.M. and Gössling, S. (2011) *Tourism and Climate Change: Impacts, Adaptation and Mitigation*. London: Routledge.

Silva, L. (2013) How ecotourism works and the community level: The case of whale watching in the Azores. *Current Issues in Tourism*; doi:10.1080/13683500.2013.786027.

Sullivan, S. (2006) The elephant in the room? Problematising 'new' (neoliberal) biodiversity conservation. *Forum for Development Studies* 33 (1), 105–135.

Sullivan, S. (2009) Green capitalism, and the cultural poverty of constructing nature as service provider. In S. Böehm and S. Dabhi (eds) *Upsetting the Offset* (pp. 255–272). London: MayFly Books.

UNWTO-UNEP-WMO (2008) *Climate Change and Tourism: Responding to Global Challenges*. Madrid: UN World Tourism Organization.

Vivanco, L.A. (2001) Spectacular quetzals, ecotourism, and environmental futures in Monte Verde, Costa Rica. *Ethnology* 40 (2), 79–92.

Vivanco, L.A. (2006) *Green Encounters: Shaping and Contesting Environmentalism in Rural Costa Rica*. New York: Berghahn Books.

WDCS (2010) *Reinventing the Whale. The Whaling Industry's Development of New Applications for Whale Oil and Other Products in Pharmaceuticals, Health Supplements and Animal Feed*. Chippenham: Whale and Dolphin Conservation Society. See www.wdcs.org/publications.php.

West, P. and Carrier, J.C. (2004) Ecotourism and authenticity: Getting away from it all? *Current Anthropology* 45 (4), 483–498.

Wheeller, B. (1994) Ecotourism: A ruse by any other name. In C. Cooper and A. Lockwood (eds) *Progress in Tourism, Recreation and Hospitality Management* (Vol. 7; pp. 3–11). London: Belhaven Press.

Williams, R. (2014) Threats facing cetacean populations: The global context. In J.E.S. Higham, L. Bejder and R. Williams (eds) *Whale-watching: Sustainable Tourism and Ecological Management* (pp. 16–29). Cambridge: Cambridge University Press.

Williams, R., Trites, A.W. and Bain, D.E. (2002) Behavioural responses of killer whales (*Orcinus orca*) to whale-watching boats: Opportunistic observations and experimental approaches. *Journal of Zoology* 256, 255–270.

Williams, R., Gero, S., Bejder, L., Calambokidis, J., Kraus S.D., Lusseau, D., Read, A.J. and Robbins, J. (2011) Underestimating the damage: Interpreting cetacean carcass recoveries in the context of the Deepwater Horizon/BP incident. *Conservation Letters* 4, 228–233.

Žižek, S. (2011) *Living in the End Times*. London: Verso.

8   Killer Whales, Theme Parks and Controversy: An Exploration of the Evidence

Jeffrey Ventre and John Jett

History of the Captive Killer Whale Industry

The practice of displaying killer whales or orcas (*Orcinus orca*) for profit began in the United States in 1965 with the killer whale, Namu, who was purchased by Ted Griffin of the Seattle Public Aquarium for US$8000 (PBS, 1997). The bull killer whale was the first to perform shows, and was named Namu after a fishing village in British Columbia near where he became entangled in a salmon net. About four months later, in October 1965, Griffin collected a young female killer whale after he harpooned and killed the animal's mother (ABC, 2007). Shamu, as Griffin named her, was intended as a companion animal for Namu, but they proved to be incompatible. Thus, Shamu was leased and then sold for US$70,000 to a new company in Southern California called SeaWorld which had opened in 1964. The profits from Namu and Shamu catalysed the formation of a multibillion-dollar marine park industry. Griffin, a young entrepreneur, combined forces with Don Goldsberry, becoming the primary whale hunters for SeaWorld. According to data comprising the Marine Mammal Inventory Report (MMIR) maintained by the National Oceanic and Atmospheric Administration (US) (NOAA), Namu survived 381 days in the Seattle Aquarium; Shamu lived for six years at the San Diego theme park.

For over a decade after capturing Namu, the whale hunters collected at least 55 killer whales from the waters of the Pacific Northwest; at least 13 whales died during capture (Center for Whale Research, 2014). However, inhumane collection methods were used which violated their capture permits, including the use of aircraft and explosives to spot and herd whales (Howard Garrett, pers. comm, 2014). Public concern over the captures (and other factors including dolphins dying in tuna fishery operations) helped trigger the passage of the Marine Mammal Protection Act by the US Congress in 1972. In Washington State, public outcry over live captures led to the ejection of SeaWorld, by court order, from those waters in 1976 (Senate Resolution 1976-222). These two events effectively ended collections in the Pacific Northwest and in US waters, but Goldsberry, and others, moved on. Wild collections continued in Iceland from 1976 to 1989, Japan in 1997 and, most recently, Russia. From September to October of 2013, Russian fisherman corralled pods of free-ranging killer whales in the Sea of Okhotsk, in two different operations, taking seven animals and reportedly dragging them up the beach by their tails (Hoyt, 2013a). (An eighth animal, dubbed Narnia, had been captured previously in August 2012 by this same group.) While the large number of killer whales taken by the marine park industry has left at least one group 'endangered' (National Marine Fisheries, 2008), the success of artificial insemination and captive breeding techniques (Robeck *et al.*, 2004) has generally reduced wild takes. It remains to be seen if collections will continue in the territorial waters of Russia and some other northern hemisphere nations.

As of November, 2014, there were 56 captive killer whales known to be living at theme parks in the United States, Canada, Japan, France, Argentina, Russia, Canary Islands (Spain) and China (WDC, 2014). Twenty-two of them (39%) began their lives in the ocean. Killer whales have historically been held at facilities in nations including Hong Kong, Switzerland, Mexico, England, Brazil, the Netherlands and Iceland. According to data within the MMIR, at least 154 killer whales have died in captivity since Namu's death in 1967, bringing the total number of captives, living and dead, to more than 200. Many more have reportedly been unaccounted for or 'lost' in the collection and display process (Kielty, 2011). Although the current value of a single whale is not generally known, a recent news report suggested that a particular adult male killer whale housed in the United States was insured for US$5,000,000 (CBS, 2010).

In summarising the killer whale captivity debate, two primary groups emerge. Pro-captivity elements include business interests that profit from the display of animals, their employees, and the tourists who fund their operations (Figure 8.1). The pro-captivity camp also includes the fishermen and trappers who collect and sell marine mammals for theme parks, traveling circuses (O'Barry, 2011), and the increasingly popular 'swim-with-dolphin' programmes around the world. Anti-captivity elements include a loosely organised collection of non-governmental organisations such as the Humane Society International, the Born Free Foundation, Whale and Dolphin Conservation, and the Marine Connection, among others. They generally advocate for stronger animal protection policies and an end to captivity for various species, but especially for cetaceans. They are funded by charitable donations and supported philosophically by animal welfarists, conservationists, scientists and animal rights activists. Former marine mammal trainers,

Figure 8.1 A captive killer whale returns a plastic object to its trainer at a theme park. The dog whistle seen is called a 'whistle bridge' and is used to let the animal know when it has completed a correct response, at which point the animal will receive a reward
Photo: Sara Childers.

including ourselves, from popular theme parks in the United States and elsewhere have also begun to emerge as an informed voice on the issue.

Contestation

In their 2009 report summarising the two sides of the issue, Rose *et al.* submit the following basic arguments:

> Pro: The public display industry maintains that marine mammal exhibits serve a valuable conservation function, people learn important information from seeing live animals, and captive marine mammals live a good life. (Rose *et al.*, 2009)

> Con: Animal protection groups, and a growing number of scientists (Hoyt, 2013b), counter that the lives of captive marine mammals are impoverished, that people do not receive an accurate picture of a species from captive representatives, and that the trade in live marine mammals negatively impacts populations and habitats.

Examination of claims of killer whale research and conservation by the marine park industry as a means of justifying captivity

Marine parks often claim the merits of their research both as a means of justifying killer whale captivity and as an important marketing strategy.

An evaluation of published peer-reviewed killer whale research either conducted or funded by a prominent marine-based theme park corporation in the United States provides insight into these claims and into their areas of focus.

Based on a readily available bibliography of peer-reviewed literature produced by the aforementioned entity (SeaWorld, 2014a), approximately 38 articles are listed as published between 1976 and 2014. Of these, four could not be located; 14 contributed to a basic understanding of captive killer whales; three focused on wild-capture techniques; seven described captive killer whale husbandry techniques; six examined various pathologies among captive killer whales; one evaluated photo-identification techniques; two examined pathologies among wild killer whales; one evaluated caloric requirements; and one was not based on science. The corporation was also involved in funding basic field research focusing on killer whales, although all of the approximately 11 reports were apparently written prior to 1988 (SeaWorld, 2014b).

The marine park industry is therefore credited with contributing to the literature regarding killer whales as they claim (SeaWorld, 2014c), although very few publications have focused directly on wild killer whales ($n = 2$), and it appears that no reports based on wild killer whale research have been generated since 1988. Over time, an increasing number of their peer-reviewed contributions have concentrated on captive killer whale pathologies (e.g. identification of West Nile infection; see St Leger et al., 2011), as well as reproductive techniques as a means of supplying captive killer whales to the theme park industry (e.g. Robeck et al., 2004). Thus, at least one US-based theme park corporation has actively engaged in various research activities since 1976. Although research emphases have changed through time, this US-based entity is credited with uniquely contributing to the scientific understanding of killer whale attributes and husbandry requirements. Some of these contributions would have been difficult without their ability to study killer whales in captive environments.

Seemingly at odds with emphases on research and conservation, however, the captive marine mammal industry is mostly absent in supporting the management and protection of wild killer whales. Notably, killer whale captures by the marine park industry have contributed to the decline of the Southern Resident population in the Pacific Northwest and its current listing as endangered (National Marine Fisheries, 2008). However, we know of no research conducted by the marine theme park industry, nor funding dedicated to developing a better understanding of, or otherwise assisting, this decimated population. The largest marine theme park corporation in the United States displays the following on their website, with no mention that their collecting activities contributed, in part, to the declining population of Southern Resident whales (National Marine Fisheries, 2008):

The research we conduct and support at SeaWorld is made available to the scientific community and may someday help researchers understand why this (*Southern Resident*) population of whales is in decline and perhaps help to reverse the trend. (SeaWorld, 2014c; our italics)

Examination of published research on the educational value of displaying killer whales in captivity

Proponents of killer whale captivity often refer to the educational value of displaying whales and dolphins in theme parks. In response to evolving public opinion regarding animal welfare, zoos and aquariums have generally shifted their marketing strategy to emphasise visitor education. For example, in their online informational booklet, a prominent theme park corporation in the United States claims:

Most people do not have the opportunity to observe these animals in the wild. Visitors are not only entertained, but also educated. The unique ability to observe and learn directly from live animals increases public awareness and appreciation of wildlife. (SeaWorld, 2014d)

However, both the specific foci and the results of research evaluating the educational efficacy of zoos and aquariums is mixed. For example, investigating knowledge and attitudes among zoo park visitors, Broad and Weiler (1998) determined that among those at a tiger exhibit, 77% perceived that they had learned something, although knowledge was not directly assessed. Contrastingly, Kidd and Kidd (1998) showed that 78% of interviewed visitors who participated in a self-guided aquarium tour reported no change in their feelings toward, or knowledge of, marine life. Theme parks housing killer whales often conduct live performances with their whales, and some zoo-based studies suggest that live animal demonstrations may be more effective than passive viewing in extending the time spent viewing an animal (which the authors state may lead to greater learning among visitors) (Anderson *et al.*, 2003). It is also thought that live animal demonstrations are most effective in garnering support towards the conservation of the animal being shown (Swanagan, 2000). Animal demonstrations may bolster emotional connections with the animal, which Ballantyne *et al.* (2011: 8) suggest is an important component in 'optimizing the long-term impact of a wildlife tourism experience'. The authors point to behaviour change among visitors as one positive, long-term impact to strive for.

Although influencing visitor behaviour may be 'the ultimate goal' of zoos and aquariums as a means of achieving conservation objectives (Povey & Spaulding, 2005), there is little evidence that this goal is being met. While visitor commitment towards conservation-oriented behaviours may increase during and immediately after a zoo experience, research suggests that these commitments generally fail to persist (Adelman *et al.*, 2000; Dierking *et al.*, 2004; Manubay *et al.*, 2002). It was once accepted that simply educating visitors was sufficient to lead to behavioural changes consistent with a conservation mission, although this is no longer considered true (Ogden & Heimlich, 2009). Consistent with this, both widely cited theories of reasoned action (Fishbein & Ajzen, 1975) and planned behaviour (Ajzen, 1991) demonstrate that intentions to perform a particular behaviour are a complex function of attitudes, subjective norms and, in the case of planned behaviour, behavioural control.

In an attempt to demonstrate the educational effectiveness of zoos and aquariums, Falk *et al.* (2007), on behalf of the American Zoo and Aquarium Association (AZA), evaluated how zoos and aquariums affect visitor knowledge and beliefs. As the primary accrediting body for many zoos and aquariums in the United States, including facilities housing captive killer whales, the AZA possessed a keen interest in the study. Their findings have since been cited as proof that 'visiting accredited zoos and aquariums in North America has a measurable impact on the conservation attitudes and understanding of adult visitors' (AZA, 2006).

Given the historically discordant approach to assessing visitor impacts, and given how little is actually known, the questions posed by Falk *et al.*'s (2007) study are certainly relevant. However, Marino *et al.* (2010) point out serious methodological flaws in the study. Among their concerns, they suggest that, although the goal of the study was to assess whether visiting zoos and aquariums affect beliefs and knowledge, Falk *et al.* only evaluated what respondents *said* they believed or knew. That is, no direct evaluations of knowledge were administered; all measures of knowledge were self-reports. Marino *et al.* (2010) elucidate at least six other methodological concerns with the study, including non-random sampling of subjects and a 14% response rate associated with long-term impacts. The findings are now widely marketed by AZA-accredited facilities. Although Falk *et al.* (2007) acknowledged that no significant gains in knowledge were identified among those comprising their sample, their rebuttal (Falk *et al.*, 2010: 417) to Marino *et al.* (2010) cites Ballantyne *et al.* (2007) and the National Research Council (2009) as growing evidence that 'visits to zoos and aquariums almost always result in enhanced scientific understanding and strengthened beliefs in the value of nature conservation.'

Concerns with Falk *et al.*'s study aside, a full exploration of the zoo education literature is beyond the scope of this chapter. However, Kellert (1997: 99) notes that 'many visitors leave the zoo more convinced than ever of human superiority over the natural world'. Whether or not zoo animal demonstrations are more effective than static displays in garnering conservation support towards the animal being shown (Swanagan, 2000), amusement parks do routinely exhibit human superiority over the killer whales in their care (Figure 8.2). It is unknown how these exhibitions of human superiority effect visitors' beliefs or anthropocentric views.

Figure 8.2 A trainer performing a 'fast swim ride' on the back of a captive killer whale
Photo: Jeffrey Ventre.

Regardless of educational efficacy, a brief evaluation of existing educational literature provided to the public by the marine park industry is useful in helping to demonstrate the accuracy of their materials. Longevity among captive killer whales is a persistent source of discord between pro- and anti-captivity factions. On the issue of killer whale longevity, one major theme park corporation in the United States states on their website:

> Scientists in the Pacific Northwest estimate life expectancies by using information derived from field observations that began in the 1970s. These scientists believe that if a killer whale survives the first six months, a female's life expectancy is 50 years and a male's is 30 years. (SeaWorld, 2014e)

These figures are consistent with systematic observations of wild killer whales in the Pacific Northwest (see Olesiuk *et al.*, 2005). In addition, these authors report that the maximum lifespan for both Northern and Southern Resident killer whales (many captive killer whales were captured from the latter population) is estimated at 80–90 years for females and 60–70 years for males. Using information contained in the MMIR, we analysed data for 201 killer whales who entered captivity between 1961 and 1 January 2014 (Jett & Ventre, in press). Our analysis of captive killer whales demonstrates that only 2% of males (dead and alive) have survived beyond 30 years once an animal enters captivity, while 5% of captive females have survived beyond 30 years (survival estimates are discussed in greater detail later in this chapter). Thus it appears that few killer whales held in captivity have neared the maximum life expectancy described among their wild counterparts. The theme park literature examined here may fail to mention estimated maximum lifespan among wild killer whales as it appears inconsistent with observations of their captive killer whales.

The collapsed dorsal fins of captive killer whales are a conspicuous consequence of captivity, where 100% of adult males demonstrate full collapse as do many adult females. In captive environments, dorsal collapse is the result of whales spending an inordinate amount of time floating at the surface of the water (also known as 'logging'), with the dorsal fin unsupported by water. In stark contrast to captive whales, it is reported that less than 1% of wild adult male killer whales in the Pacific Northwest possess the deformity (Ford et al., 1994). In her evaluation of 30 adult wild male killer whales in New Zealand, Visser (1998) found that seven (23.3%) had various stages of dorsal fin malformation. However, only one observed animal (3.3%) possessed a fully collapsed dorsal fin, with the author stating that the collapse may have been due to an apparent entanglement injury. The marine theme park industry is therefore placed in the challenging position of explaining the obvious deformities of their captive whales. Attempting to explain dorsal fin collapse among captives, one prominent theme park corporation in the United States provides the following statement on their website:

No one is exactly sure why the dorsal fins of killer whales bend, but it may have to do with genetics, injuries, or because the fins can be taller than many humans without any hard bones or muscles for support. Some killer whales (both male and female) have irregular-shaped dorsal fins: they may be curved, wavy, twisted, scarred, or bent. Of the 30 adult male killer whales that have been photo-identified in New Zealand waters, seven have collapsing or bent dorsal fins. (SeaWorld, 2014f)

While the above explanations are not necessarily untrue, they fail to accurately convey the details of the phenomenon. First, while it is true that many wild killer whales, both male and female, possess dorsal fins with slight waves, twists, bends or lean, the full collapse observed in all adult captive males is exceedingly uncommon among wild killer whales (Figure 8.3). Therefore, full collapse is, without question, a function of the captive environment. Secondly, the next statement from their educational website takes considerable liberty with Visser's (1998) findings. Visser observed only one adult male with a fully collapsed dorsal fin, whereas the other images included in her manuscript depicted wavy, leaning, hooked (at the tip) and concertina-shaped dorsal fins among the wild male killer whales she photographed.

Figure 8.3 Left image depicts the fully collapsed dorsal fin of a captive adult male killer whale, with a trainer measuring the degree of collapse. The right image demonstrates a malformed dorsal fin on an adult wild animal. Deformations as seen in 'corkscrew' are usually the result of mechanical trauma. Fully collapsed dorsal fins are rare among wild killer whales but common among captives
Photos: Jeffrey Ventre (*left*); Ingrid Visser (*right*).

Examination of killer whale survival, health effects and captivity-related stressors

A review of captive killer whale survival is useful as it allows for numerical comparisons with wild killer whale lifespan estimates, based upon known studies. Among humans, longevity positively correlates with quality of life (QOL) (Stewart *et al.*, 2013). Killer whale survival may therefore provide insight into the relative physical, emotional and psychosocial states of those animals held in captivity. Contrasting the lives of captive killer whales, free-ranging killer whales live in kin-based, stable matrilineal family units with females having an unusually long post-reproductive lifespan, similar to humans. For example, one Southern Resident matriarch (J-2), still living at time of publication, is listed in the Orca Survey field catalogue as being estimated to have been born in 1911. Female killer whales reach reproductive senescence (menopause) at about 40, with mean life expectancy of approximately 46 years, provided they survive their first six months (Olesiuk *et al.*, 2005). Male killer whales are not as long lived, with an average life expectancy of 30, again, provided they survive their first six months of life.

Using the Kaplan–Meier survival estimate model applied to the aforementioned 189 killer whales who entered captivity between 1961 and 1 January 2014, we found the overall median survival over the history of captivity to be 6.2 years (Jett & Ventre, in press). Male median survival was found to be 5.1 years, while female median survival was 10.0 years. In 1985, larger pool dimensions ushered in a modern era of successful captive killer whale breeding. This benefited free-ranging populations by decreasing the demand for wild-captured killer whales. Larger facilities also provided more space for the captives to swim. Indeed, based on our analyses, it was found that after 1 January 1985, the median survival of 11.8 years was significantly higher than prior to 1985, which was only four years. In all likelihood, the larger pool volumes, combined with improved husbandry and veterinary medicine, explain the improved, modern-era survival numbers. This aside, our analyses demonstrate several considerable departures from wild killer whale survival data. Among these, while Olesiuk *et al.* (2005) report that 41–75% of wild females survive to about 40 years of age, only two captive females (of the 55 who entered captivity prior to 1 January 1985) (3.6%) have survived more than 40 years. By nearly all metrics, when compared to data collected on free-ranging animals, killer whales in captive environments demonstrate poorer survival than wild whales.

Based on human studies, it is known, for example, that low socio-economic status is associated with cardiovascular disease, and early mortality. Similarly, environmental stressors, such as crowding, frustration and noise, are known to increase aggression in humans (Bushman & Huesmann, 2010). As killer whale trainers at a US marine park in the 1980s and 1990s, and having participated in a wild killer whale photo-identification study, we commonly witnessed health issues and behaviours not seen or described among wild animals. Indeed, since killer whales were first placed into captivity, various health and behavioural issues relating to their confinement have become apparent. These include poor dentition (from stereotypic behaviours and 'jaw popping'), excessive logging behaviour, ultraviolet radiation (UVR) exposure, exposure to biting insects, generalised social strife leading to inter-animal aggression, medication effects, and other health and wellness issues.

Steel segregation gates are the primary method of separating killer whales for breeding, training sessions, shows, or when tensions exist between animals. When separated by these gates it is common for whales to engage in a particular behaviour known as jaw-popping, which is an open-mouth threat-display of teeth followed by quick closure, or 'popping' of the upper and lower jaws. If the killer whale is charging a gate, the jaw pop can damage teeth if they contact the metal bars.

Additionally, under-stimulated whales sometimes exhibit stereotypic behaviours and will 'chew' on concrete pool corners or other protruding features of an exhibit. An analogous behaviour among horses is called 'cribbing' or 'crib biting', and is considered an abnormal 'stable vice' (Clegg *et al.*, 2008). Killer whale facilities are thus constructed to be as sterile as possible, without features that can be bitten or chewed. Tooth breakage leaves the soft pulp of some teeth exposed (Figure 8.4). If left alone, the decaying pulp can form a cavity that leads to food plugging. As a corollary, human studies show that tooth caries can create inflammation and become a focus for systemic infection (Padilha *et al.*, 2008). Thus, as a prophylactic measure, the fleshy pulp of the whale's tooth is bored out, creating an open hole into the (upper or lower) jaw (bore holes are visible in Figure 8.3). Veterinarians and trainers using a

Figure 8.4 Broken, ground and drilled teeth of a captive killer whale. These anomalies often leave the soft pulp component of their teeth exposed, which can lead to local or general infections
Photos: Ingrid Visser (*left*); Sara Childers (*right*).

variable speed drill perform this procedure, known as a 'modified pulpotomy'. This is an uncomfortable husbandry procedure for the whales, which we observed refusing to participate by sinking down into the water, shuddering, or splitting from their keepers. These bore holes are typically not filled with amalgam and thus serve as a conduit for fish debris and pathogens to penetrate into the mandible, which is highly vascular. Among humans it is known that periodontal caries result in bacteraemia and, given the large-diameter bore holes in the teeth of many captives (>4 mm) it is likely that these 'gateways' are associated with chronic bacteria loading and other health implications. In an attempt to control negative health impacts, trainers at theme parks irrigate the bored teeth two to three times each day while describing the procedures to the public as 'superior dental care'. This occurs for the rest of the whale's life, making many captive killer whales poor candidates for release into the wild.

Captive killer whales often live in sunny, low-latitude tourist destinations, in shallow pools, and in filtered, clear water. From the perspective of a park guest, clear water allows for the visualisation of the animals and their trainers (Figure 8.5). Thick clear acrylic panels are installed at most facilities to provide an optimal view from the grandstand.

Free-ranging killer whales are found in all oceans of the world; however, the majority live in high-latitude, cold-water environments such as in the North Atlantic, the North Pacific and the Southern Oceans. At these latitudes, UVR exposure is diminished, overall. Additionally, wild killer whales spend most of their time below the surface of the water, protected by suspended particles that block sunlight. At marine theme parks, such as in the Canary Islands near Africa, and US locations such as Miami, Orlando, San

Figure 8.5 The clear, shallow water of captive killer whale pools allows guests to see the animals. These attributes result in high ultraviolet radiation exposure, especially among killer whales housed in tropical and subtropical environments
Photos: Sara Childers (*left*); Ingrid Visser (*right*).

Antonio and Southern California, UVR exposure is substantial, especially given the overall lack of shade structures at these facilities. Consequently, we commonly observed sunburned dorsal surfaces on the captives we worked with, especially those prone to excessive logging. To cover up these epidermal skin lesions, black zinc oxide cream was routinely applied to the skin's surface to hide these blemishes.

It is known that UVR exposure causes immunosuppression in humans and other mammals (Kripke, 1994), which in turn can lead to severe infections from bacteria, viruses and other pathogens that do not typically cause serious infections (Sleijffers *et al.*, 2002). Exemplifying this, two captive killer whales in US theme parks died from viruses that are not typically fatal in mammals (West Nile Virus and Saint Louis Encephalitis) (Buck *et al.*, 1993; St Leger *et al.*, 2011, respectively). According to data contained within the MMIR, pneumonia is the leading cause of death among captive killer whales, and some forms of pneumonia are known to occur in other immunosuppressed mammals (Vinogradova *et al.*, 2009). Further evidence of captive marine mammal sun damage has been reported as corneal eye damage in sea lions (APHIS, 2007) and eye injuries in beluga whales (APHIS, 2002).

As killer whale trainers we commonly witnessed mosquitoes accessing the dorsal surfaces of captive killer whales in Florida. Unlike their wild counterparts that are rarely stationary, captive killer whales typically spend several hours each day and night logging (floating), during which time biting mosquitoes access their exposed dorsal surfaces. We estimate logging behaviour among captive males to often exceed 50% of their daily repertoire, and it is known that at least two captive killer whales have died as a result of mosquito-transmitted pathogens (Buck *et al.*, 1993; St Leger *et al.*, 2011).

Mosquitoes are attracted to the exhaled carbon dioxide (Dekker *et al.*, 2005), dark surfaces (Brown & Bennett, 1981), heat (Wang *et al.*, 2009) and other cues present during the logging behaviour exhibited by captive killer whales.

Social strife is magnified for killer whales in captive environments, where whales collected from different parts of the world, or who are shipped from various marine parks, are often housed together. Captive killer whales will often ram, rake and displace other animals in displays of aggression and as a means of establishing hierarchy within a group. The aforementioned jaw popping behaviour relates to the social instability created by artificial killer whale pods. In an extreme example, a female killer whale at a marine theme park in California (US) rammed another female in 1989 during a show in a display of dominance (Reza & Johnson, 1989). The impact fractured her jaw and ruptured major arteries in the whale's nasal passages, causing the whale to bleed to death. In stark contrast, a free-ranging animal can simply flee when tensions mount. The extreme spatial constraints imposed on whales in captive environments prevent a natural escape response and exacerbate incompatibilities. Along these lines, Hoyt (1992) estimated that the minimum volume of water traversed by a wild killer whale in an average 24 hours totalled 6,006,000,000 ft^3, containing over 45,302,778,000 gallons. Hoyt concluded this volume to be over 9000 times larger than the sum of the interconnecting killer whale pools at any of the SeaWorld parks.

Captive killer whale attacks

Keeping killer whales in captivity has proven to be detrimental to the health and safety of animals and trainers alike. On Christmas Eve 2009, trainer Alexis Martinez was killed by a male captive-bred killer whale named Keto, who was on loan from SeaWorld to Loro Parque in the Canary Islands, Spain. Two months later, in February 2010, trainer Dawn Brancheau was killed by SeaWorld's male killer whale, Tilikum (Figure 8.6).

This particular whale also killed trainer Keltie Byrne at a theme park in Canada prior to his arrival at SeaWorld. Tilikum additionally caused the death of park guest, Daniel Dukes, who had hidden in the park after hours. Medical Examiner (ME) reports described massive trauma to both Dawn and Alexis, and less to Daniel (Medical Examiner's Report, 1999, 2010). Deaths and serious injuries led to a US Federal judge requiring that SeaWorld end the practice of placing trainers in their pools with killer whales during shows (Welsch, 2011). In a 2-1 ruling in April 2014, the US Court of Appeals denied SeaWorld's appeal of citations issued by the occupational Safety and Health Administration. As former killer whale trainers, we conclude that there is no way to fully mitigate the safety risks associated with swimming with captive killer whales.

Figure 8.6 On 24 February 2010 the SeaWorld orca 'Tilikum' would claim his third victim, Dawn Brancheau, who is depicted here on a mural at the Orlando, Florida, International Airport in 2010. Dawn lost her life just sixty days after another trainer, Alexis Martinez, was killed by the SeaWorld orca 'Keto' in the Canary Islands. Medical examiner reports revealed brutal attacks and traumatic loss of life for both trainers, raising the question of whether killer whales should be kept in concrete enclosures for human amusement
Photo Credit: Jeffrey Ventre.

Speculation on the Future of the Industry

While demand for captive cetaceans is on the rise globally, the past five years have brought the story of cetacean captivity to millions of potential consumers of marine park entertainment. In 2009, Academy Award-winning documentary *The Cove* highlighted the ongoing capture and slaughter of small cetaceans near Taiji, Japan. Since then a non-profit activist group known as the Sea Shepherd Conservation Society has begun streaming live video feeds from the Taiji cove, exposing the practices of the hunters there to millions worldwide. This exposure has led to statements critical of these practices from the current US Ambassador to Japan, Carolyn Kennedy, as well as a letter from Yoko Ono Lennon to the fisherman of Taiji. In 2013 the documentary *Blackfish* brought the plight of killer whales in captivity to millions of viewers worldwide.

As increasing numbers of the public become educated and disillusioned with captivity, the practice is likely to slowly fall from favour, with corporations contesting changes to their business model. There is, however, a growing demand, especially in Asian markets, for captive whales and dolphins. Russia has accelerated collections of killer whales for public display, collecting eight animals since 2012. Facilities in the Middle East, such as 'Atlantis, The Palm' in Dubai, already display cetaceans and seem interested in acquiring more. In April 2013 the former CEO of SeaWorld, Jim Atchison, told the *New York Times*, 'We could take our Shamu show in Orlando and probably show it in Malaysia or Abu Dhabi or Dubai. There's a lot of interest in our brands from overseas' (Alden, 2013). Mr Atchison was forced to resign in December, 2014 due to collapsed stock value and diminished attendance at SeaWorld's US Parks. SeaWorld has continued with overseas expansion plans.

Conclusions

We acknowledge the potential for zoos and aquariums to provide critically needed educational programming to the public, and there is no doubt that zoos and aquariums can, and do, fill important conservation roles in myriad ways. Having worked within the marine park industry, we accept that there are many animal species whose environmental and social requirements can reasonably be met in a captive setting. There is, however, growing awareness globally that marine mammal captivity is unethical. As the largest and most sophisticated of the marine mammals currently in captivity, it is becoming increasingly obvious that captive environments are inadequate for killer whales. The captive marine mammal entertainment industry has strong financial incentives to continue in a business-as-usual fashion, and these same financial incentives exist in developing countries. It seems reasonable to predict that developing countries will increase the number of facilities housing captive marine mammals in the near future. However, social media is now facilitating unprecedented access to objective evidence that the practice of killer whale and other marine mammal captivity is cruel and unnecessary. As a result, the marine mammal entertainment industry now finds itself at odds with a growing number of educated citizens likely to choose alternative forms of entertainment. The practice of housing killer whales for entertainment purposes in the United States and elsewhere is clearly an unsustainable practice. It is our hope that marine parks will choose to evolve on the issue.

References

ABC (2007) SeaWorld investigation: Secrets below the surface. *American Broadcasting Corporation*, 27 May. www.10news.com/news/seaworld-investigation-secrets-below-the-surface (accessed 21 January 2014).

Adelman, L., Falk, J. and James, S. (2000) Impact of national aquarium in Baltimore on visitors' conservation attitudes, behavior, and knowledge. *Curator* 43 (1), 33–60.

Ajzen, I. (1991) The theory of planned behavior. *Organizational Behavior and Human Decision Processes* 50 (2), 179–211.

Alden, W. (2013) SeaWorld hints at overseas ambitions. *New York Times*, blog post, 19 April. http://dealbook.nytimes.com/2013/04/19/seaworld-c-e-o-hints-at-overseas-ambitions/ (accessed 3 February 2014).

Anderson, U.S., Kelling, A.S., Pressley-Keough, R., Bloomsmith, M.A. and Maple, T.L. (2003) Enhancing the zoo visitor's experience by public animal training and oral interpretation at an otter exhibit. *Environment and Behavior* 35 (6), 826–841.

APHIS (Animal Plant Health Inspection Service) (2002) *Routine Inspection Report: SeaWorld San Antonio*, March. Washington, DC: US Department of Agriculture.

APHIS (Animal Plant Health Inspection Service) (2007) *Routine Inspection Report: Los Angeles Zoo*, March. US Department of Agriculture.

AZA (2006) Groundbreaking study identifies impact of zoo and aquarium visits. Press release. Silver Spring, MD: American Zoo and Aquarium Association.

Ballantyne, R., Packer, J., Hughes, K. and Dierking, L. (2007) Conservation learning in wildlife tourism settings: Lessons from research in zoos and aquariums. *Environmental Education Research* 13 (3), 367–383.

Ballantyne, R., Packer, J. and Falk, J. (2011) Visitors' learning for environmental sustainability: Testing short- and long-term impacts of wildlife tourism experiences using structural equation modelling. *Tourism Management* 32 (6), 1243–1252.

Broad, S. and Weiler, B. (1998) Captive animals and interpretation: A tale of two tiger exhibits. *Journal of Tourism Studies* 9 (1), 14–27.

Brown, S.M. and Bennett, G.F. (1981) Response of mosquitoes (*Diptera: culicidae*) to visual stimuli. *Journal of Medical Entomology* 18 (6), 505–521.

Buck, C., Paulino, G.P., Medina, D.J., Hsjung, G.D., Campbell, T.W. and Walsh, M.T. (1993) Isolation of St. Louis encephalitis virus from a killer whale. *Clinical and Diagnostic Virology* 1 (2), 109–112.

Bushman, B.J. and Huesmann, L.R. (2010) Aggression. In S.T. Fiske, D.T. Gilbert and G. Lidzey (eds) *Handbook of Social Psychology* (pp. 833–863). New York: Wiley.

CBS (2010) SeaWorld called the best place for Tilikum. *Central Broadcasting Service*, 27 February. See www.cbsnews.com/news/seaworld-called-best-place-for-tilikum/ (accessed 3 December 2013).

Center for Whale Research (2014) Southern resident killer whales. *Center for Whale Research blog*. See www.whaleresearch.com/#!orcas/cto2 (accessed 2 February 2014).

Clegg, H.A., Buckley, P., Friend, M.A. and McGreevy, P.D. (2008) The ethological and physiological characteristics of cribbing and weaving horses. *Applied Animal Behaviour Science* 109 (1), 68–76.

Dekker, T., Geier, M. and Carde, R.T. (2005) Carbon dioxide instantly sensitizes female yellow fever mosquitoes to human skin odours. *Journal of Experimental Biology* 208, 2963–2972.

Dierking, L.D., Adelman, L.M., Ogden, J., Lehnhardt, K., Miller, L. and Mellen, J.D. (2004) Using a behavior change model to document the impact of visits to Disney's Animal Kingdom: A study investigating intended conservation action. *Curator* 47 (3), 322–343.

Falk, J.H., Reinhard, E.M., Vernon, C.L., Bronnenkant, K., Heimlich, J.E. and Deans, N.L. (2007) *Why Zoos and Aquariums Matter: Assessing the Impact of a Visit to a Zoo or Aquarium*. Silver Springs, MD: Association of Zoos and Aquariums.

Falk, J.H., Reinhard, E.M., Vernon, C.L., Bronnenkant, K., Heimlich, J.E. and Deans, N.L. (2010) Critique of a critique. *Society and Animals* 18 (4), 415–419.

Fishbein, M. and Ajzen, I. (1975) *Belief, Attitude, Intention, and Behavior. An Introduction to Theory and Research*. Reading, MA: Addison-Wesley.

Ford, J.K.B., Ellis, G.M. and Balcomb, K.C. (1994) *Killer Whales: The Natural History and Genealogy of Orcinus orca in British Columbia and Washington State*. Vancouver, BC and Seattle, WA: University of British Columbia Press and University of Washington Press.

Garrett, H. (2014) *Overview*. Freeland, WA: The Orca Network. See www.globalgiving.org/donate/12429/orca-network/info/.

Hoyt, E. (1992) *The Performing Orca – Why the Show Must Stop: An In-Depth Review of the Captive Orca Industry*. Chippenham: Whale and Dolphin Conservation Society.

Hoyt, E. (2013a) Russian Orca captures: The inside story. *Whale and Dolphin Conservation (WDC) blog*. See http://uk.whales.org/blog/erichhoyt/2013/11/russian-orca-captures-inside-story (accessed 16 November 2013).

Hoyt, E. (2013b) Scientists ponder the question of Orcas captured in Russia. *Whale and Dolphin Conservation (WDC) blog*. See http://arctic-news.blogspot.in/2014/02/mantle-methane.html (accessed 25 February 2013).

Jett, J. and Ventre, J. (in press) Captive killer whale (*Orcinus orca*) survival. *Marine Mammal Science*.

Kellert, S. (1997) *Kinship to Mastery: Biophilia in Human Evolution and Development*. Washington, DC: Island Press.

Kidd, A.H. and Kidd, R.M. (1998) General attitudes toward and knowledge about the importance of ocean life. *Psychological Reports* 82, 323–329.

Kielty, J. (2011) NOAA-NMFS failures in marine mammal inventory management for killer whales. *The Orca Project*, blog post. See http://theorcaproject.wordpress.com/page/5/ (accessed 10 November 2013).

Kripke, M.L. (1994) Ultraviolet radiation and immunology: Something new under the sun – presidential address. *Cancer Research* 54, 6102–6105.

Manubay, G., Smith, J.C., Houston, C., Schultz, K., Dotzour, A. and DeYoung, R. (2002) Evaluating exhibits that promote conservation behavior: Developing a theoretical framework. *Proceedings of the 31st Annual North American Association for Environmental Education*, 6–11 August, Boston, MA.

Marino, L., Lilienfeld, S.O., Malamud, R., Nobis, N. and Broglio, R. (2010) Do zoos and aquariums promote attitude change in visitors? A critical evaluation of the American zoo and aquarium study. *Society and Animals* 18, 126–138.

Medical Examiner's Report (1999) *Daniel Dukes*. Online document. Orlando, FL: District Nine Medical Examiner's Office. See www.scribd.com/doc/119465495/Daniel-Dukes-Medical-Examiners-Report.

Medical Examiner's Report (2010) *Dawn Brancheau*. Online document. Orlando, FL: District Nine Medical Examiner's Office. See www.scribd.com/doc/34026913/Dawn-Brancheau-Autopsy-Report.

National Marine Fisheries Service (2008) *Recovery Plan for Southern Resident Killer Whales (Orcinus orca)*. Seattle, WA: National Marine Fisheries Service, Northwest Region.

National Research Council (2009) *Learning Science in Informal Environments: People, Places, and Pursuits*. Washington, DC: National Academies Press.

O'Barry, R. (2011) SeaWorld's hypocrisy. *Save Japan Dolphins*, blog post, 24 September, See http://savejapandolphins.org/blog/post/seaworlds-hypocrisy (accessed 6 February 2014).

Ogden, J. and Heimlich, J.E. (2009) Why focus on zoo and aquarium education? *Zoo Biology* 28, 357–360.

Olesiuk, P.F., Ellis, G.M. and Ford, J.K. (2005) *Life History and Population Dynamics of Northern Resident Killer Whales* (Orcinus orca) *in British Columbia*. DFO Canadian Science Advisory Secretariat Research Document 2005/045. Ontario, BC: Fisheries and Oceans Canada.

Padilha, D.M.P., Hilgert, J.B., Hugo, F.N., Bos, A.J.G. and Ferrucci, L. (2008) Number of teeth and mortality risk in the Baltimore longitudinal study of aging. *Journals of Gerontology Series A: Biological Sciences and Medical Sciences* 63 (7), 739–744.

PBS (1997) A whale of a business. *Public Broadcasting Service Frontline*, 11 November. See www.pbs.org/wgbh/pages/frontline/shows/whales/ (accessed 28 October 2013).

Povey, K. and Spaulding, W. (2005) Message design for animal presentations: A new approach. Paper presented at the *American Zoo and Aquarium Association Annual Conference*, 13–18 September, Chicago, IL.

Reza, H.G. and Johnson, G. (1989) Killer whale bled to death after breaking jaw in fight. *Los Angeles Times*, 23 August. See http://articles.latimes.com/1989-08-23/news/mn-887_1_killer-whale (accessed 6 March 2014).

Robeck, T.R., Steinman, K.J., Gearhart, S., Reidarson, T.R., McBain, J.F. and Monfort, S.L. (2004) Reproductive physiology and development of artificial insemination technology in killer whales (*Orcinus orca*). *Biology of Reproduction* 71, 650–660.

Rose, N.A., Parsons, E. and Farinato, R. (2009) *The Case Against Marine Mammals in Captivity* (ed. N. Rose and D. Firmani; 4th edn) (pp. 1–77). Washington, DC: The Humane Society of the United States, World Society for the Protection of Animals.

SeaWorld (2014a) *Killer Whale Bibliography.* Orlando, FL: SeaWorld Parks & Entertainment. See http://i2.cdn.turner.com/cnn/2013/images/10/11/killer.whale.bibliography.10.08.13.pdf (accessed 3 January 2014).

SeaWorld (2014b) *SeaWorld and Hubbs-SeaWorld Research Institute Killer Whale Bibliography.* Orlando, FL: SeaWorld Parks & Entertainment. See http://i2.cdn.turner.com/cnn/2013/images/10/11/killer.whale.sea..hubbs.collaboration.pdf (accessed 6 January 2014).

SeaWorld (2014c) *SeaWorld's Killer Whales Benefit Killer Whales in the Wild Through Scientific Understanding and Public Engagement.* Orlando, FL: SeaWorld Parks & Entertainment. See http://seaworld.com/en/truth/global-impact/research/ (accessed 25 January 2014).

SeaWorld (2014d) *SeaWorld and Busch Gardens' Breeding Program Dedicated to Preserving Wildlife.* Orlando, FL: SeaWorld Parks & Entertainment. See www.seaworldparksblog.com/seaworld-busch-gardens-breeding-program-dedicated-preserving-wildlife (accessed 9 March 2014).

SeaWorld (2014e) *Killer Whales: Longevity & Causes of Death.* Orlando, FL: SeaWorld Parks & Entertainment. See http://seaworld.org/en/animal-info/animal-infobooks/killer-whale/longevity-and-causes-of-death/ (accessed 4 March 2014).

SeaWorld (2014f) *Killer Whales.* Busch Gardens Animal InfoBook. Orlando, FL: SeaWorld Parks & Entertainment. http://seaworld.org/en/animal-info/animal-infobooks/killer-whale/ (accessed 4 March 2014).

Sleijffers, A., Garssen, J. and Van Loveren, H. (2002) Ultraviolet radiation, resistance to infectious diseases, and vaccination responses. *Methods* 28 (1), 111–121.

Stewart, S.T., Cutler, D.M. and Rosen, A. B. (2013) US trends in quality-adjusted life expectancy from 1987 to 2008: Combining national surveys to more broadly track the health of the nation. *American Journal of Public Health* 103 (11), 78–87.

St Leger, J., Guang, W., Anderson, M., Dalton, L., Nilson, E. and Wang, D. (2011) West Nile virus infection in killer whale, Texas, USA. *Emerging Infectious Disease* 17 (8), 1531–1533.

Swanagan, J.S. (2000) Factors influencing zoo visitors' conservation attitudes and behavior. *Journal of Environmental Education* 31 (4), 26–31.

Vinogradova, Y., Hippisley-Cox, J. and Coupland, C. (2009) Identification of new risk factors for pneumonia: Population-based case-control study. *British Journal of General Practice* 59 (567), 329–338.

Visser, I.N. (1998) Prolific body scars and collapsing dorsal fins on killer whales (*Orcinus orca*) in New Zealand waters. *Aquatic Mammals* 24 (2), 71–81.

Wang, G., Qiu, Y.T., Lu, T., Kwon, H.W., Pitts, R.J., Van Loon, J.J., Takken, W. and Zwiebel, L.J. (2009) *Anopheles gambiae* TRPA1 is a heat-activated channel expressed in thermosensitive sensilla of female antennae. *European Journal of Neuroscience* 30 (6), 967–974.

WDC (2014) Orcas Currently in Captivity. Chippenham: Whale and Dolphin Conservation Society. See www.scribd.com/doc/206351248/ORCAS-Currently-in-Captivity-as-of-2014.

Welsch, K. (2011) *Judge Ken Welsch Ruling on SeaWorld Appeal.* US Court of Appeals. See www.scribd.com/doc/95427726/Judge-Ken-Welsch-Ruling-On-SeaWorld-OSHA-Appeal.

9 Dolphin Tourism and Human Perceptions: Social Considerations to Assessing the Human–Dolphin Interface

Carlie S. Wiener

Animals clearly left their imprint on our subconscious as well as the newly emerging conscious brain. We may never figure out when or how we became conscious, talking beings, but we do know that when thoughtful conversations began it would have been largely about the same old thing that preyed on everybody's mind: animals.

Meg Olmert, 2009: 9

Introduction

The allure of dolphins reflects a longstanding relationship with humans shaped by cultural, social and scientific perspectives (Wiener, 2013). In the past 20 years, swim-with-dolphin activities have dramatically grown in popularity, leading to the development of globally distributed 'hotbeds' of dolphin tourism activity. The stereotypical dolphin 'personality' fashioned in pop culture plays an important role in understanding the drive for dolphin tourism that relies on a fused portrayal of dolphins as exotic, wild, intelligent and human-like. Dolphins spark an intense desire in people to cross human–animal boundaries, which motivates the pursuit of dolphin interactions.

A long history of the dolphin–human interface ranges from early contact with lone, sociable individuals to more recent commercial swim-with-dolphin tours (Constantine, 2001). Dolphin tourism can vary dramatically depending on the type of activity pursued; there are differences between feeding, swimming and watching programmes either in captivity or in the wild (Bulbeck, 2005). The majority of dolphin swim programmes involve coastal dolphin species; however, there are a few exceptions where swimming with whales also occurs. Dolphin tourism represents single-purpose recreation where emphasis is placed on the viewing of, and/or interacting with, one particular species. Those who partake in dolphin tourism are a subgroup of wildlife tourists who differ in their involvement, familiarity and goals. Wild dolphin tourism can occur from different platforms: land-based (from the beach), boat-based (off-shore), and air-based (helicopter/small plane) (Finkler & Higham, 2004). Boat-based viewing offers swimming and snorkelling experiences, with a few rare scuba diving with dolphins options.

Dolphin interactions as part of a broader marine tourism industry (see also Wearing & Jobberns, Chapter 5 and Higham & Neves, Chapter 7, this volume) can provide psychological, economic, environmental, physiological, social and educational benefits; however, a more detailed evaluation of the tourist experience is needed to identify approaches that promote attitude and lifestyle changes among tourists (Zeppel & Muloin, 2008). Environmental educators such as Louv (2008) argue in favour of interactions with the natural world to promote a re-engagement with, and interest in, environmental conservation. Others, such as Evernden (1992), caution that these experiences do not necessarily erase the conflict between nature and present-day consumption-based culture. Perhaps it is the quality of these encounters that alters the eventual outcome; Livingston (1994) suggests that naturalists can be open to a different quality of encounter with the natural world, one where the excitement generated defines the experience. Any participant can be environmentally sympathetic; however, it is those who are most open to these experiences, regardless of the quality of the encounter, who appear to benefit the most. With human–dolphin encounters on the rise and many people reporting this event as a lifelong dream, it seems necessary to further investigate these sites of engagement and how the experiences influence the participants.

This chapter focuses on the act of swimming with dolphins and why it drives human interest in this group of animals. Previous literature has paid little attention to the actual in-water experience of the participant, de-emphasising the emotional connection that charges human–dolphin contact. Thus, the subsequent sections explore how marine tourism has perpetuated this popular leisure activity and informed current exchanges for pleasure. An introduction to the issues and attributes of these human–dolphin interfaces will be provided in the tourism context with particular attention towards the importance of eye 'gaze' and bodily contact. The chapter concludes with an overview of the debates in recent literature concerning the moral viability of dolphin swims and the motivations of swim participants.

Human Constructions of Dolphins

Marine wildlife tourism is aimed at delivering a unique experience by offering close interactions with wildlife, particularly dolphins. Evernden

(1999) and Livingston (1994) argue that engagement with the natural world fosters an ethic of care and a desire for conservation, but if this is indeed true, what is the cost to the animal that might be at the centre of this engagement? Differences in perceptions illuminate a number of dichotomies relevant to the experience: wild versus captive, mediated versus in-the-flesh, common versus endangered – not all encounters are equal. The meanings produced through the tourism experience are essential to understanding the role of wildlife in the social construction of nature. As perceptions change with time, it is these shifting opinions that help to define the place of wildlife in contemporary society.

The relationship between humans and non-human animals is formulated around shifting priorities between animals themselves and anthropocentric, capitalist initiatives. Non-human animals are blurred between representations of the real and simulated, influencing moral boundaries (Fudge, 2002). The human–dolphin interaction itself is open, based around chance and play, emphasising performance. How people behave and view this enactment of dolphins is influenced by individual perspectives of nature. According to Evernden (1992) there are three types of nature that shape human attitudes: 'nature as object', 'nature as self' and 'nature as miracle'. Nature as object conceives of the natural world in an anthropocentric manner, treating non-human animals with no subjectivity but as objects to be explored and in existence to serve human desires (Evernden, 1992; see also Burns, Chapter 2, this volume). Nature as self is rooted in a deeper, moral obligation to the natural world with concern for non-human animals as an extension of the self; nature as miracle treats the environment as unpredictable and wondrous (Evernden, 2008).

Western culture's extension of moral consideration to non-human subjects often selects pets, 'cuddly' mammals, or rare wildlife over other non-human animals (Olmert, 2009). Bekoff (2008) makes this observation by comparing human attitudes towards wolves and whales, both of which were historically persecuted. Changes in opinion towards these animals are reflective of human culture; Bekoff (2008: 397) states that 'while many people swim with dolphins, few if any truly dance or howl with wolves'. Dolphins are a good example of this selected favouritism based on their widespread appeal and famed altruism (Barney *et al.*, 2005). The promotion of dolphins as creatures that are unique from humans is explored in science fiction novels and movies such as *The Day of the Dolphins* (1973) and *The Hitchhikers Guide to the Galaxy* (2005). Contrariwise, dolphins are commonly portrayed as similar to humans as well, possessing valued human characteristics such as intelligence, altruistic behaviour and play.

Socially constructed ideas of dolphins as simultaneously exotic animals and happy friends deeply affect the way humans orient their behaviour towards this non-human animal. The problem lies in the misconceptions that these false characteristics produce. People are reluctant to allow a child to play with an unknown dog, but seem to have no problem trusting a wild dolphin (Bekoff, 2003). This example demonstrates how deeply perceptions of non-human animals are engrained into human culture. Cloke and Perkins (2005) contend that representations may not be accurate as people tend to divorce social associations from actual behaviours. Anthropomorphic depictions of popular non-human animals such as dolphins are created to fit human needs. It is precisely these historical interpretations that account for identification with certain species. Desmond (1999) pinpoints this conflicting tension regarding cetaceans (i.e. dolphins and whales) as outliers straddling the lines between being human and fish. Even among cetaceans, a hierarchy of likeability exists correlating to commonly encountered species through captive facilities and media; bottlenose dolphins and orcas tend to be favoured over less charismatic relatives such as river dolphins.

The mystery of dolphin lives has played into folklore across the globe, connecting dolphins with magical powers and merging with people on land. In South America, some view the river dolphin as a mysterious being that can shapeshift and capture souls (Montgomery, 2003). Dolphin spiritualism, the idea that dolphins have the ability to improve physical and spiritual wellbeing, has created a growing industry for those looking to participate in what has become known as dolphin therapy. Many people report the 'dolphin effect' following a dolphin swim, testifying to feelings of change or healing, including the alleviation of chronic depression, removal of pain and recovery from illness (Taylor, 2003). Burnett (2010) explains that supporters of the 'dolphin effect' believe that cetaceans have the ability to 'scan' the human body for palliative purposes. Although there is little evidence to support this, the use of sonar from dolphins has been one explanation for these reports.

Dolphin Tourism Development

The growth of dolphinaria throughout the world has increased the perception of dolphins as entertainers, extending these expectations to wild dolphins as well. These images are promoted by both captive and wild tourism facilities that falsely represent dolphins as perpetually happy and always ready to perform. Prior to interest in wild marine tourism, a longstanding history of spectator encounters with captive cetaceans is evident (see also Ventre & Jett, Chapter 7, this volume). In 1860, P.T. Barnum placed two whales on display in his American Freakshow, followed by the New York Aquarium (which first displayed dolphins in 1913) and the Florida Marine Studios in 1938 (Hughes, 2001). After the film release of *Flipper* in 1963 and the subsequent television show (1964–1967), the popularity of dolphins increased dramatically, reinforcing human interest.

Like captive exchanges, dolphin swim activities are dependent on performance. Intrigue for close encounters has contributed to the formation of destinations that have become known for opportunities to interact with dolphins. For example, locations such as Shark Bay, Australia, Kailua-Kona, Hawaii and Kaikoura, New Zealand now revolve around dolphin tourism, altering how locals and tourists value these places. Shifts in values can occur organically, like Shark Bay's feeding programme, or be produced intentionally, as exemplified by Narin, Scotland (Cater & Cater, 2007). Certain countries have prospered more than others in the popularisation of their marine tourism economies, as evidenced by infrastructure development focusing on coastal cetacean populations. The processes by which these locations are constructed rely not only on economic development, but also on the cetaceans themselves (Cloke & Perkins, 2005). An example of this is in Samadhi, Egypt, where until 2000 the dolphins were mostly a side attraction; however, as word spread, an increasing number of tourists arrived. Now up to 800 people per day visit the reef for the sole purpose of seeing the dolphins (Notarbartolo-di-sciara *et al.*, 2009). An upsurge in dolphin tourism focused on swim activities with the Hawaiian spinner dolphins (*Stenella longirostris*) has also occurred in Hawaii (Courbis, 2007; Ostman-Lind *et al.*, 2004; Wiener *et al.*, 2009) (Figures 9.1 and 9.2). Hu *et al.* (2009) validate this interest in tourists who want to swim with Hawaiian spinner dolphins based on a large jump in internet hits on dolphin swims from 2250 in 2002 to 31,400 in 2007.

Other areas such as American Samoa boast cetacean populations that have not been targeted for tourist activities; however, it is only a matter of time before these animals are considered as profitable elements. Once the

Figure 9.1 Spinner dolphin with crowd
Photo: Author.

Figure 9.2 Spinner dolphin tourism has dramatically increased among the Hawaiian Islands in several locations including Waianae, Oahu and Kailua-Kona, Hawaii
Photo: Author.

infrastructure for dolphin tourism arises, word quickly spreads and without regulation the number of tour operators jumps from one to many (Hoyt, 2001; Orams, 1997). The advertising and word of mouth from people who have previously participated build potential participants' knowledge. When the infrastructure cannot support the number of visitors and no long-term planning is implemented, tourism becomes an immediate problem.

Historically, Australia and New Zealand are two countries that have offered the greatest variety in dolphin opportunities (Wiener, 2013). Other dolphin programmes including swimming and feeding activities operate internationally, but lack the policy frameworks that exist in Australia and New Zealand. For example, New Zealand's Marine Mammal Protection Regulations (1992) enforce a no-wake zone for boats within 300 m of dolphins and allow a maximum of three boats (Lück, 2003). In Victoria, Australia, the Department of Sustainability and Environment created site-specific regulations (1998) prohibiting tour vessels from approaching dolphin schools closer than 200 m (Howes *et al.*, 2012). Elsewhere, the Great Barrier Reef Marine Protection Agency (2003) requires whale-swim operators to complete sighting sheets for every encounter (Curnock *et al.*, 2013). In the United States, it is considered illegal to feed or harass wild dolphins under the Marine Mammal Protection Act (MMPA); however, there is still a plethora of dolphin interaction programmes. To further complicate the matter, each state has its own guidelines for commercial boat tours and the five federal regions also differ in their approach regarding vulnerable species (Orams, 1995). Of greatest concern are the nations that have no protection or laws at all, such as Tonga and Brazil. In Brazil, uncontrolled feeding occurs at two locations and people swim with at least one food-provisioned dolphin (Samuels *et al.*, 2000).

Marine tourism management varies across a continuum of protection dependent on the activity, location and research availability. In the United States, state-controlled game programmes were the first to execute management following the implementation of 'wise-use' conservation brought in by federal agencies (Duffus & Dearden, 1990). International management bodies are also beginning to take an interest in the regulation of marine mammal swim programmes, including the International Whaling Commission (IWC). One of the greatest challenges for global organisations is to provide consistency in guidelines as mechanisms differ between countries. Currently, Australia, Dominica, the United Kingdom and New Zealand each have their own guidelines for marine mammal interactions (Constantine, 1999).

Many countries use marine tourism as a tool to elevate their status in international relations (Cater & Cater, 2007). Taiwan, for instance, has shifted from dolphin slaughter to marine tourism as a politically friendly way to generate income (Chen, 2011). In Zanzibar, 9% of the Indo-Pacific bottlenose dolphin population was killed annually as a result of hunting (Christiansen *et al.*, 2010). By 1992, villagers replaced the dolphin hunt with swimming activities that became a contributor to the local economy (Christiansen *et al.*, 2010). Globally, dolphin swim tourism is not developing sustainably, which is revealed by accounts of harassment towards dolphins and studies showing negative effects on populations (Christiansen *et al.*, 2010). The opposite problem exists in some communities, where the transition from harvesting practices to marine tourism is proving to be difficult. In Norway, for example, whale watching is considered a cultural attack on traditional whaling (Constantine & Baker, 1997).

Several studies have examined how attitude, environmental stimuli and physiological drives influence desires to pursue the viewing of, and interacting with, wildlife. Understanding tourist preferences is important in decision making regarding permitted activities, levels and types of interactions. Duffus and Dearden (1990) argue that innate or instinctive reactions dominate contact with wildlife, differing very little among tourists due to precognitive human responses. Amante-Helweg (1996) and Semeniuka *et al.* (2009) disagree, emphasising the heterogeneity of populations. Amante-Helweg (1996) demonstrates that most respondents interpret dolphin behaviour anthropomorphically and perceive dolphins as socio-centric: holding attributions of spirituality, altruism and interspecies sociability. Human perceptions act as important motivators for activities and do not remain static. The framing of events is vital to the tourist experience.

Specialisation is another point to consider as a growing number of people become comfortable with dolphin swim activities. Duffus and Dearden (1990) point out that as these 'rare' opportunities are sought, the generalist population of tourists becomes specialised. As more people learn about human–dolphin interactions and develop a greater comfort level with these relations, they are likely to repeat the experience. Participation in dolphin swims occurs at all swimming levels; however, those who have greater comfort in the water are able to engage easily with the dolphins. This process of specialisation has the ability to transform small-scale experiences into mass tourism, increasing the frequency and popularity by the general public.

In Hawaii, 204 participants were surveyed about their motivations for exploring a swim-with-dolphins experience. Of this group, 81% stated that the uniqueness of the opportunity was the number one reason for involvement, and 76% of those surveyed were first-time dolphin swimmers (Wiener, 2014). Over time, dolphin swims will become more common, and the skill level of participants will shift, increasing the pressure for more interactive experiences. Once people are introduced to this activity, there is a risk that they will seek out these encounters on their own, placing pressure on tour operators to discover new, less developed sites. Hawaii has already realised this trend, with once 'secret' dolphin swim bays that have become overrun with visitors pursuing dolphin swims. This has been a common trend in marine tourism, contributing to the degradation and popularisation of once unknown locations.

Negative Effects of Dolphin Tourism

A large number of studies have illuminated the negative effects of dolphin tourism on both individual and entire populations (Bejder et al., 2006; Howes et al., 2012; Lundquist et al., 2012; Lusseau et al., 2006; Stockin et al., 2008). The majority of these impacts relate to altering dolphin behaviour, effects of vessel noise, and habituation as a result of human interaction. Samuels et al. (2000) document the negative risks associated with the taming of wild dolphins; habituation has led to cetaceans being harassed by humans, decreasing maternal behaviour, increasing susceptibility to shark attacks, juveniles becoming dependent on fish hand-outs, and lower rates of calf survivorship. Specific pod reactions to dolphin tourism most notably consist of changes in dolphin activity (Constantine, 2001; Lundquist et al., 2012; Lusseau & Higham, 2004), shifts in speed (Williams et al., 2002), movement (Bejder et al., 2006), diving behaviour (Janik & Thompson, 1996; Nowacek et al., 2001), group formation (Bejder et al., 1999), and vocalisation (Buckstaff, 2004). These impacts, if continued over the long term, may result in permanent behaviour change and potentially threaten individuals and populations (Christiansen et al., 2010; Martinez & Orams, 2009).

Signs of avoidance are the most common mechanism for exploring the effects of tour boats on dolphin populations. In addition to boater presence, the way that vessels are manoeuvred (e.g. changes in speed, direction and approach), boat density and distance between dolphins and vessels are important to dolphin response (Barr, 1997; Constantine, 2001; Lusseau, 2008). Christiansen *et al.* (2010) examined the behaviour of dolphins in the presence of tour boats, concluding that dolphins are less likely to stay in resting or socialising activity when boats are near. Christiansen *et al.* (2010) also raise concerns regarding the interruption of sexual behaviour leading to a lowered rate of successful mating. Other studies have shown notable concerns regarding behaviour shifts of the Hawaiian spinner dolphin due to disturbances from tour vessels looking to interact (Courbis & Timmel, 2009; Delfour, 2007; Ostman-Lind *et al.*, 2004). As a result of the observed negative effects, the United States National Oceanic and Atmospheric Association (NOAA) has begun to consider new rules to regulate boat activity around spinner dolphins.

Tour operators have been documented manoeuvring in an aggressive manner, leading to erratic boat navigation and competition (Constantine, 2001; Lusseau, 2008). These demonstrations could be misinterpreted as predatory techniques by the animals themselves (Lusseau & Higham, 2004). Tour boats often use high speeds and frequent direction changes in order to drop off and pick up swimmers in the water, potentially leading to long-term noise disturbance (Jensen, 2009). Participants are also responsible for loud distractions through voice and physical movement. Some companies encourage swimmers to create deliberate noise, such as singing, as a form of generating interactions with wild dolphins (Martinez & Orams, 2009). Concerns have been raised regarding specific populations of dolphins that are the focus of these swim experiences. The majority of research on the effects of dolphin swim tourism has focused on boat interactions, ignoring the in-water swimmers' influence.

In-Water Dolphin–Human Connections

Pre-existing images and contemporary culture shape human expectation of a dolphin encounter. Urry (1990) explores the idea that tourists undergo their travels through an already existing frame created by representations found in the media and elsewhere. Many examples illustrate this, from the already mentioned *Flipper* movie and television series, to the resurgence of Australia's snorkel tourism following the release of the children's film *Finding Nemo* (2003) (Hahm, 2004).

Cloke and Perkins (2005) explore the mediation of dolphins in the tourism experience, highlighting the excitement associated with the anticipation of engagement, the drive for filming the encounter, and the connection felt through interactions. Other considerations not investigated include feeling the aquatic environment and the equipment needed to swim in it. Swimmers require wetsuits to keep warm, snorkels and masks to breathe and see underwater, and fins to keep pace with the dolphins. Entering the unknown ocean requires the aid of technologies to maintain what cetaceans naturally do on their own, but how do these additions change the experience? In fact, many participants in dolphin swims have little-to-no exposure to the ocean on a regular basis. In 2012, a survey in Hawaii demonstrated that 23% of participants had basic-to-no experience swimming in the ocean and 45% had basic-to-no snorkelling skills (Wiener, 2014).

Outside of the water, dolphin swimmers have reported physical and mental sensations including sensitivity to stimuli, amplified vitality and elation (Lemieux, 2009; Ocean, 1997). One of the unique characteristics related to wild dolphin tourism encounters is that autonomy for participation is given to the species itself. In previous studies exploring encounters, dolphin performance provided the single most significant characteristic of the interaction including proximity, contact, timing and acknowledgement (Amante-Helweg, 1996; Constantine, 2001; Scheer, 2010). Given this variety, the most common definition of a successful swim includes one or more dolphins within 5 m of a swimmer (Constantine & Baker, 1997). Those who participate in dolphin swims frequently have claimed to develop a continued rapport with the same dolphins. Of 47 dolphin swim operators interviewed in 2012, 70% said they recognised individual dolphins, and, 64% felt that the dolphins recognised them (Wiener, 2014).

Making Contact

Capturing photographs during the dolphin swim is a priority among many participants, actively constructing how the swimmer perceives the event (Wiener, 2013). People often become consumed by the effort to put the moment on film; they witness the experience from behind the lens. Cloke and Perkins (2005) and Warkentin (2007) observe that very few people savour the encounter without the determination of getting the right shot, trying to visually represent the peak moments in a dolphin swim that can be refabricated with family and friends. Dolphin swim companies play into this desire by adhering to particular poses to produce this exact image. Many businesses offer to take videos of participants so that the experience is guaranteed to be captured. It is this need to encapsulate the moment that places pressure on the operators to provide a close-up encounter. The nearer the participant can get to the dolphin, the better the image will be. Facial features and, in particular, eye contact seem to be the target of observation.

Making visual contact with another species is considered to be one of the deepest connections made during wild dolphin experiences (Curtin, 2006). Swimmers report a stronger emotional relationship when they feel acknowledged by the participating dolphin (Wiener, 2013). How much participants can see during their swim is a factor in the building of intimacy. Face-to-face interaction is desired to create closeness in human–dolphin relations. Unfortunately, cetacean behaviours are often misinterpreted because participants misread facial attributes when they do get close, assuming that dolphins are happy because of the upturned curve of their rostrum, or a twinkle in the eye (Desmond, 1999). Some animal species are challenged by direct eye contact and perceive this behaviour as threatening (Desmond, 1999).

Misinterpretation is common during the dolphin–human exchange because it contradicts the desired experience that people have come to expect. Emphasis on dolphin encounters often misses a critical piece of this relationship by ignoring the non-human animal's experience (Wiener, 2013). The eyes of dolphins during these interactions are represented as important social cues used to infer mental states; however, just because there is an implied understanding does not mean that the dolphins are ascribing the same meaning to their actions (Keeley, 2002).

Similar to the visual experience, reflection on tactile interaction must be considered; dolphins are sensitive to touch and are particular in how they initiate contact (Wiener, 2013). Cetaceans communicate with their bodies using flukes, pectoral fins, teeth and rostrums to demonstrate pleasure, warning and affection (Dudzinski & Frohoff, 2008). Bekoff (2000) highlights examples of interspecies communication problems during petting, feeding and swimming programmes. Visible stress and aggression can be mistaken for playful behaviour leading to human injury from being bitten or hit by a fluke (Bekoff, 2000). Additionally, humans may communicate unintentionally through their body language; e.g. increased adrenaline in the human from excitement that may cause chasing behaviours (Wiener, 2013).

The desire for connection between humans and non-human animals extends beyond facial recognition and tactile contact. The human body connects to larger networks of meaning that produce social and cultural relations through hands and bodies (Creswell, 1999). Emotions are easily evoked in the human participant; just being in the dolphin's proximity is enough to draw excitement (Besio et al., 2008). The method with which marine mammal interactions take place affects the overall perspective, and the involvement of the senses and imagined experiences are important in these occurrences. For example, the viewpoint from a boat above the ocean will be different from someone who is watching from land. Not only does proximity play into this experience, but so does the spatial plane in which the dolphin and human interact. Swimming at parallel levels and speeds will provide a more intimate encounter, compared to 'birds-eye view' observation. Cater and Cater (2007) reason that the need to get 'up close' stems from a want for connection. The desire to see animals in motion is critical to these experiences. Close interactions with marine animals whose behaviour is considered authentic are 'supposedly' unaffected by human presence (Desmond, 1999). Unfortunately, constant human influence does affect animals and the behaviours displayed are most likely not positive responses.

The Moral Viability of Dolphin Swims

Humans assume that dolphins enjoy swimming with people as much as we relish swimming with them, ignoring the fact that people can inflict unintentional harm. Warkentin (2007) notes that what is missing in dolphin swims is the etiquette of invitation, presenting a choice that acknowledges the agency dolphins possess. Even when dolphins participate of their free will, they exert energy unnecessarily that is better kept for themselves (Wursig & Wursig, 2003). The cumulative effects of these exchanges are hard to gauge based on daily disturbance, but shifts in behaviour are almost inevitable and may have long-term implications. In 2000 the IWC formally addressed in-water engagement with free-ranging dolphins, stating that even the most well intentioned human contact is accompanied by unpredictable and cumulative risks (Frohoff & Peterson, 2003).

The greatest problem with dolphin tourism is that human affection imposed on dolphins has been misplaced, causing disturbances in populations from frequent human interactions; in other words, humans are loving dolphins to death. Many fields that relate to non-human animals have dedicated courses and research for humane treatment; however, no equivalent process has appeared in marine tourism despite the central use of cetacean species (Shani & Pizam, 2008). Some wildlife-based tourism sectors such as bird and whale watching have developed ethical guidelines for their activities (Hoyt, 2003). However, dolphin tourism has evolved so quickly that the regulations have not been able to keep up.

Regardless of the type of interaction, dolphins are consumed as part of a unique experience. However, they play their own roles as independent actors in dolphin swim activities and can choose to avoid or approach boats (Cater & Cater, 2007; Shani & Pizam, 2008). Unstructured dolphin swim programmes have developed uncertainty as to how operators and participants should behave. For example, what is an acceptable distance between tourists and dolphins (Garrod, 2008)? Regulations such as a maximum approach distance are important for participants who normally do not have close encounters with wild animals and, therefore, have little experience on which to base their decision making (Garrod, 2008). The multiplicity of etiquette practised by operators is a concern considering the growth of dolphin tourism, specifically swim programmes in developing countries. While whale watching is still happening in coastal areas off larger population centres, dolphin swims are growing in much smaller and more remote areas due to ease of accessibility (Hoyt, 2003).

Conclusions

Dolphins are a well-known group of cetaceans, but a common perception of these wild animals as human-like beings sparks a desire in people to interact with them across unfamiliar environments such as the ocean. An emphasis on emotional connections during human–dolphin contact has driven the popularity of wild swims in the tourism sector. This yearning to 'swim with dolphins' has resulted in worldwide appeal, transforming marine environments into popular tourist destinations. Public attitudes towards marine mammals ultimately reflect the way dolphin tourism is developed and utilised, shadowing Evernden's (1992) three categories of attitudes towards nature. The objectification of dolphins for commercial profit has been demonstrated by businesses that put the demands of commerce ahead of dolphin needs. For the most part, dolphins have not been given subjectivity, but rather treated as objects to be explored and in existence to serve human desires (Evernden, 1992). However, even when a deeper, moralistic approach to dolphin–human interactions occurs, it can often be misguided by a romanticised notion and further fuel the commercialisation of this species. Evernden (2008) warns that the unpredictability and mystery that goes along with wild non-human animals needs to be reinforced in these situations.

The moral line between what is right and wrong during human–cetacean interaction is largely unknown, and how people affect the perceptions of dolphins will never truly be understood. Questions remain unanswered about what to do when a wild dolphin becomes aggressive or habituated. Regardless of the answer, these queries demand consideration as the traditional boundaries between humans and dolphins continue to be re-made. In both research and story, humans have demonstrated that dolphins are individuals with varied personalities and high levels of emotional, cultural and social intelligence. How humans deal with this information will greatly impact the future relationship that people will have with dolphins. Although a range of regulations has been put in place by countries that already permit dolphin swims, further investigation is needed into the long-term effects of these rules, and to better explore in-water interactions. Additionally, policy must balance the desires of the surrounding communities with protecting dolphin populations. What are the wishes of the local companies that will need to be balanced if dolphin swims are not outlawed? Dolphin swim tourism will not decrease, but if humans begin to critically examine their behaviours, then they can attempt to credit dolphins with their own agency and work towards better protection and understanding.

References

Amante-Helweg, V. (1996) Ecotourists' beliefs and knowledge about dolphins and the development of cetacean ecotourism. *Aquatic Mammals* 22 (2), 131–140.
Barney, E.C., Mintzes, J.J. and Yen, C.F. (2005) Assessing knowledge, attitudes, and behaviour towards charismatic megafauna: The case of dolphins. *Journal of Environmental Education* 36 (2), 41–55.

Barr, K. (1997) The impacts of marine tourism on the behaviour and movement patterns of dusky dolphins (*Lagenorhynchus obscurus*) at Kaikoura, New Zealand. MSc thesis, University of Otago, Dunedin, New Zealand.

Bejder, L., Dawson, S.M. and Haraway, J.A. (1999) Responses by Hector's dolphins (*Cephalorhynchus hectori*) in Porpoise Bay, New Zealand. *Marine Mammal Science* 15, 738–750.

Bejder, L., Samuels, A., Whitehead, H. *et al.* (2006) Decline in relative abundance of bottlenose dolphins exposed to long-term disturbance. *Conservation Biology* 20 (6), 1791–1798.

Bekoff, M. (2000) *The Smile of a Dolphin*. New York: Discovery Books.

Bekoff, M. (2003) Troubling *Tursiops*: Living in harmony with kindred spirits. In T. Frohoff and B. Peterson (eds) *Between Species – Celebrating the Dolphin–Human Bond* (pp. 264–274). San Francisco, CA: Sierra Club Books.

Bekoff, M. (2008) Ethics and marine mammals. In W. Pernin, B. Wursig and J.G.M. Thewissen (eds) *Encyclopedia of Marine Mammals* (2nd edn) (pp. 396–401). Burlington, MA: Academic Press.

Besio, K., Johnston, L. and Longhurst, R. (2008) Sexy beasts and devoted mums: Narrating nature through dolphin tourism. *Environment and Planning* 40, 1219–1234.

Buckstaff, K.C. (2004) Effects of watercraft noise on the acoustic behavior of bottlenose dolphins, *Tursiops truncatus*, in Sarasota Bay, Florida. *Marine Mammal Science* 20, 709–725.

Bulbeck, C. (2005) *Facing the Wild: Ecotourism, Conservation and Animal Encounters*. London: Earthscan.

Burnett, D.G. (2010) A mind in the water: The dolphin as our beast of burden. *Orion Magazine*, May/June. See http://www.princeton.edu/history/people/data/d/dburnett/profile/dgbpdfs/BurnettDG_AMind_Orion_2010.pdf (accessed 12 November 2011).

Cater, C. and Cater, E. (2007) *Marine Ecotourism: Between the Devil and the Deep Blue Sea*. Wallingford: CABI.

Chen, C.L. (2011) From catching to watching: Moving towards quality assurance of whale/dolphin watching tourism in Taiwan. *Marine Policy* 35, 10–17.

Christiansen, F., Lusseau, D., Stensland, E. and Berggren, P. (2010) Effects of tourist boats on the behaviour of Indo-Pacific bottlenose dolphins off the south coast of Zanzibar. *Endangered Species Research* 11, 91–99.

Cloke, P. and Perkins, H. (2005) Cetacean performance and tourism in Kaikoura, New Zealand. *Environment and Planning D: Society and Space* 23, 903–924.

Constantine, R. (1999) *Effects of Tourism on Marine Mammals in New Zealand*. Science for Conservation No. 106. Wellington: NZ Department of Conservation.

Constantine, R. (2001) Increased avoidance of swimmers by wild bottlenose dolphins (*Tursiops truncatus*) due to long-term exposure to swim-with-dolphin tourism. *Marine Mammal Science* 17 (4), 689–702.

Constantine, R. and Baker, C.S. (1997) *Monitoring the Commercial Swim-with-dolphin Operations in the Bay of Islands*. Science for Conservation No. 56. Wellington: NZ Department of Conservation.

Courbis, S. (2007) Effect of spinner dolphin presence on level of swimmer and vessel activity in Hawaiian bays. *Tourism in Marine Environments* 4, 1–14.

Courbis, S. and Timmel, G. (2009) Effect of vessels and swimmers on behaviour of Hawaiian spinner dolphins in Kealakeakua, Honaunau, and Kauhako bays, Hawaii. *Marine Mammal Science* 25 (2), 430–440.

Creswell, J. (1999) Mixed methods research: Introduction and application. In G.J. Cizek (ed.) *Handbook of Educational Policy* (pp. 455–472). San Diego, CA: Academic Press.

Curnock, M.I., Birtles, R.A. and Valentine, P.S. (2013) Increased use levels, effort, and spatial distribution of tourists swimming with dwarf minke whales at the Great Barrier Reef. *Tourism in Marine Environments* 9 (1–2), 5–17.

Curtin, S. (2006) Swimming with dolphins: A phenomenological exploration of tourist recollections. *International Journal of Tourism Research* 8, 301–315.

Delfour, F. (2007) Hawaiian spinner dolphins and the growing dolphin watching activity in Oahu. *Journal of the Marine Biological Association of the UK* 87, 109–112.

Desmond, J. (1999) *Staging Tourism: Bodies on Display from Waikiki to Sea World*. Chicago, IL: University of Chicago Press.

Dudzinski, K. and Frohoff, T. (2008) *Dolphin Mysteries – Unlocking the Secrets of Communication*. New Haven, CT: Yale University Press.

Duffus, D.A. and Dearden, P. (1990) Non-consumptive wildlife-oriented recreation: A conceptual framework. *Biological Conservation* 53, 213–231.

Evernden, N. (1992) *The Social Creation of Nature*. Baltimore, MD: John Hopkins.

Evernden, N. (1999) *The Natural Alien: Humankind and Environment* (2nd edn). Toronto, ON: University of Toronto Press.

Evernden, N. (2008) Nature in industrial society. In S. Armstrong and R. Botzler (eds) *The Animal Ethics Reader* (pp. 191–200). London: Continuum.

Finkler, W. and Higham, J (2004) The human dimensions of whale watching: An analysis based on viewing platforms. *Human Dimensions of Wildlife* 9, 103–117.

Frohoff, T. and Peterson, B. (eds) (2003) *Between Species: Celebrating the Dolphin Human Bond*. San Francisco, CA: Sierra Club Books.

Fudge, E. (2002) *Animal*. London: Reaktion Books.

Garrod, B. (2008) Marine wildlife tourism and ethics. In J. Higham and M. Lück (eds) *Marine Wildlife and Tourism Management* (pp. 257–271). Cambridge, MA: CABI.

Hahm, J. (2004) Assessing the impact of movies upon an individual's image formation concerning a given destination. Unpublished Master's thesis, Rosen College of Hospitality Management at the University of Central Florida Orlando, FL.

Howes, L., Scarpaci, C. and Parsons, E.C.M. (2012) Ineffectiveness of a marine sanctuary zone to protect burrunan dolphins (*Tursiops australis* sp. nov.) from commercial tourism in Port Phillip Bay, Australia. *Journal of Ecotourism* 11 (3), 188–201.

Hoyt, E. (2001) *Whale Watching 2001: Worldwide Tourism Numbers, Expenditures, and Expanding Socioeconomic Benefits*. Yarmouth Port, MA: International Fund for Animal Welfare.

Hoyt, E. (2003) Toward a new ethic for watching dolphins and whales. In T. Frohoff and B. Peterson (eds) *Between Species – Celebrating the Dolphin–Human Bond* (pp. 168–177). San Francisco, CA: Sierra Club Books.

Hu, W., Boehle, K., Cox, L. and Pan, M. (2009) Economic values of dolphin excursions in Hawaii: A stated choice analysis. *Marine Resource Economics* 24, 61–76.

Hughes, P. (2001) Animals, values and tourism structural shifts in UK dolphin tourism provision. *Tourism Management* 22, 321–329.

Janik, V.M. and Thompson, P.T. (1996) Changes in surfacing patterns of bottlenose dolphins in response to boat traffic. *Marine Mammal Science* 12 (4), 597–602.

Jensen, F.H. (2009) Acoustic behaviour of bottlenose dolphins and pilot whales. Doctoral dissertation, University of Aarhus, Denmark.

Keeley, B. (2002) Eye gaze information-processing theory: A case study in primate cognitive neuroethology. In M. Bekoff, C. Allen and G. Burghardt (eds) *The Cognitive Animal* (pp. 443–450). Cambridge, MA: Bradford Books/MIT Press.

Lemieux, L. (2009) *Rekindling the Waters: The Truth about Swimming with Dolphins*. Leicester: Troubador Publishing.

Livingston, J.A. (1994) *Rogue Primate*. Toronto, ON: Key Porter Books.

Louv, R. (2008) *Last Child in the Woods: Saving our Children from Nature Deficit Disorder*. Chapel Hill, NC: Algonquin Books.

Lück, M. (2003) Environmental education on marine mammal tours as agent for conservation – but do tourists want to be educated? *Ocean & Coastal Management* 46 (9–10), 943–956.

Lundquist, D., Gemmell, N.J. and Würsig, B. (2012) Behavioural responses of dusky dolphin groups (*Lagenorhynchus obscurus*) to tour vessels off Kaikoura, New Zealand. *PLoS ONE* 7 (7), e41969; doi:10.1371/journal.pone.0041969.

Lusseau, D. (2008) Understanding the impacts of noise on marine mammals. In J.E.S. Higham and M. Lück (eds) *Marine Wildlife and Tourism Management: Insights from the Natural and Social Sciences* (pp. 206–218). Wallingford: CABI.

Lusseau, D. and Higham, J.E.S. (2004) Managing the impacts of dolphin-based tourism through the definition of critical habitats: The case of bottlenose dolphins (*Tursiops spp.*) in Doubtful Sound, New Zealand. *Tourism Management* 25, 657–667.

Lusseau, D., Slooten, L. and Currey, R.J. (2006) Unsustainable dolphin-watching tourism in Fiordland, New Zealand. *Tourism in Marine Environment* 3, 173–178.

Martinez, E. and Orams, M. (2009) Kia angi puku to hoe i te wai: Ocean noise and tourism. *Proceedings of CMT 2009, 6th International Congress on Coastal and Marine Tourism*, 23–26 June, Nelson Mandela Bay, South Africa (pp. 211–224).

Montgomery, S. (2003) Dance of the dolphin. In T. Frohoff and B. Peterson (eds) *Between Species – Celebrating the Dolphin–Human Bond* (pp. 110–123). San Francisco, CA: Sierra Club Books.

Notarbartolo-di-sciara, G., Hanafy, M., Fouda, M.M., Afifi, A. and Costa, M. (2009) Spinner dolphin (*Stenella longirostris*) resting habitat in Samadai Reef (Egypt, Red Sea) protected through tourism management. *Journal of the Marine Biological Association of the United Kingdom* 89 (1), 211–216.

Nowacek, D., Wells, R.S. and Solow, A.R. (2001) Short-term effects of boat traffic on bottlenose dolphins (*Tursiops truncates*) in Sarasota Bay, Florida. *Marine Mammal Science* 17, 673–688.

Ocean, J. (1997) *Dolphins into the Future.* Kailua, HI: Dolphin Connection.

Olmert, M.D. (2009) *Made For Each Other: The Biology of the Human–Animal Bond.* Cambridge, MA: Da Capo Press.

Orams, M. (1995) Development and management of a wild dolphin feeding programme at Tangalooma, Australia. *Aquatic Mammals* 21 (2), 39–51.

Orams, M. (1997) Historical accounts of human–dolphin interaction and recent developments in wild dolphin based tourism in Australasia. *Tourism Management* 18 (5), 317–326.

Ostman-Lind, J., Driscoll-Lind, A. and Rickards, S. (2004) *Delphinid Abundance, Distribution and Habitat Use off the Western Coast of the Island of Hawaii.* Administrative Report No. LJ-04-02C. San Diego, CA: Southwest Fisheries Science Center.

Samuels, A., Bejder, L. and Heinrich, S. (2000) *A Review of the Literature Pertaining to Swimming with Wild Dolphins.* Contract Number T74463123. Bethesda, MD: Marine Mammal Commission.

Scheer, M. (2010) Review of self-initiated behaviours of free-ranging cetaceans directed towards human swimmers and waders during open water encounters. *Interaction Studies* 11 (3), 442–466.

Semeniuk, C., Haider, W., Beardmore, B. and Rothley, K.D. (2009) A multi-attribute trade-off approach for advancing the management of marine wildlife tourism: A quantitative assessment of heterogeneous visitor preferences. *Aquatic Conservation: Marine and Freshwater Ecosystems* 19, 194–208.

Shani, A. and Pizam, A. (2008) Towards an ethical framework for animal-based attractions. *International Journal of Contemporary Hospitality Management* 20 (6), 679–693.

Stockin, K.A., Lusseau, D., Binedell, V., Wiseman, N. and Orams, M.B. (2008) Tourism affects the behavioural budget of the common dolphin *Delphinus* sp. in the Hauraki Gulf, New Zealand. *Marine Ecology Progress Series* 355, 287–295.

Taylor, S. (2003) *Souls in the Sea: Dolphins, Whales, and Human Destiny.* Berkeley, CA: North Atlantic Books.

Urry, J. (1990) *The Tourist Gaze: Leisure and Travel in Contemporary Societies*. London: Sage.

Warkentin, T. (2007) Captive imaginations: Affordances for ethics, agency and knowledge-making in whale–human encounters. Unpublished doctoral dissertation, York University, Toronto.

Wiener, C. (2013) Friendly or dangerous waters? Understanding dolphin swim tourism encounters. *Annals of Leisure Research* 16 (11), 55–71.

Wiener, C.S. (2014) Understanding spinner dolphin marine tourism and human perceptions in Hawaii: A social approach to assessing underwater interactions. Draft unpublished doctoral dissertation, York University, Toronto.

Wiener, C.S., Needham, M.D. and Wilkinson, P.F. (2009) Hawaii's real life marine park: Interpretation and impacts of commercial marine tourism in the Hawaiian Islands. *Current Issues in Tourism* 12 (5), 489–504.

Williams, R., Trites, A. and Bain, D.E. (2002) Behavioural response of killer whales (*Orcinus orca*) to whale-watching boats: Opportunistic observations and experimental approaches. *Journal of Zoology* 256, 255–270.

Wursig, B. and Wursig, M. (2003) Being with dolphins. In T. Frohoff and B. Peterson (eds) *Between Species – Celebrating the Dolphin–Human Bond* (pp. 49–55). San Francisco, CA: Sierra Club Books.

Zeppel, H. and Muloin, S. (2008) Conservation and education benefits of interpretation on marine wildlife tours. *Tourism in Marine Environments* 5, 215–227.

10 Young Elephants in Thai Tourism: A Fatal Attraction

Erik Cohen

Introduction

The role of young animals in tourism has been little studied, despite its problematic character. Viewing young wild animals is a valued tourist experience (Farber & Hall, 2007); tourists often enjoy touching or cuddling pups or cubs of wild animals. However, that fondness may be detrimental to the animals' health and wellbeing, for reasons of which the tourists might well be unaware. Young animals 'may be particularly sensitive to stressors' (Wright *et al.*, 2007: 251), and might find human touch stressful. Kovacs and Innes (1990) indeed report that when tourists approached or touched young harp seal pups, these animals frequently exhibited a freeze response. But the fondness of tourists for young animals may have wider unanticipated ramifications for the welfare of the young animals, and even for the future of particular species. This chapter deals with those ramifications in an extended case study of the capture, treatment and display of young elephants in Thailand. I shall focus on the contradiction between the fondness of both locals and tourists for young elephants, and its fatal consequences for the animals themselves. I shall show specifically how that fondness was made use of by individual keepers and tourist establishments to exploit young elephants, and how the Thai social and legal context facilitated that exploitation, irrespective of its appalling consequences for the young animals or even for the survival of the species in the wild.

Elephants in Contemporary Thailand

Elephants suffer from a contradictory predicament in contemporary Thailand. Traditionally highly respected and valued animals, domestic elephants have served as beasts of burden in peace and fighting machines in times of war (Cohen, 2008; Warren, 1998), but they have lost both roles in modern times and have become, as Sukpanich (2000:1) succinctly put it, 'a lumbering troublesome ornament with a huge appetite and no specific function' in the contemporary Thai economy. Modernisation of the armed forces and of the transportation system reduced the need for elephants in the army and the rural economy; the logging prohibition of 1989 formally abolished the last important role of the elephants, the dragging of logs from the forest for the timber industry (Kanwanich, 1998).

With no employment for their elephants at home, the mahouts (elephant keepers) started to roam with them in the streets of Bangkok and other cities to beg for food (Cohen, 2008; Lohanan, 2002) or rented them out to entrepreneurs, who took them to the streets of tourist centres (Chadwick, 2005); this became 'so lucrative in Bangkok and Pattaya that the entrepreneurs ... are sometimes referred to as "elephant lords"' (Chadwick, 2005: 107), but had a detrimental effect on the animals, particularly the young ones. Early separation from their mothers impairs the young elephants' health: being denied their mothers' milk, they tend to develop bone diseases, which are a major cause of premature death (Atthakor, 2000; Hutasingh, 2002). Since locals as well as tourists particularly enjoyed feeding young elephants, keepers kept them for many hours on the streets, which further affected their wellbeing. Lohanan (2002: 231) describes the predicament of young elephants in the urban environment: 'Baby elephants are forced to perform on the street for money. Many of them are separated from their mothers and fed with beer and amphetamines for the entertainment of tourists.'

Elephants were frequently injured in traffic accidents in Bangkok (Bangkok Post, 2010) and caused traffic disturbances (Chadwick, 2005). Following several unsuccessful attempts throughout the early 2000s, in 2010 the urban authorities eventually succeeded in banishing elephants from the city, by imposing drastic fines on both the owners of the elephants and members of the public who fed them (Wancharoen, 2010). Since then elephants have not returned to beg in Bangkok but can still be found in the towns surrounding the capital (Kekule, 2013; Wancharoen, 2010).

However, the major alternative source of employment for elephants gradually became the tourism industry – elephant camps, theme parks and similar establishments, providing elephant rides (Duffy, 2013; Duffy & Moore, 2010) and shows (Cohen, 2008; Fang, 2006; Kontogeorgopoulos, 2009; Schliesinger, 2010; see also Bone & Bone, Chapter 4, this volume). From beast of burden the elephant became a tourist plaything (Cohen, 2008), performing various tricks for the entertainment of tourists, such as playing football (Figure 10.1), throwing darts (Figure 10.2), sitting on a stool (Figure 10.3) or even using a flush toilet. Of the estimated 4000 domestic elephants, about 2300 are presently employed in the tourist industry, in about 135 elephant camps and other tourist establishments (Wipayotin, 2012b), located around major foreign tourism centres such as Bangkok, Pattaya, Chiang Mai and on Phuket. The number of young elephants in those camps is not known, but

Figure 10.1 Young elephants playing football, dressed up in the colours of top European national teams, Samphran Elephant Ground and Zoo, 2006
Photo: Author.

Figure 10.2 Young elephant throwing dart, Nong Nooch Tropical Botanical Garden, Thai Cultural and Elephant Show, 2006
Photo: Author.

most places seek to have at least one young elephant. The bigger camps tend to offer elephant performances (Cohen, 2008); the smaller ones mainly provide elephant rides.

There are still an estimated 3700 wild elephants in Thailand's national parks and wildlife sanctuaries, but their predicament is equally problematic to that of the domestic ones: their numbers are declining and their survival is increasingly threatened (Kekule, 2013) owing to loss of habitat to expanding farmland, poisoning by farmers whose crops they invade

Figure 10.3 Young elephant sitting on stool, Nong Nooch Tropical Botanical Garden, Thai Cultural and Elephant Show, 2006
Photo: Author.

(Bangkok Post, 2013; Sukpanich, 2011), and poaching (Kekule, 2002; Satyaem, 2012). The capture of young elephants is a leading reason for poaching, owing to their great popularity with both foreign and domestic tourists.

Anthropomorphisation

In 2009, the birth of a panda cub in Chiang Mai Zoo provoked an unprecedented public craze, inspiring a mass 'pilgrimage' of domestic visitors to the zoo to see the newborn animal (Cohen, 2010). It was the most striking manifestation of the Thai people's fondness for young animals, which for a while overshadowed their more subdued, but persistent, fondness for young elephants, who are also the favourites of foreign tourists to Thailand.

Newborn elephant calves are commonly referred to as 'babies'. They are said to be playful and 'naughty' (Devakul, 1994), and are often compared to human babies. The managing director of one of the best-known theme parks, the Rose Garden, maintained that 'a baby elephant was like an infant in many ways. They love to be talked to and treated sweetly'

(Sukpisit, 1989: 21). Descriptions of young elephants are often framed in anthropomorphic language. Thus Joachim Schliesinger, who wrote extensively about Thai elephants, attributed to young elephants human discursive capacities, as can be seen from his interpretation of the way in which elephants communicate:

> I witnessed a conversation between two young elephants [in an elephant camp]. Because of a dispute between the camp manager and an elephant owner, a young elephant named Pui, at that time aged 5 years, was not allowed to perform in front of tourists as she usually did at the daily p.m. show. I was sitting on the porch of the owner's hut ... when suddenly something landed with the noise of a bomb on the tin roof of the hut. ... We checked ... and found a coconut shell. A neighbour explained that Pui, who was tied to a post a few meters away, has just used her trunk to ... throw this empty coconut shell on the roof. ... Pui was so angry about not being allowed to perform in the show and not getting her daily banana ration from the spectators that she demonstrated her anger towards her master by throwing the shell.
>
> Half an hour later, a young elephant bull, her best friend, came ... to visit Pui. He had just performed in the daily show. A stunning conversation started between the elephants, with Pui having the first word, and most probably complaining ... that she was not allowed to join the show. The young bull ... listened carefully to what Pui had to say and then took his part in the conversation by telling her what she had missed. During their conversation, both elephants used an intricate variety of sounds. (Schliesinger, 2010: 15–16)

This interpretation of the encounter between two young elephants likens it to a conversation between human children. It creates the impression that the youngsters are eager to participate in the tourist show, and to get rewarded for their performance. Such anthropomorphic interpretations support a common perception of the training of young elephants – be it for work in the logging industry of for performances in tourist settings – as 'schooling', which will prepare them to earn a living as adults, just as it does their human counterparts. Thus Vandalucci (1991: 29) referred to the Forest Industry Organization's (FIO) Young Elephant Training Center in Lampang province in northern Thailand as a 'school', and to the training of baby elephants as the 'kindergarten stage', in which 'students' go to 'classes', where they learn (among other things) how they 'should behave in front of the audience who visit the school'. By erasing the substantive differences between elephant training and human education, anthropomorphisation thus plays a crucial ideological role in masking the often cruel procedures by which the spirit of young elephants is broken, as they are made submissive to the commands of their trainers and mahouts, whether to carry logs or to perform various 'tricks' for a tourist audience.

Breaking-in Young Elephants

Elephants are wild animals; unlike dogs, cattle, horses, donkeys and sheep, they have never been fully domesticated. Hence, not only were elephants freshly captured in the wilderness in the past tamed and trained to make them subservient to humans, but elephant calves, born in captivity, are even at present subjected to breaking-in procedures, usually when they are about three years old. In the past such procedures, conducted by ethnic groups marginal to mainstream society such as the Karen in northern Thailand or the Kui in the country's Northeast (Schliesinger, 2010), were shrouded in secrecy and surrounded by complex magical rituals. They were rarely witnessed by outsiders, whether Thais or Westerners. Representative of such procedures is the *paah jaan* (also spelled *pajan*) ceremony, practised by the Karen people. The ceremony is intended to sever the strong bond between the elephant calf and its mother and to transfer it from the mother to the calf's mahout. In the process, the will of the calf is broken, and it is made docent or, in anthropomorphic language, 'disciplined' (Changyawa, 2002a). The ceremony involves several features which, although 'cruel' by Western standards, have until recently provoked little opposition or criticism.

John Hoskin (1986) was one of the first authors who witnessed the *paah jaan* ceremony in Thailand, though not in a Karen village but at the Young Elephant Training Center in Lampang province. He points out (Hoskin, 1986: 17) that even there it was 'rare to see the ancient *pajan* ceremony which accomplishes the single most difficult job in separating the baby from its mother, an essential step before schooling [of the baby] can begin'. He states that, 'As with humans, elephants begin school at the age of four or five, but the protective parent is reluctant to turn her offspring to the care of a mahout'; hence 'the desired separation can be achieved only by the performance of a magical ritual'. Hoskin describes in some detail the separation ceremony, involving magical spells and prayers 'to the god of the jungle', conducted by a *sa-lah*, a master of ceremony, and by several mahouts, in the course of which the calf is taken into a 'stall' (actually a narrow enclosure or cage; see photograph in Devakul, 1994), in which it will be kept for seven days, as its mahout makes 'friends with it by touching its body and [trying] to sit astride its neck'.

Hoskin's highly sanitised report of the *pajan* ceremony, framed in anthropomorphic terms, left out some of its more cruel features, which had come to light later on. Another reporter described the dramatic moment at which, in the course of the ceremony, 'a spell makes the mother elephant deaf to [her] child's entreaties' as it is led away into the enclosure, 'and she helplessly follows her keeper to a place so far away the loudest tearful call of her child cannot reach' (Vandalucci, 1991: 29). The reporter argues that: 'If this rite seems cruel, it's a must. And the reasons are sound. Firstly to avoid any difficulties from the mother, which may range from mere uncooperativeness to wholesale destruction. Secondly, such a crisis makes it easier to build up a relationship between a mahout and the young elephant.' The cruelty was also implicitly justified by the purpose of the Training Center, as stated by its director, i.e. 'the supply of elephants to government logging units' (Vandalucci, 1991: 29). However, as logging declined following the logging prohibition, the Center's training of young elephants in handling logs increasingly became merely a show for tourists, rather than a preparation for 'real' work in the forests.

A much more detailed report on the cruelties involved in the separation procedure was published some years later by the wildlife photographer Thoswan Devakul (1994: C1). It described the procedure as a harrowing experience, for both the young elephant and the observer, and carried explicit photographs of the calf's stubborn fight to get free, even after its seclusion in the cage. However, 'His actions did more harm than good. The centre's trainer hit him with a nailed bamboo stick on his legs and trunk', and poured holy water on his head, believed to tame him. 'Then came the first iron hook which worked more efficiently than the holy water to calm him.' Visiting the cage some time later, the author noticed that the baby elephant's 'two ears were bathed with blood from wounds made by the hook'. There were 'tears in his eyes and his neck and legs were chained. At the back of the cage was a pile of his droppings mixed with urine.'

Devakul (1994: C1) remarks that 'How much longer he has to be "trained" depends on how quickly he gets used to being manhandled, or "tamed"'. Devakul concludes with the crucial observation that 'I suddenly realized that behind the scenes of the cute, playful, intelligent and hard-working elephants in sports, tourism, the circus and the timber industry there had always been pain. What makes the elephants so tame is not the food and care they receive from the mahouts, but the fear from pain from iron hooks and the suffering they experience from being separated from their mothers before they are naturally ready' (Devakul, 1994: C1). Devakul's claim gained further support a few years later from Trakullertsathien (1996), who quoted Soraida Sarwala, the founder of the Friends of the Asian Elephant Foundation, on the training of young elephants for tourist shows: 'I went to Chayaphum Province and witnessed the training processes there. The trainer places hot steel on the young elephant's right hip to make him move left, and at his left hip to make him move right. The tourists see the elephant "dance" and it makes them smile and laugh. But the animals are suffering.'

As long as tamed elephants were seen as an important part of the 'traditional' rural way of life, and a crucial power house in the logging industry, the necessity of breaking them in has been taken for granted. The cruelty towards the young animals involved in those procedures was seen as necessary. The reports by the authors of the 1980s still reflect a discourse of humans' unquestioned right of domination over animals. The first cracks in that attitude are already noticeable in Devakul's (1994) report, at a time when young elephants were already trained to perform tricks for the amusement of the audience in tourist establishments. Although the *paah jaan* ceremony had nothing to do with the purposes to which the broken-in young elephants will be put, their consequent deployment in tourism implicitly affected its legitimacy, at a time when concerns regarding animal welfare and rights were increasingly raised on a global scale.

The terms of the discourse of elephant taming in Thailand thus took a sharp turn in 2002, when the animal rights organisation PETA (People for the Ethical Treatment of Animals) released a video, taken by two PETA volunteers during a visit to a Karen village, documenting the cruelties involved in the *paah jaan* separation ceremony. The video catapulted the issue of animal welfare in the training of young elephants, silenced in the discourse of human domination over elephants in the Thai domestic sphere, onto the international level. The narrator in the video said that 'the elephants were trained for heavy labour such as logging, and for trick shows', and explained that: 'Some elephant trainers believe a tough and cruel approach will frighten the baby elephants. Because of that fear, the animals obey to human commands', enabling the 'trainer to tame the elephant completely in only five of six days' (Jinakul *et al.*, 2002: 1). PETA showed the video to representatives of the Thai Embassy in Washington but, as Thai officials seemed uninterested in the matter, launched an 'Abusive Thailand: Elephant Cruelty' campaign in Australia (Changyawa, 2002a), and showed the video to animal protection groups in the United States and other countries (Jinakul *et al.*, 2002).

A representative of PETA, the elephant specialist Jane Garrison (2002), in an open letter to the then Thai Prime Minister Thaksin Shinawatra, drew attention to the 'horrific abuse of baby elephants in Thailand' and complained that 'we have video footage showing baby elephants being "broken" and trained in Thailand for sale to elephant camps, illegal logging and individuals who use them to beg for money on the streets. This footage is incredibly disturbing as it shows terrified baby elephants being dragged from their mothers, confined in wooden cages and tortured.' Garrison pointed out that PETA 'proposed laws to protect these highly endangered animals'. To give teeth to its demands to stop the practice, PETA launched 'a campaign urging holidaymakers to boycott Thailand'.

The unexpected attack by PETA put the Thai authorities in a quandary: by 2002, elephants had become a mainstay of the tourism industry, and young elephants were the major attraction of elephant shows. PETA's action constituted a direct threat to the employment of young elephants in the tourism industry, while its call for a boycott might even have dissuaded some people from visiting Thailand. Beyond that, however, it wrought a crack in the carefully fashioned image of Thailand on the global scene, a fundamental component of Thailand's 'regime of images' (Jackson, 2004). As in other instances of a potential offence to that regime (e.g. Cohen, 2012), the authorities reacted with a campaign that could be best described as damage control.

A representative of FIO's Thai Elephants Conservation Center initially in fact admitted that 'harsh treatment of elephants by villagers and camps was common', explaining that: 'Elephants (to be used for touristic purposes) [parenthesis in original] need to be disciplined', and adding that 'This is difficult at the beginning, and the animals need to be beaten' (Changyawa, 2002a: 2). He received support from some Karen elephant keepers, who interpreted *paah jaan* in cultural terms, as a 'sacred ceremony involving black magic and astrology', necessary to train an elephant to obey basic orders, but 'there is no intentional cruelty involved' (the implicature being that whatever cruelty is deployed was necessary). One keeper pointed out that he would not 'take care of elephants that have not gone through the *paah jaan* ceremony', because it is 'dangerous to deal with undisciplined elephants'; while another posed the rhetorical question, 'I want … those who say we tortured our baby elephants to tell me how to make them obedient if not through the *paah jaan* ceremony?' (Jinakul *et al.*, 2002: 1).

While those responses sought to reroute the controversy back to the discourse of human domination over animals, and justify whatever cruelty the ceremony involved by taken-for-granted human needs, the responses by Thai officials tended to shift responsibility for the cruelty to marginal groups or even to the accusers themselves. The chief of the FIO pointed out that the people in the video were Karen, an ethnic minority group, and not Thai. He claimed that 'Thai mahouts wouldn't do such a thing' (Changyawa, 2002b: 4), while omitting to mention that Karen mahouts have in fact served as trainers in the Young Elephant Training Center, which operated under FIO auspices. The FIO also initiated a hunt 'for the people who abused an animal in a video released by an animal rights group', found an elephant appearing to bear training wounds similar to those of the young elephant in the PETA video, and transferred it for treatment to the organisation's elephant hospital (Changyawa, 2002c: 4). The FIO's director declared that 'FIO would hold a brief elephant training course for Karen elephant owners' in the locality where the wounded elephant was found (Changayawa, 2002c: 4) – even though Karen mahouts had used similar training methods in the FIO's center, as documented earlier by Vandalucci (1991) and Devakul (1994).

But the main strategy of the authorities was to shift the blame for the alleged cruelty to PETA itself or, alternatively, to deny it altogether. In an ingenious 'clarification' as reported in the *Bangkok Post* (2002: 6), the Thai Foreign Ministry accused PETA of being 'bent on hurting the image of Thailand' by choosing 'to trek deep into the forest just to record the image of cruelty inflicted on a young elephant in one isolated and illegal incident', and accused PETA, saying that: 'Instead of quickly notifying the Thai authorities [of the perpetrated cruelty] PETA sought to video-tape the torturing and tormenting of the young elephant. By the very fact that PETA was present openly on the crime scene, PETA directly or indirectly had a part in the suffering of the young elephant.' The Ministry's clarification explains that 'when baby elephants attain a certain age they, in particularly the male calves, can be harmful to their mothers', and invokes an anthropomorphic parallel to the separation of young elephants from their mothers: 'Like [human] children attending kindergarten, baby elephants are brought to elephant camps to be with their peers', thus turning the brutal separation into a humanitarian act towards the animals.

In other instances the authorities sought to discredit the video as a staged fake. Two parliamentary committees conducted their own investigation into the incident and 'turned the case to the National Police Office, which issued a statement saying that "There was no real brutal act against elephants. It was all a total faked-up filming", in which a bucket of liquid that appeared to be blood [was poured] onto the head and legs of the elephant' (Jinakul et al., 2002: 3). The police report even threatened that 'legal action may be taken', although 'the charge remains unclear' (Jinakul et al., 2002: 3). However, the efforts to discredit the video seem to have had little effect; as the chairman of one of the elephant camps pointed out, 'the faking of the paah jaan ceremony has delivered a big blow to the tourism industry, particularly the elephant show business', as numbers of visitors 'dropped significantly after the film was aired' (Jinakul et al., 2002: 3).

However, the PETA video had no lasting impact on the treatment of young elephants for the tourism industry in Thailand. PETA's Director for Captive Animals declared that the organisation 'is very troubled by the failure to prevent the mistreatment of Thai elephants' and observed that 'There has been no serious effort to correct the core problem of exploitation [of elephants] that results in abuse' (Bangkok Post, 2004: 3). But as the decade of the 2010s progressed, the focus of attention of the animal rights activists moved from the training of young elephants to the sources of their supply.

The Procurement of Young Elephants for the Tourism Industry

With the rapid growth of both domestic and international tourism over the course of the 2010s, the number of elephant camps and other establishments featuring elephants grew rapidly, and with it the demand for elephants (Sukpanich, 2009: 4). Young elephants in particular are highly sought (Sukpanich, 2009: 5), being the star performers in elephant shows and 'a big hit with tourists' (Murray, 2004: 61), as they are easier to train to perform tricks than adult elephants (Sukpanich, 2009; Trakullertsathien, 1996). Paradoxically, although Thai domestic elephants were generally considered to be underemployed, the supply of calves from the natural reproduction of domestic elephants became insufficient to satisfy the expanding demand (Wiek, 2012). This created an incentive for poachers to capture young wild elephants in the remaining wildernesses of Thailand to be sold to camps or to individuals for begging in the streets. As Sukpanich (2009: 4), who has been following the fate of Thai elephants for many years, reports: 'With a diminishing supply of domesticated elephants, more and more wild elephants are being hunted, contributing greatly to their decline.' The captured young are then fraudulently registered and given identity certificates as the off-spring of domestic animals (Sukpanich, 2009).

Such prevarication is facilitated by loopholes in Thailand's antiquated elephant laws: 'Domestic and wild elephants in Thailand are covered under 18 laws and four ministerial regulations, leading to confusion and contra-dictions in their application' (Inchukul, 1994: 18). By an act of 1939, 'ele-phants were classified as … draught animals.… The Act required all domestic elephants to be registered with the Local Administration Department when they were eight years old.' However, 'wild elephants were later offered protection … under the Wildlife Conservation Act' (Inchukul, 1994: 18). The late registration age for domestic elephants was claimed to provide 'a legal loophole which puts baby wild elephants at risk of being kidnapped from their mother in the jungle, and subsequently reg-istered as domestic draught animals when they turn eight' (Inchukul, 1994: 18). At that age, 'it is hard to prove whether [the elephants] were really born from domesticated parents or captured in the wild and then domesticated' (Salwala, 2006). Hence, 'young elephants aged from two to seven years are commonly captured from the wild and trained, then regis-tered and certified when they turn eight years old with the claim that they were born in captivity' (Sukpanich, 2009: 5).

Wiek (2012: 13A) noted that 'The value of young elephants at camps nationwide has soared because not enough babies are being born in captivity to meet the demand'. Prices of young elephants increased rapidly over the early 2000s. In 2002 it was estimated that an elephant calf was worth as much as 250,000 baht (approx. US$8,300) (Hutasingh, 2002). By 2007 the price had doubled: a young elephant was estimated at about 500,000 baht (approx. US$16,700) (Deboonme, 2007). By 2012 the price had almost doubled again, and reached up to 900,000 baht (approx. US$30,000) (Wiek, 2012). But prices are not uniform: 'The younger the [elephants] are, the more expensive, because they can generate [more] income for their owner. Females are harder to find, so they're more expen-sive' (Thoopkrajae, 2009).

The procurement of young elephants from the wild to elephant camps became a profitable, but complex, smuggling business. It is conducted by smuggling gangs, usually acting on orders from businessmen; they employ elephant poachers, often hunters from a forest-dwelling ethnic group (Sukpanich, 2009), to capture the elephant calves and deliver them to elephant camps with the connivance of local government officials and politicians (Bangkok Post, 2012; Suksai, 2004). Such gangs presently operate mostly in western Thailand. Most baby elephant poaching takes place in the wilderness areas of the region along the mountainous border with Burma (Pollard, 2012; Wangkiat, 2013; Wiek, 2012), particularly in the huge Kaeng Krachan National Park (Bangkok Post, 2013). As work for elephants in Burma is expected to decline drastically with the recently introduced ban on timber exports, Soraida Sarwala recently 'raised concerns that many young elephants might be smuggled [from Burma] into Thailand along the border under the orders of elephant farms' (Wipatayotin, 2013).

Wild elephants live in herds. The bond between a calf and its mother is particularly strong; mothers and other members of the herd fiercely protect the calves against any intruder. The poachers are hence ordinarily forced to kill the mother, and sometimes even other adult members of the herd, in order to capture a calf. Edwin Wiek, the secretary of the Wildlife Friends Foundation Thailand (WFFT) and a renowned wild animal rights activist, describes the process of extraction and transportation of the captured elephant calf from the jungle:

> Baby elephants are being taken out of the jungle in Thailand at any cost [in elephant life]. Mothers are being shot and even their nannies and sub-adult males still with the herd, trying to protect the calves. Poachers who have been interviewed, say it is common to kill up to three elephants to take one baby from the forest. Once a few elephants are killed, the baby elephants stay close to the dead adults while the rest of the herd usually runs for safety. Poachers then have limited time to get the baby out, fearing the return of the herd and or any witnesses attracted by the sound of gunshots.... Once the babies have been taken away from the forest, they are moved to 'safe houses' in border areas controlled by corrupt politicians, government officials and influential businessmen. Here the young are tamed through week-long torture rituals [i.e. the *paah jaan* ceremony] to break their spirit. In many cases they are then introduced to a 'foster mother,' a captive [domesticated] female elephant. This introduction is particularly important for the future transportation of the [baby] elephant out of areas controlled by the criminals' since they can be said 'to be the offspring of the captive (legally owned) older female'. (Wiek, 2012: 13A)

Wiek claims that the poachers 'will receive about 300,000 baht [approx. US$10,000] for baby elephants', so 'the profit [of the smuggling] gangs is huge, with elephant camps paying up to 900,000 baht [approx. US$30,000]. . . . Aside from some "costs" such as bribing officials on the way, they can make up to 500,000 baht [approx. US$16,700] per [baby] elephant' (Wiek, 2012: 13A).

In 2012 animal rights activists alleged that 'up to half of the young tuskers in Thailand have been smuggled in [from Burma and Thai national parks] alongside "fake" surrogate mothers that already have identity papers' (Pollard, 2012: 13A). However, 'The government's response to these allegations was to hit back at the two key accusers by raiding [animal rescue] centers that they operate' (Pollard, 2012: 13A). As in the case of the *paah jaan* ceremony, the authorities turned against the whistle-blowers. As Pollard (2012: 13A) points out: 'some elephant parks are run by business people with money and influence. They have a lot to lose. And tourism chiefs may also fear a backlash if tourists decide they don't want to visit elephant camps with "captive" babies made docile and compliant by a violent "breaking of their spirit" by mahouts.'

Nevertheless, 2012 the national parks authorities have begun raiding elephant camps in quest of smuggled young elephants, and have confiscated some elephants without proper identification documents (Wipatayotin, 2012a). However, their action soon encountered resistance: a group of elephant park owners threatened to 'block major roads with their jumbos if wildlife officials continue to seize animals from private shelters' and a local politician, claiming to represent the elephant parks, 'said that the group would . . . petition [the] Prime Minister . . . to dismiss the [National Parks] department chief, for alleged misconduct involving the confiscation of elephants from private shelters' (Wipatayotin, 2012a: 4).

The chief of the National Parks Department was not dismissed as demanded (Pongrai & Sarnsamak, 2012), but retired in September 2012 (Wipatayotin, 2012c). Under the new department chief the raids on elephant camps were renewed. In the course of 2013 the police seized a total of 26 undocumented elephants from camps in several provinces – considered the biggest seizure ever (Bangkok Post Online, 2013). But considering the number of young elephants smuggled into the camps, estimated by one activist minimally at 100 annually (Wiek, 2012), this only scratches the surface of the problem. To deal more effectively with the issue, a change in the antiquated elephant laws was proposed, according to which the legal distinction between domestic and wild elephants would be abolished, and all the animals would fall under the jurisdiction of the Department of National Parks. The new law would allow wildlife authorities better control over elephant poaching. However, the proposed change immediately incited massive opposition among elephant camp owners, who worried that their undocumented animals might be confiscated (Sukpanich, 2013). As they 'threatened to bring 100 elephants to surround Government House [in Bangkok]', the authorities relented and consented to 'negotiate with the owners and formed a new committee to revise the draft [of the law]' (Kongrut, 2013).

Conclusions

The fondness of the Thai people and foreign tourists for young elephants is a fatal attraction – since it indirectly and inadvertently causes suffering and even death to the much-loved animals. But that conjecture has only penetrated slowly into the public sphere, and is even at present only partially recognised. As long as domestic elephants were perceived as 'cattle', needed by humans for work and warfare, their taming, training and employment was taken for granted within a broader discourse of human domination over animals. The ingrained cultural premises, in both the ethnic minorities dealing directly with elephants and in wider Thai society, have allotted no 'voice' to the animals. The tendency to anthropomorphically liken young elephants to children and their taming and training to 'schooling' helped inadvertently to make the cruelty involved in these practices acceptable to the broader public.

No wonder then that, when outsider activists introduced the discourse of animal rights and welfare into the Thai public sphere, they met with incomprehension by the representatives of the elephant training establishments, who claimed that the alleged 'cruelty' in taming young elephants is part of an ancient tradition, even as the higher authorities sought, somewhat disingenuously, to deny the exercise of any cruelty in the taming of young elephants, and condemned the allegations of cruelty as vicious recriminations. However, the activists' allegations of cruelty in the taming process would not be granted much attention if they did not bear indirectly upon the tourist industry, which employed growing numbers of young elephants in tourist shows.

The continued popularity of those shows was predicated upon a thorough segregation between the public display of young elephants, apparently eagerly performing various tricks, and the painful methods deployed in their training. This was facilitated by the spatial separation between the two activities: the taming took place in secluded localities to which outsiders had little, if any, access. Unlike the case of the 'Tiger Temple', no volunteers, who could directly observe and then disclose the methods used (Cohen, 2013), were present at the taming and training sessions. This is why the video taken by some PETA volunteers who witnessed a *paah jaan* ceremony caused such a sensation: it threatened the carefully maintained boundary between the front and the back stages in the taming, training and presentation of young elephants in tourist shows.

However, as the attention of animal rights activists turned from the treatment of young elephants to their procurement, the breaching of a different boundary was highlighted: the distinction between domestic and wild elephants. While the cruelty deployed in the taming and training of young domestic elephants affected the image of Thailand, it was not considered illegal, but the poaching of wild elephant babies and fraudulently documenting them as domestic was a crime. Even as they turned against the whistle-blowers as troublemakers, the authorities started to take steps against those illegal activities. However, owing to the fierce opposition on part of the camp owners, they failed in their attempt to put elephant ownership on a new legal basis. As a deepening political crisis gripped the nation's attention, the fate of young elephants came off the public agenda.

Acknowledgement

Thanks are due to David Fennell of Brock University for his comments on an earlier draft of this chapter.

References

Atthakor, P. (2000) Baby elephants not fit for shows. *Bangkok Post*, 20 December, p. 4.

Bangkok Post (2002) Thai ministry counters PETA's claims. *Bangkok Post, Perspective*, 15 December, p. 6.

Bangkok Post (2004) Enforcement needed to stop abuse. *Bangkok Post, Perspective*, 20 June, p. 3.

Bangkok Post (2010) Rescuing a proud symbol. *Bangkok Post*, 18 September, p. 8.

Bangkok Post (2012) Elephants in need of help. *Bangkok Post*, 17 March, p. 8.

Bangkok Post (2013) The problem with elephants. *Bangkok Post*, 5 April, p. 9.

Bangkok Post Online (2013) 16 illegal elephants seized from tourist areas. *Bangkok Post Online*. See www.bangkokpost.com/news/local/365776/police-swoop-illegal-elephants (accessed 21 August 2004).

Chadwick, D.H. (2005) Thailand's urban giants. *National Geographic* 208 (4), 98–117.

Changyawa, P. (2002a) Animal rights group urges tourist boycott. *Bangkok Post*, 16 October, p. 2.

Changyawa, P. (2002b) Link to torture video denied. *Bangkok Post*, 19 October, p. 4.

Changyawa, P. (2002c) FIO finds abused elephant. *Bangkok Post*, 28 October, p. 4.

Cohen, E. (2008) The Thai elephant: From beasts of burden to tourist plaything. In E. Cohen, *Explorations in Thai Tourism* (pp. 135–179). Bingley: Emerald.

Cohen, E. (2010) Panda and elephant – contesting animal icons in Thai tourism. *Journal of Tourism and Cultural Change* 8 (3), 154–171.

Cohen, E. (2012) Fetuses in a Thai temple as chaotic irruption and public embarrassment. *Asian Anthropology* 11, 1–20.

Cohen, E. (2013) 'Buddhist compassion' and 'animal abuse' in Thailand's Tiger Temple. *Society and Animals* 21 (3), 266–283.

Deboonme, A. (2007) Jumbo love. *The Nation* [Bangkok], 9 April, p. 3D.

Devakul, M.L.T. (1994) Taming the wild. *The Nation* [Bangkok], 18 January, p. C1.

Duffy, R. (2013) The international political economy of tourism and the neoliberalization of nature: Challenges posed by selling close interactions with animals. *Review of International Political Economy* 20 (3), 605–626.

Duffy, R. and Moore, L. (2010) Neoliberalizing nature? Elephant-back tourism in Thailand and Botswana. *Antipodes* 42 (3), 742–766.

Fang, S. (2006) *Thai Elephants: Tourism Ambassadors of Thailand*. Chiang Mai: Fang S.T. Samuel.

Farber, M.E. and Hall, T.E. (2007) Emotions and environment: Visitors' extraordinary experiences along the Dalton Highway in Alaska. *Journal of Leisure Research* 39 (2), 248–270.

Garrison, J. (2002) Letter to PM Thaksin on the abuse of baby elephants in Thailand. *The Nation* [Bangkok], 31 October, p. 6A.

Hoskin, J. (1986) The time an elephant has to forget its mum. *Bangkok Post*, 22 June, p. 17.

Hutasingh, O. (2002) Ayutthaya's nursery gives jumbos hope. *Bangkok Post*, 17 March, p. 2.

Inchukul, K. (1994) Beasts of burden: The rights of elephants. *Bangkok Post*, 29 May, p. 18.

Jackson, P. (2004) The Thai regime of images. *Sojourn: Journal of Social Issues in Southeast Asia* 2, 181–218.

Jinakul, S., Charasdamrong, P. and Kanwanich, S. (2002) The memory of elephants. *Bangkok Post, Perspective*, 15 December, pp. 1, 3.

Kanwanich, S. (1998) Jobless giants. *Bangkok Post*, 3 May, pp. 1, 8.

Kekule, L.B. (2002) Killing for cash. *Bangkok Post, Outlook*, 16 December, pp. 1, 8.

Kekule, L.B. (2013) A dying breed. *Bangkok Post, Life*, 31 July, p. 12.

Kongrut, A. (2013) Jumbo problems. *Bangkok Post, Life*, 6 November, p. 12.

Kontogeorgopoulos, N. (2009) Wildlife tourism in semi-captive settings: A study of elephant camps in northern Thailand. *Current Issues in Tourism* 12 (5–6), 229–249.

Kovacs, K.M. and Innes, S. (1990) The impact of tourism on harp seals (*Phoca groenlandica*) in the Gulf of St. Lawrence, Canada. *Applied Animal Behaviour Science* 26 (1), 15–26.

Lohanan, R. (2002) The elephant situation in Thailand and a plea for cooperation. *Giants on Our Hands; Proceedings of the International Workshop on the Domesticated Asian Elephant*. Bangkok: Food and Agriculture Organization of the UN.

Murray, S. (2004) Saving the elephants. *Fah Thai* 13 (6), 60–66.

Pollard, J. (2012) Furore intensifies over elephant trade in Thailand. *The Nation* [Bangkok], 12 March, p. 13A.

Pongrai, J. and Sarnsamak, P. (2012) National parks chief faces transfer. *The Nation*, 1 August.

Salwala, S. (2006) Elephant's true friend. *Bangkok Post*, 23 July, p. 3.

Satyaem, Ch. (2012) Suspected elephant killers caught. *Bangkok Post*, 19 February, p. 3.

Schliesinger, J. (2010) *Elephants in Thailand. Vol. 1: Mahouts and their Cultures Today.* Bangkok: White Lotus.

Sukpanich, T. (2000) At the mercy of man. *Bangkok Post, Perspective*, April, p. 1.

Sukpanich, T. (2009) Hunted in the wild. *Bangkok Post, Spectrum*, 8 March, pp. 3–5.

Sukpanich, T. (2011) Jumbo dilemma. *Bangkok Post, Spectrum*, 31 April, pp. 3–5.

Sukpanich, T. (2013) Beasts of burden. *Bangkok Post, Spectrum*, 27 October, pp. 8–9.

Sukpisit, S. (1989) '*Riak kwan chang*' ceremony: The blessing of a newborn elephant. *Bangkok Post*, 9 September, p. 21.

Suksai, S. (2004) Alarm as trade in calves grows. *Bangkok Post*, 1 July, p. 6.

Thoopkrajae, V. (2009) One jumbo job finished. *The Nation* [Bangkok], 24 December, p. 4B.

Trakullertsathien, Ch. (1996) National icon on the brink of extinction. *Bangkok Post*, 10 May, p. 36.

Vandalucci, V. (1991) New kids on the logs. *Bangkok Post*, 3 February, pp. 29, 38.

Wancharoen, S. (2010) Residents face B10,000 fine for feeding elephant. *Bangkok Post*, 10 July, p. 2.

Wangkiat, P. (2013) Chaiwat says jumbo deaths a conspiracy by officials. *Bangkok Post*, 20 April, p. 2.

Warren, W. (1998) *The Elephant in Thai Life and Legend*. Bangkok: Monsoon Editions.

Wiek, E. (2012) Thai elephants are being killed for tourist dollars. *The Nation* [Bangkok], 24 January, p. 13A.

Wipatayotin, A. (2012a) Elephant operators threaten blockade. *Bangkok Post*, 1 March, p. 4.

Wipatayotin, A. (2012b) State agencies vow better safety for jumbos. *Bangkok Post*, 13 March, p. 5.

Wipatayotin, A. (2012c) New dept chief opens door to compromise. *Bangkok Post*, 20 December, p. 1.

Wipatayotin, A. (2013) Timber ban sparks jumbo trading fears. *Bangkok Post*, 23 October, p. 4.

Wright, A.J., Soto, N.A., Baldwin, A.L., *et al.* (2007) Anthropogenic noises a stressor in animals: A multidisciplinary perspective. *International Journal of Comparative Psychology* 20, 250–273.

11 Drama Over Large Carnivores: Performing Wildlife Tourism in a Controversial Space

Outi Ratamäki and Taru Peltola

Introduction

Large carnivores, brown bears, lynx, wolverines, eagles and wolves have a new role in Finland – they have become business partners with entrepreneurs who run small nature tourism businesses. These controversial animals, admired as symbols of wilderness and hated as rogues, are part of the rural transformation and reshaping of human economic relations. This has not taken place without friction. On the contrary, the new role for these animals has provoked a debate on what kinds of human–wildlife relations are appropriate. In addition, this debate has led to a set of questions related to what sort of lifestyles and ways of making a living have a right to prosper in the remote, rural areas of Finland.

We explore these tensions in terms of the 'politics of belonging' (Lavau, 2011; Lien, 2005). By this, we mean the questions, choices and negotiations of what constitutes rural life and appropriate human–wildlife relations. Eastern Finland's remote rural landscapes, which form the stage for these activities, have gone through a major restructuring of livelihoods and lifestyles (Rannikko, 1999). The traditional rural lifestyle of this region, based on the combination of small-scale agriculture and forest work, has disappeared along with the mechanisation of forestry and the restructuring of farming, and has been replaced by what sociologist Pertti Rannikko (2008) calls a 'drop-by rurality'. As a place for recreation, the rural has a new role and identity in society.

Wildlife tourism is part of this post-productivist development and transformation of rural space. Yet it has been reported as having both positive and negative ecological, economic and sociocultural consequences (Buckley, 2004). Conflicts arise not only between recreation and other forms of land use, but also between various forms of recreation and tourism (Bunce, 1994; Butler *et al.*, 1998; Kauppila, 2007; Puhakka *et al.*, 2009; Roberts & Hall, 2001; Urry, 1995).

Against these broader developments, we explore how remote rurality is negotiated through the performances of belonging and 'not-belonging' in a case study of Erä-Eero, a small nature tourism enterprise in Eastern Finland. The business is run by its sole proprietor, Eero Kortelainen. We analyse Eero's practices of place-making, that is, how he prepares the rural space for touristic consumption, negotiates with landowners, local residents and hunters and arranges relations between humans and animals. Through these practices, he attempts to facilitate tourists' attachment to the place, while simultaneously coordinating and regulating the movements of other actors. In addition, we also analyse how the actors challenge these attachments and arrangements. For Erä-Eero, earning the right to make a living in a place is thus by no means self-evident but an effect of constantly making, reordering and unmaking interactions that enable or disable particular naturecultures.

Performing Human–Wildlife Relations in a Tourism Space

Many scholars have aligned together the concepts of performance and tourism (e.g. Coleman & Crang, 2002a; Edensor, 2001, 2007; Lacy & Douglass, 2002; Olsen, 2002). Performativity of tourism means that the aesthetic, social, cultural and physical organisation of the tourist space suggests particular touristic activities (Edensor, 2001). At the same time, the routines of tourism create and maintain the social and material organisation of a space. This mutual enactment of a tourism act, occurring within a particular environmental and societal setting, also constitutes tourism as a phenomenon. Taking a photograph of an animal, for example, is not a singular, isolated event. It is part of the process of making and maintaining the tourism industry (Edensor, 2000). Similarly, entrepreneurs, when introducing their practice to visitors, are not only talking about their business, but simultaneously making it real (Diamond, 1996). Through this making, tourism routines and practices also become attached to the various societal contexts in which they take place. After a trip, when a tourist explains his/her experiences to friends and family, s/he is not only describing things; s/he is also remaking the tourism experience and relocating it (Coleman & Crang, 2002b).

This approach puts a focus on the practices that ultimately constitute tourism. Coleman and Crang (2002b) explain that tourism is not only about a tourist going to a place to see something. Tourism is a practice in which the tourist and the natural and social environments are co-produced. Together, the tourist and the environment create the space for, and the experience of, tourism. Further, Coleman and Crang (2002b: 10) state: 'We want to open

up the possibilities of understanding tourism as an event that is about mobil-
ising and reconfiguring spaces and places, bringing them into new constella-
tions and therefore transforming them.'

Coleman and Crang (2002b: 6) stress that local cultures have always been
both conscious and reflexive in the process of continuous becoming, rather
than being. The same applies to the notions of 'authentic nature' (Lavau,
2011), which often form a resource for nature tourism. The actors in tourism,
the tourists themselves and the operators, are often not aware of the performativity of their actions. Tourists may, for example, create a reason for the
locals and entrepreneurs to maintain, reconstitute and negotiate their local
culture and practices (Lacy & Douglass, 2002). On the other hand, performances can also be used as political tools in very conscious ways (Langellier,
1999; Morison & Macleod, 2013). For example, particular public wildlife discourses can be used as a resource in touristic storytelling (see Taylor, 2006 for
a discussion about discursive resources). What is particularly interesting in our
case study is how the tourists, the operator and other related actors also live,
experience and make real their wildlife attitudes and beliefs while participating in this storytelling.

Performances are not, however, only discursive. They are a combination
of existing material and discursive resources (Crouch, 2002; Lloyd, 1999;
Morison & Macleod, 2013). For example, a touristic space can be performed
by the physical configuration of the space that welcomes and suggests particular activities. Similarly, human–wildlife relations are made real through
the practical arrangements that make the animals viewable. The everyday
routines perform a particular version of naturecultures, organising the relationship between society and nature, humans and non-human animals as
well as ideas about that relationship. This idea arises from a theoretical perspective that acknowledges the multiplicity of reality (Mol, 2002) and that
the reality is enacted rather than pre-existing (Hinchliffe, 2007; Lavau, 2011;
Lien & Law, 2011).

In the following, we analyse the wildlife tourism business as a performance of belonging, through which it claims space and the right to prosper
for the naturecultures that emerge from its socio-material practices. The recognition of the multiplicity of co-existing realities enables us to view the
inherent contradictions not as contradictions of thinking, but as overlapping
ways of configuring and arranging things, people, animals and their stories.

The Case Study of Erä-Eero

The wildlife tourism operator Erä-Eero provides multiple recreational services including hiking, canoeing and rock climbing, but the most special
activity offered is photographing large carnivores, in particular the wolverine, from a hide. The presence of wolverines differentiates Erä-Eero from

other similar enterprises. This is one of the few places in the world where this rare animal can be photographed in the wild.

Our research data consist of three separate interview and observation rounds. The first visit to the location was carried out by one of the authors when she visited Erä-Eero as a customer in the spring of 2010, spending one night in a hide. At this time, the entrepreneur did not know that the visitor was a researcher. During the second visit, in the summer of 2011, the entrepreneur was approached by both of us as researchers. This visit included a long interview aided by illustrative maps of the place. The interview themes included questions about the enterprise, its marketing and customers, as well as the entrepreneur's relations to other local and regional actors and their cooperation. Furthermore, a lot of time was spent discussing the ecological and material conditions of the business. During this visit, it was also possible to see how the entrepreneur welcomed foreign visitors. We were able to assist him by preparing sandwiches and by doing the dishes. A third round of interviews was conducted during the summer of 2012 when actors related to the Erä-Eeros' activities were interviewed. These included: two local residents and private landowners; two local hunters; the executive director of the local game management association; the park superintendent of Metsähallitus (a state enterprise that administers state-owned land and water areas); a public health inspector; a local veterinarian; the financial manager and forest manager of the local parish (a landowner); and the sales director of Karelia Expert Tourist Service (a tourist bureau).

In the following sections, we analyse how the actors manage, maintain and create practices, possibilities and constraints among themselves and between humans and wildlife. We address the significant distinctions produced by the routines, practices and accounts of using and being in the rural landscape and their interrelations. These distinctions are a means to invoke accounts of what kinds of rural naturecultures are welcome and what kinds are not.

Performances of Belonging

Presenting the place

Erä-Eero is located in a very remote corner of the easternmost province of North Karelia, Finland, close to the Russian border. It is a small wonder that a tourist ever finds their way to this remote, boggy area. Heading towards it, the roads get narrower – the paved roads become gravel roads. The two authors were even misled by the GPS to take a wrong forest road. There are no permanent human residents there except for two neighbours. How can a place like this be made attractive and accessible to tourists?

Erä-Eero's website has a number of photographs illustrating the location and the possibilities for different activities (Figure 11.1). Pictures work well

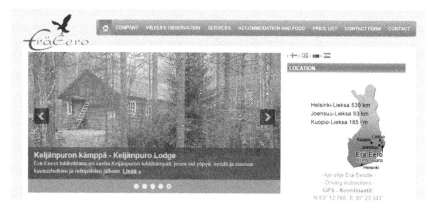

Figure 11.1 Front page of Erä-Eero's website, www.eraeero.com/

for communication, but illustrative texts are still required to better lure the tourist. The business is presented in four different languages (Finnish, English, Russian and Spanish); this makes it possible for visitors outside Finland to approach the place. The multi-language website is a means of connecting the place and the business with the outside world. These connections are important in configuring the place for touristic consumption.

The practices of presenting a business can be understood as place-making. They attach new meanings to a place, connecting it with the needs and hopes of potential visitors. Another example of such place-making is provided by the practices of promotion. Eero, the entrepreneur, has tried to build a network of cooperation around his business. Recently, the local hotels and other tourism businesses found a shared interest with him. For example, the superintendent of Metsähallitus stated that the Erä-Eero enterprise brought added value to their marketing of the natural parks and other recreational services in the region. If tourists ask what they can do in the area, it is good advertising for the region to be able to offer something as exciting as viewing and photographing large carnivores.

The responsibility of marketing Erä-Eero is increasingly shifting from Eero himself to a collective of regional enterprises. The role of Karelia Expert Tourist Service is important in advancing these cooperative opportunities. However, the sales director admits that the time she can dedicate to a single enterprise is very limited. Instead of creating a strong individual profile for Erä-Eero, she advertises Erä-Eero's services within a larger 'service package'. These choices and practices influence what sort of tourists will be attracted. Wildlife tourism operators may themselves choose highly specialised marketing strategies. Through selective marketing, they are able to build connections to the target groups, for example, British bird enthusiasts, that best suit their business profile. Erä-Eero's strategy is different. Eero's business is not based on offering tourists highly specialised expertise on specific animals but, rather, he sells the possibility of experiencing Finnish wildlife. This experience is intimately tied to the specific location and its history.

Practices of representation do not only refer to text and speech, but also to the physical configuration of the rural landscape. En route to Erä-Eero, one drives along a beautiful sandy ridge through scenery decorated by lakes and pine forest. Upon reaching Erä-Eero, the traveller faces a semi-natural court-yard and old-looking wooden buildings. There is neither electricity nor water or a sewer system. Erä-Eero has participated in designing the location by either relocating pre-existing buildings or constructing appropriate new ones. One can find a smoke sauna, huts and outdoor toilets. A brook runs through the location so you can start your canoeing on site. The main building, which in the early 20th century served as quarters for loggers, now welcomes visitors. Classified as a heritage building, it also has facilities for visitors to dine and sleep in a very original atmosphere.

The landscape and the physical infrastructure underline the transforma-tion from productivism to post-productivism that the place has gone through. At the same time, their design presents the business as part of a long, and at least to some extent romanticised, continuum of using the remote wilderness areas. In this way, the configuration of the landscape and location is a performance of belonging – the business is claiming a right to exist in the wilderness by connecting with the history of the place. It is also manifest in the name of the business: 'erä' refers to the ancient traditions and skills of making one's living in the wilderness. However, Erä-Eero also dis-tinguishes its business from the traditional consumptive use of wildlife. Eero has decorated the place with wildlife-related objects, such as binoculars, pic-tures and books. These objects make it impossible to confuse the place with a hunting hut, often decorated with animal skins and trophies. The place welcomes those who want to observe the animals and who are interested in their ecology and life.

The hides are located some kilometres from the 'headquarters' on rental land (Figure 11.2). One, constructed on a slope, is a fairly large double-bar-relled log house with different spaces reserved for photographing and sleep-ing. Toilet facilities are also available. The swamp area, where the carnivores come to eat the carcasses, is located below the hide. The carcasses are used to lure the animals into the open space so they can be more easily viewed and photographed. The landscape behind the swamp is a dense old spruce forest, part of Natura 2000, a European ecological network of protected areas. There are three other hides, not as sophisticated when compared to the log house; they are on the ground level for better photography opportunities. The hides enable Erä-Eero to receive both professional and non-professional photographers. Some visitors only want to watch; even families with chil-dren may visit. The infrastructure maintenance is costly and ultimately affects the price of the service, but it is what makes the wildlife accessible to the various different groups.

Figure 11.2 The hides from which wildlife such as wolverines can be observed
Photos: Outi Ratamäki.

While we visited Erä-Eero, a middle-aged couple from France arrived and Eero and his nature guide welcomed them. The couple had visited other similar businesses further north, and had come to Erä-Eero to see wolverines. The nature guide was essential for the couple's experience since Eero does not speak French or English. The guide, Eero's part-time employee, described the practicalities to the visitors. While this communicative challenge might add to the touristic experience and emphasise the rurality of the location, the sales director of Karelia Expert Tourist Service sees it as a problem. She describes how effective it would be if the entrepreneur could personally communicate with the customers – not only at the location, but also in every possible marketing situation. The language issue is at the heart of different performances of belonging. The tourist service aims to perform a modern rurality with an international profile, one in which Erä-Eero has difficulty making its place.

Setting the scene, performing legitimacy

Eero spends a lot of time and effort in educating all the visitors about proper behaviour in the hides. You have to be very silent; whispering is the only proper way to communicate and you must avoid excessive walking. One's own food and drink are not allowed. Long pipes from the hides deliver the scent of humans high up in the air. This is one precaution against the wildlife becoming familiarised to human presence. Only Eero is allowed to walk in the photographing area and he wears rubber gloves when placing the carcasses. This careful manoeuvring is needed to persuade Eero's business partners (that is, the predators) to perform their share of the touristic experience: without the animals there would be no tourists (Figure 11.3).

The business is based on using carcasses. The wolverine favours fish, and is mostly lured by it, whereas bears are attracted by offal and whole

Figure 11.3 Setting the scene
Photos: Outi Ratamäki (*left*); Taru Peltola (*right*).

carcasses of slaughtered animals (mainly pigs, sometimes horse or moose). Several laws and rules regulate the use of carcasses (Pohja-Mykrä & Kurki, 2009): one needs to have permission from the landowner; there are restrictions as to what kind of animal by-products are allowed as a carcass (e.g. cattle are not allowed); one needs to notify the municipal veterinarian who supervises the operation; and if there is a risk of environmental damage, an environmental permit is required. Also, the collection and storage of carrion is regulated.

The growth of carcass-enabled photographing businesses has not gone without criticism. Eskelinen (2009), Pohja-Mykrä and Kurki (2009) and Suonpää (2002) have studied this business sector in Finland and found that some people fear the practice of keeping carcasses because of the potential danger that wild animals will become too familiarised with humans. Some also express concern that these predatory animals will start associating the smell of humans with easy food. However, this kind of dynamic also may be established by other, more ordinary, everyday practices. For example, careless recycling of compost waste or insufficient waste-storage equipment may accustom bears to feeding on waste disposed by humans (Peltola *et al.*, 2013). Another problem is that there are many unsupervised, illegal carcass sites in the forests. According to Eero, these sites are not only bad for the business but also for the entire reputation of carcass-enabled photographing.

Eero's careful handling of the carcasses and strict instructions for tourists who might not be accustomed to wildlife can be understood as a performance of legitimacy. Although the local parish has rented the land to Erä-Eero, they have many concerns over wildlife tourism. In their personal opinion, the interviewees think it is more valuable to see the wild animal 'in the wild' than at a site where animals are lured with bait. The ideas of wildness can be used in determining belonging (see also Lavau, 2011). Therefore, emphasising the distinction between wildlife that is dependent on humans and wildlife that is genuinely wild can be interpreted as a performance of non-belonging. Also the interview with the Park superintendent of Metsähallitus suggests this: 'The entrepreneur should, indeed, keep in mind not to create any opportunity for anyone to say he is accustoming the bears to humans. He should be very aware of this. Not to give any reason for this kind of talk.' Although his business is dependent on feeding the animals, Erä-Eero needs to regulate feeding and avoid making the animals too dependent on him.

Furthermore, Erä-Eero's practices have been regarded as being risky for people who are unaware of the site and arrive there to pick berries or mushrooms. Employees of the parish, including one of the interviewees, have come across bears in the location. We were also told a story about a woman picking branches to decorate graveyards who, when meeting a bear, became so scared that she lost her way in the woods. Yet the interviewees find it difficult to estimate the influence of Erä-Eero's feeding practice on the frequency of sightings, particularly because the region's bear population is dense. To avoid risk and to increase the legitimacy of the business, Eero has placed signs about the photographing activity (Figure 11.4).

Local hunters have a strong interest in participating in this discussion. They feel that they have been accused of hunting too much of the bear population and thus negatively impacting the success of enterprises such as Erä-Eero. The hunters wish to emphasise their role as game managers working for the state government. The executive director of the local game management association, for example, underscored the distinction between private business interests and public interests: 'Well, he is running a business there [...] Our job is to take care of the assignments given by the ministry. It is a bit different then.' The hunting permits given out by the

Figure 11.4 Signs informing of camera surveillance in the area and the feeding of large carnivores for photographic purposes
Photos: Outi Ratamäki (*left*); Taru Peltola (*right*).

Ministry of Agriculture and Forestry are based on annual population estimates. Another 'public servant' role the hunters have is to assist the police in removing unwanted wild animals roaming too close to housing. The distinction implies that the human–wildlife relationships made real by the wildlife tourism business are not necessarily regarded as appropriate from the public interest perspective. On the other hand, we interviewed two local hunters, who also believed that maintaining hunting pressure in the region upholds the timidity of the bears. In their opinion this helps to sustain the legitimacy of Erä-Eero's business, and thus contribute to Erä-Eero's belonging in the place.

Performing Enclavic Spaces and Community Support

Edensor (2000, 2001) reminds us that performances of touristic space cannot be totally controlled. Tourists and other involved actors employ and approach the space with their attitudes, values, expectations and practices that might create surprises. Eero has realised that he needs to control the tourists and 'outsider' encounters in order to maintain a suitable space for wildlife tourism. Hunters in action and landowners harvesting wood disturb the wildlife tourism performance by giving alternative meanings to the space and by occupying it.

For example, the hunting season for bears starts on 20 August. The local parish, as a landowner, sells hunting permits for their land. Since hunters are not allowed to use carcasses as bait, Eero has agreed to remove all the carcasses, which are attractive to the bears. Otherwise, it would be difficult for the hunters to prove that they have not used the carcass in their hunting. However, Eero continues feeding wolverines and welcoming tourists. Eero has had to negotiate with hunters who have taken up their stand very close to the hides. Not only the presence of people, but also the noise they create by driving vehicles, slamming vehicle doors and using hunting dogs, increases the risk of tourists not seeing any wild animals the following night. After negotiations with Eero, the local hunters have recognised their potential disturbance to the business and agreed that it is not appropriate to hunt close to the hides. However, the executive director of the local game management association reminded us in our interview that they cannot control all hunters and especially not 'tourist hunters' coming from other regions in Finland.

One very concrete way of controlling unexpected encounters is to block the road leading to the hide. The local parish, on whose land the road runs, has not been sympathetic to Eero's attempts to regulate the regional traffic. The parish has also had disputes with Eero about the road's maintenance costs. In Edensor's words, Eero is trying to create and maintain an 'enclavic space' (Edensor, 2000), that is, a single-purpose space. It needs continuous upkeep but, when successfully maintained, an enclavic space minimises ambiguity and contradiction. Enclavic spaces also require policing and monitoring; technological equipment, such as surveillance cameras, may help in this (Figure 11.4). The 'security performance' introduced to the tourists when they arrive to the location also encourages the visitors to self-monitor. The rural location and small number of local residents help Eero in his efforts to maintain control.

Eero has also suggested to the landowner, the local parish, that it suspend any forest management activities and hunting in the surrounding area while he is running his business. This would help him to maintain the wilderness idea. Instead, the rental agreement states that Eero must remove the carcasses before the hunting season, and his suggestion to broaden the 'hunting-free' area surrounding the hides has not been supported. The parish's reason for renting the land in the first place was to be supportive of multiple use of the forests, but it regards one hectare of land as enough space for the tourism activity. The parish representatives feel that Eero does not himself honour the idea of multiple use, but rather is looking at the situation too strongly from the perspective of his own personal needs. In their opinion, Eero cannot be described as a very community-oriented entrepreneur (Borch et al., 2008).

Hallak et al. (2013) introduce the concept of 'enlightened self-interest', which refers to the diverse ways an entrepreneur can support the community surrounding a business, e.g. making donations and organising public events. According to their study, a business offering support to the community correlates positively with the business' success because this behaviour creates a symbiotic relation between the business and the people of the place. Hallak et al. (2013) quote geographer Peter E. Murphy (1983: 181), who considers tourism as a 'resource industry' where 'the industry gives back to the community while extracting a living from it'. However, this support cannot be one-sided. The way the community operates may also attract entrepreneurs to the region. With good cooperation, small enterprises can become catalysts for community development. 'Place attachment' is an important idea behind the analysis of Hallak et al. (2013). An entrepreneur's strong place attachment will positively influence his/her relations with the community; on the other hand, one with a low place attachment may be a reason for the community offering limited support.

Erä-Eero's cooperation with other regional enterprises can be seen as a form of 'community entrepreneurship'. By this we refer to the entrepreneur's attempts to mobilise resources for local development, and to encourage others to be more entrepreneurial (Hallak et al., 2013: 661). Community networks and relations are important in these attempts. Such commitment to the community can be seen as a counter-performance for Eero's very regulative attempts to construct an enclavic space.

Conclusions

The particular arrangements of making wildlife viewable make Erä-Eero's kind of business possible, but they also constitute a space for critical discussion about proper human–wildlife relations in rural areas and, thus, also about the concept of rurality. The ecosystem of our case study area provides plenty of opportunities for nature tourism and also holds some globally specific characteristics. Positive attitudes towards building nature tourism in rural areas can be seen as a performance where productivist spaces are turned into post-productivist spaces. Single entrepreneurs are seen as part of a large, regional entrepreneurial network. However, many everyday encounters create challenges for the entrepreneur, who then has to develop and maintain creative socio-material solutions for these situations. Further challenges are created by the performative ambitions of other social actors who share the same space. This shows that the transition from productivist to post-productivist space is not a straightforward process, but rather a process in which the different practices of place-making overlap, suggesting different belongings.

Landowners, local residents and hunters bring their own nuances to the ambiance of the activities. Due to conflicting beliefs, attitudes and practices, the public debates over large carnivores in Finland cannot be avoided. These actors make their ambitions and values come alive, not only by discursive means, but also by battling over restrictions for land use and 'marking' the landscape with their own signs, e.g. voices, use of vehicles and walking in the area. Erä-Eero struggles with the challenge of creating a tourist-friendly and a credible space for wildlife tourism, while at the same time it has to perform a wildlife-safe space. These performances require balancing between autonomic and collective place-making. Disturbing activities close to the tourist site pose the most relevant threat for breaking the autonomy of wildlife tourism performance. Negotiations with the nearby actors, especially hunters and the parish landowner, have been very challenging for Erä-Eero. Building good community relations has been easier with the broader, 'out-of-place' audience, i.e. other entrepreneurs. It seems that building good community relations is not only about the entrepreneur 'giving' to the community, but also about how to consolidate different ways of place-making.

By looking at tourism practices from the perspective of performativity, we have been able to take into account not only the tourists and the entrepreneurs, but also other actors, including their needs and values, and we have been able to analyse the power relations between these actors. Furthermore, this approach has encouraged us not to forget the meaning of the material and ecological spaces where all of this takes place. Animals are not just objects of viewing and photographing; they are also active participants in the making of this specific type of tourism. As with any other participant, they can be influenced, but not totally controlled. Performing a space where animals can be seen requires constant effort and a routine to maintain a particular kind of human–animal relationship. Yet the tourism business cannot focus only on the interactions between the tourists and the animals; performances of touristic space always take place in relation to other, co-existing realities performed through the everyday practices of other social actors. Approaching tourism as a performative practice enables the identification of the routines, rhythms and scales of these co-existing naturecultures, which intersect and produce overlapping arrangements between things, people, animals and their stories. This, we hope, may provide keys to resolving tensions between them.

Acknowledgements

This work was supported by the Academy of Finland under Grant No. 251341.

References

Borch, O.J., Førde, A., Rønning, L., Vestrum, I.K. and Alsos, G.A. (2008) Resource configuration and creative practices of community entrepreneurs. *Journal of Enterprising Communities: People and Places in the Global Economy* 2 (2), 100–123.

Buckley, R. (ed.) (2004) *Environmental Impacts of Ecotourism*. Wallingford: CABI.

Bunce, M. (1994) *The Countryside Ideal. Anglo-American Images of Landscape*. London: Routledge.

Butler, R., Hall, C.M. and Jenkins, J.M. (1998) Introduction. In R. Butler, C.M. Hall and J.M. Jenkins (eds) *Tourism and Recreation in Rural Areas* (pp. 3–16). Chichester: John Wiley.

Coleman, S. and Crang, M. (eds) (2002a) *Tourism. Between Place and Performance*. New York and Oxford: Berghahn Books.

Coleman, S. and Crang, M. (2002b) Grounded tourists, travelling theory. In S. Coleman, and M. Crang (eds) *Tourism. Between Place and Performance* (pp. 1–17). New York and Oxford: Berghahn Books.

Crouch, D. (2002) Surrounded by place. Embodied encounters. In S. Coleman and M. Crang (eds) *Tourism. Between Place and Performance* (pp. 207–218). New York and Oxford: Berghahn Books.

Diamond, E. (1996) Introduction. In E. Diamond (ed.) *Performance and Cultural Politics* (pp. 1–12). New York: Routledge.

Edensor, T. (2000) Staging tourism. Tourists as performers. *Annals of Tourism Research* 27 (2), 322–344.

Edensor, T. (2001) Performing tourism, staging tourism. *Tourist Studies* 1 (1), 59–81.

Edensor, T. (2007) Mundane mobilities, performances and spaces of tourism. *Social and Cultural Geography* 8 (2), 199–215.

Eskelinen, P. (2009) *Karhut elinkeinona – millaisia ovat katselupalveluja tarjoavat yritykset? [Finnish Brown Bear Watching Tourism Entrepreneurship in Numbers]*. Helsinki: Riista- ja kalatalouden tutkimuslaitos.

Hallak, R., Brown, G. and Lindsay, N.J. (2013) Examining tourism SME owners' place attachment, support for community and business performance: The role of the enlightened self-interest model. *Journal of Sustainable Tourism* 21 (5), 658–678.

Hinchliffe, S. (2007) *Geographies of Nature. Societies, Environments, Ecologies*. London: Sage.

Kauppila, J. (2007) From a forgotten corner to a world famous community conservation success story. Situating the co-management of the Makuleke region of the Kruger National Park, South Africa. Licentiate thesis, University of Tampere, Finland.

Lacy, J.A. and Douglass, W.A. (2002) Beyond authenticity: The meanings and uses of cultural tourism. *Tourist Studies* 2 (1), 5–21.

Langellier, K.M. (1999) Personal narrative, performance, performativity: Two or three things I know for sure. *Text and Performance Quarterly* 19 (2), 125–144.

Lavau, S. (2011) The nature/s of belonging: Performing an authentic Australian river. *Ethnos: Journal of Anthropology* 76 (1), 41–64.

Lien, M. (2005) 'King of fish' or 'feral peril': Tasmanian Atlantic salmon and the politics of belonging. *Environment and Planning D* 23 (5), 659–671.

Lien, M. and Law, J. (2011) 'Emergent aliens': On salmon, nature, and their enactment. *Ethnos: Journal of Anthropology* 76 (1), 65–87.

Lloyd, M. (1999) Performativity, parody, politics. *Theory, Culture & Society* 16 (2), 195–213.

Mol, A. (2002) *The Body Multiple: Ontology in Medical Practice.* Durham, NC: Duke University Press.

Morison, T. and Macleod, C. (2013) A performative-performance analytical approach: Infusing Butlerian theory into the narrative-discursive method. *Qualitative Inquiry* 19 (8), 566–577.

Murphy, P.E. (1983) Tourism as a community industry: An ecological model of tourism development. *Tourism Management* 4 (3), 180–193.

Olsen, K. (2002) Authenticity as a concept in tourism research. The social organization of the experience of authenticity. *Tourist Studies* 2 (2), 159–182.

Peltola, T., Heikkilä, J. and Vepsäläinen, M. (2013) Exploring landscape in-the-making: A case study on the constitutive role of animals in society–nature interactions. *Landscape Research* 38 (4), 461–475.

Pohja-Mykrä, M. and Kurki, S. (2009) *Suurpetojen haaskaruokinnan yhteiskunnallisen kestävyyden haasteet [The Sustainable Social Environment and its Challenges in Carrion Baiting of Large Carnivores].* Seinäjoki: University of Helsinki, Ruralia-Institute.

Puhakka, R., Sarkki, S., Cottrell S.P. and Siikamäki, P. (2009) Local discourses and international initiatives: Sociocultural sustainability of tourism in Oulanka National Park, Finland. *Journal of Sustainable Tourism* 17 (5), 529–549.

Rannikko, P. (1999) Combining social and ecological sustainability in the Nordic forest periphery. *Sociologia Ruralis* 39 (3), 394–410.

Rannikko, P. (2008) Sivakan metsät avoimina ja suljettuina tiloina. In S. Knuuttila and P. Rannikko (eds) *Kylän paikka. Uusia tulkintoja Sivakasta ja Rasimäestä.* Helsinki: Suomalaisen Kirjallisuuden Seura.

Roberts, L. and Hall, D. (eds) (2001) *Rural Tourism and Recreation: Principles to Practice.* Wallingford: CABI.

Suonpää, J. (2002) *Petokuvan raadollisuus. Luontokuvan yhteiskunnallisten merkitysten metsästys [Brutal Reality of Photographing Carnivores. Hunting for the Societal Meanings of Wildlife Photography].* Tampere: Vastapaino.

Taylor, S. (2006) Narrative as construction and discursive resource. *Narrative Inquiry* 16 (1), 94–102.

Urry, J. (1995) *Consuming Places.* London: Routledge.

12 Conflicts Between Cultural Attitudes, Development and Ecotourism: The Case of Bird Watching Tours in Papua New Guinea

David Newsome

Introduction

The island of New Guinea, which comprises Irian Jaya and Papua New Guinea (PNG), is rich in birds. According to Beehler *et al.* (1986), 1 km² of lowland forest can support up to 150 different species including parrots, fruit pigeons, ground pigeons, cassowaries, megapodes and the iconic birds of paradise. The latter group comprises 42 species and these are especially attractive to wildlife enthusiasts and bird watchers because of spectacular courtship displays involving the use of colourful and elongated tail, breast and head feathers. Mating behaviour often involves several males displaying at a favoured site which is attended by females that are attracted to the displaying males.

Birds of paradise have featured in the lives of Papuan people for more than 2000 years (Everett, 1987). Their attraction is related to the intensity of nuptial displays exhibited by courting males. Various species such as Stephanie's astrapia, blue, King of Saxony and Raggiana birds of paradise have been and continue to be, hunted for their tail feathers, breast and head plumes for use in ceremony, festivals and traditional dances (Beehler *et al.*, 1986; Frith & Frith, 2009). Skins of birds of paradise are stored and the trading of plumes is widespread and they may be hired from their owners in exchange for goods and services (Frith & Frith, 2009). Other species such as ground pigeons are hunted for food as well as their plumes and certain species, such as cassowaries, may be captured or taken as eggs for captive rearing. Cassowaries are also hunted for their feathers, quills, claws and meat and feature in Papuan rituals and legends (Folch, 1992).

Over the last few decades the exposure of PNG's birdlife on television documentaries and the rise of international bird watching tourism have introduced a new dimension to the importance of Papuan birdlife. Moss (2009) estimates that at the very least there are now hundreds of thousands of birdwatchers travelling overseas to watch birds. Given the number of countries that are visited, this makes the economic importance of bird watching significant. Steven *et al.* (2013) note that bird watching is a rapidly expanding component of the nature-based tourism industry and that bird watchers will organise travel itineraries to visit sites with high avifaunal biodiversity and travel to see rare and endemic species. PNG contains 725 species of birds, around 80 of which are endemic, including spectacular parrots, bowerbirds, ground pigeons and birds of paradise.

Bird watching tour companies, based in the UK, the USA, South Africa and Australia, market and run bird watching tours to PNG with a view especially to see endemic parrots, crowned pigeons, jewel babblers and birds of paradise. This type of tourism generally does not take place in protected areas as 97% of the land in PNG is, and has been, owned by different families for generations (Van Helden, 2001). Some local communities have seen the potential for diversifying their income and have set up lodges at key locations where bird watchers can stay (Figure 12.1). Kumul Lodge in the

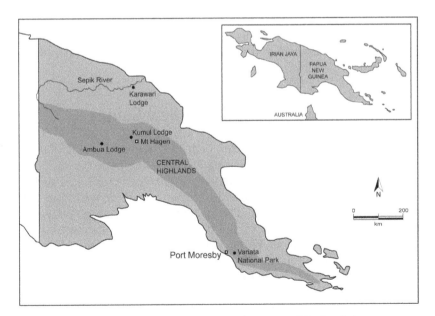

Figure 12.1 Map of Papua New Guinea showing locations of birding lodges
Source: Author.

Mount Hagen area, for example, is now a world famous bird watchers' lodge where clients are able to obtain close views of birds of paradise at a feeding station. Local bird watching guides, most of whom are former hunters, provide guiding services for tourists. Such guides liaise with the foreign tour group leader to maximise species identification and engage in daily excursions into the surrounding environment in order to see and identify different species of birds.

Today bird watching tourism provides income for a significant number of people who are associated with such lodges and who own the land on which the bird watching takes place. What at one level may seem to be a successful and sustainable wildlife tourism operation is, however, troubled by a number of issues such as disputes as to which family owns various parcels of land and arguments over boundaries. Moreover, the deeply engrained culture of hunting larger species of birds, and especially birds of paradise for their feathers, threatens the abundance, population viability and the ability to view many species of birds at close range. In addition to these issues, as the population of PNG grows there is more demand for land and forest resources and consequently areas of forest are cleared to make way for the provision of food crops and areas for living. The central New Guinea highlands, where many birds of paradise occur, extend across altitudes of 1200–2300 m and there is a significant demand for firewood for cooking and heating. Accordingly, the combined impacts of hunting and forest loss are diminishing bird numbers and their habitats (BirdLife International, 2000; Frith & Frith, 2009). The purpose of this chapter is to explore in detail the nature of bird watching tourism in PNG and to consider the threats to this locally important sustainable industry. The chapter also considers what steps can be taken to ensure its viability in the future.

Bird Watching Tourism in Papua New Guinea

As at 2013 there were at least 2000 'high-end' (spending US$10,000+ on the trip) bird watchers per year visiting PNG (Wakra, pers. comm, 2013). Substantial local community benefits via the provision of services such as guiding, accommodation, catering and transport can be derived from such visitors. As previously mentioned, PNG is an increasingly sought after bird watching destination because of the presence of many spectacular and endemic species. Furthermore, bird watching tourism has increased in PNG because of media profiling, the rise of bird watching tour companies and increased access to previously inaccessible areas and cheap travel. Some local communities in PNG have responded to this rising tide of interest in bird watching. Several lodges have been built and over time have become particularly well known and even famous bird watching locations in PNG, for example, Kumul and Ambua Lodges.

Table 12.1 provides an overview of some international tour companies serving bird watching tourism in PNG. Potential clients in Europe, South Africa, USA, Canada and Australia can visit tour company websites that describe the nature of the tour and list targeted birds. Tours generally comprise 7–12 people who have a special interest in birds. Specific birds are on the list of species that can be seen as advertised in tour itineraries (for example, see Birdquest Tours, 2013; Field Guides Birding Tours Worldwide, 2013; Zoothera, 2012). Table 12.2 provides an indicative list of birds that can be seen on various organised bird watching tours. Many of these species can be seen at the world famous Kumul Lodge at Mount Hagen and Ambua Lodge at Tari in the central highlands. Many of the costs involved in a bird watching trip are for the provision of services at the local level and thus the local community is able to profit especially if they own and operate a lodge that is the focal point of bird watching activity.

Table 12.1 Bird watching tour companies operating in Papua New Guinea

Tour company	Sites visited	Reference
Birdquest Tours (2013)	Varirata NP, Kumul and Ambua	www.birdquest-tours.com/Papua-New-Guinea-birding-tours-1/2013
Kirrama Wildlife Tours (2013)	Varirata, Ambua Lodge Kumul Lodge, Tabubil, Kiunga	www.kirrama.com.au/newgui.html
Rockjumper Birding Tours (2013)	Varirata NP, Kumul and Ambua	www.rockjumperbirding.com/tours/destinations/papua-new-guinea
PNG Tourism Promotion Authority (2008)	Kumul, Ambua, Karawari	www.pngtours.com/birding.html
Papua Expeditions (2012)	Arafak Mountains, Baliem Valley, Northern Lowlands	www.bird-watching-papua-adventure-travel.com/papuabirdtours.html
Tropical Birding (2014)	Varirata NP, Kumul and Ambua	www.tropicalbirding.com/australasia-tours/new-guinea/papua-new-guinea/
Victor Emanuel Nature Tours (2013)	Varirata NP, Kumul and Ambua	www.ventbird.com/birding-tour/2013/08/20/papua-new-guinea-highlights
Field Guides Birding Tours Worldwide (2013)	Varirata NP, Kumul and Ambua	http://fieldguides.com/bird-tours/new-guinea
Sicklebill Safaris (2013)	Varirata NP, Kumul and Ambua	http://sicklebillsafaris.com/index.php/about
Zoothera (2012)	Varirata NP, Kumul, Ambua, Makara and Karawari	www.zootherabirding.com/page_2580969.html

Table 12.2 Examples of sought-after species that bird watching tour companies advertise as target species for sightings

Black-billed brushturkey (*Talegalla fuscirostris*)
Gurney's eagle (*Aquila gurneyi*)
Southern crowned pigeon (*Goura scheepmakeri*)
Palm cockatoo (*Probosciger aterrimus*)
Goldie's lorikeet (*Psitteuteles goldiei*)
Black-capped lory (*Lorius lory*)
Brehm's tiger parrot (*Psittacella brehmii*)
Eclectus parrot (*Eclectus roratus*)
Brown-headed paradise kingfisher (*Tanysiptera danae*)
Rufous-bellied kookaburra (*Dacelo gaudichaud*)
Arcbold's bowerbird (*Archboldia papuensis*)
MacGregor's bowerbird (*Amblyornis macgregoriae*)
Loria's satinbird (*Cnemophilus loriae*)
Crested berrypecker (*Paramythia montium*)
Spotted jewel-babbler (*Ptilorrhoa leucosticta*)
Mountain peltops (*Peltops montanus*)
Lesser melampitta (*Melampitta lugubris*)
Lawes's parotia (*Parotia lawesii*)
King of Saxony bird of paradise (*Pteridophora alberti*)
Superb bird of paradise (*Lophorina superba*)
Black sicklebill (*Epimachus fastosus*)
Brown sicklebill (*Epimachus meyeri*)
Black-billed sicklebill (*Drepanornis albertisi*)
Magnificent bird of paradise (*Diphyllodes magnificus*)
King bird of paradise (*Cicinnurus regius*)
Twelve-wired bird of paradise (*Seleucidis melanoleucus*)
Greater bird of paradise (*Paradisaea apoda*)
Raggiana bird of paradise (*Paradisaea raggiana*)
Lesser bird of paradise (*Paradisaea minor*)
Blue bird of paradise (*Paradisaea rudolphi*)
Golden myna (*Mino anais*)

Kumul Lodge (Figure 12.2), for example, may receive tour groups of 8–15 people led by an expatriate who works in conjunction with local guides affiliated with the lodge. The lodge is a community-owned hotel and bird watching service. Kumul Lodge has several guides who are local landowners and who lead the group, provide orientation and facilitate movement along tracks in the forest that is frequently their own land. The guides also know where the birds can be found, help to identify calls and confirm sightings, and

Figure 12.2 View from the main reception area of Kumul Lodge. The line of photographs represents birds which ostensibly can be seen during a stay at the lodge
Photo: Author.

know how to locate (often with the assistance of associated landowners) bird of paradise display trees. Kumul Lodge advertises and promotes the chance of successful sightings of at least eight species of bird of paradise.

Ambua Lodge, comprising 40 roundhouses, opened in 1985 and is owned and operated by Trans-Niugini Tours, a tour company with joint PNG and foreign ownership/investment. The lodge employs some 30 staff including guides, drivers and catering staff. The adjacent forest in which bird watching takes place is locally owned. Ambua, with a bird list of 217 species including 13 birds of paradise, is probably the most highly visited bird watching lodge in PNG (St Louis *et al.*, 2012).

A popular bird watching site that contrasts with the before-mentioned lodges is Variata National Park (for location, see Figure 12.1). It is unusual as it is one of the only government-owned protected areas in PNG. Most bird watching tour companies (Table 12.1) target Variata because of the relative ease of access from Port Moresby and the capacity for reliable sightings of male Raggiana birds of paradise at a regular display site. Given its high profile in the international bird watching web data it is disappointing that the park has been neglected and facilities are run down (Figure 12.3). It is apparent that the park is understaffed and underfunded; that the park was in a poor condition was acknowledged in 2013. The Environment and Conservation Minister was recorded as saying that his department has been underfunded for many years and that there were plans to upgrade facilities such

Figure 12.3 Degraded and abandoned visitor centre facilities at Variata National Park
Photo: Author.

as walking trails (Variata National Park Transformation Plan, 2013). Although statements were made and the intentions are somewhat positive, there remains insufficient funding to upgrade the core facilities at this important national park. This problem is perhaps symptomatic of a failure to recognise the importance of conservation and the relative importance of sustainable tourism in the PNG economy. Furthermore, the aforementioned situation at Variata reflects the findings of Leverinton *et al.* (2010), who found that park facilities in many countries around the world are at risk of such neglect or are already neglected due to inadequate park funding and management capacity.

Sustainability of Bird Watching Tourism in PNG

Following on from the aforementioned observations at Variata National Park, there are a number of ongoing factors that are going to hinder and ultimately prevent the expansion of a viable and sustainable bird watching tourism industry in PNG. Although Kumul Lodge is a highly successful bird watching tourism enterprise, further investigation reveals that there are a number of issues that threaten sustainability. These issues relate to land ownership, the problem of land disputes and the use of land that is owned by the local community.

Bird watching clients staying at Kumul Lodge in 2013 would no doubt have observed a notice inside their rooms. The content of the notice reflects the tenuous local political situation that bird watching tour group providers such as the management of Kumul Lodge and international bird watching companies have to contend with (Figure 12.4). In simple financial terms, 'everyone wants a piece of the action', meaning that when there are good profits to be made within a poor economy many different players seek some way in which they can also benefit from the profits of tourism. The boundaries between differently owned lands are often poorly defined and several different communities may use the same parcel of land. Kinch (2003) notes that past disputes have been associated with the economic value of the land and there are clear implications for tourism business development. Disputes over potential tourism profits are avoided by locating lodges on land that is clearly owned by a particular family group.

Even if land disputes can be avoided, there remain several land use issues that threaten birds, their habitats and the viability of tourism. One of these issues is the cultural use of birds for ceremony and food. Recognising that hunting is a threat to the viability of bird watching, the owners and associates of Kumul Lodge discourage hunting. Several approaches are used, such as, the provision of information and assistance to local schools, on better ways to develop sustainable economies like tourism. Given that the community lives off the land and hunting is a way of life, it is easy to foresee many difficulties.

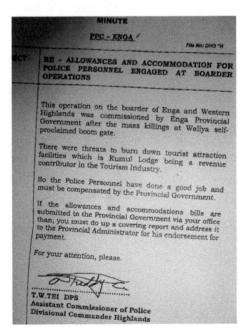

Figure 12.4 Information leaflet posted inside Kumul Lodge accommodation in July 2013
Photo: Author.

For example, many people live in a state of poverty and are dependent on clearing the forest to grow vegetables. There is also the wider issue of deforestation for resources and mineral extraction in the wider political landscape.

Positive aspects in favour of bird watching tourism occur when Kumul Lodge guides undertake tours onto land owned by different people and these landowners are paid per tourist that visits the site. Furthermore, with regard to hunting pressures, nowadays the preservation of feathers used in ceremonies is more effective than it had been in the past, and in the Kumul area there is an increasing trend for using hired and recycled feathers. Because of the economic success of Kumul Lodge, much of the local community is interested in protecting birds, but various individuals still hunt birds of paradise. In addition there remains a continuous demand for timber that is sourced from surrounding forests.

The same issues as indicated above surround Ambua Lodge and are complicated further by road construction, increased traffic volumes and on-shore gas developments. A combination of hunting and timber extraction in and around the Tari Gap area in the central highlands threatens the survival of restricted-range birds of paradise such as the sicklebills (Figure 12.5). The Tari Gap area, served by Ambua Lodge, is promoted as an iconic bird watching site in the online bird watching literature (Table 12.1). At the time of writing, in early 2014, habitat is being lost, hunting continues and more recently there are many trucks, which service an on-shore gas project, passing through the area.

Figure 12.5 Timber being sold by private landowners in the vicinity of Ambua Lodge. This privately owned forest which contains several restricted-range birds of paradise is gradually being depleted of trees for timber and firewood
Photo: Author.

Perhaps a case that strongly illustrates the point about the sustainability of bird watching tourism in the context of hunting can be found at Karawari Lodge on the Sepik River (for location, see Figure 12.1). The lodge is situated among 100,000 ha of riverine lowland forest. Although first impressions from the balcony of the lodge convey a sense of wilderness, some 8000 people live in the forest viewscape, most of them along the banks of the Sepik River. The local economy comprises subsistence living based on forest products and tourism. Previously a lot of hunting activity took place with the use of guns but this practice has now been banned, mainly due to conflicts with tourism and conservation and because of the expense associated with using shotguns. The Victoria crowned pigeon, a target species, is protected by law in PNG, but enforcement with regard to hunting is poor due to the dispersed nature of villages and human activity along the riverbanks and in the adjacent forest (BirdLife International, 2014). Hunting around the lodge is discouraged as it conflicts with bird watching activities and those communities that benefit from tourism tend to reduce hunting pressure.

Birds of paradise are also protected but the hunting pressure remains, with hunters using bows and arrows and slingshots. Populations of the Victoria crowned pigeon have been heavily reduced due to hunting (Figure 12.6). At the same time, it is one of the main species that bird watchers would like to see and is profiled by bird watching tour companies. Attempts to locate and view this bird by a tour group in 2013 failed to record a sighting

Figure 12.6 Captive Victoria Crowned Pigeon at a village situated on the boundary of Karawari Lodge, Sepik River. Birds are often trapped and kept in villages
Photo: Author.

but many traps were found and there was much evidence of feral pigs and the disturbance that they cause. Baptista *et al.* (1997) noted more than a decade ago that despite 'protection' the Victoria crowned pigeon has been significantly depleted due to hunting and was absent from large areas of the forest and around villages in the middle Sepik River.

Hunting as a Problem for Bird Watching Tourism

Beehler *et al.* (1986) noted that hunting pressure is extensive and ongoing, aided by the use of snares, shotguns and bows and arrows. Larger species (ground pigeons, megapodes and cassowary) are taken as a source of protein and birds of paradise (and other species) are taken for their breast plumes, tail feathers and wings. Although it is to be acknowledged that hunting of wildlife is a central part of PNG culture and livelihood, its continuance according to historical and individually desired levels under current sociopolitical conditions, such as poverty and resource development, poses a significant challenge for the sustainability of bird watching tourism into the future. Impacts on wildlife in the past have been low where there have been no commercial demands but today hunting must be viewed in the context of an increasing human population, habitat loss and climate change (Butchart *et al.*, 2010). The available evidence, although data are poor due to a dearth of accurate estimates of bird populations, suggests that continued hunting will continue to deplete populations of birds in PNG (BirdLife International, 2000; Butchart *et al.*, 2010; Frith & Frith, 2009). The depletion of birds due to a continuation of hunting is therefore not likely to be sustainable in terms of a viable bird watching tourism industry. Table 12.3 highlights the role of hunting in depleting the populations of certain species and causing a serious decline in birds that are of high tourism interest.

Baptista *et al.* (1997) report on the decline of western and southern crowned pigeons due to hunting for plumes and food. All three species of crowned pigeon are reported to be highly prized by hunters yet at the same time profiled by bird watching tour companies as birds to see. The dwarf cassowary is rare or absent in many areas due to hunting and the southern cassowary has declined to threatened status due to a combination of hunting and the predation of its eggs by feral pigs (Folch, 1992). The birds of paradise that bird watchers visiting PNG want to see more than any other group are also in decline due to hunting and rapid modernisation; this last factor is one that negates any long-term local interest in sustainability (Frith & Frith, 2009). Especially at risk are those birds of paradise with restricted altitudinal ranges. Adult males of the blue bird of paradise, ribbon-tailed astrapia, Stephanie's astrapia, King of Saxony bird of paradise, black sicklebill and the brown sicklebill are all targeted by hunters and this selective hunting pressure is likely to bring about an imbalance in the population structure with

Table 12.3 Threatened and declining populations of birds in Papua New Guinea and Irian Jaya (West Papua) which are of ecotourism importance

Species	Estimated population	Threats and cause of decline	Conservation measures
Southern cassowary (*Casuarius casuarius*)	>10,000	Hunting in PNG and Irian Jaya. Habitat fragmentation in Australia.	Most remaining populations in Australia confined to protected areas.
Northern cassowary (*Casuarius unappendiculatus*)	2500–10,000	Hunting for meat and feathers. Eggs collected and chicks reared in villages.	None known.
New Guinea harpy eagle (*Harpyopsis novaeguineae*)	2500–10,000	Hunting for tail and flight feathers. Hunting pressure increasing due to the availability of guns and decline also associated with loss of larger mammals due to human hunting.	Present in Crater Mtn Wildlife Management Area and some other protected areas. Protected by law in PNG but this is poorly enforced.
Western crowned pigeon (*Goura cristata*)	2500–10,000	Hunting, capture and trade in live specimens. Degradation and loss of habitat.	Present in a few existing protected areas.
Victoria crowned pigeon (*Goura victoria*)	2500–10,000	Hunting, capture and trade in live specimens. Degradation and loss of habitat.	Protected by law in PNG plus education and research.
Southern crowned pigeon (*Goura scheepmakeri*)	>10,000	Hunting and loss of habitat.	Protected by law in PNG plus education and research.
Pesquet's parrot (*Psittrichas fulgidus*)	42,000	Hunting for feathers. Nestlings captured by felling trees or enlarging nest cavities coupled with scarcity of suitable nest trees. Demand for feathers grows as a result of increasing population and increases in tourist and cultural shows.	None specified.
Fire-maned bowerbird (*Sericulus bakeri*)	2500–10,000	Hunting and loss of habitat.	None specified.

Table 12.3 (Continued)

Species	Estimated population	Threats and cause of decline	Conservation measures
Macgregor's bird of paradise (*Macgregoria pulchra*)	2500–10,000	Hunting and loss of habitat.	Protected by law in PNG and IJ.
Black sicklebill (*Epimachus fastosus*)	2500–10,000	Hunting and loss of habitat. Hunting pressure is increasing as skins become more valuable.	Protected by law.
Wahne's parotia (*Parotia wahnesi*)	2500–10,000	Loss of forest associated with increasing human population.	Protected by law and proposed forest reserves.
Blue bird of paradise (*Paradisaea rudolphi*)	2500–10,000	Hunting and loss of habitat.	Protected by law in PNG.

Source: Derived from BirdLife International (2000).

negative consequences on breeding success resulting in further population declines (Table 12.3; Frith & Frith, 2009).

A curious aspect of this growing endangerment of some species is that some bird watchers set themselves a new baseline in hoping to see some species as they continue to decline or before the birds become extinct (Newsome & Rodger, 2012). At the same time, and in the context of a new baseline of available species that can be seen, while ground pigeons and some birds of paradise are 'written off', bird watchers might continue to visit PNG to see and record the more tolerant and robust species. Even if some natural areas are reserved as protected areas, this may not be a reliable form of protection due to illegal hunting as is the case in many other parts of the world (for example, see Aiyadurai *et al.*, 2010; Corlett, 2009; Primack & Corlett, 2005). In addition to this, where there is hunting pressure, birds are shy and have low visibility making them difficult to find and, as mentioned before, may be totally absent even in the presence of suitable habitat.

Wider Environmental Issues and the Search for Solutions

Beehler *et al.* (1986) indicated that logging, road construction, the opening up of previously inaccessible land, mining and the expansion of permanently cleared areas posed a threat to many species of birds in PNG and Irian Jaya. These problems continue today at an ever-increasing rate (Butchart et al., 2010; Corlett, 2009; Frith & Frith, 2009). The central highlands in particular are subject to loss of habitat because such areas are the most suited to cultivation (Primack & Corlett, 2005). Such loss of important bird habitat is resulting in bird tour companies altering their itineraries. As reported by Tropical Birding (2014), the continued loss of habitat in the Tabubil area of the central highlands is likely to make a preferred bird watching site for certain birds of paradise obsolete.

The demand for land is linked to an increasing population that sits in the context of men sometimes having two to three wives; with a fertility rate of four children per woman there can be up to 10 children in a single family (UNICEF, 2014). Large families necessitate land that can be cleared for agriculture. There is a rising demand for fuelwood and timber is removed from the forest adjacent to a patch of land that a particular family group live on and farm. These population-driven environmental changes are also occurring alongside increasing demands for energy and fuels and associated resource development projects. Moreover, traditional hunting sits within this wider context and the cumulative impact of all these pressures on the environment especially threatens those birds of paradise and other species with limited distributions in the central highland zone.

One answer to the rising problems of land clearing, resource development and hunting pressure might be the designation of protected areas such as national parks. Corlett (2009) notes that Irian Jaya (West Papua) has designated some large protected areas but also observes that much of the 'frontier forest' is rapidly being lost and that the population of this region will have increased to 11 million by 2050. However, the scope for protecting public lands as national parks is different in PNG because of the very high ownership by private landowners/local people. This makes the acquisition of land for conservation and national parks in PNG very difficult (Corlett, 2009; Van Helden, 2001). With 97% of land in PNG under local community ownership, there are 44 protected areas but this comprises only 1.6% of PNG. These areas fall under the categories 'wildlife management areas', 'conservation cooperative societies' and protected natural areas such as Variata National Park (Corlett, 2009).

Given that it is unlikely that government-owned and managed national parks will be gazetted in the sense that they have been in other countries (such as Indonesia, Malaysia and Thailand), the conservation of birds for tourism will be dependent on the interests and will of local landowners such as those who own Ambua and Kumul Lodges. It is apparent, however, that there are ongoing problems associated with land disputes and wider landscape degradation that threaten the success of sustainable bird tourism.

BirdLife International (2000), in recognising the threats posed to birds by hunting and habitat loss, suggest the establishment, expansion and ongoing management of protected areas as a solution to these problems. Such actions can then be enhanced further by the development and application of ecotourism by adding value to the role and purpose of such reserves. A starting point in attempting to achieve more protection for natural areas and develop ecotourism is to design and implement 'big picture' policy directions towards maintaining PNG as a viable bird watching tourism destination in the future.

These directions might take the form of:

(1) The development of a regional tourism framework that takes account of actual and potential future nature-based tourism programmes that are threatened by mining, resource development such as on-shore gas developments and logging activity.
(2) The need to identify additional important tourism areas that require proactive and funded conservation measures to be put into place. Such areas will need to be well-managed protected areas with reliable conservation outcomes.
(3) There is the need for a threat assessment to birds (especially in relation to hunting pressures) and bird watching habitats (loss and fragmentation) of high tourism value.

Such overarching policy development would need funding, staff, training and conservation legislation to be effective. There is still a lot of education work and negotiation that needs to be done at the local level to engage landowners and create the sociopolitical environment for successful bird watching tourism to become part of a broader sustainable economy.

Conclusions

PNG is an iconic bird watching destination that provides the opportunity to see many endemic species as well as the spectacular birds of paradise. In the global context, bird watching tourism continues to expand as a tourism business with an ever-increasing market of wealthy clientele who wish to see exotic birds in overseas locations. The demand for bird watching opportunities in PNG has seen the development of bird watching lodges like Kumul and Ambua. At the local level these lodges have proved to be lucrative enterprises and are now internationally recognised bird watching locations.

Unfortunately, what seem to be highly successful and sustainable tourism enterprises are troubled and threatened in the longer term by a combination of sociocultural, political and environmental issues. Where profits are being made on community-owned land there is the risk of land disputes about derived economic values. The land tenure system in PNG is such that as much as 97% of land is in family/community group ownership and this land is the livelihood and a source of food and materials for the community.

An increasing population is driving further land clearing, especially in the central highlands, and this is resulting in the loss of habitat for many species of birds.

The necessity to live off the land and a deeply ingrained tradition of hunting birds for food and their feathers means that there is ongoing pressure on the populations of many species of birds. Hunting pressure continues to deplete what are considered to be iconic species by bird watchers and it is already, and will become, increasingly difficult to see certain birds as they become rare or are eliminated from certain areas due to the combined impacts of hunting and habitat loss.

These aforementioned pressures are intensified when wider landscape changes, such as road construction and resource extraction projects, are taking place which result in additional forest loss. The loss of natural environments around the world has to some degree been offset by the creation of protected areas such as national parks. Such places, when funded and well managed, can be important conservation reserves and provide for a wide range of nature-based tourism activities. The creation of such reserves in PNG is, however, limited by widespread local community land ownership. Perhaps the only way forward is to recognise these inherent limitations and develop a suite of high-level policy frameworks that can assist in conserving the birds that sustainable nature-based tourism depends upon. Given the poor funding status of the Ministry of Environment and Conservation and the greater priorities given to resource development that holds the promise of people being able to materially improve their lives within a backdrop of widespread poverty and a rising population, this grand vision for successful bird watching tourism is not likely to be realised.

References

Aiyadurai, A., Singh, N. and Milner-Gulland, E.J. (2010) Wildlife hunting by indigenous tribes: A case study from Arunachal Pradesh, Northeast India. *Oryx* 44, 564–572.

Baptista, L.F., Trail, P.W. and Horblit, H.M. (1997) Columbiformes. In J. del Hoyo, A. Elliott and J. Sargatal (eds) *Handbook of the Birds of the World, Vol. 4: Sandgrouse to Cuckoos* (pp 60–243). Barcelona: Lynx Ediciones.

Beehler, B., Pratt, T. and Zimmerman, D. (1986) *Birds of New Guinea*. Princeton, NJ: Princeton University Press.

BirdLife International (2000) *Threatened Birds of the World*. Barcelona and Cambridge: Lynx Ediciones and Birdlife International.

BirdLife International (2014) Species factsheet: Goura victoria. *Birdlife.org*. See www.birdlife.org (accessed 5 December 2013).

Birdquest Tours (2013) *Papua New Guinea Birding Tour*. See www.birdquest-tours.com/Papua-New-Guinea-birding-tours-1/2013 (accessed 5 December 2013).

Butchart, S., Collar, N., Stattersfield, A. and Bennun, L. (2010) Conservation of the world's birds: A view from 2010. In J. del Hoyo, A. Elliott and D.A. Christie (eds) *Handbook of the Birds of the World, Vol. 15: Weavers to New World Warblers* (pp.13–68). Barcelona: Lynx Ediciones.

Corlett, R. (2009) *The Ecology of Tropical East Asia*. Oxford: Oxford University Press.

Everett, M. (1987) *The Birds of Paradise and Bowerbirds*. London: New Burlington Books.
Field Guides Birding Tours Worldwide (2013) *Papua New Guinea Birding Tour*. See http://fieldguides.com/bird-tours/new-guinea (accessed 5 December 2013).
Folch, A. (1992) Struthioniformes. In J. del Hoyo, A. Elliott and J. Sargatal (eds) *Handbook of the Birds of the World, Vol. 1: Ostrich to Ducks* (pp. 76–103). Barcelona: Lynx Ediciones.
Frith, C.B. and Frith, D.W. (2009) Family Paradisaeidae (birds of paradise). In J. del Hoyo, A. Elliott and D.A. Christie (eds) *Handbook of the Birds of the World, Vol. 14: Bush-Shrikes to Old World Sparrows* (pp. 404–492). Barcelona: Lynx Ediciones.
Kinch, J. (2003) *Marine Tenure and Rights to Resources in the Milne Bay Province, Papua New Guinea*. CMT and rights to resources. 2nd Pacific Regional International Association for the Study of Common Property Conference, Brisbane.
Kirrama Wildlife Tours (2013) *Papua New Guinea Bird Tour*. See www.kirrama.com.au/newgui.html (accessed 5 December 2013).
Leverington, F., Costa, K.L., Pavese, H. and Hockings, M. (2010) A global analysis of protected area management effectiveness. *Environmental Management* 46 (5), 685–698.
Moss, S. (2009) Birding past, present and future – a global view. In J. del Hoyo, A. Elliott and D.A. Christie (eds) *Handbook of the Birds of the World, Vol. 14: Bush-shrikes to Old World Sparrows*. Barcelona: Lynx Ediciones.
Newsome, D. and Rodger, K. (2012) Vanishing fauna of tourism interest. In R.H. Lemelin, J. Dawson and E.J. Stewart (eds) *Last Chance Tourism: Adapting Tourism Opportunities in a Changing World* (pp. 55–70). London and New York: Routledge.
Papua Expeditions (2012) *West Papua Birding Expeditions*. See www.bird-watching-papua-adventure-travel.com/papuabirdtours.html (accessed 5 December 2013).
PNG Tourism Promotion Authority (2008) *Birding in Papua New Guinea*. See www.pngtours.com/birding.html (accessed 5 December 2013).
Primack, R.B. and Corlett, R. (2005) *Tropical Rain Forests: An Ecological and Biogeographical Comparison*. Oxford: Blackwell.
Rockjumper Birding Tours (2013) *14 Tours Available in Papua New Guinea*. See www.rockjumperbirding.com/tours/destinations/papua-new-guinea (accessed 5 December 2013).
Sicklebill Safaris (2013) *About Sicklebill Safaris*. See http://sicklebillsafaris.com/index.php/about (accessed 5 December 2013).
Steven, R., Castley, J.G. and Buckley, R.C. (2013) Tourism revenue as a conservation tool for threatened birds in protected areas. *PLoSOne* 8 (5), e62598.
St Louis, R., Bernard Carillet, J. and Starnes, D. (2012) *Lonely Planet Guide to Papua New Guinea and the Solomon Islands*. London: Lonely Planet Publishing.
Tropical Birding (2014) *Papua New Guinea: Paradise Untamed*. See www.tropicalbirding.com/australasia-tours/new-guinea/papua-new-guinea/ (accessed 18 February 2014).
UNICEF (2014) *At a Glance: Papua New Guinea*. See www.unicef.org/infobycountry/papuang_statistics.html (accessed 25 February 2014).
Van Helden, P. (2001) *A Policy and Planning Needs Assessment for the Milne Bay Conservation Project* (PNG/99/G41). Marine Conservation in Milne Bay Province, Papua New Guinea. Copenhagen: UNOPS.
Variata National Park Transformation Plan (2013) See www.youtube.com/watch?v=cqsoSDuKoJo (accessed 9 February 2014).
Victor Emanuel Nature Tours (2013) *Papua New Guinea Highlights: Aug 20–Sep 02, 2013*. See www.ventbird.com/birding-tour/2013/08/20/papua-new-guinea-highlights (accessed 5 December 2013).
Wakra, D. (2013) *Professional Tour Guide, Port Moresby, PNG*.
Zoothera (2012) *Papua New Guinea – An Easy Tour!* See www.zootherabirding.com/page_2580969.html (accessed 5 December 2013).

13 'Eating the Animals You Come to See': Tourists' Meat-eating Discourses in Online Communicative Texts

Muchazondida Mkono

Introduction

In this chapter I examine tourists' online exchanges, and the discourses that are discerned within them, in relation to their meat-eating experiences at a variety of global tourist destinations. In particular, I focus on discourses that reflect their struggle to overcome internal moral/ethical conflict over meat-eating. In the context of wildlife tourism experiences, these tourists acknowledge, in varying ways, the irony of eating the meat of animals they travel to see in the wild. By examining these discourses, I also gain access to tourists' underlying attitudes towards animals. Further, I highlight the role of the internet as a conduit for expressing, sharing and debating reflective thought and experience.

I adopt netnography, a qualitative and interpretive online methodology, thus tapping into a novel medium of communicative behaviour. Such a medium works well within the new 'mobilities' paradigm (Büscher & Urry, 2009; Cresswell, 2011; Elliott & Urry, 2010; Sheller & Urry, 2006; Urry, 2007), which sees the movement of tangible and intangible entities as a defining characteristic of contemporary society. Specifically, the movement of texts within online communities has become a central aspect of contemporary human interactional behaviour.

The study is important for several reasons. First, meat consumption discourses are yet to be studied in depth in the context of tourist behaviours and experience. On a broader level, exploring meat-eating discourses, as Bastian *et al.* (2012) note, provides a novel perspective from which to observe psychological processes associated with everyday moral behaviour. Further, the research is expedient in light of increased consciousness around what we eat, wherein people, especially in developed countries, are learning to ask tough questions about their food choices (Singer & Mason, 2006). In particular, people are becoming more curious about whether animals that provide the meat they eat suffer needlessly (Bulliet, 2005).

Furthermore, the topic of meat-eating acquires increased relevance to tourism research amid calls for non-consumptive forms of wildlife experience, which are viewed as more sustainable than consumptive forms (Mau, 2008; Walpole & Thouless, 2005; Wilson & Tisdell, 2001). While the dichotomy between consumptive and non-consumptive tourism activities remains a contentious one, partly due to a lack of clarity of the meaning of the term 'non-consumptive', it is argued that the former, characterised by direct intervention in an animal's life, in most cases killing it, has undesirable ecological consequences, as it immediately impacts on wildlife numbers (Tremblay, 2001; Wilson & Tisdell, 2001).

Analysing discourses also provides a more nuanced understanding of the data, adding a critical edge to interpretive research on tourist experience (Hannam & Knox, 2005). Discourses capture the complexity of tourists' communicative acts as they have both a linguistic and a socially inspired meaning; language can therefore be seen as a form of social practice (Stamou & Paraskevopoulos, 2004). As such, understanding discourses, premised on an epistemology of plural and subjective truths and realities, is useful for demonstrating the social construction of meanings, perspectives and debates around meat-eating (Gössling & Peeters, 2007).

Human Attitudes Towards Animals

Understanding the range of attitudes towards animals aids in the comprehension of tourists' reflections on their meat-eating behaviours while touring. Research indicates that attitudes shape behaviours and perspectives linked to the humane (or otherwise) treatment of animals (Serpell, 2004). However, attitudes are complex, and structured approaches help to deal with that complexity. For example, Kellert and Berry (1980: 42) identified nine attitudinal dimensions that illustrate the multifaceted nature of human attitudes towards animals. These dimensions are: *naturalistic* (primary interest and affection for wildlife and the outdoors); *dominionistic* (interest in exerting control and mastery over animals, as in sporting situations); *ecologistic* (concern for the environment as a system, for interrelationships between wildlife species and natural habitats); *utilitarian* (concern for the practical and material value of animals or the animals' habitat); *humanistic* (strong affection for individual animals); *moralistic* (concerned with the subjective right and wrong treatment of animals, characterised by strong opposition to exploitation or cruelty towards animals); *scientistic* (formed around the physical attributes and biological functions of animals); *aesthetic* (primary interest in the artistic and symbolic attributes of animals); and *negativistic/neutralistic* (the active or passive avoidance of animals due to indifference, dislike or fear).

Later work proposed simpler scales. For example, Serpell (2004) developed a model of human attitudes to animals that is described by two primary motivational considerations, namely *affect*, which represents people's affective and/or emotional responses to animals, and *utility*, representing people's perceptions of animals' instrumental value. The role of *affect* in particular is receiving increasing interest in studies of tourist experience (for example, Hosany & Gilbert, 2010; Prayag *et al.*, 2013). *Affect* helps us understand, for instance, why certain foods cause particular emotional reactions.

Serpell (2004) argues that animal attributes influence people's affective response towards them. Specifically, animals that are phylogenetically close to humans, or that are physically, behaviourally or cognitively similar to them, tend to evoke more positive affect than those that are phylogenetically distant or dissimilar. Further, those animals that are perceived as 'cute', or otherwise aesthetically appealing or admirable, as well as those that are seen as particularly vulnerable, rare, fragile or sensitive, also tend to be preferred. Serpell (2004) further observes that positive affect is weakest and utility concerns strongest when people are engaged in consumptive or coercive rather than non-consumptive or affectionate interactions with animals. In addition, childhood exposure to affectionate or affiliative relationships with animals, for example in pet keeping, tends to predispose people to develop more positive affect and weaker utility orientations. The obverse appears to apply to individuals exposed to consumptive, coercive or abusive interactions with animals during childhood, although the research is not conclusive (Herzog, 2010; Serpell, 2004). Other factors which have been found to affect attitudes towards animals include individual personality, age, history, religious beliefs, culturally defining practices and cultural representations (Mathews & Herzog, 1997; Serpell, 1996, 2004).

In relation to meat-eating, Joy (2011) suggests that our reactions to meat vary according to our perception of the species of animals from which it came. The variations, she adds, are a result of our *schema*, which refer to psychological frameworks which shape our attitudes, beliefs, ideas, perceptions and experiences (DiMaggio, 1997). Our schema will determine whether we classify an animal as prey, food, pet, pest or predator. This classification in turn determines whether we hunt it, flee from it, exterminate it, love it or eat it (Joy, 2011). Similarly, Herzog (2010) notes that our relationships with animals offer a lens into the quirks of human nature: we love some animals, hate some animals and are ambivalent to others. Thus, individual attitudes towards animals have also been described as highly idiosyncratic (Serpell, 2004).

At societal level, attitudes towards animals have evolved over time. Specifically, Bulliet (2005) argues that attitudes of 'domesticity' have given way to 'post-domesticity'. He describes domesticity as referring to the social, economic and intellectual characteristics of communities in which most members consider daily contact with domestic animals, other than pets, a normal part of life. Post-domesticity, on the other hand, refers to an existence characterised by the physical and psychological distancing of people from the animals that produce foods, even though they may maintain very close relationships with companion animals or pets (Bulliet, 2005; Chou, 2012). Bulliet (2005) argues that domestic society takes the killing of animals for granted, and has few moral qualms about consuming animal products. Post-domestic societies, however, which are growing, especially in the West, are completely immersed in the emotional contradictions inherent in post-domesticity: they find it hard to give up meat, leather and the use of animals in medical and other 'tests', but they are revolted by details of what goes on behind the scenes to provide these goods (Bulliet, 2005; Peters, 2006; Sax, 2009). This reveals a double standard, Bulliet (2005) suggests, in relation to domestic and wild animals.

Meat-eating in Tourism Experience

Food and eating constitute an important part of tourist experience. However, in the case of meat-eating, a paradox arises when tourists venerate and express admiration for the animals they see in the wild yet, ironically, they will also eat the meat of the same animals – this has been termed the 'meat paradox' (Loughnan *et al.*, 2010). It must be emphasised that my intent in engaging with this paradox is not to debate whether eating game meat is ethically/morally/religiously right or wrong, but rather to explore the discourses which surround tourists' experiences of eating meat.

The 'meat paradox' offers a lens through which to understand the nature of cognitive dissonance that occurs when an individual's behaviour and integral beliefs are in conflict or tension. Cognitive dissonance, arising in the context of the meat paradox, is therefore a useful framework for understanding internal conflict linked to human behaviour. However, it has only been minimally applied to tourism theorising in relation to tourist experience, although, as a concept per se, the theory has received a lot of attention in research, since Festinger (1957) first conceptualised it. Festinger argued that where there is perceived inconsistency within an individual's cognition, a negative interpersonal state is generated (dissonance), which in turn motivates the individual to seek and implement a means to alleviate this aversive state (Bastian *et al.*, 2012; Elliot & Devine, 1994; Festinger, 1962). However, the negative affect associated with dissonance is not easily overcome (Bastian *et al.*, 2012).

When behaviours and values are incongruent, to deal with the moral discomfort which ensues, Joy (2011) states, we have three options: we can change our values to match our behaviours; we can alter our behaviours to match our values; or we can change our perception of our behaviours so that they appear to match our values. Through a process of psychic numbing, we can disconnect mentally and emotionally from our experiences. Joy (2011) further suggests that this numbing is a defence mechanism by which we practice avoidance and denial. This mechanism affords us what she terms invisibility, which enables us, in her view, to consume meat without envisioning the animal that we are eating.

Nevertheless, the meat paradox is a complex phenomenon. Its complexity is what makes it a particularly fitting concept for demonstrating that wildlife experiences entail cultural, moral, ethical and historical dilemmas. For example, as Franklin (2006: 226) observes, the brumby (feral horse) 'holds a particular place in Australia's affections, something of a defining place that emerges out of legends, stories, poetry, war times and hard times'. Franklin explains that animals may therefore embody environmental anxiety in a particular moment, a craved-for dinner item in the next, and the object of a hunting trip in yet another moment, highlighting the dilemmas and paradoxes that are part of the ethics of what we eat.

Herzog (2010) believes that the paradoxes that haunt our interactions with animals are a result of the fact that much of our thinking is a product of a combination of instinct, learning, culture, language, intuition and mental shortcuts. The influences on human–animal relations therefore vary with context, so that tourist behaviours in relation to their interactions with animals can only be fully understood when the combination of elements of their individual and collective circumstances are factored in. The issues presented in the ensuing discussion therefore are not a matter of right or wrong, good or bad, but represent instead an acknowledgement of the different standpoints, opinions, experiences and worldviews which operate in any human–animal interaction and, more specifically, in situations where tourists consume meat while travelling.

Methodology

As stated earlier, the study's methodology is netnographic. Netnography involves searching for and analysing online narratives for the purposes of answering specific research questions (Björk & Kauppinen-Räisänen, 2012; Kozinets, 2002). Kozinets (2002: 62) defines netnography as 'ethnography on the Internet'; 'a new qualitative research methodology that adapts ethnographic research techniques to study cultures and communities that are emerging through computer-mediated communications'. Compared to traditional offline qualitative methods, netnography is faster and cheaper (Dwivedi, 2009; Kozinets, 1997, 1998, 2006). Further, it provides access to a virtually global pool of internet user data, as well as typically rich, candid narratives, especially where the data are in the form of user-generated content. These online narratives, like 'visitors' books', constitute 'a rich source of qualitative data by being unsolicited and spontaneous personal narratives' (Stamou & Paraskevopoulos, 2004: 108).

Netnography engages with the mobilities paradigm in useful ways. In an era where the internet is a significant, if not the dominant, medium of communication, the movement of information and ideas in online texts is at the centre of interactive behaviour. It therefore makes sense to deploy methods that engage synergistically with this platform. Unlike with traditional interpretive methodologies, where there is an assumption that connections between people are based on physical propinquity or a 'metaphysics of presence', a mobilities perspective recognises that in contemporary society this is not always the case, as virtual proximity becomes increasingly more relevant to social interaction, characterised by an 'imagined presence' (Büscher & Urry, 2009). Thus a mobilities model, or 'mobilities turn' (Urry, 2003; Wiley & Packer, 2010) challenges sedentarist production of knowledge and, as such, mobilities research encompasses mobility across a wide range of forms, practices, scales, locations and technologies. The mobilities paradigm interrogates the politics of mobility and immobility, the material contexts within which they are embedded, and their representational and non-representational dynamics (Blunt, 2007).

Data generation and analysis

For the study, the netnographic format used was passive and covert. In other words, I did not actively participate in the relevant online forums and I did not disclose my research activity to members of the relevant online communities. This has been described as the *lurker* format (Björk & Kauppinen-Räisänen, 2012; Bowler, 2010; Jawecki & Fuller, 2008; Quinton & Harridge-March, 2010). Given that the data were already in the public domain, and were not of a sensitive nature, it was not necessary to seek individual consent from the individual members whose texts were used in the analysis.

Data were generated from keyword searches on TripAdvisor.com, using combinations of terms related to meat-eating as part of tourism experience, such as 'game meat' and 'eating meat'. The results were printed and read through to identify recurrent themes. The process continued until no new relevant insights could be gleaned from further searches. For rigour, the username of the relevant tourist, the website from which it was extracted and, where available, the provenance of the tourist are provided at the end of each quote given in the presentation and discussion of findings.

Challenges and weaknesses of netnography

The study's methodological weaknesses must be noted. First, as an online methodology, the absence of the face-to-face interface poses challenges in relation to the authenticity of data, particularly in terms of its provenance (for example, the age and nationality of the online participants). Further, in the lurker format adopted in the present study, it is not possible to probe online users for further detail or clarification. However, these limitations do not undermine the rigour of the present study, as its intended outcomes were not contingent on specific details about online participants. The data were also sufficiently rich, for the purposes of the study, to obviate the need for further probing.

A further challenge associated with netnography is the lack of clarity regarding ethical requirements. For example, there is no consensus on the requirement for informed consent. My sentiment is that, unless personal and sensitive data are actively solicited from participants, it is not necessary to seek their consent for texts that are publicly available. As indicated earlier, for the present study, as the texts were already in the public domain and no personal information was solicited from participants, individual consent was not sought. Further, no identifying information is given, apart from online usernames/pseudonyms.

Tourists' Online Exchanges and Discourses

Confronting the meat paradox

It is not surprising that tourists would reflect on their eating behaviours while touring, as food is invariably an important part of tourism experiences. Within that reflection, the relevance of the meat paradox is evident in tourists' exchanges online. For example, a Scottish tourist writes:

> If you have no conscience and fancy eating the creatures you came to Africa to see in the wild, then the Boma is the culinary experience for you. (*Raycarstairs, Scottish tourist, Igougo*)

The role of 'conscience' evoked by the tourist as a conduit for self-reflection points to the psychological impact of meat-eating behaviours and, indeed, any behaviours in which tourists engage. The tourist here suggests that people who possess a conscience (as humans should) would refrain from a culinary experience characterised by eating 'the animals you came to see'. Another tourist, referring to the experience offered by a restaurant which serves African cuisine for lunch and dinner at Disney's Animal Kingdom Villas – Kidani Village in Walt Disney World Resort – notes:

> There is some irony in eating (meat, in my case) while watching wild game. The food and service were great, but the views of wildebeest, zebra and giraffes while eating were a unique experience. The way the animals

are 'caged' in the terrain, with no bars or glass makes for such a free feeling. It's like having dinner on the Animal Kingdom Kilimanjaro experience (without the predators). Also, be prepared to experiment with the cuisine. It's different and delicious. No negatives, except the long walk from the parking deck. (*415SecondStreet, North Carolina, TripAdvisor*)

By highlighting the irony in eating meat while watching wild game, the tourists above explicitly confront the meat paradox. The tourists perceive dissonance between the admiration or even veneration of animals implied in visits to wildlife attractions, and the behaviour of eating these same animals. Tourism in this instance acts as a precipitant of internal conflict of what may otherwise be 'normal' day-to-day food consumption behaviours.

In some tourism experiences, such as the safari, or the Disney experience described above, the degree of cognitive dissonance might be heightened by the immediacy of the connection between live animals tourists travel to see and game meat consumed in tourist restaurants. As such, it is not easy for tourists to disengage mentally from the origins of meat (as would be easier in the case of city restaurants, for instance, where the animals from which the meat comes are distanced from the environment of consumption) in an effort to reduce the dissonance aroused by eating meat. Tourists would then be motivated to find ways of reducing such dissonance, although in their texts it was not clear how they might have sought to accomplish this. In this relation, Bastian *et al.* (2012) found in three studies that this dissonance motivates people to deny minds to animals, when they are reminded of the link between eating meat and animal suffering.

However, tourists' moral/ethical concerns should not be overstated. Indeed, many tourism activities are hedonistic and, as such, it is also no surprise that the majority of tourists' reflections on meat-eating dwelt on their culinary enjoyment of meat, without any express ethical/moral concern, for example:

Cape Town is a city for foodies, and for meat it just doesn't get better than the Husssar Grill. There are several locations, we ate at the Greenpoint location 3 times this visit because it was walking distance to where we were staying. First off, there is no corkage fee. This is great as we bought some terrific wines when visiting Stellenbosch and we could enjoy them for no additional charge. Their Game selection is out of this world – The Kudu melts in your mouth, the escargot is divine, and the beef is delicious. (*Wrldtvlr27, Washington DC, TripAdvisor*)

This restaurant changed owners recently and my wife and I can vouch for the current (as of April 6, 2013) food. The meats in particular are fantastic! Try the ostrich. Or the 'trio of game' – ostrich, kudu and springbok. The meat is delicious and the sauces were amazing as well.

Even the sides were delectable. Large portions. Add a bottle of fine wine and our total was still less than half of what we would have spent in the USA. (*Ori B, San Francisco, TripAdvisor*)

Nonetheless, whether or not tourists enjoy meat with a hedonistic mindset, their texts suggest varying levels of affective attachment to animals, which makes the meat paradox even more apparent. In other words, the meat paradox is clearer when one considers the admiration, and even adulation, of animals, that is a common theme in the majority of tourist texts:

Cute animals.*** Loved it. If you like woodland animals, go see it! (*Californiafamilypv, TripAdvisor*)

San Diego Zoo definitely delivered tons of awesome animals and habitats that make viewing them usually easy with multiple viewing spots if they are hiding. The layout doesn't feel well planned as you have to meander in few places. We loved the tram though that saved us from having to walk back to the front of the zoo. (*Scott L, Minnesota, TripAdvisor*)

The San Diego Zoo is definitely one of the best zoos I've been to. They have some amazing animals and attractions. The Giraffe feeding was our favorite part. (*SS220, Colorado, TripAdvisor*)

In the above texts, animals are described as 'cute', 'outstanding', 'amazing' and 'awesome'. Indeed, discourses on the ethics of eating meat are often constructed around the 'cuteness' of animals. For example, there is continuing criticism in the West of the practice of eating dog meat in some Asian countries (Brandt & Jenks, 2011), because 'dogs are cute' (Begeç, 2012; Beverland et al., 2008; Sherman et al., 2009). Research has shown that 'cuteness' plays an important role in our attitudes towards animals (Herzog, 2010).

Animals are also accorded emotional states such as 'happy' and 'unhappy', which means they are seen as possessing minds and affective capabilities:

I've seen much better zoos, and a major problem with this place is that single and small group animal displays prevail. This is a problem especially for the monkeys, who look very unhappy. We were pretty sure too that the regular double deck noisy buses around the place accounted for why most animals were 'no shows'. (*LPNSW, Australia, TripAdvisor*)

When animals are seen as possessing affective capacity, they are then capable of suffering, a reality that, for some individuals, can lead to the experience of cognitive dissonance. It is clear that tourist reflections involve, on various levels, a negotiation between preferred behaviours and moral cognition. The emergent conflict creates a tension that tourists seem at a loss to resolve. It does not appear that tourists go beyond simply acknowledging such tension, however – resigning themselves to the irony, but not renouncing meat-eating as a result of experiencing dissonance.

Non-meat Eaters and Vegetarian Discourses

Vegetarianism emerged as a recurrent topic of discussion within meat-eating exchanges. Vegetarian discourses are of direct relevance to the meat paradox in that some vegetarians could have been motivated to quit meat-eating precisely as a result of the dissonance between the behaviours of admiration of animals and eating their meat at the same time. One tourist wrote, in response to a question posed by another: 'Anywhere to eat game meat in Kenya?'

> My preference is to see the game alive and kicking on the plains rather than on my plate! (*Tembofan, Somerset, TripAdvisor*)

Other members responded in support of the above:

> Hear hear, Tembo! (*FLFourOneZero, Kenya, TripAdvisor*)

> Totally agree Tembofan I also go to Kenya to see live animals. I personally can't understand why people would want to eat such beautiful creatures, mind you I'm vegetarian. (*Poppyr, Scotland, TripAdvisor*)

The tourist who had originally asked the question was compelled to clarify his position, adding:

> Just as clarification, I wouldn't want to support the slaughter of endangered animals but as a meat-eater I was looking to experience something I've never tried before if it was a (legal) opportunity ... much like when a friend went to northern Canada and tried Moose and Bear. Stuff I can't get in Toronto, Canada! In any case thanks for the advice and the continued source of information! (*Stevenjbull, Toronto, TripAdvisor*)

Divergent attitudes towards animals are especially evident between meat-eaters and non-meat eaters. Non-meat eaters, including elective vegetarians, as in the above quote, often refer to the guilt that comes from taking the life of another creature, which Herzog (2010) also highlights. Such behaviour and consciousness, as Bulliet (2005) argues, are expressions of post-domesticity. In such a social system, Bulliet asserts, the hunting and killing of wild beasts in particular seems worse than unnecessary; it is seen as wanton, excessive, cruel, vicious and primitive (Bulliet, 2005).

Encompassing both affective and utilitarian facets, a complex combination of naturalistic, aesthetic, moralistic and ecologistic considerations, on the part of tourists, can be gleaned from the above communicative exchanges. There are those who emphasise, in their criticism of eating game, the aesthetic qualities of animals in the wild. Also, among tourists who express reservations about eating meat, a 'care ethics' assumption, proposing that we should at least show sympathy to animals, and that such sympathy is morally compulsory (Engster, 2006; Hills, 1993; Serpell, 2004), is apparent. Indeed, Joy (2011) argues that the vast majority of us care about animals, in our different ways. With further information about the different backgrounds of the online users, it would be interesting to examine more closely the individual influences for these attitudes.

It is also notable that even tourists who enjoy eating meat are not unconcerned about other potential implications of their behaviours. Therefore, the source of cognitive dissonance is not limited to the act of eating meat, but the consciousness of the short- and long-term impacts of the activities at the destination. Meat-eating is therefore one of many activities that might be implicated, as the tourists attempt to balance their pleasure-seeking behaviours with a characteristic post-domestic awareness and uneasiness about the consequences of those behaviours.

Endangered Animal Discourses

The 'endangered animals' discourse in the tourist's commentary above is a controversial and widely debated topic among scholars (Dansky, 1999; Wasser *et al.*, 2004). However, the degree of dissonance felt by tourists in the case of consumptive uses of wild animals is likely to be particularly significant, given that many of these, especially in African destinations, are threatened with extinction. Indeed, much of the criticism directed at consumptive tourism practices apply to contexts involving endangered species (Tremblay, 2001). In this relation, one tourist asks:

> Game meat? First, let me say thank you for your help in planning our trip to Botswana and Zimbabwe. As we get closer to our trip (just 3 weeks!), I have a few remaining questions. I have seen some posters mentioning eating game meat during their stay such as warthog. Are these animals raised for their meat? Or, are they wild game that have been shot and killed for their meat? Are there any concerns about the effect of eating game meat on the numbers in the wild? What about concerns about disease transmission from animals to humans (e.g. parasites, viruses – see Nathan Wolfe on TED)? I know my adventuresome husband will be interested in trying game meat if on the menu, but, want to know if I need to say anything in advance. Thanks so much. (*lacontessa1, Maryland, TripAdvisor*)

The tourist above is conscious of the impact of eating game meat on the numbers of animals left in the wild in Zimbabwe and Botswana. On a practical level, it would be useful for the tourist's planning and decision making to have access to information about wildlife management practices at the respective destinations where game is served. It is also notable that tourists might feel accountable for the ecological impact of game meat consumption, even though they do not directly determine the wildlife consumption policies at destinations.

The extent to which someone feels responsible for the ecological impact reflects their ethical framework. This opens up the whole question of ethical tourism: to what extent do people leave their ethics at home and participate in activities out of the norm for them, when they are displaced in time and space?

The endangered species discourse is more complicated when it relates to tourism contexts where bushmeat is a significant component of local diets, as in the case of areas surrounding the Serengeti National Park in Tanzania (Mfunda & Røskaft, 2010). In such contexts, when tourists project their ethical concerns for endangerment of species to local wildlife, this may be in direct confrontation with locals who may seek to consume meat because they feel rightfully entitled to wildlife resources in their local environments. The agency of tourists is clearly limited, but so is the agency of the locals, in terms of the impact of their voices and behaviour on wildlife resource utilisation. However, as has been frequently expressed in tourism studies, it is often that local needs and preferences are sacrificed for the benefits of the commercial tourism industry. The tensions among stakeholders, for instance in environments where meat is consumed by tourists but where locals cannot hunt, make the ethical paradoxes of human–animal interactions in tourism spheres even more glaring.

Therefore, to be rigorous and comprehensive, the meat-eating debate as a part of the endangered species discourse should occur within the larger context of historical, aesthetic, ecological, educational, recreational and scientific considerations of the different stakeholders. Views on animals are contingent on a range of factors, including the context of consumption, the species and its ecological circumstances, as well as on the individual characteristics of the tourist (for example, whether they are vegetarian or not). As Franklin (2006) notes, we move between a variety of viewpoints and discourses on animals and they become different objects in the process. In other words, people draw boundaries for moral concern in relation to their interactions with animals in a motivated, rather than absolute, fashion (Loughnan et al., 2010).

Conclusions

The chapter has explored three discourses in relation to meat-eating behaviours within tourist experience: tourists' direct engagement with the meat paradox; vegetarian standpoints; as well as the concern over endangered species. Within these discourses were located various dilemmas linked to meat-eating, which also help to reveal some of the varying and complicated human attitudes towards animals. In particular, tourist texts point to a struggle of the conscience that accompanied their decision to eat the very animals they marvel at and admire in wildlife experiences. The central point made in the discussion is that the adulation of animals, juxtaposed with the culinary enjoyment of meat, creates a paradox, from which cognitive dissonance results. It was not clear, however, how tourists sought to deal with this dissonance. Also, consistent with Herzog's (2010) assertion, the chapter has shown that our attitudes, behaviours, and relationships with animals are more complicated than we often realise.

The discourses presented in the discussion highlight the need to investigate further the ethics, morals, public reactions and emotions that inform tourist encounters with wildlife. The complexity of these issues can best be tackled with more critically oriented approaches that acknowledge the subjectivities of human experience, sense-making and meaning-making. It is not the eating of meat alone that creates the paradox; other consumptive practices (such as trophy hunting, popular in sub-Saharan Africa), might create the same kind of moral dilemma. These practices could be explored to enhance understanding of the tourist experience, beyond the simplistic hedonist framework. It is legitimate to represent tourists more as morally, culturally, religiously and ecologically reflective agents in the tourism system.

On a methodological level, the discussion has showcased the internet's potency as a communicative and reflective platform – a space within which tourism experience itself inspires introspection and retrospection over day-to-day behaviours such as meat-eating. The ease of exchange of information and viewpoints on the internet has enabled the rapid expansion of online communities, which make the internet a viable fieldwork site for researchers, in its own right. It is, however, surprising that, in the case of meat-eating discussions reported in this chapter, relevant foodservice managers have not engaged with online users, even though sites such as TripAdvisor allow them to respond to users' comments. For instance, where tourists seek information about the impact of serving game meat in restaurants on the numbers of animals in the wild, it might be beneficial for managers to acknowledge and respond to such concerns.

As social science continues to embrace the 'mobilities turn', it is envisaged that methodologies that engage with the movement of texts in virtual space would be increasingly adopted in tourism studies, and in the social sciences in general. The potential to access global datasets, which are not dependent on the physical proximity of users, significantly enhances the scale at which researchers can frame their research approaches. Online media are becoming a core aspect of communicative activities, and research methodologies would do well to reflect that.

Future research could also examine the food security implications of meat-eating, in tourist experience and more broadly. There is potential for research on our relationships with animals to enhance our understanding of the quirks of human cognition and behaviour, especially where the two are not consistent. Furthermore, as society progresses on a post-domestic path, where more and more of us actively question where our food comes from, discourses that might appear relatively trivial might become central in the future. It will be interesting to observe in future how these changes will be reflected in tourist experience and reflections thereof.

References

Bastian, B., Loughnan, S., Haslam, N. and Radke, H.R. (2012) Don't mind meat? The denial of mind to animals used for human consumption. *Personality and Social Psychology Bulletin* 38 (2), 247–256.

Begeç, S. (2012) The use of dogs in defense and security management in Turkey. *Veteriner Fakültesi Dergisi, Uludağ Üniversitesi* 31 (2), 51–61.

Beverland, M.B., Farrelly, F. and Lim, E.A.C. (2008) Exploring the dark side of pet ownership: Status- and control-based pet consumption. *Journal of Business Research* 61 (5), 490–496.

Björk, P. and Kauppinen-Räisänen, H. (2012) A netnographic examination of travelers' online discussions of risks. *Tourism Management Perspectives* 2, 65–71.

Blunt, A. (2007) Cultural geographies of migration: Mobility, transnationality and diaspora. *Progress in Human Geography* 31 (5), 684–694.

Bowler, G.M. (2010) Netnography: A method specifically designed to study cultures and communities online. *Qualitative Report* 15 (5), 1270–1275.

Brandt, A. and Jenks, C. (2011) 'Is it okay to eat a dog in Korea … like China?' Assumptions of national food-eating practices in intercultural interaction. *Language and Intercultural Communication* 11 (1), 41–58.

Bulliet, R.W. (2005) *Hunters, Herders, and Hamburgers: The Past and Future of Human–Animal Relationships*. New York: Columbia University Press.

Büscher, M. and Urry, J. (2009) Mobile methods and the empirical. *European Journal of Social Theory* 12 (1), 99.

Chou, Y. (2012) The changing social meanings of pets and their alternative futures. *Journal of Futures Studies* 17 (2), 1–14.

Cresswell, T. (2011) Mobilities I: Catching up. *Progress in Human Geography* 35 (4), 550–558.

Dansky, S.M. (1999) The CITES 'objective' listing criteria: Are they 'objective' enough to protect the African elephant? *Tulane Law Review* 73, 961–980.

DiMaggio, P. (1997) Culture and cognition. *Annual Review of Sociology* 23 (1), 263–287.

Dwivedi, M. (2009) Online destination image of India: A consumer based perspective. *International Journal of Contemporary Hospitality Management* 21 (2), 226–232.

Elliot, A.J. and Devine, P.G. (1994) On the motivational nature of cognitive dissonance: Dissonance as psychological discomfort. *Journal of Personality and Social Psychology* 67 (3), 382.

Elliott, A. and Urry, J. (2010) *Mobile Lives*. New York: Routledge.

Engster, D. (2006) Care ethics and animal welfare. *Journal of Social Philosophy* 37 (4), 521–536.

Festinger, L. (1957) *A Theory of Cognitive Dissonance*. New York: Row, Peterson & Co.

Festinger, L. (1962) *Cognitive Dissonance*. Redwood City, CA: Stanford University Press.

Franklin, A. (2006) *Animal Nation: The True Story of Animals and Australia*. Sydney: UNSW Press.

Gössling, S. and Peeters, P. (2007) 'It does not harm the environment!' An analysis of industry discourses on tourism, air travel and the environment. *Journal of Sustainable Tourism* 15 (4), 402–417.

Hannam, K. and Knox, D. (2005) Discourse analysis in tourism research – a critical perspective. *Tourism Recreation Research* 30 (2), 23–30.

Herzog, H. (2010) *Some We Love, Some We Hate, Some We Eat: Why It's So Hard to Think Straight About Animals*. New York: HarperCollins.

Hills, A.M. (1993) The motivational bases of attitudes toward animals. *Society and Animals* 1 (2), 111–128.

Hosany, S. and Gilbert, D. (2010) Measuring tourists' emotional experiences toward hedonic holiday destinations. *Journal of Travel Research* 49 (4), 513–526.

Jawecki, G. and Fuller, J. (2008) How to use the innovative potential of online communities? Netnography – an unobtrusive research method to absorb the knowledge and creativity of online communities. *International Journal of Business Process Integration and Management* 3 (4), 248–255.

Joy, M. (2011) *Why We Love Dogs, Eat Pigs, and Wear Cows: An Introduction to Carnism*. San Francisco, CA: Conari Press.

Kellert, S.R. and Berry, J.K. (1980) *Phase III: Knowledge, Affection, and Basic Attitudes Toward Animals in American Society*. Arlington, VA: National Technical Information Service.

Kozinets, R.V. (1997) 'I want to believe': A netnography of the X-Philes' subculture of consumption. *Advances in Consumer Research* 24, 470–475.

Kozinets, R.V. (1998) On netnography: Initial reflections on consumer research in investigations of cyberculture. *Advances in Consumer Research* 25, 366–371.

Kozinets, R.V. (2002) The field behind the screen: Using netnography for marketing research in online communities. *Journal of Marketing Research* 39, 61–72.

Kozinets, R.V. (2006) Netnography. In R.W. Belk (ed.) *Handbook of Qualitative Research Methods in Marketing B2* (pp. 129–142). Cheltenham and Northampton, MA: Edward Elgar Publishing.

Loughnan, S., Haslam, N. and Bastian, B. (2010) The role of meat consumption in the denial of moral status and mind to meat animals. *Appetite* 55 (1), 156–159.

Mathews, S. and Herzog, H.A. (1997) Personality and attitudes toward the treatment of animals. *Society and Animals* 5 (2), 169–175.

Mau, R. (2008) Managing for conservation and recreation: The Ningaloo whale shark experience. *Journal of Ecotourism* 7 (2–3), 208–220.

Mfunda, I.M. and Røskaft, E. (2010) Bushmeat hunting in Serengeti, Tanzania: An important economic activity to local people. *International Journal of Biodiversity and Conservation* 2 (9), 263–272.

Peters, T. (2006) The return of the chimera. *Theology and Science* 4 (3), 247–259.

Prayag, G., Hosany, S. and Odeh, K. (2013) The role of tourists' emotional experiences and satisfaction in understanding behavioral intentions. *Journal of Destination Marketing & Management* 2 (2), 118–127.

Quinton, S. and Harridge-March, S. (2010) Relationships in online communities: The potential for marketers. *Journal of Research in Interactive Marketing* 4 (1), 59–73.

Sax, B. (2009) The magic of animals: English witch trials in the perspective of folklore. *Anthrozoos: A Multidisciplinary Journal of The Interactions of People & Animals* 22 (4), 317–332.

Serpell, J. (1996) *In the Company of Animals: A Study of Human–Animal Relationships*. Cambridge: Cambridge University Press.

Serpell, J.A. (2004) Factors influencing human attitudes to animals and their welfare. *Animal Welfare* 13, S145–S152.

Sheller, M. and Urry, J. (2006) The new mobilities paradigm. *Environment and Planning A* 38 (2), 207.

Sherman, G.D., Haidt, J. and Coan, J.A. (2009) Viewing cute images increases behavioral carefulness. *Emotion* 9 (2), 282.

Singer, P. and Mason, J. (2006) *The Ethics of What We Eat*. Melbourne: Griffin Press.

Stamou, A.G. and Paraskevopoulos, S. (2004) Images of nature by tourism and environmentalist discourses in visitors books: A critical discourse analysis of ecotourism. *Discourse & Society* 15 (1), 105–129.

Tremblay, P. (2001) Wildlife tourism consumption: Consumptive or non-consumptive? *International Journal of Tourism Research* 3 (1), 81–86.

Urry, J. (2003) Social networks, travel and talk. *British Journal of Sociology* 54 (2), 155–175.

Urry, J. (2007) *Mobilities*. Malden: Polity Press.

Walpole, M.J. and Thouless, C.R. (2005) Increasing the value of wildlife through non-consumptive use? Deconstructing the myths of ecotourism and community-based tourism in the tropics. *Conservation Biology Series* 9, 122.

Wasser, S.K., Shedlock, A.M., Comstock, K., Ostrander, E.A., Mutayoba, B. and Stephens, M. (2004) Assigning African elephant DNA to geographic region of origin: Applications to the ivory trade. *Proceedings of the National Academy of Sciences of the USA* 101 (41), 14847–14852.

Wiley, S.B.C. and Packer, J. (2010) Rethinking communication after the mobilities turn. *Communication Review* 13 (4), 263–268.

Wilson, C. and Tisdell, C. (2001) Sea turtles as a non-consumptive tourism resource especially in Australia. *Tourism Management* 22 (3), 279–288.

Part 3

Shifting Relationships

14 From the Recreational Fringe to Mainstream Leisure: The Evolution and Diversification of Entomotourism

R. Harvey Lemelin

Introduction

Although a number of researchers (Berenbaum, 1995; Hogue, 1987; Lockwood, 2013; Lorimer, 2007; Raffles, 2010) have highlighted positive human–insect encounters, most discussions pertaining to human–insect interactions suggest that these are largely negative (see Kellert, 1993, for a discussion pertaining to entomophobia and anthropomorphism). In the spirit of appreciative inquiry and advocacy, this chapter highlights how insects and arachnids draw people from all walks of life into various leisure and tourism activities. Entomotourism encompasses the pursuit of specific insects for one's specimen collection, as pets, and the deliberate, seeking out of encounters with insects in controlled settings such as butterfly pavilions and insectariums, or in natural settings such as national parks (Corley, 1993; Lemelin, 2013a; Raffles, 2010). Elsewhere, 'insect hotels' and 'pollinator parks' (designated natural areas aimed at attracting certain pollinators like insects and birds), butterfly gardens and dragonfly ponds have been established in urban environments (Daniels, 2013; Lemelin, 2007, 2013a).

It could be argued that the activities listed above are undertaken by an eccentric few operating on the recreational fringe (activities that lie outside of the leisure commonplace, but are nevertheless practised by a number of communities and are organised through associations, social media and activities) (Lemelin & Fine, 2013). After all, travellers go to great means to avoid such insects as cockroaches, mosquitoes and bed-bugs during their leisure and tourism outings (Lemelin & Williams, 2012). Yet, each year, millions of people around the world visit the currently existing 250 insectariums and butterfly pavilions, pollinator parks, beekeeping museums, and attend more than 100 insect-based festivals and special events (e.g. Hampyeong Butterfly Festival and the Firefly Festival, Korea) and volunteer for the 50 citizens' science projects dedicated solely to insects (Hvenegaard et al., 2013; Johansen & Auger, 2013; Kim et al., 2008; Lemelin, 2013a). According to Parsons (1992) and Slone et al. (1997), the worldwide retail sales of butterflies alone may be as high as US$100m per annum, employing thousands of people in developed and in developing nations. The annual beetle trade worldwide is also estimated at US$100m (Tournant et al., 2012). These economic figures, when combined with the number of enthusiasts participating in recreational entomology worldwide (Lemelin, 2009; Pearson, 2013), suggest that this type of leisure activity should not be relegated to the recreational fringe for it is a multimillion dollar global industry involving millions of participants worldwide. Rarely investigated, entomotourism provides important educational and interpretive opportunities, when properly developed.

Supported by ethnographic studies, interviews and discussions with experts in entomology, this chapter begins by providing an overview of the literature pertaining to human–insect interactions. The ensuing section commences with a description of how insects can be viewed in both controlled and natural settings. Controlled environments are defined as butterfly pavilions and insectariums where insects are featured and, in some cases, raised in regulated situations. The focus of these exhibitions is the featuring of insects and spiders in semi- and fully controlled settings to the general public. Although butterfly gardens, dragonfly ponds and pollinator gardens are all examples of insects being featured in natural settings, the discussion on viewing insects in natural environments focuses solely on wildlife sanctuaries and national parks. Examples of where insects are featured as the prime attraction are also provided. Later, the chapter discusses how interactions with insects, while challenging in some instances, can be educational and transformative and, in the long run, be beneficial to all animals, whether they be human, insect or otherwise.

Learning About and Interacting with Insects, in a Tourism Context

Attitudes towards insects arise from a complex interplay of factors involving cultural, biological, physiological attributes of the insects (aposematic attributes such as bright colours, larger sizes), education and knowledge (Barua et al., 2012; Lemelin, 2013b). Bixler et al. (2002), Measham (2006), and Tunnicliffe and Reiss (1999) argue that basic knowledge about insects is influenced by early childhood experiences, field experiences and parental support. These early childhood experiences are critical in cultivating sympathetic or proactive support towards the environment (see Bögeholz, 2006; Chawla, 1999; Ewert *et al.*, 2005; Kals *et al.*, 1999; Tanner, 1980). Other researchers like Barua *et al.* (2012), Rule and Zhbanova (2012) and Zoldosova and Prokop (2006) suggest that children's preference for insects is strongly correlated with their representation in modern popular culture and in scientific literature.

Tourism experiences providing opportunities for direct contact with wildlife create a 'strong and positive educational message to their visitors' (Ballantyne *et al.*, 2011: 770), as well as securing 'long-term conservation of wildlife and wildlife habitats' (Ballantyne *et al.*, 2009: 658). Wildlife tourism has been defined as tourism that includes trips with the purpose of observing, feeding, touching, photographing and/or otherwise interacting with wildlife in a non-consumptive manner. According to Hvenegaard (2002), wildlife tourism is most empowering when it is guided by ecotourism principles of sustainable development, experiential philosophy, cultural respect and environmental ethics. Wildlife tourists partaking in captive (aviaries, zoos, oceanaria, aquaria, petting zoos), semi-captive (wildlife parks, rehabilitation centres) and in natural settings (national parks, protected areas, migratory routes) experiences, have described the importance of a variety of responses to their experience. Such experiences often involve sensory impressions (vivid visual, auditory, olfactory or tactile memories of their experience often brought about by proximity to wildlife), emotional affinity (emotional connections with the experience), reflective responses (new insights derived from the experience or through conversation with other participants) and behavioural responses (a heightened awareness of the need for action and conservation measures) (Ballantyne *et al.*, 1998, 2011).

Whether it is early childhood experiences, education, partaking in a wildlife tourism experience or a combination of all three, researchers agree that human–animal encounters can often prompt curiosity, inquisitiveness and exploration and that such encounters can lead to a greater willingness to learn, greater tolerance and even, in some cases, changed behaviours (Ballantyne *et al.*, 2011; Lemelin, 2013b). From an invertebrate perspective, awareness of and support for insects are essential to our recognition of these animals in our own daily lives and for the inclusion of invertebrates in conservation programmes (Huntly *et al.*, 2005). Although awareness does not guarantee protection, awareness and knowledge of the natural world are nevertheless crucial for the recruitment of the next generation of naturalists and conservationists (Balmford *et al.*, 2002; Cheesman & Key, 2007; Kawahara & Pyle, 2013; Snaddon *et al.*, 2008; Sodhi *et al.*, 2004). In many cases, these interactions can be facilitated through experiential education, interpretation, guided outings and through the help of specialised equipment like bug nets and technology (micro-lenses on cameras), and apps on tablets and smartphones (Lemelin, 2013a; Mitchell, 2013).

Viewing Insects and Spiders in Controlled Environments

The first live exhibit of butterflies and other insects to be established in Europe was at the London Zoo in 1897. Other zoos soon followed thereafter (Lemelin, 2013a; Veltman, 2013). In 1960, the first butterfly pavilion at Sherborne, Dorset was established (Lemelin, 2013a). Today there are over 250 stand-alone butterfly pavilions, insectariums and museums (e.g. beekeeping museums) solely dedicated to insects, around the world (Corley, 1993; Lemelin, 2013a). Butterflies and certain types of moths are permitted to fly freely and interact with visitors in large open areas, while leaf-cutter ants, stick-insects, honey bees, cockroaches, praying mantis and spiders (e.g. orb weavers, black widows, tarantulas) are featured in various enclosed settings (i.e. terrariums). While visitation figures are hard to acquire, the examples featured in this chapter (e.g. Audubon Butterfly Garden and Insectarium, the Cambridge Butterfly Conservatory, the McGuire Center for Lepidoptera and Biodiversity) have hosted nearly three million visitors throughout the past two decades. In other instances, special displays like 'The Romance of Ants' display at the Field Museum of Natural History in Chicago, IL, attracted 500,000 individuals in 2012/2013 (Moreau, 2013 pers. comm). These figures, however, do not account for zoos and museums like the San Diego Zoo, CA or the Royal Ontario Museum in Toronto, Canada that have also integrated insects and spiders into their permanent displays.

Consisting of a free-flight butterfly garden, numerous live animal exhibits (roughly 100 arthropod species are viewable on any given day), and an edible insect area appropriately named 'Bug Appétit', the Audubon Butterfly Garden and Insectarium (established in 2008) located in the city of New Orleans, LA, is a specialised entomotourism attraction offering informal science education programmes designed to help guests appreciate and value insects and invertebrates. Apart from interaction with insects in the butterfly garden and animal exhibits, the 200,000 annual visitors can also partake in special events like the ANTiversary (birthday celebration for the museum held on milestone years) and Hoppy Thanksgiving (bug-based twist on traditional holiday fare) (Necaise, 2014, pers. comm).

Located in Cambridge, Canada, the Cambridge Butterfly Conservatory (established in 2001) features 2000–3000 different types of invertebrates along with turtles, fish and 15 free-flying species of birds in the butterfly conservatory. The site also offers two exhibition areas featuring live animal displays (including a functional bee hive), and temporary exhibits. A seasonal pollinator garden and an environmentally sensitive bog are also located on the property. Dedicated to education and outreach, the Cambridge Butterfly Conservatory offers a number of curriculum-based educational programmes from kindergarten to high school, from preschool to home schooling, and special events like BugFeast, Hug-a-Bug, Monarch Tagging Weekend and the Flight of White. The conservatory also supports various graduate student projects and is actively involved in the reintroduction of the Karner blue butterfly in Ontario (Brewster, 2014, pers. comm). Approximately 125,000 people visit the conservatory on an annual basis (Brewster, 2014, pers. comm).

Established in 2004 on the University of Florida campus in Gainesville, FL, the McGuire Center for Lepidoptera and Biodiversity features a butterfly rainforest, a research laboratory and a collection space. Attracting between 80,000 and 125,000 visitors annually, the butterfly rainforest is home to over 1200–1500 free-flying butterflies from around the world along with an assortment of birds, fish and turtles. Public programming (school tours, teacher training, interpretation for visitors) along with annual festivals including a fall Butterfly Fest and spring Earth Day Celebration attracts thousands of visitors and helps promote environmental literacy (Daniels, 2014, pers. comm).

Staffed by professional staff and dedicated volunteers, these centres, along with the hundreds of butterfly pavilions and insectariums worldwide, provide excellent opportunities to engage visitors through various interpretive strategies and showcase potentially dangerous or endangered animals in a secure setting (Cushing & Markwell, 2011). In certain instances, tarantulas and hissing cockroaches may be taken out of their cases to interact with visitors. Connecting with these animals in controlled settings is quite important since these guided interactions provide opportunities for discussion, address certain preconceptions, engage other senses (like tactile senses) and diminish 'distances' between us and 'other animals'.

Discussions with managers of insectariums and butterfly pavilions suggest that some of the critiques of these sites, including the presentation of insects in contrived fashions, the focus on exotic, utilitarian and aposematic species rather than less flamboyant, local species, and even the environmental footprint of these establishments, are far outweighed by the generation of awareness, education and tolerance. In those instances where insects have to be imported, these specimens can be purchased from licensed distributors working with partners located in developing nations – a business which, if managed appropriately, can be a form of sustainable wildlife harvesting which has positive outcomes for both community and economic development (Veltman, 2013; Young, 1986). Butterfly pavilions and insectariums, the managers explained, must also comply with regional, national and international laws for animal husbandry. Some sites like the St Louis Zoo have even participated in the reintroduction of formerly extirpated species back into the environment (Spevak, 2010, pers. comm).

Viewing Insects in Natural Environments

The opportunity to view, chase, hold and otherwise interact with these creatures provides various experiential opportunities to discover the relationship between insects and their environments, and to learn more about the conservation of these animals. This is why so many bug camps, citizen science events and festivals like the Shionoe Firefly Festival in Japan are often hosted near or in these protected areas. Each year thousands of visitors travel to rural areas in North America and Asia to view fireflies (Rykken & Farrell, 2013), while approximately 600,000 and 700,000 enthusiasts, respectively, visit the glow worm caves in Australia and New Zealand (Hall, 2013), and butterfly sanctuaries in Mexico, South Africa and Taiwan (Lemelin, 2007; Monterrubio et al., 2013). Dragonfly sanctuaries like the Dragonfly Kingdom at Nakamura (the world's first dragonfly nature preserve and museum), the Wicken Fen in Cambridgeshire, England, and the dragonfly awareness trails at the KwaZulu-Natal National Botanical Garden in Pietermaritburg, South Africa (Willis & Samways, 2013) attract thousands of 'dragon hunters' from around the world (Huntly et al., 2005; Lemelin, 2007, 2009; Samways, 2013).

The few studies examining human interactions with insects in protected areas (see Kerley et al., 2003 in the Addo Elephant National Park; Huntly et al., 2005 in the Ndumu Game Preserve and the Pietermaritburg Botanical Gardens, South Africa) suggest that visitor interests in insects is predicated upon effective management and interpretation strategies. In those instances where people actually reported being interested in certain insects like the flightless dung beetle, this interest was a consequence of 'the information brochures and road signs which draw attention to both the threatened conservation status of this species as well as their intriguing behavior of dung-ball rolling' (Kerley et al., 2003: 19). Building on this approach, the 'Little 5' (i.e. elephant shrew, ant lion, rhinoceros beetle, buffalo weaver, leopard tortoise) marketing strategy (including a webpage and interpretive pamphlet) capitalises on the charismatic 'Big 5' theme by introducing visitors to charismatic microfauna (Loon, 2013). Although the idea of 'charismatic microfauna' is less well developed than the concept of 'charismatic species' (see also Skibins, Chapter 16, this volume), the idea of 'charismatic microfauna' has been associated with bees, butterflies and some dragonflies (Hall et al., 2011; Lemelin, 2013a).

Despite this growth and diversity, challenges to conducting entomotourism in natural areas do exist, for parks staff and managers typically know very little about their invertebrate fauna (Kerley *et al.*, 2003), and may even reinforce the fear that insects and their relatives are a threat to the health of humans and landscapes (Huntley *et al.*, 2005). As Lemelin (2013b) argues, intolerance of insects, even in natural environments, can result in the application of pesticides and other management strategies aimed at controlling or even eliminating these animals from these habitats. Last, viewing insects in their natural environment is subject to seasonal variations and weather conditions and in some cases may require sophisticated equipment and some specialised knowledge of the species behaviours.

Like the wildlife tourism and ecotourism opportunities discussed earlier, visits to butterfly farms can contribute to economic diversification opportunities (SEED, 2014), promote local conservation initiatives, and provide local employment opportunities through handicrafts and accommodations (Young, 1986). In other situations, entomotourism can educate and entertain youth living in urban areas: armed with butterfly nets, collection tools, field guides and an identification sheet unique to the park and surrounding area, 700 students a year are sent out to various locations throughout the Boston Harbor Islands National Recreation Area, MA, USA and Thompson Island Outward Bound Education Center to collect, examine and identify species of different members of the micro-fauna (producers, herbivores, carnivores, scavengers and decomposers). Students must then identify the species and determine what types of adaptations each animal group fits into (Albert & Colby, 2014, pers. comm).

Discussion and Conclusions

The goal of this chapter was to illustrate the growth and diversification of human–insect encounters in leisure settings through an examination of entomotourism. Various examples of human–insect interactions in both captive and natural settings showcase the importance of these educational encounters. These educational strategies are used to increase public awareness of insects by emphasising their ecological and socio-economic roles (Barua *et al.*, 2012). But these experiences, as Ballantyne *et al.* (2011) and Lemelin (2009) suggest, can go far beyond education, for human–animal encounters in natural settings can provide multi-sensorial experience while promoting a sense of belonging with nature. In captive settings, the social aspect of human–wildlife encounters provides opportunities for participants to express their concerns and direct questions to the staff, volunteers and fellow group members in controlled and safe environments (Ballantyne *et al.*, 2011).

In some instances, these experiences can be transformative, resulting in visitors altering their behaviours by becoming more tolerant to the presence of insects on their property or home, reducing or eliminating pesticide use or introducing integrated pest management into their gardening practices (i.e. the deliberate introduction of predatory insects for pest control), joining an insect association, participating in citizen science projects on insects, conducting backyard safaris (looking for insects in one's domain) or building an insect hotel, butterfly garden or dragonfly pond on their property. In most instances, interest and changed behaviours must be sustained beyond the on-site experience through feedback and ongoing support (Ballantyne & Packer, 2005). The Cambridge Butterfly Conservatory does this by providing an interactive website and using various types of social media which help to keep visitors connected and up to date on the latest news from the entomological world.

For some local populations, entomotourism provides employment opportunities, revenue through the sales of arts and crafts, regional economic diversification strategies (through the incorporation of tourism with local practices) and the conservation of habitat. In other instances, relatively large, conspicuous, colourful, mostly diurnal, charismatic, aposematic micro-fauna (such as bees, beetles, butterflies and dragonflies) are excellent subjects for conservation strategies, nature interpretation and public education. As these examples provided in the earlier sections suggest, the concept of flagship species in entomotourism should be based upon popular invertebrates like the flightless dung beetle or certain types of endemic and/or threatened butterflies (e.g. Monarchs, Karkloof blue, Karner blue), that will resonate with visitors, increase further opportunities for entomotourism and lead to sustained interest in conservation and research programmes through funding and public support (Barua *et al.*, 2012; Pullin, 2012). By recognising and integrating insects into recreation activities, curiosity and openness towards insects can be fostered in both young and old, creating a positive cycle of change where insects are not only tolerated but respected for their utility, diversity and adaptability.

Acknowledgements

The author would like to thank the following contributors for their contributions to this chapter: Jayme Necaise and Zack Lemann at Audubon Butterfly Garden and Insectarium; Elisabeth Colby and Marc Albert from the Boston Harbor Islands National Park Area; Adrienne Brewster from the Cambridge Butterfly Conservatory; Jaret Daniels from the Florida Museum of Natural History's McGuire Center for Lepidoptera and Biodiversity and Butterfly Rainforest; and Christopher Willis and the KwaZulu-Natal National Botanical Garden, managed by the South African National Biodiversity Institute.

For further information on the collaborators of this chapter, readers are encouraged to visit the following websites:

Audubon Butterfly Garden and Insectarium	www.auduboninstitute.org/visit/insectarium
Boston Harbor Island National Recreation, Area	www.nps.gov/boha/index.htm
Cambridge Butterfly Conservatory	www.cambridgebutterfly.com/
Florida Museum of Natural History McGuire Center for Lepidoptera and Biodiversity	www.flmnh.ufl.edu/mcguire/
KwaZulu-Natal National Botanical Garden	www.sanbi.org/gardens/kwazulu-natal

References

Ballantyne, R. and Packer, J. (2005) Promoting environmentally sustainable attitudes and behaviour through free-choice learning experiences: What is the state of the game? *Environmental Education Research* 11 (3), 281–295.

Ballantyne, R., Packer, J. and Beckmann, E. (1998) Targeted interpretation: Exploring relationships among visitors' motivations, activities, attitudes, information needs and preferences. *Journal of Tourism Studies* 9 (2), 14–25.

Ballantyne, R., Packer, J. and Hughes, K. (2009) Tourists' support for conservation messages and sustainable management practices in wildlife tourism experiences. *Tourism Management* 30 (3), 658–664.

Ballantyne, R., Packer, J. and Sutherland, L.A. (2011) Visitors' memories of wildlife tourism: Implications for the design of powerful interpretive experiences. *Tourism Management* 32 (4), 770–779.

Balmford, A., Clegg, L., Coulson, T. and Taylor, J. (2002) Why conservationists should heed Pokémon. *Science* 295, 2367–2367.

Barua, M., Gurdak, D.J., Ahmed, R.A. and Tamuly, J. (2012) Selecting flagships for invertebrate conservation. *Biodiversity and Conservation* 21 (6), 1457–1476.

Berenbaum, M.R. (1995) *Bugs in the System: Insects and their Impacts on Human Affairs.* Cambridge, MA: Helix Books.

Bixler, R.D., Floyd M.F. and Hammitt, W.E. (2002) Environmental socialization – quantitative tests of the childhood play hypothesis. *Environment and Behaviour* 34, 795–818.

Bögeholz, S. (2006) Nature experience and its importance for environmental knowledge, values and action: Recent German empirical contributions. *Environmental Education Research* 12, 65–84.

Chawla, L. (1999) Life paths into effective environmental education. *Journal of Environmental Education* 31, 15–26.

Cheesman, O.D. and Key, R.S. (2007) The extinction of experience: A threat to insect conservation? In A.J.A. Stewart, T.R. New and O.T. Lewis (eds) *Insect Conservation Biology: Proceedings of the Royal Entomological Society's 23rd Symposium* (pp. 322–350). Wallingford and Cambridge, MA: CABI.

Corley, T. (1993) *Let's Go Buggy.* Los Angeles, CA: Corley Publications.

Cushing, N. and Markwell, K. (2011) I can't look: Disgust in the zoo visit experience. In W. Frost (ed.) *Zoos and Tourism* (pp. 167–178). Bristol: Channel View Publications.

Daniels, J. (2013) Gardening and landscape modification: Butterfly gardens. In R.H. Lemelin (ed.) *The Management of Insects in Recreation and Tourism* (pp. 153–168). Cambridge: Cambridge University Press.

Ewert, A., Place, G. and Sibthorp, J. (2005) Early-life outdoor experiences and an individual's environmental attitudes. *Leisure Sciences* 27, 225–239.

Hall, C.M., James, M. and Baird, T. (2011) Forests and trees as charismatic mega-flora: Implications for heritage tourism and conservation. *Journal of Heritage Tourism* 6 (4), 309–323.

Hall, M. (2013) Glow-worm tourism in Australia and New Zealand: Commodifying and conserving charismatic micro-fauna. In R.H. Lemelin (ed.) *The Management of Insects in Recreation and Tourism* (pp. 217–232). Cambridge: Cambridge University Press.

Hogue, C. (1987) Cultural entomology. *Annual Review of Entomology* 32, 181–199.

Huntly, P.M., Van Noort, S. and Hamer, M. (2005) Giving increased value to invertebrates through ecotourism. *South African Journal of Wildlife Research* 35, 53–62.

Hvenegaard, G.T. (2002) Birder specialization differences in conservation involvement, demographics, and motivations. *Human Dimensions of Wildlife* 7 (1), 21–36.

Hvenegaard, T.A., Delamere, T., Lemelin, R.H., Brager, K. and Auger, A. (2013) Insect festivals: Celebrating and fostering human–insect interactions. In R.H. Lemelin (ed.) *The Management of Insects in Recreation and Tourism* (pp. 198–216). Cambridge: Cambridge University Press.

Johansen, K. and Auger, A. (2013) Citizen science and insect conservation. In R.H. Lemelin (ed.) *The Management of Insects in Recreation and Tourism* (pp. 252–273). Cambridge: Cambridge University Press.

Kals, E., Schumacher, D. and Montada, L. (1999) Emotional affinity toward nature as a motivational basis to protect nature. *Environment and Behavior* 31, 178–202.

Kawahara, A.Y. and Pyle, R.M. (2013) An appreciation for the natural world through collecting, owning and observing insects. In R.H. Lemelin (ed.) *The Management of Insects in Recreation and Tourism* (pp. 138–152). Cambridge: Cambridge University Press.

Kellert, S.R. (1993) Values and perceptions of invertebrates. *Conservation Biology* 7, 845–855.

Kerley, G.I.H., Geach, B.G.S. and Vial, C. (2003) Jumbo or bust: Do tourists' perceptions lead to an under-appreciation of biodiversity? *South African Journal of Wildlife Research* 33 (1), 13–21.

Kim, Y., Kim, S.S. and Agrusa, J. (2008) An investigation into the procedures involved in creating the Hampyeong Butterfly Festival as an ecotourism resource, successful factors, and evaluations. *Asia Pacific Journal of Tourism Research* 13 (4), 357–377.

Lemelin, R.H. (2007) Finding beauty in the dragon: The role of dragonflies in recreation, tourism, and conservation. *Journal of Ecotourism* 6 (2), 139–145.

Lemelin, R.H. (2009) Goodwill hunting? Dragon hunters, dragonflies & leisure. *Current Issues in Tourism* 12 (3), 235–253.

Lemelin, R.H. (ed.) (2013a) *The Role of Insects in Recreation and Tourism*. Cambridge: Cambridge University Press.

Lemelin, R.H. (2013b) To bee or not to bee: Whether 'tis nobler to revere or to revile those six-legged creatures during one's leisure. *Leisure Studies* 32 (2), 153–172.

Lemelin, R.H. and Fine, G.A. (2013) Leisure on the recreational fringe: Naturework and the place of amateur mycology and entomology. *Philosophy, Activism, Nature (PAN)* 10, 77–86.

Lemelin, R.H. and Williams, G. (2012) Blossoms and butterflies, waterfalls and dragonflies: Integrating insects in the hospitality and tourism industries through swarm supposition. In P. Sloan, C. Simons-Kaufmann and W. Legrand (eds) *Sustainable Hospitality and Tourism as Motors for Development: Case Studies from Developing Regions of the World* (pp. 198–212). New York: Routledge.

Lockwood, J. (2013) *The Infested Mind: Why Humans Fear, Loathe, and Love Insects*. Oxford: Oxford University Press.

Loon, R. (2013) *The Small 5005 of Southern Africa*. Johannesburg: Jacana Media.

Lorimer, J. (2007) Nonhuman charisma. *Environment and Planning Development: Society and Space* 25 (5), 911–932.

Measham, T.G. (2006) Learning about environments: The significance of primal landscapes. *Environmental Management* 38, 426–434.

Mitchell, F.L. (2013) May you live in interesting times: Technology and entomology. In R.H. Lemelin (ed.) *The Management of Insects in Recreation and Tourism* (pp. 235–251). Cambridge: Cambridge University Press.

Monterrubio, J.C., Rodriguez-Munoz, G. and Menondoza-Ontiveros, M.M. (2013) Social benefits of ecotourism. The Monarch butterfly reserve in Mexico. *Enlightening Tourism: A Pathmaking Journal* 3 (2), 105–124.

Parsons, M.J. (1992) The butterfly farming and trading industry in the Indo-Australian region and its role in tropical forest conservation. *Tropical Lepidoptera* 2, 1–31.

Pearson, D.L. (2013) Tiger beetles: Lessons in natural history, conservation and the rise of amateur involvement. In R.H. Lemelin (ed.) *The Management of Insects in Recreation and Tourism* (pp. 56–75). Cambridge: Cambridge University Press.

Pullin, A. (ed.) (2012) *Ecology and Conservation of Butterflies.* New York: Springer.

Raffles, H. (2010) *Insectopedia.* New York: Pantheon Books.

Rule, A. and Zhbanova, K.Z. (2012) Changing perceptions of unpopular animals through facts, poetry, crafts and puppet plays. *Early Childhood Education* 40, 223–230.

Rykken, J.J. and Farrell, B.D. (2013) Discovering the microwilderness in parks and protected areas. In R.H. Lemelin (ed.) *The Management of Insects in Recreation and Tourism* (pp. 306–323). Cambridge: Cambridge University Press.

Samways, M.J. (2013) Dragonflies: Their lives, our lives, from ponds to reserves. In R.H. Lemelin (ed.) *The Management of Insects in Recreation and Tourism* (pp. 108–120). Cambridge: Cambridge University Press.

SEED (2014) Seed Award 2011: Butterfly farming for pro-poor tourism: Tanzania. *SEED Initiative.* www.seedinit.org/awards/all/butterfly-farming-for-pro-poor-tourism-and-environment-conservation.html (accessed 24 January 2014).

Slone, T.H., Orsak, L.J. and Malver, O. (1997) A comparison of price, rarity and cost of butterfly specimens: Implications for the insect trade and for habitat conservation. *Ecological Economics* 21 (1), 77–85.

Snaddon J.L., Turner E.C. and Foster W.A. (2008) Children's perceptions of rainforest biodiversity: Which animals have the lion's share of environmental awareness? *PLoS ONE* 3 (7), e2579; doi:10.1371/journal.pone.0002579.

Sodhi, N.S., Koh, L.P., Brook, B.W. and Ng, P.K.L. (2004) Southeast Asian biodiversity: An impending disaster. *Trends in Ecology & Evolution* 19, 654–660.

Tanner, T. (1980) Significant life experiences: A new research area in environmental education. *Journal of Environmental Education* 11, 20–24.

Tournant, P., Joseph, L., Goka, K. and Courchamp, F. (2012) The rarity and overexploitation paradox: Stag beetle collections in Japan. *Biodiversity Conservation* 21, 1425–1440.

Tunnicliffe, S.D. and Reiss, M.J. (1999) Building a model of the environment: How do children see animals? *Journal of Biological Education* 33, 142–148.

Veltman, K. (2013) Butterfly conservatories, butterfly ranches and insectariums: Generating income while promoting social and environmental justice. In R.H. Lemelin (ed.) *The Management of Insects in Recreation and Tourism* (pp. 189–197). Cambridge: Cambridge University Press.

Willis, C.K. and Samways, M.J. (2013) *Dragonfly and Damselfly Trail Guide: KwaZulu-Natal National Botanical Garden.* Pretoria: South African National Biodiversity Institute.

Young, A.M. (1986) Eco-enterprises: Eco-tourism and farming of exotics in the tropics. *Ambio* 15 (6), 361–363.

Zoldosova, K. and Prokop, P. (2006) Education in the field influences children's ideas and interest toward science. *Journal of Science Education and Technology* 15, 304–313.

15 From Dinner Plate to T-shirt Logo: The Changing Role of a Flagship Turtle Species in One of Brazil's Most Popular Tourism Destinations

Fernanda de Vasconcellos Pegas

Introduction

The loss of biodiversity is a problem of global magnitude (Sachs *et al.,* 2009). Efforts to stem this decline include the use of flagship animal species as catalysts to gain local and political support for biodiversity conservation. Flagship species are characterised as species that have widespread social appeal, and their success is determined by their ability to raise funds, enhance awareness and help achieve myriad conservation and sustainable development goals (Walpole & Leader-Williams, 2002; see also Skibins, Chapter 16, this volume). While the applicability of flagship species to raise awareness and funds for conservation as well as the importance of destination image in tourism promotion (e.g. Beerli & Martin, 2004; Echtner & Ritchie, 1993; Pike, 2002) have been popular research topics, few studies (e.g. Tisdell & Wilson, 2002a) have conducted detailed assessments of the factors that help shape the image of a tourist destination via the use of flagship species. This chapter identifies the factors that have influenced changes in local values and uses of one of Brazil's iconic group of animals, sea turtles, over a 30-year period, and demonstrates how the flagship species approach has influenced the local tourism industry.

The fishing village of Praia do Forte, in Northern Bahia, is a prime ecotourism and coastal tourism destination as well as an important reproduction and feeding site for four of the five species of sea turtles found in Brazil: the endangered loggerhead (*Caretta caretta*), olive Ridley (*Lepidochelys olivacea*), green (*Chelonia mydas*) and the critically endangered hawksbill (*Eretmochelys imbricata*) turtles. Nine months of ethnographic research conducted between 2006 and 2008 allowed the assessment of how the Praia do Forte community used sea turtles and how the tourism industry made use of the sea turtle image.

Flagship Species

Flagship species are iconic and are 'catalysts for change in the human dimension' (Eckert & Hemphill, 2005: 122). Public acceptance of flagship species is based on the emotional connection with and charisma of the animal, compounded by the species' diminishing populations (Eckert & Hemphill, 2005). Tigers, pandas and lions are typical of charismatic mammal flagship species (Barua, 2011; Clucas *et al.*, 2008; Woods, 2000). However, this mammal-centric selection has been criticised (Simberloff, 1998) with studies demonstrating that birds, fish, reptiles and amphibians can also be effective conservation ambassadors. Examples include crocodiles (Tremblay, 2002), lizards (Walpole & Leader-Williams, 2002), snakes (Frynta *et al.*, 2011) and, as I illustrate in this chapter, sea turtles.

Flagship species help tourism businesses achieve their financial, educational and marketing goals (Castley *et al.*, 2012; Pegas & Stronza, 2010; Tisdell & Wilson, 2002a). Wildlife tour operators, for example, depend on flagship species (Curtin, 2010) to enhance wildlife viewing experiences (Higginbottom & Buckley, 2003), to promote a destination via online marketing (Castley *et al.*, 2012), and to promote a destination image more generally (Boshoff *et al.*, 2007; Lindsey *et al.*, 2007). The linkage between tourism and conservation can also be mutually beneficial. Tourism initiatives can contribute to species conservation by helping to generate funding and enhance public awareness, conserve areas that rely on tourism activities, and raise political support for species protection (Buckley *et al.*, 2012; Landry & Taggart, 2010; Pegas & Buckley, 2012; Pegas *et al.*, 2013; Tisdell & Wilson, 2005). Some studies have analysed the use of wildlife visual imagery as a complementary tool for promoting destinations (e.g. Castley *et al.*, 2012).

Some of these studies analysed the contribution that flagship species make to the image visitors have of a destination (Boshoff *et al.*, 2007; Higginbottom & Buckley, 2003; Lindsey *et al.*, 2007). Castley *et al.* (2012) analysed online images of flagship species, but stopped short of assessing how these images influenced tourism development or how these images might influence local wildlife values and uses. However, it is well established that tourism can also be detrimental to species and ecosystems (Davenport & Davenport, 2006; Sorice *et al.*, 2006). While coastal tourism can cause ocean pollution, sea turtle habitat loss and degradation, and nest disturbance (Pegas & Stronza, 2010; Tisdell & Wilson, 2005), a flagship species approach can minimise these environmental problems. Nevertheless, we remain limited in our understanding of the factors that contribute to the successful adoption of a species as a flagship species from a community perspective as well as how this change helps promote a tourist destination.

The TAMAR Project

In Brazil, despite sea turtles being protected by federal law since 1967, historical sea turtle harvesting accounts indicate an illegal practice that was done frequently, throughout the species' range, and without quota limits. This practice is associated with the overall depletion of turtle population numbers in the country (Marcovaldi & Marcovaldi, 1999). Efforts to reverse this illegal practice included the establishment of the National Sea Turtle Conservation Programme (TAMAR) by the Brazilian Government in 1980. TAMAR is short for '**TA**rtaruga **MAR**inha' or sea turtle, in Portuguese. TAMAR's mission is to protect the species within the national territory. The use of sea turtles as a flagship species facilitates this mission.

TAMAR is a collaborative effort between the Brazilian Government's Institute of Renewable Resources (IBAMA-ICMBio), Chico Mendes Institute of Biodiversity (ICMBio) and Ministry of the Environment (MMA) and the non-profit organisation, *'Fundação Pró-TAMAR'* (Pró-TAMAR Foundation). TAMAR operates 23 research stations in nine states and employs approximately 1300 people nationwide. In 1982 TAMAR opened a conservation research station in Praia do Forte (Marcovaldi & Marcovaldi, 1999). In the early 1980s the village was small, without electricity, and home to approximately 600 residents (Marcovaldi & Laurent, 1996). Tourism development was still in its early stages with few tourism-related establishments and limited infrastructure (e.g. no paved road access). The presence of sea turtles had little influence on the local tourism industry as the tourist focus was on local beaches, not turtle watching. A few years later, tourists started to demonstrate an interest in turtle conservation. Interest took place in various ways including the act of asking TAMAR researchers questions about turtle conservation and by offering financial support via the purchase of TAMAR products. Such activities created an incentive for TAMAR to open a visitor centre (VC) in the village soon after.

The VC started small with a few marine exhibits containing exemplars of local marine life (e.g. sea turtles) as well as interpretative media on turtle conservation; T-shirts with the turtle logo were the main products offered for sale (Pegas & Stronza, 2010). Improvements in the local infrastructure and greater regional coastal tourism development led to an increase in the number of tourists (Pegas, 2012). This growth in tourist numbers generally directly influenced visitor numbers at the VC and provided a financial opportunity for TAMAR to use the flagship species approach to raise awareness, political support (e.g. establishment of state laws that prohibit traffic of cars along sea turtle nesting beaches), and funds for species conservation. Praia do Forte is, in fact, the most visited of TAMAR's 11 VCs with 368,000 visitors in 2011 (Fundação Pró-TAMAR, 2012).

The village of Praia do Forte

The village of Praia do Forte was formed when families moved to the area to work on the coconut plantation at the end of the 19th century (Pegas et al., 2013). The plantation was sold in 1972 with the new owner ceasing plantation operations soon after. As a result, local families relied more extensively on local resources, including marine turtles, for their subsistence needs. Changes in land tenure led to a shift in the local economy from agriculture to tourism and, years later, to also include sea turtle conservation and tourism. The establishment of the local tourism industry helped place Praia do Forte on the domestic and international coastal tourism map. As a result, the village is no longer a small, isolated and little known coastal destination; instead it has become one of Brazil's top 10 best small beach destinations (Veja, 2007) and has the highest number of hotel rooms in the state. As a result of the booming development of secondary homes and hotel lodging options in the village, the population of about 2000 permanent residents rises to over 14,000 people during the peak summer season (Prefeitura Municipal de Mata de São João, 2004).

Methods

Information presented in this chapter is part of a larger research effort on the impacts of ecotourism on local livelihoods and turtle conservation across generations. Information on the methodology used and the findings are provided in greater detail in Pegas and Stronza (2010) and Pegas et al. (2013). I collected the data presented in this chapter using a mixed method approach. I captured changes in the uses of and values attached to turtles by the local community via face-to-face interviews, visual ethnography and participant observation. I conducted face-to-face interviews with 77 local families during nine months of ethnographic research between 2006 and 2008. Face-to-face interviews provided detailed information about the ways in which the community used turtles prior to the arrival of TAMAR in 1982 as well as contemporary uses.

Historical household uses of turtles were based on anecdotal information provided by local fishing families as these were the residents living in the community during that period. I gathered contemporary uses and values from all respondents as this information was relevant to the period in which I conducted the study. Due to a scarcity of publically accessible visual archival data, I relied on photographs provided by local families. I then triangulated the photographic images, narrative interview data and available literature to validate emergent themes. Unfortunately, impoverished living conditions during the plantation period precluded most families from keeping visual records of their lives and community. Residents who were able to capture that period via photographs provided me with additional valuable insights. Unlike my experience with archival data, I found it easier to obtain contemporary turtle images as these are widely depicted outside businesses, on local houses, and as part of tourist merchandising. Likewise, I found turtle images linked to local tourism development enterprises. I also assessed the use of turtles in advertisements from the hotel industry and by the local and state tourism agencies. Participant observation gave me the opportunity to witness interactions between local residents and turtles, local residents and tourists, and between local residents and TAMAR. This information complemented the data I gathered via visual ethnography and interviews.

Results

Out of 77 residents, 32 are members of Praia do Forte's traditional fishing families, also known as the native residents of the village. Eight of the 32 native respondents were at least 18 years old in 1982 and 15 are fishermen. Of the 34 women in the study, 19 are either wives or daughters of fishermen. The remaining participants have limited or no ties with the local fishing culture and/or with the native families. These residents have lived in the village an average of 15 years and are from adjacent villages or from Salvador, the state capital 80 km south of the village.

When asked their perspective on turtle conservation in the village and its impacts on local livelihoods, almost all respondents, native (99%) and not-native (98%), said they supported conservation actions by TAMAR. The drivers of this extraordinary level of support seem to be a combination of a shift in the sources of livelihood needs and community ties with the founders of TAMAR. For example, respondents said that harvesting, consumption and display of turtle shells were once traditional local practices and symbols of pride but they are no longer socially acceptable. When asked to elaborate upon this socially acceptable concept, they made statements like 'we don't need to eat turtle anymore because there is food at the grocery store', 'it is not right because the founders help us' and 'we need live turtles because of the tourism'. Another factor appears to be directly linked with the growing popularity and economic profitability of TAMAR sea turtle ecotourism and conservation initiatives. To better illustrate these changes, results are presented in two distinct sections: (1) the period before and (2) the period after the establishment of TAMAR's conservation research station in 1982. The use of turtles as a flagship species by the tourism industry is demonstrated in section (2) as this industry was inchoate until the late 1980s and early 1990s.

Traditional uses and values before 1982

Turtle consumption has a long history within the local fishing families. According to these families, turtles were a common component of their diet. There were no quota limits on the number of turtles and turtle eggs acquired per individual and household. However, turtle meat was not valued over other types of meat; respondents indicated preferring fish over turtle meat. Sea turtles were apparently harvested because they were easily found on the nearby reef and, individually, provided a greater amount of meat than most harvested fish species. As noted by one respondent: 'Nobody cared about them in the past. They were just food.' His recollection of harvesting indicates values and uses directly linked to subsistence needs.

There was no indication that turtle meat and its consumption had any religious or ceremonial meaning. Although men in the village associated consuming turtle eggs with virility and sexual benefits, this was not the main driver of egg consumption. Overall, both eggs and meat were considered very good sources of protein and energy, particularly to the fishermen whose work was physically demanding. Many respondents noted that, despite the bad smell and unpleasant taste of turtle meat, they consumed the meat for its recognised beneficial attributes.

Some respondents remembered using turtle shells for ornamentation (e.g. to hang on the walls of their house) and as storage containers (e.g. laundry). There were reports that turtles were also used to make jewellery but none of the study respondents said they did so. Turtle meat and eggs were also used as a form of currency to barter with residents who lived in inland villages (e.g. Açú da Torre). When asked why they engaged in turtle harvesting and put turtle products to such uses, respondents noted that economic hardship made it necessary during the plantation period. Praia do Forte and Açú da Torre residents commonly exchanged tapioca roots, tapioca flour, fruit and vegetables. Hence, consumption and use of turtles was primarily driven by necessity in Praia do Forte rather than as a means of providing an intercommunity or regional market for turtle products.

Contemporary uses and values

Before the opening of the VC, turtle images were initially used by TAMAR as education tools. Turtle images on posters and signs were placed along local beaches and at the research station. At this stage, sea turtle images were linked with educational messages to raise awareness about existing turtle conservation laws and activities as well as ecological reasons for protecting, rather than consuming the species. Hence, the main goal was to control turtle and egg harvesting, not to develop turtle tourism.

TAMAR visitor centre

If turtles were a traditionally valued food source, the arrival of TAMAR in the village and later tourism demand for turtle watching activities introduced a new financial incentive to protect the species. Today, the VC offers a plethora of educational sources to raise awareness about and gain support for turtle conservation at the local and national levels (Figure 15.1). At the VC, visitors can watch and learn about marine life via large tanks and aquariums, presentation of documentaries at the movie theatre, displays of photographs and interpretative panels in English and Portuguese, and guided tours. There is also a large retail store that sells only TAMAR products, a restaurant and a cultural area used by artists during conservation awareness events. The VC is also used as an open classroom for local children and youth enrolled on TAMAR's environmental education programmes (e.g. the Tamarzinho Program) (Pegas et al., 2012). The community is welcome to visit and use the VC's learning facilities free of charge. Captive-born turtles are displayed year-round, while hatchling releases occur between September and April.

The retail store at this VC is TAMAR's most popular, selling hundreds of turtle-related items from popular mass-produced items to handcrafted items produced by 12 community cooperatives located in four states.

Figure 15.1 Replica of a leatherback sea turtle at Praia do Forte's VC
Photo: Author.

Disseminating the flagship species concept at the community level

The popularity and expansion of the VC provided the community with an opportunity to earn income from the flagship species phenomena. It appears that turtle conservation and tourism also generate direct benefits to the community as a whole through improvements to local infrastructure and economic and educational opportunities for children and youth (e.g. Finn Larsen Kindergarten, the Tamarzinho Program).

Out of the 45 non-local respondents, 33 moved to the village for employment reasons. Thirty-two out of these 33 respondents earned income from tourism, 12 were employed by TAMAR, and 11 sold products with a turtle logo and/or turtle outline. These outcomes, said 74 (96%) respondents, were part of why they support the work of TAMAR in the village. In fact, there seems to be a strong association between the economic profitability of turtle tourism at TAMAR and the community's perception of the economic sustainability of the village. The following are some of the statements provided by both native and newcomer residents to the village: 'The turtles now have a different value... the people here in the village need tourism'; 'People need the turtles because of tourism'; 'They value [turtles] more now because of the tourism. The identity of Praia do Forte is connected with preservation, especially with the turtles'; and 'People here value the turtles in a different way now because of tourism, because it is from tourism that they make a living'. For some respondents, the linkage between the TAMAR VC and the local tourism industry is crucial:

> If a person comes to Praia do Forte and does not see a turtle, this person has not come to Praia do Forte. Turtles are Praia do Forte. They value [Praia do Forte] because the main point of Praia do Forte is TAMAR. TAMAR is the post card for the community. If it was not for TAMAR for certain the tourism level here would not be as high as it is today.

A similar perspective was presented by this respondent: 'The biggest tourist attractions here in the village are the turtles. Besides the turtles, the village does not have anything that the tourist would like to come and see.'

These perceptions appear to influence the way locals specifically value turtles. When asked if there is a change in the value of turtles from the period when they were harvested, the majority (97% of the native and 93% of the non-native respondents) agreed that this is true. They were also asked whether this change in value (i.e. support for the conservation rather than the harvesting of sea turtles) is associated with the economic value of live turtles. Respondents replied: 'People in the past did not give them value. They were of no importance. Now, they are very important. Valuing them is fundamental'; 'People value the turtles more now than before. This is because of TAMAR. TAMAR brings tourism, so they value them more.'

For one respondent, the popularity of sea turtles has created a shift in priorities: 'Turtles are now more important than the people here.' While such a perception could cause a backlash towards turtle conservation efforts, such feelings seem to be associated with a long history of government neglect. As explained by the native residents in this study, most of the resources allocated by the local government have targeted the tourism industry, not the needs of the impoverished members of the community. Consequently, the community has long been deprived of good education, health and safety resources. On the other hand, resources allocated to protect sea turtles and their habitat have been enhanced over the past years. Despite this perspective, this respondent and most of the respondents support turtle conservation because this practice has been generating direct socio-economic benefits for the community and residents. Some of these economic benefits take place via turtle marketing, offering visitors a variety of products and prices. Examples include items carved from stone, coconut and wood used for house ornamentation, jewellery, magnets, toys, soaps and t-shirts. While most are turtle-related goods not locally produced, turtle ecotourism has been providing the community with a viable and somewhat reliable income opportunity not found within the local fishing industry.

Turtle images are also been used by the local services industry, particularly the retail, food and transportation sectors (Figure 15.2). Most of these logos are used to attract visitors to these businesses; however, some logos are incorporated into the official trademark of the business, such as the Oliveira

Figure 15.2 Sea turtles displayed at the entrance of a pharmacy
Photo: Author.

businesses in the village (i.e. coffee shop, grocery store) and the transportation company Cootexlibra.

The hotel industry also capitalises on the 'flagship species phenomena', integrating the turtle image in their logos. Examples include the B&Bs, Pousada Farol das Tartarugas, Pousada Brasil and Pousada Tia Helena. The 5-star resort IberoStar took another approach. Rather than displaying turtles in its logo, images are displayed at some strategic areas along its golf course. Turtles are also used by social media, including the official websites of local and regional tourism advertisements, advertisements linked to the hotels and activities in the region, and information presented by tour operators to promote the village as a tourist destination. For example, Praia do Forte's main tourism website carries a turtle image on its official logo (i.e. www.praiadoforte.org.br).

Discussion

Using a flagship species to facilitate expected marketing, financial and educational goals means relying on the species' charisma and on external factors often unrelated to the ecological needs of the species. In the case of turtle conservation and tourism in Praia do Forte, five key factors appear to be critical drivers to changes in the way turtles are used and valued by the community: (i) active law enforcement by TAMAR researchers; (ii) a positive relationship between the community and the founders of TAMAR; (iii) the establishment of a profitable tourism and conservation initiative at the VC; (iv) a strong financial value; and (v) lack of a religious significance.

Enforcement continues to be a critical conservation strategy because sea turtle protection laws were poorly enforced and communicated to the community by the responsible environmental federal agency, the IBAMA. Enforcement of federally enacted turtle protection laws has been carried out by TAMAR researchers since 1982, who monitor local beaches and fishing activities, conduct meetings and informal dialogue with local fishermen, and provide education about the consequences of illegal harvesting (e.g. fines) to the greater community.

While conflicts between communities and government agencies as well as conservation organisations have been known to occur elsewhere (e.g. Gusset et al., 2009; Hemson et al., 2009), this seems not to have occurred in Praia do Forte. According to Pegas et al. (2013), the generation of employment opportunities and provision of livelihood resources (e.g. food, transportation, medical supplies) helped develop and maintain a positive relationship between the community and TAMAR founders for over 30 years.

Unlike in Mexico (Senko et al., 2014), consumption of sea turtle meat and eggs is not a cultural or religious tradition among Brazilian society. Therefore, the society's perception of sea turtles as non-food sources has had a significant influence on sea turtle conservation efforts and the efficiency of the flagship concept in Brazil. Positive ties and feelings of trust also allowed constructive dialogue between the fishermen of Praia do Forte and TAMAR researchers to take place. This helped enhance researchers' understanding of local socio-economic needs and traditions as well as the community's knowledge about turtles. This understanding is critical to reducing human impacts on sea turtles (Hamann *et al.*, 2010).

Lastly, the establishment of the TAMAR VC provided a key venue for turtle watching and a new source of income for both TAMAR and the community. This venture resulted in direct economic benefits from conservation. Hence, it is unlikely that the image of a turtle would have become so ubiquitous had the VC not been in place. With almost half a million annual visitors, turtle tourism and conservation make TAMAR's VC a signature destination for both 'specialist' and 'generalist' tourists (Wilson & Tisdell, 2001).

Tourism: A vital link

In Praia do Forte, whereas turtles are no longer consumed for their meat and eggs, they still support local livelihoods. Changes in value and uses are strongly associated with the economic profitability of turtle conservation via TAMAR. In fact, the image and conservation awareness of turtles are inseparable in the village. Turtle shells have been replaced by mock turtle imagery that dominates local businesses and tourist merchandise markets. This clearly indicates a conservation buy-in at the community level. While the preponderance of turtle images is primarily a marketing tactic, flagship species marketing also aids turtle conservation by highlighting the important role the species plays in the local tourism economy. This is a shift from valuing turtles for products that may have only 'family' benefits.

As in Mon Repos, Australia, tourism is a vital aspect of the successful promotion of turtles as iconic images of a destination. The profitability of turtle watching not only influences current activities, it also influences the way the local communities (e.g. traditional owners in the case of Mon Repos; Tisdell & Wilson, 2002b), perceive turtle conservation efforts. In Brazil, residents associated the establishment of TAMAR VC with the growth and profitability of the local tourism industry. They also recognise the presence of live turtles as a key attraction and tourism marketing component, and therefore the wide adoption of turtle images as logos. Beyond the local scale, the popularity of turtle conservation at TAMAR was a strong factor in the establishment of environmental state laws specifically tailored towards turtle conservation (e.g. no artificial lights on nesting beaches). Political support is also vital in controlling for illegal coastal tourism development within turtle reproduction areas. These are indicators that the flagship species concept has helped TAMAR gain political ground for turtle conservation across scales. TAMAR activities also ensured that turtles became the 'tourist ambassadors' for the village and helped secure the image of Praia do Forte as a turtle conservation tourist destination. The important marketing role of visual wildlife images to promote a tourist destination has also been noted by Castley *et al.* (2012).

As part of the definition of a flagship species, TAMAR VC also acts as a venue for educational programmes to take place (Pegas *et al.*, 2012). This mimics the situation in Mon Repos, where an information centre was established and a formal turtle watch organised in response to growing tourist interest over turtle nesting in the area (Tisdell & Wilson, 2002a). In most countries where harvesting, both legal and illegal, is prevalent, conservation efforts have yet to achieve similar results (e.g. Mancini & Koch, 2009; Nada & Casale, 2011).

The hope is that information presented in this chapter can be used to support the notion that reptiles can be successful flagship species candidates. Sea turtles seem to have an almost universal appeal. In Brazil, sea turtles are included in the national currency and TAMAR's turtle logos have been placed on the covers of chocolate bars and instant noodle packages. At the international level, sea turtles are pictured in postage stamps (Amr, 2013), agency logos, and flags (Eckert & Hemphill, 2005). From a species perspective, hatchlings are a powerful draw. In Praia do Forte, hatchling release ceremonies are TAMAR's most popular activities. Seeing large numbers of a flagship species in one place enhances tourists' viewing opportunities and experiences (Higginbottom & Buckley, 2003).

Perhaps attention to 'undervalued' species can help raise awareness about conservation needs for species not included in the cuddly category. As suggested by Home *et al.* (2009), other reptile species can be efficient conservation ambassadors. These charismatic species can act as drivers for the conservation of various endangered and non-endangered species where harvesting can threaten species survival. Businesses, including those in the tourism industry, can help with financial support through corporate social responsibility (CSR) initiatives (Buckley & Pegas, 2012). A prime example is the case of the IberoStar Resort which, in addition to displaying colourful sea turtles along its golf course, also funds a small interpretative sea turtle conservation centre located adjacent to the resort's golf course and staffed with TAMAR researchers.

Despite the successful case presented here, the presence of charismatic species is not sufficient to guarantee their survival or conservation of their habitat. This chapter describes just one successful conservation strategy. In this example, the use of flagship species enhances conservation awareness, raises funds and promotes a tourist destination. We know that the marketing potential of flagship species using visual imagery can heighten the pre-visit experience of destinations (Choi *et al.*, 2007). As in the case of koalas and kangaroos in Australia (Higginbottom *et al.*, 2004; Jenkins, 2003; Murphy, 2000), lions and elephants in Africa (Goodwin & Leader-Williams, 2000) and the Komodo dragon in Indonesia (Walpole & Leader-Williams, 2002), sea turtles are established iconic species of Praia do Forte and the adjacent region. This achievement is, in part, due to the effective role flagship species play in promoting both species conservation awareness and the village as a tourist destination.

Conclusions

While the efforts of TAMAR have been recognised on a national and international scale, Praia do Forte's framework may not be applicable to other turtle nesting sites. As noted by Hamann *et al.* (2010), effective sea turtle protection strategies are indeed not universal but may vary with each species, each management unit and perhaps even each nesting rookery. Still, some of the lessons learned from this case study have global applicability. Specifically: (i) it is critical to acquire and sustain a positive relationship between conservation programmes and the community if positive changes are to occur; (ii) the linkage between the image of the live species and enhancement of livelihood conditions must include provision of direct benefits to the local community; (iii) the implemented ecotourism initiatives must have a strong sustainable foundation to control negative impacts on the species and community in the event mass tourism development takes places in response to flagship marketing popularity; and (iv) it is vital that support from the tourism industry and government officials controls development impacts to the species and maintains active conservation efforts.

In closing, results from this study demonstrate that the effectiveness of flagship species does not only promote, generate funding for and raise awareness about conservation, but that flagship species are also an effective vehicle to promote a tourism destination.

Acknowledgments

I am grateful to the families of Praia do Forte for their generosity and for sharing their life stories about their beautiful community, as well as TAMAR for the support and assistance provided throughout the study. This study was partially funded by the NSF Cultural Anthropology Programme (#0724347; PI: Amanda Stronza), PADI Foundation, Viillo and Gene Phillips Scholarships, and funding from the Graduate Student Research Grant and The Center for Socioeconomic Research and Education at Texas A&M University.

References

Amr, Z.S. (2013) Reptiles on postage stamps in Arabian countries in western Asia and north Africa. *Russian Journal of Herpetology* 20 (1), 27–32.
Barua, M. (2011) Mobilizing metaphors: The popular use of keystone, flagship and umbrella species concepts. *Biodiversity and Conservation* 20 (7), 1427–1440.

Beerli, A. and Martin, J.D. (2004) Factors influencing destination image. *Annals of Tourism Research* 31 (3), 657–681.

Boshoff, A., Landman, M., Kerley, G. and Bradfield, M. (2007) Profiles, views and observations of visitors to the Addo Elephant National Park, Eastern Cape, South Africa. *South African Journal of Wildlife Research* 37, 189–196.

Buckley, R.C. and Pegas, F. (2012) Tourism and corporate social responsibility. In A. Holden and D. Fennell (eds) *Handbook of Tourism and Environment* (pp. 521–530). Oxford: Routledge.

Buckley, R.C., Castley, J.G., Pegas, F., Mossaz, A.C. and Steven, R. (2012) A population accounting approach to assess tourism contributions to conservation of IUCN-redlisted mammals. *PLoS ONE* 7 (9): e44134.

Castley, J.G., Bennet, A. and Pickering, C. (2012) Wildlife visual imagery: Do pictures used to promote destinations online match on-site species visibility at two geographic destinations? *Geographical Research* 51 (1), 59–70.

Clucas, B., McHugh, K. and Caro, T. (2008) Flagship species on covers of US conservation and nature magazines. *Biodiversity and Conservation* 17 (6), 1517–1528.

Curtin, S. (2010) What makes for memorable wildlife encounters? Revelations from 'serious' wildlife tourists. *Journal of Ecotourism* 9 (2), 149–168.

Davenport, J. and Davenport, J. (2006) The impact of tourism and personal leisure transport on coastal environments. *Estuary Coastal Shelf Science* 67, 280–292.

Echtner, C.M. and Ritchie, J.B. (1993) The measurement of destination image: An empirical assessment. *Journal of Travel Research* 31 (4), 3–13.

Eckert, K. and Hemphill, A. (2005) Sea turtles as flagship for protection of the wider Caribbean region. *MAST* 3 (2) and 4 (1), 119–143.

Frynta, D., Marešová, J., Řeháková-Petrů, M., Šklíba, J., Šumbera, R. and Krása, A. (2011) Cross-cultural agreement in perception of animal beauty: Boid snakes viewed by people from five continents. *Human Ecology* 39 (6), 829–834.

Fundação Pró-TAMAR (2012) *Annual Report – 2011*. Praia do Forte, Brazil: Projeto TAMAR.

Goodwin, H. and Leader-Williams, N. (2000) Tourism and protected areas: Distorting conservation priorities towards charismatic megafauna? In A. Entwistle and N. Dunston (eds) *Priorities for the Conservation of Mammalian Diversity: Has the Panda Had its Day?* (pp. 257–275). Cambridge: Cambridge University Press.

Gusset, M., Swarner, M.J., Mponwane, L., Keletile, K. and McNutt, J.W. (2009) Human–wildlife conflict in northern Botswana: Livestock predation by endangered African wild dog *Lycaon pictus* and other carnivores. *Oryx* 43 (1), 67–72.

Hamann, M., Godfrey, M.H., Seminoff, J.A., Arthur, K. and Barata, P.C. (2010) Global research priorities for sea turtles: Informing management and conservation in the 21st century. *Endangered Species Research* 11, 245–269.

Hemson, G., Maclennan, S., Mills, G., Johnson, P. and Macdonald, D. (2009) Community, lions, livestock and money: A spatial and social analysis of attitudes to wildlife and the conservation value of tourism in a human–carnivore conflict in Botswana. *Biological Conservation* 142 (11), 2718–2725.

Higginbottom, K. and Buckley, R. (2003) *Terrestrial Wildlife Viewing in Australia*. Wildlife Tourism Report Series No. 9. Nathan, Queensland: CRC for Sustainable Tourism, Griffith University.

Higginbottom, K., Northrope, C., Croft, D., Hill, B. and Fredline, L. (2004) The role of kangaroos in Australian tourism. *Australian Mammology* 26, 23–32.

Home, R., Keller, C., Nagel, P., Bauer, N. and Hunziker, M. (2009) Selection criteria for flagship species by conservation organizations. *Environmental Conservation* 36 (2), 139–148.

Jenkins, O. (2003) Photography and travel brochures: The circle of representation. *Tourism Geographies* 5, 305–328.

Landry, M. and Taggart, C. (2010) 'Turtle watching' conservation guidelines: Green turtle (*Chelonia mydas*) tourism in near shore coastal environments. *Biodiversity Conservation* 19, 305–312.

Lindsey, P., Alexander, R., Mills, M., Romanach, S. and Woodroffe, R. (2007) Wildlife viewing preferences of visitors to protected areas in South Africa: Implications for the role of ecotourism in conservation. *Journal of Ecotourism* 6 (1), 19–33.

Mancini, A. and Koch, V. (2009) Sea turtle consumption and black market trade in Baja California Sur, Mexico. *Endangered Species Research* 7 (1), 1–10.

Marcovaldi, M. and Laurent, A. (1996) A six season study of marine turtle nesting at Praia do Forte, Bahia, Brazil, with implications for conservation and management. *Chelonian Conservation & Biology* 2 (1), 55–59.

Marcovaldi, M.A. and Marcovaldi, G. (1999) Marine turtles of Brazil: The history and structure of Projeto TAMAR-IBAMA. *Biological Conservation* 91, 35–41.

Murphy, L. (2000) Australia's image as a holiday destination: Perceptions of backpacker visitors. *Journal of Travel and Tourism Marketing* 8, 21–45.

Nada, M. and Casale, P. (2011) Sea turtle bycatch and consumption in Egypt threatens Mediterranean turtle populations. *Oryx* 45 (1), 143–149.

Pegas, F. (2012) Carrot-and-stick approaches to biodiversity conservation: The case of sea turtles in Brazil. *Applied Biodiversity Science Perspective Series* 2 (3).

Pegas, F. and Buckley, R.C. (2012) Ecotourism in the Americas. In S. Beavis, M. Dougherty and T. Gonzales (eds) *The Berkshire Encyclopedia of Sustainability: Vol. 8. The Americas and Oceania: Assessing Sustainability* (pp. 90–91). Great Barrington, MA: Berkshire Publishing.

Pegas, F. and Stronza, A. (2010) Ecotourism and sea turtle harvesting in a fishing village of Bahia, Brazil. *Conservation and Society* 8 (1), 15–25.

Pegas, F., Coghlan, A. and Rocha, V. (2012) An exploration of a mini-guide program: Training local children in sea turtle conservation and ecotourism in Brazil. *Journal of Ecotourism* 11 (1), 48–55.

Pegas, F., Coghlan, A., Stronza, A. and Rocha, V. (2013) For love or for money? Investigating the impact of an ecotourism programme on local residents' assigned values towards sea turtles. *Journal of Ecotourism* 12 (2), 90–106.

Pike, S. (2002) Destination image analysis – a review of 142 papers from 1973 to 2000. *Tourism Management* 23 (5), 541–549.

Prefeitura Municipal da Mata de São João (2004) Adequação do Plano Diretor Urbano de Mata de São João ao Estatuto da Cidade. Mata de São João, Bahia, Brazil: Prefeitura Municipal de Mata de São João. Internal Report.

Sachs, J., Baillie, J., Sutherland, W., Armsworth, P. and Ash, N. (2009) Biodiversity conservation and the millennium development goals. *Science* 325, 1502–1503.

Senko, J., Mancini, A., Seminoff, J.A. and Koch, V. (2014) Bycatch and directed harvest drive high green turtle mortality at Baja California Sur, Mexico. *Biological Conservation* 169, 24–30.

Simberloff, D. (1998) Flagships, umbrellas and keystones: Is single species management passé in the landscape era? *Biological Conservation* 83, 247–257.

Sorice, M., Shafer, C. and Ditton, R. (2006) Managing endangered species within the use–preservation paradox: The Florida manatee (*Trichechus manatus latirostris*) as a tourism attraction. *Environmental Management* 37, 69–83.

Tisdell, C. and Wilson, C. (2002a) *Economic, Educational and Conservation Benefits of Sea Turtle Based Ecotourism: A Study Focused on Mon Repos.* Wildlife Tourism Research Report Series No. 20, Nathan, Queensland: CRC for Sustainable Tourism, Griffith University.

Tisdell, C. and Wilson, C. (2002b) Ecotourism for the survival of sea turtles and other wildlife. *Biodiversity and Conservation* 11, 1521–1538.

Tisdell, C. and Wilson, C. (2005) Does tourism contribute to sea turtle conservation? Is the flagship status of turtles advantageous? *MAST* 3 (2) and 4 (1), 145–167.

Tremblay, P. (2002) Tourism wildlife icons: Attractions or marketing symbols? *Proceedings of the 2002 CAUTHE Conference*, Fremantle, Western Australia.

Veja (2007) *Praia: O Melhor Destino.* See http://veja.abril.com.br/especiais/brasil_2007/p_018.html (accessed 25 November 2013).

Walpole, M.J. and Leader-Williams, N. (2002) Tourism and flagship species in conservation. *Biodiversity and Conservation* 11 (3), 543–547.

Wilson, C. and Tisdell, C. (2001) Sea turtles as a non-consumptive tourism resource especially in Australia. *Tourism Management* 22, 279–288.

Woods, B. (2000) Beauty and the beast: Preferences for animals in Australia. *Journal of Tourism Studies* 11 (2), 25–35.

16 Ambassadors or Attractions? Disentangling the Role of Flagship Species in Wildlife Tourism

Jeffrey C. Skibins

Introduction

Wildlife tourism (WT), by definition, is reliant on tourists. Therefore, WT venues must be attractive to tourists. And, in order to be attractive, venues must have species that have broad public appeal. Often these considerations result in a disproportionate emphasis being placed on just a few species. Additionally, many venues have embraced a more active role in biodiversity conservation, and thus seek to deliver outcomes aligned with sustainability principles, the goal being to extend conservation benefits to species beyond those in the limelight.

And therein lies the rub. The juxtaposition of tourist attraction and conservation goals has led to a great deal of confusion surrounding the role of certain animals in WT. To enhance their public appeal, parks, protected areas and zoos rely on a small handful of charismatic species. And this seems to be a highly effective strategy, as the combined annual visitation for these venues exceeds several hundred million visitors (Higginbottom, 2004a). Subsequently, a growing trend in WT is to link these charismatic species with conservation campaigns. This strategy is based on the assumption that the public's attraction to a species will translate into pro-conservation behaviours (such as philanthropy and volunteering).

The link of a species' public appeal with conservation outcomes is the basis of conferring flagship species status. Flagships are a surrogate species concept rooted in conservation biology, and can be used to address a wide range of anthropogenic threats to biodiversity conservation (Caro &

O'Doherty, 1999; Simberloff, 1998; see also de Vasconcellos Pegas, Chapter 15, this volume). Flagship species are selected for their ability to raise public awareness and action. As such, they are ideally suited to the task of blending the role of tourist attraction and animal ambassador, thus delivering sustainable outcomes from WT.

The success of flagship-based tourism is often attributed to the formation of a connection to nature, within the tourist, that is derived from these encounters with wildlife (Saunders, 2003). Tourists have been shown to develop a strong connection to individual animals observed in wild and captive settings, and this connection has been shown to extend to the species as a whole (Curtin, 2006; Schanzel & McIntosh, 2000; Skibins & Powell, 2013). The effects of such encounters are often enhanced when in the presence of large mammals. Several studies have shown that visitors are strongly attracted to animals such as big cats, giraffes and great apes, and that viewing these animals is a primary motivation for a trip (Figures 16.1 and 16.2) (Kerley *et al.*, 2003; Lindsey *et al.*, 2007).

However, there is often a disconnect between simple attraction and flagship outcomes. Critics point out that conflating popularity with conservation outcomes at best dilutes, and at worst entirely fails to deliver the objectives in using flagship species. Russell and Ankenman (1996: 71) note, 'if a certain species of animal is seen only as a commodity, there exists the danger that once the value of that commodity decreases, there will be less

Figure 16.1 A shared gaze? Charismatic megafauna such as giraffes attract the bulk of wildlife tourists who participate in safaris in a number of African nations
Photo: Betty Weiler.

Figure 16.2 Tourists observing and photographing a chimpanzee, Uganda
Photo: Betty Weiler.

rationale for conservation efforts on that species' behalf'. Additionally, practitioners are left to struggle with how best to garner attraction, awareness and action for non-charismatic species such as reptiles and insects – species that Myers *et al.* (2004) refer to as 'biophilically challenged' (see also Lemelin, Chapter 14, this volume).

Wildlife Tourism

Nature-based tourism may be defined as tourism in which the natural environment is the principal attraction (Buckley, 1994). WT is a recognised subset of activities within nature-based tourism. These activities may be taxon specific such as whale watching, or broadly based such as African safaris. Additionally, activities may be categorised based on impacts (consumptive/non-consumptive), venue (e.g. natural area, wildlife sanctuary or zoo/aquarium), or type of animals encountered (e.g. domesticated/non-domesticated, avian, marine) (Higginbottom, 2004a).

Due in part to the wide range of activities and venues, there has been some difficulty in developing a consensus definition of wildlife tourism. Roe *et al.* (1997) provide a broad definition that includes uses, participation rates, sustainability, impacts and duration as qualifiers to distinguish WT from ecotourism. Higginbottom (2004a) has modified this definition to be more

Table 16.1 Non-consumptive wildlife viewing activities and venues

Wildlife viewing activity	Representative venues
Unguided experiences (no direct involvement of commercial tour operators)	National parks, protected areas
Visits to captive settings	Zoos, [a]aquariums, [a]wildlife sanctuaries
Specialised wildlife viewing outings	Whale watching, safaris, birding
Managed localised natural phenomena	Migratory routes, breeding colonies, caves
Guide-led tours to view wildlife in natural settings	National parks, protected areas, private reserves
Volunteer assistance for universities and conservation NGOs	National parks, protected areas, private reserves

Notes: [a]Refers to zoos and aquariums that are members of the Association of Zoos and Aquariums (AZA) and/or the World Association of Zoos and Aquariums (WAZA).

reflective of the experience. For the purposes of this chapter, WT will be defined as tourism that provides encounters with non-domesticated animals in wild (*in situ*) or captive (*ex situ*) settings. The following discussion of WT will be limited to non-consumptive activities (i.e. activities that do not result in the intentional death or removal of animals from the wild). This abbreviated version is supported by the definitions of Roe *et al.* (1997) and Higginbottom (2004a). Table 16.1, adapted from Valentine and Birtles (2004), provides a brief overview of commonly recognised non-consumptive wildlife viewing activity categorisations and their respective venues.

Supporters of WT argue that exposing massive numbers of the public to wildlife creates memorable experiences and stimulates a connection to nature (Curtin, 2010; Ryan *et al.*, 2000; Zaradic *et al.*, 2009). This offsets any negative impacts and produces a net overall positive impact for conservation. However, several studies have documented the severity of negative impacts to wildlife from WT (Berman *et al.*, 2007; Sandbrook & Semple, 2006), and note that the increased public demand for the rare and exotic have exposed previously untrammelled areas to tourism's heavy footprint (Markwell, 2001; Terborgh, 2004). Thus, the very popularity of a species that draws tourists to a site may prove to hasten the extirpation of that species.

Conservation Outcomes

When managed for sustainability, WT is purported to produce direct conservation outcomes such as increased funding, educational opportunities, political support and sociocultural initiatives for species of concern (Higginbottom *et al.*, 2003; Orams, 1997; Wilson & Tisdell, 2003).

Additionally, encounters with animals during a tourism experience are claimed to stimulate a connection to nature, increase awareness and create peak experiences (Miller, 2005; Russell, 1994; Russell & Ankenman, 1996). Such encounters are hypothesised to drive support, within the participants, for conservation action (Saunders, 2003; Saunders & Myers, 2003; Saunders et al., 2006).

As the primary activity of WT is viewing wildlife, most initiatives are designed to support species of visitor interest. To that end, both *in situ* and *ex situ* WT venues have relied on charismatic megafauna (CMF) to anchor conservation outcomes. For example, Myers et al. (2004) found that zoo visitors who observed gorillas or okapis expressed increased levels of care and a strong desire to see them preserved in the wild. Ballantyne et al. (2011) found visitors developed an emotional affinity for dolphins, and that this connection can be applied to broader levels of biodiversity. After observing lion behaviour, Cousins et al. (2009) report that tourist volunteers express a deep sense of wonder, awe and a connection with nature. Additionally, Orams (1997) found that education programmes, in conjunction with direct animal encounters, increased visitors' willingness to adopt 'green' behaviours. These findings support the premise that exposure to CMF can elicit positive affects in tourists and such responses can be stimuli for pro-conservation behaviour.

The most common pro-conservation behaviour is the generation of funds through direct fees and/or philanthropy (Newsome et al., 2005; Okello et al., 2008; Tisdell et al., 2007). Willingness to pay is a frequently used metric to assess individuals' acceptance of increased fees and their level of intended financial contribution. Willingness to pay has been shown to be extremely high for *in situ* conservation of the giant panda (Kontoleon & Swanson, 2003), endangered Australian mammal, bird and reptile cohorts – regardless of likeability (Tisdell et al., 2005, 2007), and increased entrance fees to Komodo National Park (Walpole & Leader-Williams, 2002). Additional examples of conservation outcomes that can be enhanced through WT include:

- habitat preservation (Caro & Girling, 2010);
- green consumerism (Ballantyne et al., 2011);
- increased participation in venue sponsored events (Dickie et al., 2007);
- volunteering (Cousins et al., 2009);
- political activism (Higginbottom et al., 2003).

A more generalised source of financial benefits is through increased visitation. East African national parks enjoy exceptionally high visitation rates and much of this is attributed to the presence of CMF. Zoos that house and display CMF also report similar patterns of visitation. Increased visitation carries with it increases in gate revenue, special fees and donations. Ideally, these funds can be directed towards conservation efforts.

Conservation Psychology

The field of conservation psychology provides a framework to better understand the conservation outcomes associated with WT. The goal of conservation psychology is to understand the interdependence of humans and nature and to promote a healthy and sustainable relationship. This addresses the theme pointed out by Mascia et al. (2003: 650) that 'Biodiversity conservation is a human endeavor: initiated by humans, designed by humans, and intended to modify human behavior to achieve a socially desired objective – conservation of species, habitats, and ecosystems'. However, one challenge that arises is in understanding what humans value and how much human presence is compatible with conservation goals (Saunders et al., 2006).

Conservation psychology is well suited to addressing this challenge because it is both an applied and basic discipline. It is applied because the primary goal is to address and ameliorate environmental issues; basic because it is based on theory (Clayton & Myers, 2009). In an early and definitive treatise, Saunders (2003: 138) defines conservation psychology as:

> the scientific study of the reciprocal relationships between humans and the rest of nature, with a particular focus on how to encourage conservation of the natural world. Conservation psychology is an applied field that uses psychological principles, theories, or methods to understand and solve issues related to human aspects of conservation. It has a strong mission focus in that it is motivated by the need to encourage people to care about and take care of the natural world.

Conservation psychology specifically focuses on how to actively encourage the conservation element of the human–environment relationship. The empirical testing of the relationship between caring for and conserving a resource is one avenue of research promulgated by conservation psychology (Saunders, 2003; Vining, 2003). Several studies have begun to investigate this relationship. DeMares (2000) found that interactions with cetaceans led tourists to seek an outlook that overcame the perceived estrangement between humans and nature. Bruni et al. (2008) found that zoo visits can stimulate an individual's connectedness to nature. Skibins and Powell (2013) measured zoo visitors' connection to a species. Not only were visitors capable of forming a connection to a species during a zoo visit, but this connection was strongly predictive of pro-conservation behavioural intent.

However, a connection to nature itself may not always produce the desired conservation outcomes. For example, Chapman (2003) states that wildlife viewers in Elk Island National Park were only concerned with large wildlife and were dismissive of birds and smaller species. Okello et al. (2008) report that tourists' strong desire to see cheetahs can severely restrict cheetah hunting and ultimately decrease survival. Cohen (2010) presents a fascinating case study of Thai zoos inadvertently pitting elephant and panda interest groups against one another. The public's connection to these two species was enmeshed with several social movements and led to a nationwide critique of conservation.

WT provides an ideal laboratory to examine how tourists' wildlife viewing experience influences a connection with a species and stimulates the adoption of pro-conservation behaviours. Understanding this relationship can provide greater insight for differentiating the role of species as simple tourist attraction or ambassador for conservation.

Attractions or Ambassadors

Animals such as bears, big cats and marine mammals are the lifeblood of WT and an easily identifiable icon for conservationists (Figure 16.3). But what is it about these animals that the public finds so appealing or, more precisely, charismatic? Lorimer (2007: 915) defines animal charisma thus: 'Nonhuman charisma can best be defined as the distinguishing properties of a non-human entity or process that determine its perception by humans and its subsequent evaluation.' Non-human charisma is subject to anthropogenic manipulation and consists of three dimensions: ecological, aesthetic and corporeal. Within these dimensions, certain characteristics are often used to promote a species' role as attraction or ambassador. Table 16.2 provides an overview of common characteristics associated with species' charisma and which positively influence public perception.

Figure 16.3 A lion crossing a road among tour vehicles in Tanzania
Photo: Betty Weiler.

Table 16.2 Characteristics of wildlife charisma

Characteristic	Reference
Taxonomic grouping/ similarity to humans	Caro and Girling, 2010; Leader-Williams and Dublin, 2000; Sitas *et al.*, 2009; Tisdell *et al.*, 2005; Woods, 2000
Large bodied/body mass	Fuhrman and Ladewig, 2008; Kellert, 1996; Leader-Williams and Dublin, 2000; Sitas *et al.*, 2009; Woods, 2000
Level of endangerment	Sitas *et al.*, 2009; Tisdell *et al.*, 2005
Activity level/movement/ understandable behaviour	Bowen-Jones and Entwistle, 2002; Fuhrman and Ladewig, 2008; Jacobs, 2009; Kellert, 1996; Lorimer, 2007; Rolston, 1987; Woods, 2000
Carnivorous/dangerous	Caro and Girling, 2010; Goodwin and Leader-Williams, 2000; Kaltenborn *et al.*, 2006; Kellert, 1996; Okello *et al.*, 2008; Rolston, 1987; Woods, 2000
Large eyes	Lorimer, 2007; Rolston, 1987
Connection to ecosystem/ cultural association	Bowen-Jones and Entwistle, 2002; Caro and Girling, 2010; Kaltenborn *et al.*, 2006; Kellert, 1996; Leader-Williams and Dublin, 2000; Rolston, 1987; Woods, 2000
Aesthetics	Goodwin and Leader-Williams, 2000; Kellert, 1996; Lorimer, 2007; Tisdell *et al.*, 2005; Woods, 2000
Intelligence	Kellert, 1996; Woods, 2000

Historically, CMF have simply served as tourist attractions (Beardsworth & Bryman, 2001; Draper, 2005). The desire to see CMF, *in situ* and *ex situ*, is a driving force behind the massive participation rates in WT (Valentine & Birtles, 2004). Moreover, the presence of CMF is a major determinant of visitation rates, particularly for zoos and aquariums, which is a common metric of success (Zimmermann, 2010). However, as WT venues adopt a wider conservation role, the trend is to embrace a more conservation-based role for these species, that of 'animal ambassador' (Hutchins *et al.*, 2003; Shani & Pizam, 2010).

As a tourist attraction, a species' primary role is to drive attendance and revenue. As an ambassador, a species is expected to be a catalyst for a conservation campaign. Both roles rely on a species' charisma. However, charisma in an ambassador species is expected to deliver more than attendance. An ambassador's charisma should facilitate an emotional connection between the tourist and the species. This emotional connection is expected to provide the basis for a more long-term concern for the species' conservation. However, the temptation to transition an attraction-based species to an ambassador is often too great for many venues to resist. This strategy is based on the assumption that species which are wildly popular with the public will, by default, stimulate public action. Thus, animals that garner the most attention are linked to conservation campaigns that the venue is promoting. While this strategy may be effective, it is often so only due to chance.

This is because the chain linking simple charisma to direct action is tenuous at best and dependent on the individual WT experience. Additionally, the role of popularity as a catalyst for conservation action has been called into question. As Lorimer (2007) points out, charisma is subject to anthropogenic manipulation. Thus, what defines charisma may differ between tourist subgroups and/or cultures. For example, more experienced tourists may enter experiences with higher levels of awareness, and thus not be influenced by 'popular' ambassadors (Beaumont, 2001; Lee & Moscardo, 2005). Furthermore, 'traditional' charisma features (Table 16.2) may not resonate with experienced tourists who often seek exposure to a wider numbers of species (i.e. less popular/traditionally charismatic) versus focusing on a few select attractions (Curtin, 2009).

So, although a species' charisma is a fundamental building block of generating support for conservation campaigns, assuming public popularity will translate to an emotional connection, which in turn will translate into action, is a poor strategy. A better approach is to select potential ambassador species on the basis of the target market, sociocultural norms, appropriate linkages to the conservation messages and relevant charismatic features. The purposeful link of these elements, prior to a campaign, can provide a greater effectiveness of the ambassador species to deliver conservation outcomes such as garnering political support, altering consumer behaviours and funding habitat preservation.

Flagship Species and Wildlife Tourism

A more technically specific and appropriate term for 'animal ambassador' is flagship species. As mentioned earlier, flagship species is a surrogate species concept borrowed from conservation biology. Other surrogate species categories include keystone, umbrella, focal and indicator. What differentiates flagship species from these other concepts is that the conservation outcomes associated with flagships are social and not ecological in nature.

Heywood (1995: 491) defines the concept of flagship species as 'popular, charismatic species that serve as symbols and rallying points to stimulate conservation awareness and action'. Additionally, Heywood provides two examples of flagship scales. The first is the traditional CMF such as large cats and primates. The second addresses smaller sized and less traditional taxa such as plants and insects. This is a critical, but often overlooked, element of the definition. More recently, Caro and Girling (2010) have clarified the types of conservation outcomes flagships tend to deliver. They propose promotion of conservation awareness, self-promotion, raising funds and setting up reserves as the principal objectives in using flagship species.

Because flagship species are expected to produce certain outcomes, it is possible to measure their effectiveness. However, this assumes that a species has been chosen as a flagship a priori. Too often, increased revenues and attendance are accepted as flagship conservation outcomes. Thus the public demand for viewing a species is erroneously assumed to be a conservation commitment. When simple popularity is mistaken for a flagship outcome, the long-term impacts can be quite severe for wildlife and conservation projects may be prioritised on unscientific grounds (Sergio et al., 2006).

The popularity of certain species can hinder sustainability due to the increase in negative impacts from high visitation rates such as changes in diversity, population declines, increased predation and increased mortality (Berman et al., 2007; Haysmith et al., 1995; Heil et al., 2007). Increased visitation may also compromise the effectiveness of conservation outcomes for sympatric species. Often, venues may focus so heavily on maximising viewing options for popular species that other species on site suffer. This can include maintaining artificially high populations, or exotic introductions (Sims-Castley et al., 2005). Conflating popularity with flagship outcomes can also have a negative impact on neighbouring communities. Broader socio-economic issues such as livestock losses, human deaths and neglect of high conservation priority areas have been linked to increasing pressure from WT (Sergio et al., 2006; Wilkie & Carpenter, 1999). As Walpole and Leader-Williams (2002) point out, if benefits are contingent on visitation rates, and not behaviour change, what happens when visitors stop coming?

However, when species are purposefully selected and flagship outcomes are aligned with specific conservation campaigns, the results can be incredibly positive. In order to be an effective flagship, a species should have charismatic features that resonate with the target audience and culture in which the flagship is to be launched. These features should be interpreted in such a way as to help the audience develop an emotional connection to the animal. Based on this connection, direct calls to action, which align with specific conservation objectives, can then be made of tourists.

The intentional selection of a species to serve as a flagship is the most critical step in the process. To understand which species are viable candidates, one must know the context in which the flagship is to be marketed. Bowen-Jones and Entwistle (2002) provide 10 criteria for selecting 'locally appropriate' species. Regardless of context, the flagship should be a species that the intended audience is willing to support and/or tolerate restrictions for surrounding its management (Home et al., 2009).

Several studies have shown the differential responses of wildlife tourists. For example, Ballantyne et al. (2009) report that tourists to the Mon Repos Conservation Park were willing to limit their own interaction with turtles in order to minimise impacts. Myers et al. (2004) found zoo visitors were capable of linking specific emotional responses with different species.

Gorillas and okapis generated feelings of beauty and peacefulness, whereas snakes generated feelings of fear and disgust. Beh and Bruyere (2007) provide an overview of safari tourists and their preferences for WT experiences. Across all three tourist types, each was more interested in general nature viewing relative to species-specific sightings. This runs contrary to traditional 'Big 5' marketing and reinforces the caveat of not confusing popularity as flagship status.

Not only is it important to understand contextual responses, it is necessary to know what will stimulate desired responses. Size is one of the most basic features known to elicit a connection in tourists, hence the term 'megafauna'. Zoo visitors tend to prefer larger animals, and report size, activity level and biogeographical information were strong traits in facilitating a connection (Fuhrman & Ladewig, 2008; Ward et al., 1998). In a study of Australian tourists, Woods (2000) concludes that there is a general trend for large species with human similarities and behaviours that are readily understandable. Kaltenborn et al. (2006) propose that cultural and religious traditions associated with flagship species can be strong motivations for accepting sometimes unpopular management actions.

Intentionally structuring WT experiences on the basis of contextual responses and charismatic features is a powerful tool to elicit an emotional connection in tourists. In a study of a swim-with-dolphin experience, tourists reported feelings of euphoria and peak experiences (Curtin, 2006). Visitors to Penguin Place (Otago, New Zealand) expressed feelings of 'pleasure, curiosity, privilege, amazement and fascination' following a viewing experience (Schanzel & McIntosh, 2000: 49). Zoo visitors also expressed an increase in an 'implicit connectedness with nature' (Bruni et al., 2008: 143). Smith et al. (2008b) sought to understand both psychological and physiological responses of zoo visitors who attended shows featuring birds of prey. A combination of self-reports and physiological monitoring revealed that visitors experienced increases in emotional arousal as indicated by increased levels of happiness, pleasantness, heart rate and breathing patterns.

In an early call for conservation psychology-based research, Vining (2003) makes an eloquent case for understanding the value of an emotional connection to wildlife. One of her key points is in determining how an emotional connection with a species can be a catalyst to broader behaviours. Since then, several authors have provided examples of how an emotional connection can lead to flagship outcomes. In the transition from connection to awareness and action, interpretation can be a highly effective tool (Ballantyne et al., 2007; Ham & Weiler, 2002; Skibins et al., 2012b).

Swanagan (2000) reports that zoo visitors who are actively engaged in interpretive experiences (e.g. attend first-person interpretive programmes) were more likely to support elephant conservation than visitors who simply observe elephants and read signage. Smith and Sutton (2008) found exposure to interpretive material raised awareness and led to the formation of behavioural intent. Interpretation has also been shown to be effective at converting behavioural intention into action (Orams, 1997).

Generating action is the ultimate objective of flagship species. This is a more recent line of enquiry but is producing promising results. After participating in the free flight 'Spirits of the Sky' programme at Healesville Sanctuary, Australia, visitors were more likely to adopt behaviours specific to avian conservation. Six months after the visit, 68% reported starting or increasing a conservation action (Smith *et al.*, 2008a). Tourists who had positive interactions with grizzly bears were more supportive of management actions and had a greater awareness of conservation initiatives in Denali National Park (Skibins *et al.*, 2012a). Following encounters with sea turtles, tourists were more likely to adopt conservation monitoring behaviours.

There was also a general trend for increased philanthropy and political support (Wilson & Tisdell, 2003). Ballantyne *et al.* (2011) reported that 7% of tourists adopted a new conservation behaviour (e.g. altering household and consumer practices, and volunteering), and 11% reported a heightened awareness of the need to adopt conservation behaviours following a marine-based WT experience. Their study also provides a solid blueprint for designing WT experiences that can provide 'powerful memories, enhance the visitor experience, and encourage visitors to adopt environmentally responsible behaviours in response to their visit' (Ballantyne *et al.*, 2011: 778).

Other studies have also explored the types of behaviours WT venues should seek. Pro-conservation behaviours that tourists are likely to adopt should be simple to perform and available on site. Additionally, behaviours should be relevant to the experience. Broad generic calls to action are not as effective. Rather, actions that are linked to the species observed and that reinforce messaging are more likely to be adopted (Powell & Ham, 2008; Smith *et al.*, 2010). Skibins *et al.* (2013) tested these trends between wild and captive venues and found no differences.

Another promising line of WT experiences designed to deliver flagship outcomes is the exploration of non-traditional species (Cristancho & Vining, 2004; Huntly *et al.*, 2005; Lemelin, 2007, and this volume, Chapter 14). Within Western cultures, plants, insects, amphibians and reptiles often fail to make the list of popular and/or charismatic species. As such, they are often excluded from consideration for flagship status. This is unfortunate because these taxa are often in desperate need of conservation and contain many features that are known to be charismatic (Table 16.2). Recent studies suggest that wildlife tourists are capable of forming a connection to a much broader array of species than traditionally utilised (Skibins & Powell, 2013; Skibins *et al.*, 2013). WT venues that begin to purposefully explore 'biophilically challenged' species as potential flagships could not only improve conservation outcomes for a greater degree of biodiversity, but also attract a wider market share of experienced tourists.

Conclusions

WT is often a victim of its own success. *In situ* sites are experiencing constant pressure as tourists press into pristine environments. *Ex situ* sites are often relegated to competing with theme parks as mere entertainment options. However, the public's continued demand for wildlife viewing experiences can be a diamond in the rough for conservationists. There is strong evidence to suggest that tourists can: (i) form an emotional connection to a species; (ii) a wide array of species (i.e. not only CMF) can elicit this connection; and (iii) this connection can lead to the adoption of pro-conservation behaviours. Coupled with tourists' expectations that WT venues actively contribute to conservation (Tribe, 2004; Zimmermann, 2010) these data suggest flagship-based experiences are ideally positioned to make significant and lasting contributions to biodiversity conservation.

Through the intentional design of experiences, coupled with strategically aligned interpretation, venues can create a setting wherein tourists are likely to form a connection to an animal and participate in actions to conserve that species. As venues purposefully select flagship species, they should explore those that are lesser known and can benefit from the types of pro-conservation behaviours tourists can perform. Having the ability to execute action on site is a critical element for delivering flagship outcomes. To this end, interpretation can be a very useful tool. Through a strategic communication plan, a species' unique conservation story may be told and tourists can be presented with an opportunity to perform the desired conservation-related behaviours.

As venues and tourists continue to co-evolve, we are in the enviable position of being partners in a common conservation mandate. Building synergies between *in situ* and *ex situ* sites may be another role for flagships. Flagship species can serve as a bridge to developing a stronger conservation ethic, garnering a greater appreciation for biodiversity as a whole, and moving both managers and tourists to action.

References

Ballantyne, R., Packer, J., Hughes, K. and Dierking, L. (2007) Conservation learning in wildlife tourism settings: Lessons from research in zoos and aquariums. *Environmental Education Research* 13 (3), 367–383.

Ballantyne, R., Packer, J. and Hughes, K. (2009) Tourists' support for conservation messages and sustainable management practices in wildlife tourism experiences. *Tourism Management* 30 (5), 658–664; doi:10.1016/j.tourman.2008.11.003.

Ballantyne, R., Packer, J. and Sutherland, L.A. (2011) Visitors' memories of wildlife tourism: Implications for the design of powerful interpretive experiences. *Tourism Management* 32 (4), 770–779.

Beardsworth, A. and Bryman, A. (2001) The wild animal in late modernity: The case of the Disneyization of zoos. *Tourist Studies* 1 (1), 83–104.

Beaumont, N. (2001) Ecotourism and the conservation ethic: Recruiting the uninitiated or preaching to the converted? *Journal of Sustainable Tourism* 9, 317–341.

Beh, A. and Bruyere, B.L. (2007) Segmentation by visitor motivation in three Kenyan national reserves. *Tourism Management* 28 (6), 1464–1471; doi:10.1016/ j.tourman.2007.01.010.

Berman, C.M., Li, J., Ogawa, H., Ionica, C. and Yin, H. (2007) Primate tourism, range restriction, and infant risk among macaca thibetana at Mt. Huangshan, China. *International Journal of Primatology* 28 (5), 1123–1141.

Bowen-Jones, E. and Entwistle, A. (2002) Identifying appropriate flagship species: The importance of culture and local contexts. *Oryx* 36 (2), 189–195; doi:10.1017/ s0030605302000261.

Bruni, C., Fraser, J. and Schultz, P. (2008) The value of zoo experiences for connecting people with nature. *Visitor Studies* 11 (2), 139–150.

Buckley, R. (1994) A framework for ecotourism. *Annals of Tourism Research* 21 (3), 661–665.

Caro, T.M. and Girling, S. (2010) *Conservation by Proxy: Indicator, Umbrella, Keystone, Flagship, and Other Surrogate Species.* Washington, DC: Island Press.

Caro, T.M. and O'Doherty, G. (1999) On the use of surrogate species in conservation biology. *Conservation Biology* 13 (4), 805–814.

Chapman, R. (2003) Memorable wildlife encounters in Elk Island National Park. *Human Dimensions of Wildlife: An International Journal* 8 (3), 235–236.

Clayton, S. and Myers, O.G. (2009) *Conservation Psychology: Understanding and Promoting Human Care for Nature.* Hoboken, NJ: Wiley-Blackwell.

Cohen, E. (2010) Panda and elephant – contesting animal icons in Thai tourism. *Journal of Tourism and Cultural Change* 8 (3), 154–171.

Cousins, J.A., Evans, J. and Sadler, J.P. (2009) 'I've paid to observe lions, not map roads!' – an emotional journey with conservation volunteers in South Africa. *Geoforum* 40 (6), 1069–1080.

Cristancho, S. and Vining, J. (2004) Culturally defined keystone species. *Human Ecology Review* 11 (2), 153–164.

Curtin, S. (2006) Swimming with dolphins: A phenomenological exploration of tourist recollections. *International Journal of Tourism Research* 8 (4), 301–315.

Curtin, S. (2009) The self-presentation and self-development of serious wildlife tourists. *International Journal of Tourism Research* 12 (1), 17–33.

Curtin, S. (2010) What makes for memorable wildlife encounters? Revelations from 'serious' wildlife tourists. *Journal of Ecotourism* 9 (2), 149–168.

DeMares, R. (2000) Human peak experience triggered by encounters with cetaceans. *Anthrozoos: A Multidisciplinary Journal of The Interactions of People and Animals* 13 (2), 89–103.

Dickie, L.A., Bonner, J.P. and West, C. (2007) *In situ* and *ex situ* conservation: Blurring the boundaries between zoo and the wild. In A. Zimmermann, M. Hatchwell, L. Dickie and C. West (eds) *Zoos in the 21st Century: Catalysts for Conservation?* (pp. 220–235). Cambridge: Cambridge University Press.

Draper, M. (2005) African Wilderness Pty Ltd: A authentic encounter with the big five, death and the meaning of life. In C. Ryan, S.J. Page and M. Aicken (eds) *Taking Tourism to the Limits* (pp. 113–128). Oxford: Elsevier.

Fuhrman, N.E. and Ladewig, H. (2008) Characteristics of animals used in zoo interpretation: A synthesis of research. *Journal of Interpretation Research* 13 (2), 31–42.

Goodwin, H. and Leader-Williams, N. (2000) Tourism and protected areas – distorting conservation priorities towards charismatic megafauna? In A. Entwistle and N. Dunstone (eds) *Priorities for the Conservation of Mammalian Diversity: Has the Panda Had its Day?* (pp. 257–275). Cambridge: Cambridge University Press.

Ham, S.H. and Weiler, B. (2002) Interpretation as the centerpiece of sustainable wildlife tourism. In R. Harris, T. Griffin and P. Williams (eds) *Sustainable Tourism: A Global Perspective* (pp. 35–44). Oxford: Elsevier Science.

Haysmith, L., Hunt, J.D., Knight, R.L. and Temple, S.A. (1995) Nature tourism: Impacts and management. In R.L. Knight and K.J. Gutzwiller (eds) *Wildlife and Recreationists* (pp. 203–221). Washington, DC: Island Press.

Heil, L., Fernandez-Juricic, E., Renison, D., Cingolani, A.M. and Blumstein, D.T. (2007) Avian responses to tourism in the biogeographically isolated high Cordoba Mountains, Argentina. *Biodiversity and Conservation* 16 (4), 1009–1026.

Heywood, V.H. (ed.) (1995) *Global Biodiversity Assessment*. Cambridge: Cambridge University Press.

Higginbottom, K. (2004a) Wildlife tourism: An introduction. In K. Higginbottom (ed.) *Wildlife Tourism: Impacts, Management and Planning* (pp. 1–14). Altona: Common Ground Publishing.

Higginbottom, K. (2004b) *Wildlife Tourism: Impacts, Management and Planning*. Altona: Common Ground Publishing.

Higginbottom, K., Tribe, A. and Booth, R. (2003) Contributions of non-consumptive wildlife tourism to conservation. In R. Buckley, C. Pickering and D. Weaver (eds) *Nature-based Tourism, Environment and Land Management* (Vol. 1) (pp. 181–195). Wallingford: CABI.

Home, R., Keller, C., Nagel, P., Bauer, N. and Hunziker, M. (2009) Selection criteria for flagship species by conservation organizations. *Environmental Conservation* 36 (2), 139–148; doi:10.1017/s0376892909990051.

Huntly, P.M., Van Noort, S. and Hamer, M. (2005) Giving increased value to invertebrates through ecotourism. *South African Journal of Wildlife Research* 35 (1), 53–62.

Hutchins, M., Smith, B. and Allard, R. (2003) In defense of zoos and aquariums: The ethical basis for keeping wild animals in captivity. *Journal of the American Veterinary Medical Association* 223 (7), 958–966.

Jacobs, M.H. (2009) Why do we like or dislike animals? *Human Dimensions of Wildlife* 14 (1), 1–11.

Kaltenborn, B.P., Bjerke, T., Nyahongo, J.W. and Williams, D.R. (2006) Animal preferences and acceptability of wildlife management actions around Serengeti National Park, Tanzania. *Biodiversity and Conservation* 15 (14), 4633–4649; doi:10.1007/s10531-005-6196-9.

Kellert, S.R. (1996) *The Value of Life*. Washington, DC: Island Press.

Kerley, G.I.H., Geach, B.G.S. and Vial, C. (2003) Jumbos or bust: Do tourists' perceptions lead to an under-appreciation of biodiversity? *South African Journal of Wildlife Research* 33 (1), 13–21.

Kontoleon, A. and Swanson, T. (2003) The willingness to pay for property rights for the Giant Panda: Can a charismatic species be an instrument for nature conservation? *Land Economics* 79 (4), 483–499.

Leader-Williams, N. and Dublin, H.T. (2000) Charismatic megafauna as 'flagship species'. In A. Entwistle and N. Dunstone (eds) *Priorities for the Conservation of Mammalian Diversity: Has the Panda Had its Day?* (pp. 53–84). Cambridge: Cambridge University Press.

Lee, W.H. and Moscardo, G. (2005) Understanding the impact of ecotourism resort experiences on tourists' environmental attitudes and behavioural intentions. *Journal of Sustainable Tourism* 13 (6), 546–565.

Lemelin, R.H. (2007) Finding beauty in the dragon: The role of dragonflies in recreation and tourism. *Journal of Ecotourism* 6 (2), 139–145.

Lindsey, P.A., Alexander, R., Mills, M.G.L., Romañach, S. and Woodroffe, R. (2007) Wildlife viewing preferences of visitors to protected areas in South Africa: Implications for the role of ecotourism in conservation. *Journal of Ecotourism* 6 (1), 19–33.

Lorimer, J. (2007) Nonhuman charisma. *Environment and Planning D: Society and Space* 25 (5), 911–932.

Markwell, K. (2001) 'An intimate rendezvous with nature?': Mediating the tourist–nature experience at three tourist sites in Borneo. *Tourist Studies* 1 (1), 39–57.

Mascia, M.B., Brosius, J.P., Dobson, T.A., Forbes, B.C., Horowitz, L., McKean, M.A. and Turner, N.J. (2003) Conservation and the social sciences. *Conservation Biology* 17 (3), 649–650.

Miller, J. (2005) Biodiversity conservation and the extinction of experience. *Trends in Ecology and Evolution* 20 (8), 430–434.

Myers, O.E., Saunders, C.D. and Birjulin, A.A. (2004) Emotional dimensions of watching zoo animals: An experience sampling study building on insights from psychology. *Curator* 47, 299–321.

Newsome, D., Dowling, R. and Moore, S. (2005) *Wildlife Tourism*. Clevedon: Channel View Publications.

Okello, M.M., Manka, S.G. and D'Amour, D.E. (2008) The relative importance of large mammal species for tourism in Amboseli National Park, Kenya. *Tourism Management* 29 (4), 751–760.

Orams, M.B. (1997) The effectiveness of environmental education: Can we turn tourists into 'Greenies'? *Progress in Tourism and Hospitality* 3, 295–306.

Powell, R.B. and Ham, S.H. (2008) Can ecotourism interpretation really lead to pro-conservation knowledge, attitudes and behaviour? Evidence from the Galapagos islands. *Journal of Sustainable Tourism* 16 (4), 467–489.

Roe, D., Leader-Williams, N. and Dalal-Clayton, D.B. (1997) *Take Only Photographs, Leave Only Footprints: The Environmental Impacts of Wildlife Tourism*: London: International Institute for Environment and Development.

Rolston, H. (1987) Beauty and the beast: Aesthetic experiences of wildlife. In D. Decker and G. Goff (eds) *Valuing Wildlife: Economic and Social Perspectives* (pp. 187–196). Boulder, MO: Westview Boulder Press.

Russell, C.L. (1994) The social construction of other animals. *The Trumpeter: Journal of Ecosophy* 11 (3), 136–140.

Russell, C.L. and Ankenman, M.J. (1996) Orang-utans as photographic collectibles: Ecotourism and the commodification of nature. *Tourism Recreation Research* 21 (1), 71–78.

Ryan, C., Hughes, K. and Chirgwin, S. (2000) The gaze, spectacle and ecotourism. *Annals of Tourism Research* 27 (1), 148–163.

Sandbrook, C. and Semple, S. (2006) The rules and the reality of mountain gorilla *Gorilla beringei beringei* tracking: How close do tourists get? *Oryx* 40 (4), 428–433; doi:10.1017/s0030605306001323.

Saunders, C.D. (2003) The emerging field of conservation psychology. *Human Ecology Review* 10, 137–149.

Saunders, C.D. and Myers, O.E. (2003) Exploring the potential of conservation psychology. *Human Ecology Review* 10 (2), 137–149.

Saunders, C.D., Brook, A.T. and Myers Jr, O.E. (2006) Using psychology to save biodiversity and human well-being. *Conservation Biology* 20 (3), 702–705.

Schanzel, H. and McIntosh, A. (2000) An insight into the personal and emotive context of wildlife viewing at the Penguin Place, Otago Peninsula. *New Zealand. Journal of Sustainable Tourism* 8 (1), 36–52.

Sergio, F., Newton, I., Marchesi, L. and Pedrini, P. (2006) Ecologically justified charisma: Preservation of top predators delivers biodiversity conservation. *Journal of Applied Ecology* 43 (6), 1049–1055; doi:10.1111/j.1365-2664.2006.01218.x.

Shani, A. and Pizam, A. (2010) The role of animal-based attractions in ecological sustainability: Current issues and controversies. *Worldwide Hospitality and Tourism Themes* 2 (3), 281–298.

Simberloff, D. (1998) Flagships, umbrellas, and keystones: Is single-species management passe in the landscape era? *Biological Conservation* 83 (3), 247–257.

Sims-Castley, R., Kerley, G.I.H., Geach, B. and Langholz, J. (2005) Socio-economic sig-
    nificance of ecotourism-based private game reserves in South Africa's Eastern Cape
    Province. *Protected Areas Programme 6.*
Sitas, N., Baillie, J.E.M. and Isaac, N.J.B. (2009) What are we saving? Developing a stan-
    dardized approach for conservation action. *Animal Conservation* 12 (3), 231–237;
    doi:10.1111/j.1469-1795.2009.00244.x.
Skibins, J.C. and Powell, R.B. (2013) Conservation caring: Measuring the influence of zoo
    visitors' connection to wildlife on proconservation behaviors. *Zoo Biology* 32 (5),
    528–540.
Skibins, J.C., Hallo, J.C., Sharp, J.L. and Manning, R.E. (2012a) Quantifying the role of
    viewing the Denali 'Big 5' in visitor satisfaction and awareness: Conservation impli-
    cations for flagship recognition and resource management. *Human Dimensions of
    Wildlife* 17 (2), 112–128; doi:10.1080/10871209.2012.627531.
Skibins, J.C., Powell, R.B. and Stern, M.J. (2012b) Exploring empirical support for inter-
    pretation's best practices. *Journal of Interpretation Research* 17 (27), 25–44.
Skibins, J.C., Powell, R.B. and Hallo, J.C. (2013) Charisma and conservation: Charismatic
    megafauna's influence on safari and zoo tourists' pro-conservation behaviors.
    Biodiversity and Conservation 22 (4), 959–982; doi:10.1007/s10531-013-0462-z.
Smith, A. and Sutton, S. (2008) The role of flagship species in the formation of conserva-
    tion intentions. *Human Dimensions of Wildlife* 13, 127–140.
Smith, L., Broad, S. and Weiler, B. (2008a) A closer examination of the impact of zoo visits
    on visitor behaviour. *Journal of Sustainable Tourism* 16 (5), 544–562.
Smith, L., Weiler, B. and Ham, S. (2008b) Measuring emotion at the zoo. *Journal of the
    International Zoo Educators Association* 44, 26–31.
Smith, L., Curtis, J. and van Dijk, P. (2010) What the zoo should ask: The visitor perspec-
    tive on pro-wildlife behavior attributes. *Curator: The Museum Journal* 53 (3),
    339–357.
Swanagan, J.S. (2000) Factors influencing zoo visitors' conservation attitudes and behav-
    ior. *Journal of Environmental Education* 31 (4), 26–31.
Terborgh, J. (2004) *Requiem for Nature.* Washington, DC: Island Press.
Tisdell, C., Wilson, C. and Nantha, H.S. (2005) Association of public support for survival
    of wildlife species with their likeability. *Anthrozoos* 18 (2), 160–174.
Tisdell, C., Nantha, H.S. and Wilson, C. (2007) Endangerment and likeability of wildlife
    species: How important are they for payments proposed for conservation? *Ecological
    Economics* 60 (3), 627–633.
Tribe, A. (2004) Zoo tourism. In K. Higginbottom (ed.) *Wildlife Tourism: Impacts,
    Management and Planning* (pp. 35–56). Altona: Common Ground Publishing.
Valentine, P.S. and Birtles, A. (2004) Wildlife watching. In K. Higginbottom (ed.) *Wildlife
    Tourism: Impacts, Management and Planning* (pp. 15–34). Altona: Common Ground
    Publishing.
Vining, J. (2003) The connection to other animals and caring for nature. *Human Ecology
    Review* 10, 87–99.
Walpole, M.J. and Leader-Williams, N. (2002) Tourism and flagship species in conserva-
    tion. *Biodiversity and Conservation* 11 (3), 543–547.
Ward, P.I., Mosberger, N., Kistler, C. and Fischer, O. (1998) The relationship between
    popularity and body size in zoo animals. *Conservation Biology* 12 (6), 1408–1411.
Wilkie, D.S. and Carpenter, J.F. (1999) Can nature tourism help finance protected areas
    in the Congo Basin? *Oryx* 33 (4), 332–338.
Wilson, C. and Tisdell, C. (2003) Conservation and economic benefits of wildlife-based
    marine tourism: Sea turtles and whales as case studies. *Human Dimensions of Wildlife*
    8 (1), 49–58.
Woods, B. (2000) Beauty and the beast: Preferences for animals in Australia. *Journal of
    Tourism Studies* 11 (2), 25–35.

Zaradic, P.A., Pergams, O.R.W. and Kareiva, P. (2009) The impact of nature experience on willingness to support conservation. *PLoS ONE* 4 (10), e7367.
Zimmermann, A. (2010) The role of zoos in contributing to *in situ* conservation. In D.G. Kleiman, K.V. Thompson and C.K. Baer (eds) *Wild Mammals in Captivity: Principles and Techniques for Zoo Management* (2nd edn) (pp. 281–287). Chicago, IL: University of Chicago Press.

17 Pooches on Wheels: Overcoming Pet-related Travel Constraints Through RVing

Ulrike Gretzel and Anne Hardy

Introduction

An increasing number of people in the Western world own pets; for instance, it is estimated that Australians alone own over 3.4 million dogs (36% of households) and 2.3 million cats (23% of households) (Australian Companion Animal Council, 2010). In the United States, pet ownership is even more common, with 40% of households owning dogs and 33% including cats. Pet ownership triggers a number of decisions (such as food, medical care, toys, carriers) to form a complex purchase-consumption system (Woodside & King, 2001). It is estimated that Americans spend almost US$60bn on their pets each year (American Pet Products Association, 2014). To an ever greater extent, travel decisions are part of the system. About 14% or 29 million Americans travel with their pets (eHotelier.com, 2005).

Although the travel industry is slowly catching on to the fact that pet ownership is on the rise and that an increasing number of people would like to bring their pets with them when they travel, lodging establishments that accept pets are still not readily available at all destinations. Pet friendliness is often used as a unique selling point, and comes with a hefty price tag (Elliot, 2014). Examples include luxury boutique hotels that differentiate themselves by offering services such as special towels, Versace crystal bowls, welcome biscuits tied with a bow, take-home toys, pet sitting, dog walking, doggie day spa visits, designer pet beds and special pet gift and dining menus (Lobley, 2014). Constraints when travelling with pets are not only encountered with respect to accommodation; while some airlines are pet friendly (e.g. United Airlines offers a programme called PetSafe), transportation can also be an issue and significantly expensive. Consequently, pet transport companies offer their services to ease these hurdles and online websites like

PetFriendlyTravel.com and Bringfido.com list pet-friendly destinations, lodging, restaurants and attractions. Moreover, countries differ markedly in their willingness to allow pet-related travel; Australia has a special reputation as an extremely pet-unfriendly country when it comes to travelling, even domestically (Tulloch, 2013).

Although exceptions such as boutique hotels exist, most commonly pet-friendly accommodation is offered by roadside motels or caravan parks, which fall under the category of drive tourism. The often extensive advice given by automobile clubs on travelling with pets illustrates that 'pooches on wheels' is indeed a common phenomenon in the context of drive tourism. Independent travel in a motor vehicle offers the flexibility needed for pet travel and allows one to mostly evade restrictions imposed by the tourism, hospitality and transportation industries. Consequently, RVing can be seen as one, if not *the*, most pet-friendly way to travel, especially over longer periods of time, as it combines pet-friendly transport with pet-friendly accommodation. This chapter seeks to shed light on the extent to which RVing may be conceptualised as a way of travelling to accommodate pets and overcome the pet-related constraints of other forms of travel. It does so by examining qualitative interview and netnographic data from RVers with respect to references to pets and their influence in making travel-related decisions.

Background

Carr (2009) argues that as our relationship to pets changes and intensifies, understanding the role of these animals in tourism and leisure experiences is becoming increasingly important. Yet the academic tourism literature has largely ignored pet travel as a phenomenon. A Google Scholar search conducted by the authors only yielded a handful of mostly peripheral references to pets in tourism-related publications. For instance, research on visitor information centres that focuses on motivations to stop at and use these facilities often identifies 'exercising pets' as an important factor (e.g. Pennington-Gray & Vogt, 2003). Pan *et al.* (2007) found that pet-friendly is a very common keyword used in online accommodation searches. Kaplanidou and Vogt (2006) suggest that pet policies constitute important information to include on travel websites. Yet, despite extensive focus on travel planning and decision making in the general tourism literature, very little is known as to if and how travellers consider pets when making travel-related decisions. Carr and Cohen (2009) present a study that shows substantial desire to bring pets on holidays but also a general lack of actual realisation of such yearnings, mainly because of the dearth of pet-friendly accommodation offerings. Chen *et al.* (2013) also looked into constraints related to pet travel and suggest that these can be conceptualised as pet-specific constraints, interpersonal constraints and structural constraints. Not surprisingly, the greater the attachment to the animal, the more likely travellers are to negotiate the constraints (Hung et al., 2012).

This lack of research on pet travel stands in stark contrast to literature in other disciplines that clearly emphasises the significant role pets play in modern households. Haraway's (2003) companion species manifesto provides a convincing account of the significance these pets play in our lives. Specifically, she illustrates how humans and dogs are historically linked, on a social, biological and behavioural level, and argues that there is a visible implosion of nature and culture in the joint lives of dogs and humans. Greenebaum (2004) describes pets' elevation in status to 'fur babies' and the resulting integration of pets into leisure activities. Belk (1996) investigates the various metaphors people use to describe their relationships with companion animals and finds that 'members of the family' is a commonly used one.

A look at human dwellings reveals that 'homes are not home just to humans but that they are home to humans living very closely and purposefully with other species, particularly cats and dogs' (Franklin, 2006: 138). Franklin further notes that for the majority of adults the main motivation for keeping pets is indeed for company and as such that cohabitation results in new ways of accommodating and relating to each other, including changes in space management and home aesthetics. Power (2012) also stresses the key place these pets occupy in human familial relations and draws attention to the impacts of pet ownership on practices of family and home. Albert and Bulcroft (1988) show that pets can become central to family life, especially in certain household structures, and are often anthropomorphised.

A special issue in the *Journal of Business Research* (Holbrook & Woodside, 2008) suggests that such anthropomorphising and the accompanying love for pets opens up various opportunities for marketing. An ever greater number of products and services are available to ensure that pets enjoy the comforts of modern life just as their human companions do. Their influence is not only restricted to purchases directly related to them; they have to be considered when choosing places to live, buying cars, selecting furniture and home decorations and purchasing clothing. They are integrated into household routines such as mealtimes and activity scheduling. Thus, one can assume that, as significant members of the household, pets also influence travel consumption decisions and practices.

RVing is growing in importance, with more consumers than ever selecting this travel style in order to meet their travel needs (Hardy et al., 2013). RVing as an activity has been defined as a 'form of tourism where travellers take a camper trailer, van conversion, fifth wheel, slide-on camper, caravan or motor home on holiday with them, and use the vehicle as their primary form of accommodation' (Hardy & Gretzel, 2011: 194). RVing is generally seen as a form of travel that allows travellers to break free from various travel constraints such as the fixed schedules of tours, the need to make accommodation bookings and the reliance on tourism infrastructure (especially transportation). Freedom, flexibility and independence are prominent themes in RVers' descriptions of their motivations to engage in this specific type of travel.

However, while these notions of freedom and flexibility are central motives reoccurring in justifications for the choice of RVing as the preferred travel modus operandi (Hardy & Gretzel, 2011; Hillman, 2013), there is also a strong theme of wanting to feel like home while on the road (Counts & Counts, 2001; Viallon, 2012). The recreational vehicle affords RVers an opportunity to overcome this apparent contrast between freedom/flexibility/ novelty and the desire for home by providing an opportunity to bring familiar physical objects on the road and to encapsulate oneself in foreign terrains. It therefore challenges the notion of travel as being liminal, as there is no clear distinction between the everyday and the trip when the RV is basically an extension of the home.

If, for more and more people, home has a strong association with pets, then pets should prominently feature in RVers' accounts of their activities and the meanings associated with them. They should also play an important role in the decision-making processes of RVers. Indeed, the US-based Recreation Vehicle Industry Association (RVIA, 2012) reports that being able to bring anything they want on vacation is a big motivating factor for RVers and that 54% of them actually bring pets along when they travel. Specifically, of those who travel with pets in their RVs in the United States, 92% bring dogs and 14% cats, while other pets travelling with RVers include birds, ferrets, snakes and horses. This is also reflected in the many tips and resources provided by RV-related websites in relation to RVing with pets (e.g. www.fmca.com/122-motorhome/motorhoming-with-pets.html; www.woodalls.com/articledetails.aspx?sectionName=Featured+RV+Cam ping+Articles&articleID=2441773 and http://rvtravel.com/publish/cat_ index_78.shtml). There are even websites solely dedicated to camping and RVing with pets, for example, http://www.petcamping.com/ is aimed at providing tips and making the search for pet friendly campgrounds easy. The RV industry advocacy platform GoRVing explicitly states that 'With RVing, one of the great benefits is that you can satisfy your wanderlust while bringing along your furry friends'. We set out to explore how prominently this idea of bringing pets really features among RVers.

Methods

The results presented in this chapter are derived from ethnomethodological research (Gurbrium & Holstein, 2000), which sought to interpret how RVers construct RVing as a travel style, how they enact it, and what they identify as motivating factors to engage in this particular form of travel. Therefore, our research did not set out to uncover the relationship between RVing and pet ownership. Rather, our analysis, which was qualitative and inductive in nature, was conducted in such a manner that it allowed for themes to emerge from the data. Pet ownership and the impact that it played on travellers' decisions to RV and their choice of destinations was found to be such an emergent theme and the data were subsequently coded to capture it.

We conducted our research into RVing in two countries. The first was Canada where we conducted 50 interviews of RVers at Dawson Creek in northern British Columbia. This township marks the start of the famous Alaska Highway, which is regarded as a mecca for North American RVers. Our interviews were semi-structured in nature and were conducted at three RV overnight stops, including one free camping site and two commercial RV parks.

The second dataset that we used for this research was from research conducted at three RVing destinations on the east coast of Tasmania, an island state of Australia. Comparable to the Canadian research study, disparate camping grounds were selected as the study sites to reflect the variety of overnight RV sites and styles. These included a national park camping ground, a free camping site maintained by Parks Tasmania and a low-cost overnight camping area comprising one sports field in a small town. Like the Canadian research, our Australian research sought to uncover the meanings and behaviours different RVers associate with RVing. We undertook 50 qualitative in-depth interviews in each country. In both countries, our interviews were conducted at RV campsites mostly at around 5pm, which is widely regarded as 'happy hour', when RVers gather at the end of the day to drink and discuss issues of interest.

We also undertook netnographic research (Kozinets, 2010) to gain further insights into the consumption culture of RVing with pets from a more general group of RVers. Following the principles outlined by Kozinets, we selected two popular RVing forums used by RVers from the two countries: Good Sam's (www.goodsamclub.com/forums/) for Canada and the Caravaners Forum (http://caravanersforum.com/) for Australia. We conducted searches for 'pets' and 'pet friendly' and extracted contents from forum areas specifically dedicated to pet-related RVing as well as pet-related quotes that appeared in general forum areas, e.g. those dedicated to trip planning. The qualitative data derived through these steps was then analysed with respect to common themes prominent in the expressions/discussions of RVers. The goal was to provide a general overview of how much pets feed into discourses of travelling with a 'home on wheels' and overcoming the constraints of regular travel as well as the actual travel planning processes.

Results

Our findings confirm the strong link between pet travel and RVing that we hypothesised. The fact that 'pets' emerged as a theme by itself from very open-ended questions during interviews about RVing suggests that it is a rather prominent concept in the minds of RVers. The following presentation of specific findings delves further into its importance and the specific role pets play in relation to travel decision making and the choice of RVing as a form of travel.

Pet-related themes from the Australian data

Tasmania, an island state located to the south of the Australian mainland, is widely regarded as an RVing 'mecca' due to its vast tracts of wilderness and plentiful supply of free or low-cost RVing opportunities. We conducted our interviews in three locations: a national park which did not allow dogs; a dog-friendly local council campground; and a dog-friendly site that was managed by the Tasmanian Parks and Wildlife Service but was not inside a national park. The interview data suggest that around 15% of RVers travelled with pets. The themes that emerged for the Australian data are illustrated below:

Theme 1: For RVers who travel with their dogs, the destination and overnight camping choice is made according to dog friendliness

RVers indicated that their ownership of a dog drives the choice of where to stay overnight and which destination to visit. The comments reveal that pet ownership and ability to travel with their pet are important to them but that even RVing still puts a lot of constraints on pet travel that need to be negotiated, which causes some degree of frustration.

> *Respondent 1, staying in a dog-friendly site*: That's what's good about here – you can bring your dog. You see most people can't go camping for long periods of time because they have to get their dog babysat. If your dog is sociable you can bring it.

> *Respondent 24, staying in a dog-friendly site, talking about the reasons that influenced their choice of overnight site*: The main would be the weather. We also need to be able to take our dogs.

Dog ownership for RVers is clearly very restrictive, particularly for those who are traveling in larger rigs for extended periods of time. For some respondents, their ability to travel to the capital city of Tasmania was hampered because of their pet, combined with their large rig size.

Respondent 25, staying in a dog-friendly site: There's only one place in Hobart that takes dogs, and they've got no sites for a big van like this so we couldn't go there.

Further, the data which emerged from these interviewees revealed that RVers' desire to visit natural locations such as national parks is severely restricted by owning a dog. There was a strong desire for this restriction to be eased.

Respondent 38, staying in a dog-friendly site, when asked if they ever stay in national parks: I just wish more National parks would be a little more interested with the dog, if I could stay at a National park with the dog, go walking, and leave him in the van, that would be sweet. Unfortunately we are all criminals.

Theme 2: Dog-friendly campsites also act as an indicator to some RVers that the campsite may be undesirable

Interestingly, while there was a strong desire for more access to be given to dogs by RVers who travelled with their dogs, a convergent set of opinions emerged from some RVers who were staying in the national park, which did not allow dogs. This suggests that there is also resistance within the RVing community towards pets as RVing companions.

Respondent 18, staying in a national park: It sounds awful, but sometimes you drive in and you look at the people that are already there and you think you don't want to stay there. If there were a lot of dogs or something.

Respondent 17, staying in a national park: A lot of the ones we've rejected lately – one was dodgy, feral looking (people) – i.e. dogs/guns. Dogs particularly, dogs are usually a sign of not happy times. All boys (young guys).

Thus, for these travellers, the presence of dogs also guided their decision-making process, albeit in a different manner. To them, the presence of dogs was an indicator that the campsite may attract 'unsavoury' campers.

Pet-related themes from the Canadian data

The themes which emerged from these interviews with RVers in Canada were similar to those which emerged in Australia, whereby pets featured prominently in the accounts of RVers and pet ownership was a primary factor in the choice of destinations and choice of overnight stops. Interestingly, the presence of dogs as an indicator for unsavoury campers did not emerge as an indicator among Canadian RVers. Perhaps with the fact that Canadian RV parks, national, provincial and local RV park options generally allow dogs, there was less focus on the difficulties that dog ownership created for RVers and more focus on the importance of the role that the dog played as a core family member and a motivating factor to engage in RVing.

Theme 1: For RVers who travel with their dogs, the destination and overnight camping choice is made according to dog friendliness

While dog friendliness seems not usually to constitute a problem for Canadian RVers, it still features prominently in their decision making.

Interviewer: What RV facilities do you look for?

Respondent 12: Grass. Dog friendly with walking areas. We were in one where they had a fenced off area that went into the lake. That was nice. Most places will allow dogs, so we didn't have many problems that way.

Respondent 45: We were able to leave our dogs inside because we could run air conditioner, so we could go into town and have a big steak.

Theme 2: The dog as a core member of the family unit

Respondents talked about dogs as significant family members and therefore also significant travel companions. They identified these pets as playing an important role in characterising what the RV travel style is about.

Respondent 7: We all like to travel, and see what there is to see and have comforts of our home at the same time. Most of the RVers are like that. They travel with their dogs and cats.

Respondent 2: We socialize as we walk through campground. Our dog is a great conversation starter.

Respondent 39: We are travelling with a group – paid group (Tracks). My wife and I and a dog. We are going to Alaska.

Respondent 41: It's the two of us travelling and one very spoiled dog.

Theme 3: RVing was chosen as an activity because it allowed travellers to take their dog with them

The Canadian data contained explicit references to RVing specifically being chosen as a form of travel because of its affordances for pets.

Respondent 19: [We chose RVing because] we can drive around and see the country and we can bring our two dogs.

Respondent 44: You are in your own bed, in your own shower, on your own toilet and in your own kitchen. It's a healthier living style, same with eating habits. You can take your pet with you.

These comments are embedded in a broader discussion of how RVing allows the home to come along on trips.

Respondent 22 Canada: It's the convenience of having your own living quarters and at night like being at home. We feel comfortable. It feels like our second home.

Respondent 34 Tasmania: Good shower, got a loo, got air-conditioning, got a leather recliner, a good cook. Comfort and space. Nice bed.

Respondent 41 Tasmania: Comfort, size is just good, reliable, seats and beds are comfortable it's wonderful. We have our own stove, have everything at our fingertips, microwave, gas stove. Own toilet and own showers in a 5 meter rig.

Respondent 31 Tasmania: It follows us wherever we go! Comfortable, homely, extra bed for relatives.

Respondent 20 Canada: It's more like home when you stop at night, because you can do your own cooking and you have your own bed. It's just so much better, than travelling in a car, because you have your home behind you.

Pet-related subthemes from the online communities

The search on the Good Sam's forum site allowed us to identify 320 pet-related posts in the last six months alone, some of which had hundreds of replies. There is also a dedicated pet forum called the 'RV Pet Stop'. The search on the Caravaners Forum resulted in 533 posts related to RVing with pets. The following themes emerged very clearly from these online conversations held by RVers in North America and Australia.

Theme 1: A great desire to bring the fur babies along

The forums are full of expressions of how important it is for these RVers to be able to travel with their pets. As a consequence, pet friendliness of the caravan parks and campgrounds is a clearly stated decision criterion and pet unfriendliness is detested. While some amenities are 'nice to have', pet friendliness is seen as a 'must have' when selecting routes and destinations.

> We just took delivery of a 2014 Jayco 20MRB travel trailer and have a GMC 2500HD Duramax. We've never been campers and this is our first TT, although we are experienced horse haulers. We live in south Surrey and are looking for suggestions for a first place to set up camp for 2 or 3 nights. We are looking for a well-run place within 2 hours drive with full hookup (30 amp power, water and sani) minimum, plus any other goodies to help us ease into this e.g. wifi, cable, store, room service (just kidding) – whatever helps! It has to be pet friendly or we won't get a vote from our black lab. (Good Sam)

> I personally wouldn't go without the dog ... (Caravaners)

> We travelled over east and back again with our German Shepherd, the few times that we did want to stay in a park we of course only looked at those that were listed as 'pet friendly', never booked ahead. (Caravaners)

Theme 2: Appropriation of the RV to make it a home for pets

While the RV allows travellers to take their pets along with them, their vehicles are often not seen as ideal by some of the pet owners and therefore require modifications. Just like homes are changed to accommodate pets, the forums are full of posts that describe efforts to make the RV itself more pet friendly. Some posts are as mundane as where in the RV to put a litter box, whereas others suggest significant modifications to the structure of the vehicle and quite creative solutions to making the 'home on wheels' a real home for the pooch.

> I have seen described a pet box made from a lower storage compartment. Screens are fashioned for when the access doors are open, and access is made through the floor of the coach, into the lower storage. The pets can be confined in the lower storage at will. They can be protected by the screens when the outer access is open. I suppose that when you fabricate the screens, you could provide exit to the ground outside. (Good Sam)

> As the DW and I prepare to go full time I am trying to brainstorm a doggie door for our RV. So far I envision a doggie door for our small dogs in our coach. I don't think it would work in the coach door, too much traffic. I am actually thinking about a system where the door is installed in the side of the coach, perhaps through the bedroom wall. Outside there would be a ramp to the doggie door and a standard portable fence like pets mart sells. The ramp and portable fence could be folded up and easily stored flat in the basement when on the move. (Good Sam)

Theme 3: A great need for pet-related travel information

The desire to take pets on the road with them translates into very specific information needs for RVers. While most of the posts refer to questions regarding the pet friendliness of campgrounds, there are also requests for more general information on what should be taken into consideration when travelling with pets. The fact that information requests such as these are posted on these forums suggests that these needs are not being sufficiently met by other information sources and that pet friendliness is far from common when it comes to campgrounds and caravan parks.

> Hi All, My hubby is flying out of Charlotte NC in June. We have never been in the State. Can anyone recommend any RV parks. Looking for something no further out than an hour from Airport, full hook ups for 36 ft and 33 ft motorhomes, pet friendly, laundry facilities and a pool would be nice but not a deal breaker. (Good Sam)

> … I'm in the process of planning an itinerary of where to stay that is pet friendly in our own 18'6 van and what to see and do for a 5 week trip we're planning for October/November … (Caravaners)

> Thought I'd ask, I've never taken my cats camping. I have a new cat, but he has some special needs, namely he's missing one leg and has to take blood pressure medication daily. He doesn't mind traveling to the vet's office in the car and he's very relaxed when we're at the vet's office. Knowing him, he'd probably be happy as a clam stretching out on the bunk soaking up rays. Just wondering how many others take their cats camping and what experiences they've had. (Good Sam)

Theme 4: Constraints and potential conflicts

Similar to the interviews, the forum posts also suggest that RVing with pets is not constraint-free. The term 'pet friendly' is open to interpretation and not all kinds of pets or breeds are automatically included. The posts also suggest that conflicts can arise when RVers impose their pets on a campground community.

> I love to see families take their dogs camping. Our kids take theirs along. What I don't like are those who have no respect for other campers or their pet and let them bark all day. It only upsets others camping but worse is hard on the dog. (Good Sam)

> Many members travel with dogs. You are limited when it comes to National Parks, and you have to look for pet friendly caravan parks. Plenty of discussion on these here too, and Complete List of Caravan Parks from link above left shows which ones allow pets, and this had a

link to Badger's Caravan Park reviews submitted by us, the caravan park users, where pet friendly is also noted where known. (Caravaners)

Even if a park is listed as pet friendly it is always up to management's discretion whether they allow any pets at any time, application is either by phone or in person. When checking at reception to see if there were firstly any suitable sites for our van we always told them we had a dog with us, only once were we asked what breed we had and when we stated a German Shepherd we were asked to pay a refundable $50 bond for him, which we gladly did and collected when leaving. The same park had a sign in the laundry saying that they didn't allow any breeds or large dogs that may be perceived to be frightening to others, yet they allowed our boy to stay. Perhaps management had a liking to our breed, never asked. (Caravaners)

I might add that in the same park while we were there, there was a little dog which I think was a fluffy cross breed, gorgeous looking little thing – but it was allowed to roam free several times, obviously to exercise itself, they never picked it's poop up unless reminded by others to do so, yapped and barked in a high pitch incessantly – and then it bit a lady and quite a nasty bite it was too. I think they were asked to leave the park and rightly so. Some people have no idea or just don't care about others or even their own pets. (Caravaners)

Conclusions

Our research confirmed that for many RVers, the ability to bring pets with them is a great desire and strong motivating factor in choosing RVing as a form of travel. However, it is not constraint free. National parks, campgrounds, caravan parks and tourist attractions are limited in their pet friendliness and information about where pets are welcome is not readily available. Also, certain animals or breeds can impose additional constraints. Further, the RV itself, while often containing all the amenities one would find in a home, is not a very pet-friendly space and needs to be modified to accommodate pet needs. And, last but not least, other RVers and general travellers often do not appreciate the presence of pets. The results therefore confirm the presence of the full spectrum of constraints (pet-specific, interpersonal, structural) as identified by Chen *et al.* (2013). Still, the RVers we interviewed and observed online seem to be very willing to overcome such constraints in order to travel with their pets and make the RV a real home for the whole family, i.e. including the fur babies.

The findings clearly suggest that pet-related travel is a phenomenon that is growing in importance but remains understudied. They also provide some theoretical insights related to the increasing potential to recreate the home when away, especially when RVing, which challenges the notion of liminality often seen as a defining characteristic of tourism experiences. In addition, they suggest that pet-related travel decision making differs from traditional models and requires further analysis. For example, theoretical models related to tourism decision making often assume that accommodation and transportation decisions are lower level decisions rather than primary considerations when travellers plan their vacations (Woodside & King, 2001). This is clearly not the case for RVing in general and certainly not for pet-related RVing. Where one goes or what other amenities are offered by a campground are secondary considerations, while the primary focus is on ensuring freedom and flexibility, which often includes the freedom to bring a pet.

Finally, the importance of bringing pets on the road is also manifested in the many risks these RVers are willing to incur as a result: the risk of not finding a suitable caravan park or being asked to leave; the risk of someone being injured by the pet; and, most significantly, the risk of the pet dying or being injured in the course of a trip. How travellers justify and/or negotiate these added risks and how the tourism industry responds to them are topics that certainly need more investigation in order to be able to fully understand the phenomenon of travelling with pets.

References

Albert, A. and Bulcroft, K. (1988) Pets, families, and the life course. *Journal of Marriage and the Family* 50 (2), 543–552.

American Pet Products Association (2014) *Pet Industry Market Size & Ownership Statistics*. Greenwich, CT: American Pet Products Association. See www.americanpetproducts. org/press_industrytrends.asp (accessed 2 March 2014).

Australian Companion Animal Council (2010) *Contributions of the Pet Care Industry to the Australian Economy* (7th edn). Victoria: Australian Companion Animal Council. See www.acac.org.au/pdf/ACAC%20Report%200810_sm.pdf (accessed 2 February 2014).

Belk, R. (1996) Metaphoric relationships with pets. *Society & Animals* 4, 121–145.

Carr, N. (2009) Animals in the tourism and leisure experience. *Current Issues in Tourism*, Special Issue, 12 (5–6), 409–411.

Carr, N. and Cohen, S. (2009) Holidaying with the family pet: No dogs allowed! *Tourism and Hospitality Research* 9 (4), 290–304.

Chen, A.H., Peng, N. and Hung, K.P. (2013) Developing a pet owners' tourism constraints scale: The constraints to take dogs to tourism activities. *International Journal of Tourism Research* 16 (4), 315–324; doi:10.1002/jtr.1959.

Counts, D.A. and Counts, D.R. (2001) *Over the Next Hill – An Ethnography of RVing Seniors in North America*. Peterborough, ON: Broadview Press.

eHotelier.com (2005) Luxury travel & vacations have gone to the dogs. *eHotelier.com*, 16 May. See http://ehotelier.com/hospitality-news/item.php?id=A5102_0_11_0_M (accessed 5 March 2014).

Elliott, C. (2014) Beware: Traveling with pets may cost you more than you think. *Washington Post*, 4 April. See www.washingtonpost.com/lifestyle/travel/beware-traveling-with-your-pets-may-cost-you-more-than-you-think/2014/04/03/7e7380e8-b69f-11e3-8cc3-d4bf596577eb_story.html (accessed 5 April 2014).

Franklin, A. (2006) 'Be[a]ware of the dog': A post-humanist approach to housing. *Housing, Theory and Society* 23 (3), 137–156.

Greenebaum, J. (2004) It's a dog's life: Elevating status from pet to 'fur baby' at Yappy Hour. *Society & Animals* 12 (2), 117–135.

Gurbrium, J.F. and Holstein, J.A. (2000) Analysing interpretive practice. In N. Denzin and Y. Lincoln (eds) *Handbook of Qualitative Research* (2nd edn) (pp. 487–508). London: Sage.

Haraway, D. (2003) *The Companion Species Manifesto.* Chicago, IL: Prickly Paradigm Press.

Hardy, A. and Gretzel, U. (2011) Why we travel this way: An exploration into the motivations of recreational vehicle users. In D. Carson and B. Prideaux (eds) *Drive Tourism: Trends and Emerging Markets* (pp. 194–223). London: Routledge.

Hardy, A., Gretzel, U. and Hanson, D. (2013) Travelling neo-tribes: Conceptualising recreational vehicle users. *Journal of Tourism and Cultural Change* 11 (1–2), 48–60.

Hillman, W. (2013) Grey nomads travelling in Queensland, Australia: Social and health needs. *Ageing and Society* 33 (4), 579–597.

Holbrook, M.B. and Woodside, A.G. (2008) Animal companions, consumption experiences, and the marketing of pets: Transcending boundaries in the animal–human distinction. *Journal of Business Research* 61 (5), 377–381.

Hung, K.-P., Chen, A. and Peng, N. (2012) The constraints for taking pets to leisure activities. *Annals of Tourism Research* 39 (1), 487–495.

Kaplanidou, K. and Vogt, C. (2006) A structural analysis of destination travel intentions as a function of web site features. *Journal of Travel Research* 45, 204–216.

Kozinets, R.V. (2010) *Netnography: Doing Ethnographic Research Online.* London: Sage.

Lobley, K. (2014) Have pet, will travel. *Qantas Inflight Magazine*, January, pp. 122–125.

Pan, B., Litvin, S. and O'Donnell, T.E. (2007) Understanding accommodation search query formulation: The first step in putting 'heads in beds'. *Journal of Vacation Marketing* 13 (4), 371–381.

Pennington-Gray, L. and Vogt, C. (2003) Examining welcome centre visitors' travel and information behaviours: Does location of centres or residency matter? *Journal of Travel Research* 41, 272–280.

Power, E.R. (2012) Domestication and the dog: Embodying home. *Area* 44 (3), 371–378.

RVIA (2012) Survey shows RVers will be on the road this spring and summer, will adjust to higher fuel prices. Reston, VA: Recreation Vehicle Industry Association. See www.rvia.org/?ESID=tforecst&pinrtable=true (accessed 18 March 2014).

Tulloch, L. (2013) Australian airlines' pet hate. *Sydney Morning Herald*, 20 July. See www.smh.com.au/travel/australian-airlines-pet-hate-20130718-2q5sb.html (accessed 31 March 2014).

Viallon, P. (2012) Retired snowbirds. *Annals of Tourism Research* 39 (4), 2073–2091.

Woodside, A.G. and King, R.I. (2001) An updated model of travel and tourism purchase-consumption systems. *Journal of Travel & Tourism Marketing* 10 (1), 327.

18 Exploited Elephants and Pampered Pets: Reflecting on Tourism–Animal Relationships

Kevin Markwell

Contemplating Crocodiles

The murky water which had been until a moment ago, deceptively calm, erupts suddenly with the enormous force of a 1000 kg, black leathery body, torpedoing skywards, higher than the sides of the boat I am sharing with 15 other tourists. Water splashes over the aluminium hull as passengers surge forward, their smartphones, tablets and cameras positioned shield-like between themselves and the great reptile they have paid to see. With its front legs held close by its sides, the 4 m long crocodile clamps its massive jaws around a small cube of buffalo meat dangling from a stick offered by the boat's captain (Figure 18.1). In freefall now, it smacks its head hard against the side of the boat, slides into the depths of the river and disappears. Passengers look at each other in astonishment, not quite sure that they can believe what had just happened, before turning their attention to their cameras and phones to relive the experience through the photos they had just taken. The captain shifts the boat's motor into gear and chugs further down the river in search of more crocodilian action. The tour has just begun.

The following morning, with the Darwin sun already high in the sky and the air heavy with humidity, I walk into the centre of town to visit Crocosaurus Cove, the 'ultimate urban wildlife experience', sandwiched between bars, cafes and souvenir shops along part of the city's tourist strip. The Cove has an impressive display of tropical reptiles and fish but it's the crocs that pull in the crowds. Huge adult males, delicate babies and all sizes in between can be viewed in comfort from walkways above crystal-clear ponds and from below, through thick, acrylic windows.

I watch visitors dangle bits of meat from fishing rods into a pool filled with snappy metre-length youngsters, while others pose for photographs

Figure 18.1 A large estuarine crocodile lunges vertically out of the water to eat a piece of buffalo meat secured to a wire during a 'Jumping Croc' boat tour near Darwin, Australia
Photo: Author

as they hold baby crocodiles, their jaws firmly secured by a thick rubber band (Figure 18.2). The ultimate experience, though, is the Cage of Death, an acrylic cylinder that is lowered into one of two pools inhabited by several very large adult animals. Operating 12 times per day, the 'Cage' (which can accommodate up to two visitors) gives visitors an idea of what it might be like to be crocodile food. Customers hope that one of the crocodiles will swim right up to the plastic cylinder and open its mouth in a vain attempt to extricate the human flesh contained safely inside. This can be a bit hit and miss, however, with the crocodiles often preferring to stay on the other side of the pool, much to the disappointment of the paying 'prey' and the crowds of people watching the spectacle from the viewing gallery below the pool.

Leaving the Cove through the gift shop, I pause to look at the variety of crocodile skin products on display – handbags, wallets, belts and key rings. Most of the merchandise appears to be high quality and has price tags to

Figure 18.2 Feeding crocodiles using meat attached to fishing rods is a visitor activity at Crocosaurus Cove, Darwin
Photo: Author

match. The gift shop is busy with visitors who don't find any incongruity between the living crocodiles they had just been viewing and the crocodile skin-based products they were now buying. Indeed, of the 415 postings on TripAdvisor for the attraction [as of 1 June 2014], only two commented negatively about the sale of crocodile skin merchandise at the gift shop. Hungry, I find a café further up the road to have a meal, my eyes scanning a menu that includes dishes created from barramundi, chicken, beef and, of course, crocodile.

As Ryan (1998) and Tremblay (2008) have shown, the saltwater crocodile (*Crocodylus porosus*) has become an important player in the tourism industry of Australia's Northern Territory. Tourists, predominantly originating from urban centres where animals do not normally regard humans as food, are eager to see these large, prehistoric and dangerous animals in close proximity. 'Salties' as they are known locally, are charismatic megafauna par excellence; a large male, in particular, is a compelling and awe-inspiring sight (Figure 18.3). However, crocodiles typically do not engender the same emotional responses that the sight of whales, elephant, orang-utan or even sea turtles evokes. In the case of crocodiles, feelings of awe and astonishment might be accompanied by feelings of disgust or revulsion. However, as Cushing and Markwell (2011) suggest, negative emotions have the capacity to play a part in creating overall satisfaction for tourists.

Figure 18.3 The massive bulk of an adult male estuarine crocodile is a spectacular animal attraction in many of the rivers of Australia's Top End in the Northern Territory
Photo: Author

Judging from comments on TripAdvisor, the overwhelming majority of tourists are very satisfied with their crocodile encounters in the Northern Territory. These include 'jumping crocodile' river tours, ecotourism and Indigenous cultural cruises, visits to commercial crocodile farms and viewing crocodiles in captivity. A high-end 'safari-hunting' trial had also been planned by the Northern Territory Government but this has been vetoed by the federal Environment Minister on the grounds that there was a risk of inhumane treatment to crocodiles (ABC News, 2014). Tourists can nevertheless eat their flesh at restaurants, purchase souvenirs such as crocodile-foot letter openers and backscratchers and buy their likenesses on tea towels, t-shirts, mugs and postcards. And, if they are happy to part with AU$160.00, they can spend 15 minutes dangling in a submerged plastic cylinder, hoping for one to swim up and terrorise them.

The crocodile is clearly a versatile 'product' which is valued by the tourism industry in many ways: as a living animal; as a carcass that can be butchered for its meat and skin; as a spectacular performer, whether in the wild or in captivity; and as a symbol around which place identity can be shaped. The peril that the species presents to humans can also translate into a threat to the economic viability of the tourism industry if tourists perceive the risk of danger to their own lives as being too great. Somewhat paradoxically, however, there is evidence that this threat works in the opposite direction, reaffirming the image of the Northern Territory as one of the last great frontiers and enticing tourists to visit (see ABC Stateline, 2003 for a discussion involving NT tour operators and Dr Pascal Tremblay, Charles Darwin University).

Given the fascination that tourists have with death, disaster and atrocity, as shown through the popularity of thanatourism, it is hardly surprising that many should be drawn to the compelling sight of a dangerous apex predator which has the capacity to kill and eat people. Some are satisfied to see them under natural conditions without any interventions to enhance their experience other than a knowledgeable guide and a safe boat. Touristic pleasure, in this case, is derived from seeing such an impressive animal at close quarters behaving entirely naturally within the context of its natural habitat as well as through gaining a greater knowledge of aspects of their biology and ecology. Such an encounter is an example of Cohen's (2009: 114) 'authentic Otherness of wild animals', in which animals are not framed by explicit anthropomorphic and anthropocentric assumptions and characteristics and are viewed in wild settings. Others are satisfied with viewing them in captivity, where they are able to admire them at close hand and where they might also learn something about them.

There is also strong demand for crocodile-based experiences that present the animal in some kind of spectacular performance for the entertainment of tourists. The settings in which these tourist encounters occur are contrived or manufactured in some way and are sustained through a variety of careful interventions. The sudden appearance of a large crocodile jumping from the river to take a piece of meat is without question a spectacular and, for many people, thoroughly enjoyable encounter. The animals which form the basis of this tourism product live wild lives apart from being conditioned to take food from tour boat operators and the behaviour of jumping out of the water is one which is natural to them; crocodiles can leap from the water to capture birds and bats roosting in overhanging trees. However, provisioning otherwise wild animals with food is a contentious practice (see Newsome *et al.*, 2005 for a comprehensive summary of the impacts of provisioning wildlife with food) which has significant risks both to wildlife and for humans. Mild controversy erupts in Darwin from time to time over the potential risks that provisioning large crocodiles create for people living near or visiting the river systems (see, for example, NT News, 2011). Others view the activity as a needless manipulation of the behaviour of a species simply to create an amusing spectacle for tourists and on that basis it cannot be supported.

This brief discussion of crocodilian involvement in the northern Australian tourism industry raises a number of broader questions that the authors contributing to this book have themselves sought to address. Is it permissible to intervene in the lives of wild animals in order to create pleasure for tourists? Can we admire a living animal and yet enjoy eating its flesh or wear its skin and maintain moral consistency? Can tourism encounters with animals be personally transformative and lead to nature conservation outcomes or are they more likely to reinforce power inequalities between humans and non-human animals? Does tourism by its very nature as a form of capitalist activity inevitably lead to the commodification and exploitation of animals? Are there alternative ways of creating tourism practices which are more respectful of, and empathic towards, animals? The following section draws together the important conceptual and empirical insights that have emerged from the studies contributed by the authors of the various chapters in order to reach some conclusions.

Towards an Understanding of Human–Animal Relationships in Tourism

As I stated in Chapter 1, my aim in compiling this book was to throw light onto the diverse ways in which humans and animals intersect through tourism spaces and places, practices and structures. The model of tourism–animal relationships presented in Chapter 1 elucidates the array of intersections that occur between animals and tourism at all spatial and temporal components of the overall tourism experience. The eclectic mix of chapters that comprise the book examine a variety of forms of tourism–animal relationships: wildlife tourism; the eating of animals within tourism experiences; the ramifications of including companion animals on holidays; connections between tourism and wildlife conservation; and conflicts that arise between the various actors or stakeholders that are involved, both human and non-human. However, the dominance of studies targeted at aspects of wildlife tourism is evident with over three-quarters of the chapters addressing this topic. The dominance of mammals as research subjects is also apparent, with just over 70% of the chapters focusing on this group of animals, with chapters on cetaceans, elephants, wolverines, dingoes, seals, goats and domestic dogs and cats. Of the remaining three chapters that featured specific animal groups, only one involved birds, one sea turtles and one invertebrates. The geographical spread of contributions was rather more diverse, with studies set in Australia, Africa, Brazil, Canada, Finland, Iceland, New Zealand, Papua New Guinea and Thailand. Importantly, the book benefits from the critical insights of many of the contemporary leading authorities working in tourism–animal research.

How then does this book contribute to our understanding of human–animal relationships as they are constituted within tourism? What conceptual and empirical insights have been gained from this diverse collection of studies? One dominant theme that emerges from the book relates to the ethical and moral treatment of animals by tourists and the tourism industry. Ethical issues concerning the treatment of animals arise in each of the geographical regions and in the constituent phases of the total tourism experience, as depicted in Figure 1.1. Yet, as Fennell (Chapter 2) argues, very little attention has been directed to these ethical issues by tourism researchers or by the tourism industry itself. What moral frameworks permit the creation of 'living souvenirs' that can be bought in China, mentioned in Chapter 1, or sustain the interest by tourists in posing for photographs with (apparently drugged) tigers at tourist attractions at a number of Thai destinations? Fennell identifies five theoretically informed ethical positions and demonstrates how each can be applied to tourism–animal interactions. He contends that, in order for a more ethical and sustainable tourism industry to emerge, our taken-for-granted relationships with animals have to be subjected to critical scrutiny.

Burns (Chapter 3) continues this exploration of ethical positions by focusing particularly on the processes by which animals are objectified and commodified by an industry that largely values animals instrumentally. The two case studies she presents highlight the alternative ways by which animal–tourist interactions can be managed if an ecocentric, as opposed to anthropocentric, approach is adopted by the tourism industry and by other agencies charged with the management of wild animals such as national park managers. Both she and Fennell advocate for stronger involvement and leadership from peak tourism bodies in order to advance the interests of animals, which are seen to be legitimate stakeholders in tourism systems.

The ethical issues of commodification, objectification and exploitation are explored in the context of specific studies of elephants in Thailand (Bone & Bone, Chapter 4), whales (Wearing & Jobberns, Chapter 5) and the heli-hunting of a species of goat (Lovelock, Chapter 6). Each of these chapters demonstrates how the interests and agency of animals can be diminished through their involvement in tourism as objects of the tourist gaze, as performers in contrived spectacles, regardless of whether or not they are living wild or in some form of captive situation, or as hunted quarry. In the case of the Thai elephants, Bone and Bone show that the processes of objectifying and Othering oppress both women and elephants, the bodies of whom are disciplined and managed in order to create the spectacles that tourists seemingly want to see. In their assessment of whale watching, both captive and wild forms, Wearing and Jobberns argue that both forms present problems for whales. They argue that, while captivity does not provide whales with lives that can genuinely replicate wild conditions, whales living free lives might still be impacted by the unintended consequences of whale watching. They advocate for a new form of ecotourism that takes into account the welfare of animals as individuals which are respected for their intrinsic value.

In the only chapter to address hunting specifically, Lovelock carefully dissects the debates that are associated with heli-hunting, a form of high-yield tourism that has been criticised for being unethical through its deleterious effects on the welfare of individual tahr, a species of wild goat previously introduced into New Zealand. The ethically fragile nature of recreational hunting is exacerbated in a form of hunting in which the hunter is spatially disconnected from their quarry and in which the method of hunting creates stress for the animals. He argues that the legitimacy of what might be considered more ethical forms of recreational (and subsistence) hunting is placed under pressure by heli-hunting, which turns living animals into targets to be shot at from the sky.

The second theme dealt with by this book concerns the ambiguities, inconsistencies, contradictions and contestations that so often exemplify human–animal relations in tourism, as indeed they do our relationships with animals generally. Many of the ethical issues that were dealt with by authors in Part 1 emerge again in the second part of the book, as there are frequently ethical and moral implications arising from the ambiguous and often contested relationships between tourism and animals. The interconnections between ecotourism, which they position as a form of neoliberal capitalism, and nature conservation are critiqued by Higham and Neves (Chapter 7). From their analysis they conclude that rather than fixing or ameliorating the environmental and social problems that they purport to do, mainstream or conventional forms of ecotourism actually tend to reproduce these problems. They argue that new ways of 'doing ecotourism' (which was also advanced by Wearing and Jobberns) should be at the forefront of contemporary research and innovation, stressing that such tourism has to 'uncouple' itself from the petroleum industry if it is to ever become truly sustainable.

The involvement of cetaceans in tourism was the focus of Jett and Ventre in Chapter 8 and Weiner in Chapter 9. Jett and Ventre's chapter complements the earlier chapters by Wearing and Jobberns and Higham and Neves by providing a critical, insider view of the practice of exhibiting captive killer whales at oceanaria. Although they don't explicitly position the keeping of killer whales within a neoliberal framework, they suggest that the logic of capitalism underpins the rationale for sustaining a form of entertainment that is exploitative of a species that is so demonstrably unsuited to captivity. Yet millions of visitors attend these attractions each year and most, it seems, accept the legitimacy of such entertainment, although the keeping of killer whales and dolphins has become a controversial practice in many countries.

Weiner's chapter explores some of the contradictions and ambiguities in tourist encounters with dolphins. Her micro-scale analysis of tourist–dolphin interactions reveals the culturally constructed (and often highly romanticised) expectations of dolphins as always happy animals, eager to interact with humans, and harbouring some kind of spiritual dimension that can be 'tapped into' through embodied practices such as swimming. Her chapter explicitly invokes the emotional and embodied experiences of a wildlife encounter, an aspect which was not foregrounded in most of the chapters in the book. Yet the tactile encounters offered by swimming with dolphins can expose these animals to unintentional harm which Weiner argues needs to be managed through codes of ethical practice and through stronger policy frameworks and associated legislation.

Cohen's analysis of the use of young elephants in Thai tourism (Chapter 10) details the disciplining practices that are required to produce a compliant animal amenable to performing tricks for the amusement of tourists and reinforces some of the arguments established earlier by Bone and Bone (Chapter 4). However, his analysis demonstrates that two aspects of these elephant shows serve to sustain a demand for them: that the tourists themselves are unaware of the cruelty involved in these disciplinary practices which remain out of sight in the metaphorical backstage and that anthropomorphic discourses used to frame the elephants and their 'antics' reassure tourists that the elephants are enjoying their performance work. A paradox is revealed based on the affection that tourists have for baby animals, which translates into demand for the supply of young elephants for tourism spectacles in which the animals are subjected to practices that cause considerable suffering. While animal welfare organisations openly criticise the ongoing use of these animals in this way, tourists still provide a market for their continued existence.

Contestation and conflict between the interests of tourism and locals, underpinned by interactions by tourism–animal interactions, were explored within two very different countries, and two very different wildlife encounters: carnivorous mammal watching in Finland by Ratamäki and Peltola in Chapter 11 and bird watching tourism in Papua New Guinea by Newsome in Chapter 12. Acceptance and accommodation of wildlife tourism within local districts is not always straightforward, as these chapters show. Conflicting attitudes towards large carnivorous animals such as bears and wolverines complicate the ongoing sustainability of a wildlife enterprise in Finland, which is itself caught up in the transition of a landscape from a productive to a post-productive agricultural space. In the case of Papua New Guinea, a range of internal and external factors such as the cultural significance of hunting, conflict over land ownership and logging and mining threaten to jeopardise bird watching tourism in that country. The lesson from these two studies is that successful and sustainable wildlife tourism depends upon paying close attention to the needs and expectations of individuals in surrounding communities and, wherever possible, seeking productive, collaborative relationships with them.

The remaining chapter in this part of the book examined tourists' relationships with meat. While an ever-expanding literature critiques the food choices that we are confronted with within a framework of ethical eating and sustainable food systems, Mkono (Chapter 13) pointed out that little research has been directed at meat eating within tourism settings. Once again an ethical question, in this case that of eating meat and, in particular, the meat of non-domesticated animals, is evoked in her chapter, although engaging with the ethics of eating such meat was not her focus. Her study, which involved the analysis of reviews of eating 'game animals' in African destinations that were posted on TripAdvisor, revealed some of the dilemmas and paradoxes that tourists were confronted with when deciding on whether or not to eat the animals which they also valued as living beings that they admired on the savannah.

The final theme dealt with by the book explored the changing relationships between animals and tourism, and here we find the most optimistic and positive examinations of tourism–animal relationships. Lemelin (Chapter 14) showed that human interactions with insects, arachnids and other invertebrates are not always negative and that there is a growing demand for managed encounters with butterflies, fireflies, dragonflies and spiders. Such encounters, if supported by effective and creative interpretation can, he argued, be transformative, leading to a greater appreciation of invertebrates and a more sympathetic understanding of them. Lemelin also maintained that certain species which are attractive or endearing in some way – 'charismatic microfauna' – can be used to promote regional biodiversity conservation.

Pegas' research (Chapter 15) showed how substantial shifts have occurred in the ways by which marine turtles have been valued by residents of a Brazilian coastal district that has had its economy reoriented towards ecotourism. Turtles were no longer valued for their meat or shells, but as living animals from which people could make a reasonable living through their involvement, either directly or indirectly, with turtle tourism. This substantial shift in the way the turtles are socially constructed and valued has led to them being used as flagship species which can encourage people, both local and tourists, to support broader biodiversity conservation initiatives. While most flagship species are mammals, Pegas argues that charismatic reptiles such as turtles, which are non-threatening and endearing, can also perform this role effectively.

The concept of flagship species was further explored by Skibins (Chapter 16). He argued that conservation programmes should make much greater use of charismatic megafauna as flagship species that can promote broader conservation goals. Skibins argued that a shift in the way these animals are conceived in wildlife tourism is warranted, from simply attractions that generate visitor numbers to ambassadors, which can be catalysts for conservation campaigns. However, the success of such an approach is dependent, he contended, on taking a nuanced and strategic approach to tourist markets and matching animal ambassadors to particular tourist market segments. An animal which might have great appeal to specialised wildlife watchers may have little to no appeal to a mass tourist market.

The remaining chapter (Chapter 17) by Gretzel and Hardy shifted focus from wild animals to the animals that share our domestic spaces, pets. While pet keeping is an activity with a very long history, significant shifts in the way pets are constructed have recently occurred in Western societies in particular. The terms 'companion animals' or, more recently, 'fur babies' signal a change in the way we position these animals, suggesting a closer, more intimate, familial, relationship. Gretzel and Hardy examined the growing popularity of including pets (mostly dogs and cats) in holidays, using recreational vehicular travel as their particular focus. Their findings suggested that desiring the company of a pet while travelling can act as a constraint affecting travel routes and accommodation and consequently decisions about where to stay become very important. Inclusion of a pet in the holiday can also create greater risk for both the owner and the pet itself.

In summary, the key insights that can be drawn from this wide-ranging set of studies are that, first, we cannot ignore the fact that tourism, as a form of capitalist endeavour providing hedonistic experiences, has a tendency to value animals instrumentally which frequently leads to their commoditisation, exploitation and mistreatment. Secondly, economic practices take place within particular social and cultural contexts at particular moments in history and we must not ignore the effects of sociocultural constructions of animals on their intersections with tourism. Thirdly, it is clear that, for many animals involved in tourism, their role is that of a performer or entertainer, whether they are held in captivity or living wild lives. The expectations held by tourists of the nature of these encounters can seriously compromise the interests of the animals – something which is not often understood by tourists who are only given access to the 'front stage' performance space. Social media, however, is playing, and will increasingly play, an important role in raising awareness among people, of touristic practices that have significantly damaging effects on animals as individuals and at the population level. Through their engagement with user-generated content sites, tourists have the capacity to influence tourism industry practices. Fourthly, a number of authors demonstrate that tourism can also bring benefits to animals, especially at a species level. The creation of sustainable and ethically responsible forms of animal-based tourism does have the potential to contribute positively towards nature conservation, whether by changing attitudes to species considered less likeable such as spiders and crocodiles or shifting the economic basis of interactions from consumptive to non-consumptive as in the case of sea turtles.

Future Research Directions

This book has been published at a time in the history of the earth that many physical and social scientists have termed the Anthropocene, an epoch characterised by unprecedented human domination and subsequent transformation of global biophysical and ecological processes (see Burns, 2014; Zalasiewicz *et al.*, 2011), such as anthropogenic climate change. It is also a period in which growing numbers of people in Western nations are actively questioning our relations with non-human animals, particularly around the use of animals in food systems. Historian Richard W. Bulliet (2005) argues that such questioning is characteristic of the post-domestic phase in the West's relations with animals. Our sociocultural relations with animals are constantly in flux (Barrow, 2010; Franklin, 1999) but it appears that the early 21st century is witnessing significant transformations in how we relate to animals. The emergence of terms like 'ethical eating', 'humane meat' and 'compassionate conservation' signal new ways of thinking about our relations with animals that shifts them from being constructed predominantly as property to be owned and commodities to be used or consumed to subjects with agency with whom we share the planet. Yet many of the studies presented in this book demonstrate that the tourism industry continues to position animals mostly as objects that can be transformed into commodities that can generate revenue for businesses, paying little regard to the interests of the animals themselves. Ethical questions concerning how animals should be used in tourism emerged in the majority of the chapters.

More interdisciplinary research, drawn from the humanities and the social and natural sciences and informed not only by conventional theories but engaging with emerging theoretical frameworks such as, but not limited to, post-human and post-domestic perspectives, is called for that continues to seek greater and more nuanced understandings of tourism–animal relationships at each space and stage of the tourism experience, as illustrated in Figure 1.1. A whole-of-tourism approach is called for and the value of carefully designed case studies is demonstrated by several of the chapters in this book. The insights of scholars (and the experiences of industry practitioners) from cultures outside a White, Eurocentric ontology must be welcomed and facilitated into the research conversation about tourism–animal relationships.

Clearly a broadening of the types of animals that intersect with tourism and the types of interactions that occur is also warranted. More tourism-focused research is needed on taxa such as invertebrates, fish, amphibians and reptiles and on interactions beyond those contextualised within wildlife tourism, such as the use of animals as food, animals as workers, and the relationships between companion animals and tourism. Empirical studies on both the supply and demand side of the industry are called for that identify new ways of involving animals that are based on respect and inherent value and which do not diminish the quality of life of those animals, or impact on species security. Research also needs to continue to understand how encounters with animals and the profound emotional responses that can result can help to shape stronger positive attitudes towards animal welfare and ecosystem sustainability.

There is also an enormous amount of work yet to be done on the way people engage with representations of animals in the pre-tour decision-making processes and how these shape subsequent interactions with animals at destinations and beyond, upon return home. Web 2.0 facilitates an enormous array of opportunities for tourists to share their experiences of animals and to engage in conversations and debates about the treatment of animals within tourism. Researchers' appropriate use of user-generated content sites and other forms of new media, through netnographic approaches, coupled with well-designed field-based studies, will provide rich and fascinating datasets that can be used to gain more nuanced understandings of interactions and interrelationships, impacts and issues. The internet itself will profoundly affect and shape our understandings and experiences of animals. Already, radical reinventions of hunting are being proposed such as 'web-based hunting' where 'hunters' could remotely manipulate high powered rifles set up on game ranches via a digital camera and their computer, hundreds or even thousands of kilometres from the actual game ranch. Research attention must be focused on understanding the seemingly unlimited ways by which the internet will reconfigure human-animal relations within the related domains of leisure and tourism.

Our contemporary relationships with animals are the outcome of complex historical, cultural, social, economic and political structures, processes and practices that underlie an enormous array of individual attitudes and beliefs. The meanings we attach to animals and the moral status we give to them varies across times, spaces and cultures. We turn animals into symbols, commodities, myths, competitors, collaborators, enemies and friends; we pay enormous attention to the interests of some, and little, if any attention, to the interests of others. Tourism is a realm in which these inconsistencies, contradictions and ambiguities are continuously played out but with varying degrees of recognition, acknowledgement or concern. There is, therefore, a clear need for much greater research attention focused on better understanding these complicated relationships and for the evidence-based outcomes of this research to inform shifts in government policy and regulation and industry practice. These shifts in government policies and industry practices are necessary if the interests of non-human animals are to be taken more seriously by the tourism industry, and by individual tourists, themselves.

References

ABC News (2014) Crocodile safari hunting: Environment minister scuppers NT plan. *ABC News*, 27 March. See www.abc.net.au/news/2014-03-27/croc-safari-hunting-ruled-out-environment-minister-greg-hunt/5349122 (accessed 2 July 2014).

ABC Stateline (2003) Croc tourism. *ABC Stateline*, 4 April. See www.abc.net.au/stateline/nt/content/2003/s826663.htm (accessed 2 July 2014).

Barrow, M.V. (2010) The alligator's allure, changing perceptions of a charismatic carnivore. In D. Brantz (ed.) *Beastly Natures, Animals, Humans and the Study of History* (pp. 127–152). Charlottesville, VA: University of Virginia Press.

Bulliet, R.W. (2005) *Hunters, Herders and Hamburgers: The Past and Future of Human–Animal Relationships*. New York: Columbia University Press.

Burns, G.L. (2014) Anthropomorphism and animals in the Anthropocene. In G.L. Burns and M. Paterson (eds) *Engaging with Animals: Interpretations of a Shared Experience* (pp. 3–20). Sydney: Sydney University Press.

Cohen, E. (2009) The wild and the humanized: Animals in Thai tourism. *Anatolia* 20 (1), 100–118.

Cushing, N. and Markwell, K. (2011) I can't look: Disgust in the zoo visit experience. In W. Frost (ed.) *Zoos and Tourism, Conservation, Education, Entertainment?* (pp. 167–178). Bristol: Channel View Publications.

Franklin, A. (1999) *Animals and Modern Cultures: A Sociology of Human–Animal Relations in Modernity.* London: Sage.

Newsome, D., Dowling, R. and Moore, S. (2005) *Wildlife Tourism.* Clevedon: Channel View Publications.

NT News (2011) Northern Territory 'Brutus' cruises raising risks of savage attacks on tourists, says croc expert. *NT News*, 16 July. See www.theaustralian.com.au/archive/news/sink-brutus-boats-safety-alert/story-e6frg6po-1226095855416 (accessed 4 July 2014).

Ryan, C. (1998) Saltwater crocodiles as tourist attractions. *Journal of Sustainable Tourism* 6 (4), 314–327.

Tremblay, P. (2008) Wildlife in the landscape: A top end perspective on destination-level wildlife and tourism management. *Journal of Ecotourism* 7 (2–3), 179–196.

Zalasiewicz, J., Williams, M., Haywood, A. and Ellis, M. (2011) The Anthropocene: A new epoch of geological time? *Philosophical Transactions of the Royal Society A: Mathematics, Physical and Engineering Sciences* 369 (1938), 835–841.

Index